Shifts in the Welfare Mix

Public Policy and Social Welfare
A Series Edited by Bernd Marin

European Centre
for Social Welfare Policy and Research

Volume 1

A. Evers, H. Wintersberger (Eds.)

Shifts in the Welfare Mix

Their Impact on Work, Social Services
and Welfare Policies

Campus Verlag · Frankfurt am Main
Westview Press · Boulder, Colorado

Printed with the financial support by the "Jubilee Fund" of the Austrian National Bank.

Library of Congress Cataloging-in-Publication Data

Shifts in the welfare mix: their impact on work, social services, and
welfare policies / edited by Adalbert Evers and Helmut Wintersberger.
p. cm.
  ISBN 0-8133-7959-8
  1. Public welfare-Cross-cultural studies. 2. Welfare state-
Cross-cultural studies. I. Evers, Adalbert. II. Wintersberger,
Helmut
HV40.S5834 1990   89-70534
361.793-dc20   CIP

CIP-Titelaufnahme der Deutschen Bibliothek

Shifts in the welfare mix: their impact on work, social services
and welfare policies / A.Evers ; Helmut Wintersberger (eds). –
Frankfurt am Main : Campus Verlag ; Boulder, Colorado :
Westview Press, 1990
  (Public policy and social welfare ; Vol. 1)
  ISBN 3-593-34243-X (Campus Verlag)
  ISBN 0-8133-7959-8 (Westview Press)
NE: Evers, Adalbert [Hrsg.]; GT

© 1990 by European Centre for Social Welfare Policy and Research, 1090 Vienna, Berggasse 17.
Composition: Werner L. Laudenbach. Printed by Interpress – Dabasi Nyomda, Hungary.

Contents

Introduction

Shifts in the Welfare Mix – Introducing a New Approach for the Study of Transformations in Welfare and Social Policy

Adalbert Evers

If future historians will look at the two decades beginning in the mid 1960s, they may realize better than we do today, that many changes that occurred in those days did not only happen in the outer world, but also in the minds of people. One important sign might be the masses of literature on the welfare state, its problems, crises, end, transformation or whatever. One of the things which are so up-stirring about these publications is the fact that while research is evermore detailed, the theoretical and political assumptions as well as the values which guide this research have multiplied. Given these circumstances, it seems already difficult to undertake studies of a comprehensive nature on a theme like the welfare state; but it is even more difficult to do so by a comparative study about differing realities and changes in welfare in Eastern and Western European countries. Furthermore, if such a comparative project has to be done by working groups comprising more than twenty social scientists from eight different countries,[1] the most urgent question is, how to unify the plurality of interests and perspectives. Therefore, a kind of background concept has been worked out, which is presented in this introduction. This framework, wherein the specific national studies have been placed according to the situation they refer to, is described in the title we found for the whole research project: "Shifts in the Welfare Mix – Their Impact on Work, Social Services and Welfare Policies"[2]. By outlining this common background, it might be easier for the reader to detect more or less similar and comparative elements but also shortcomings in the contributions presented in this book than the review of the co-authors at the end of this volume.

The first part of this introduction recapitulates the basic assumptions of the concept of 'welfare mix' as well as a number of topics related to welfare policies and directly connected with it. It also presents some of the arguments why the research group – beyond pragmatic reasons – concentrated on the concept of work and social services.

The second part of the introduction tries to transform the debate on 'shifts in the welfare mix' into a social policy debate. By introducing values, concepts and strategies the reasoning cuts through the limits of a sometimes quite economistic discourse on new welfare mixes. We intend to highlight five dimensions of such a social policy debate which were fundamental to the research as a whole. The last part will be devoted to some methodological questions of comparative research and to the path the research groups tried to follow.

The Welfare Triangle. On the Socio-economics of a Shifting Welfare Mix

If one defines the 'welfare mix' with Rose basically as "the contribution that each of three very different social institutions – the household, the market and the state – make to total welfare in society" (1985: 4), this simple definition does not reveal directly its far-reaching implications. They consist in a widening of the look, society takes on its own development, be it the look of public discourses or scientists. In social science and especially in economic reasoning for a long time a 'bi-sectoral' view had predominated, where economic development and strategies were exclusively discussed in terms of changes in formal economies (be they market or planned ones) and state institutions. Since many societal strategies are built on economic reasoning, it is needless to say that their visions and concepts privileged the (market) economy and/or the state as places for action, while the 'third sector', constituted by the economy of households, figured mainly as a place of consumption. A well-developed household economy in terms of a productive unit was defined as a traditional element in modern societies and not as an element of their future. There is yet one point of view from where elements outside of state institutions and markets have always been seen as decisive, if not for 'welfare', so at least for personal 'well-being': the people's and citizens' point of view. But since until today numerous performances around households, help, advice, care and affection look more as self-evident parts of everyday life or as prerequisites for 'real' work, defined as employment, they have been rarely considered as *productive* action to be respected by market or state.

Yet at the beginning of the 1970s, the households and their surrounding networks were introduced not only as consumers, but as a third active economic factor (see the literature on what has been called 'voluntary', 'autonomous', 'informal' sector, e. g.: Matzner 1980). But this happened only in a minority of publications and often enough this 'third sector' was conceived in residual terms without defining its own contribution to welfare development in a more positive and detailed manner. Meanwhile, we are in the midst of a process, where the geography of social life around households is being measured and conquered by scientists and politicians, by time-budget studies, estimations on household production, reflections on how to make more conscious use of the family as a resource for social

8

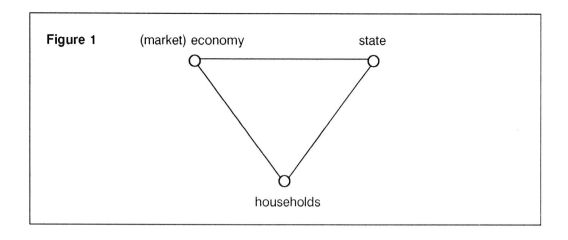

Figure 1 (market) economy   state

households

integration and similar. In a way this trend follows the market actors, which detected quite early the use of dealing with 'informal self-production' in one or the other way – be it by undermining it, offering ready-made products and services, or by instrumentalizing and extending it through the expansion of all kinds of self-service. But social and family life have also been seen as a space to be defended from outside interventions. Self-help and the small networks of social support developed not only as an element in defence of people's well-being but also as a medium to express new needs and to claim new rights. Given such contradictory trends within the 'third sector', we are about to leave the shores of a tradition, where informal economies were seen as a residual or passive phenomenon, to be structured or eaten up in a one-sided relationship, where economic or state actors are turning everything into a commodity, a professional service or a part of formal production and business. Such an embarkment is just beginning to change our views on the inherited institutions and concepts of welfare, but it is still quite uncertain where we will go, if we begin to think informal household economies not as a fading phenomenon of yesterday but as an active element of future welfare development.

Relying especially on the publications by Rose (1985) and Gershuny (1983), one can discuss what can be called a *welfare triangle,* a system which works by its respective inter-relations: "Insofar as the household, the market and the state are each imperfect providers of welfare, then the existence of a multiplicity of resources can be beneficial" (Rose 1985: 4). If we discuss welfare in terms of goods, services, the generation and distribution of income, work and time, shifts concerning the respective share and role of household, (market) economy and state can be perceived.

Conceiving households (see figure 1) as one *integral* part of a complex entity, presupposes the evidence of two basic facts:

• Household economies are not vanishing but changing, even stabilizing in an economic dimension.

• Households are everless an outer commodity but they undergo a process from formal towards real integration.

Concerning the first of these two basic facts, Polanyi (1978) has already shown, that in contrast to many ideologies the market development with its destruction of informal social ties and boundaries nourishes the expansion of state regulations, which have to compensate for this destruction process of 'community' in the social sphere. This mutual strengthening of state and formal economy became prolonged in forecasts and visions like 'the service society', where a process of further monetarization and job creation was supposed to be without limits, centring evermore around a tertiary sector while reducing step by step the role of households, be it in terms of household production or work time to be spent there. Yet Gershuny (1983) has shown that such utopias are far too simple. On the one hand, he demonstrated, that consumer-oriented services as an important part of the heterogeneous tertiary sector increase lesser in terms of productivity than the industrial sector. Limited possibilities to serialize services and to reduce here the relative input of labour and wages (rising in accordance to the overall development) result in an overproportional increase of costs or prices for consumer-oriented services (see also Muysker and Wagener 1986). This affects the consumer either directly if the services are marketed, or through taxes if they are public. Facing those developments households won possibilities for substitution which grew with household goods getting cheaper and services more expensive. The trend towards a *modern* type of "informal household production", as analyzed by Gershuny, breaks the linear trend of a presupposed service economy.

Relating now to the second process mentioned above, the monetarization of households, their further integration in a complex economy and welfare system can be observed. "Households increasingly acquire their services by a combination of unpaid work with capital goods and materials purchased with money earned in paid employment" (Gershuny 1983: 48). With respect to personal services households rely on a number of "social support networks" (Whittacker and Garbarino 1983) which rank in size and structure from the micro-systems of informal neighbourhoods to the macro-systems of public health institutions. Consequently, studies have shown that the household economy of a white-collar employee may be more developed than the one of a marginal worker. Even if additional public services are created, they do not simply abolish or reduce household work but create new types of complementary service work like e. g. helping the children in school, bringing the elderly to a hospital, acquiring skills needed for good treatment in health institutions, etc. (see Balbo 1987). Taking part in the labour markets and the systems of public provision is the complementary side of a household economy, which is important for the majority of people and their "divisions of labour" (Pahl 1984) whatever its acknowledgement in public policies and welfare concepts may be.

The process of industrialization and modernization with its contemporary shifts can therefore be introduced not as a bipolar one of increased marketization and etatism, but in terms of a triangular relation, where informal household production has a changing yet stable place and is far from vanishing. This is a first step in making clear, why we used the 'welfare mix' concept as a background. Explaining why we concentrated on the issues 'work' and 'social services' will be the next step of our argumentation.

First of all, it can be stated that a tight link exists between *work/employment* and the 'mix' between the responsibilities of formal and informal systems, especially with respect to services. The issue of work has, in the context of the ongoing employment crisis, one central dimension which could be formulated by: how to get to new jobs? So simple and short the question, so diverse and complicated the answers. Even if the simple hope on the tertiary revolution and its employment effects have been considerably silenced both by the potential for rationalization in production-oriented services and the possibilities of substitution through informal household production, as described by Gershuny, experts and politicians agree on the fact that the personal and social services are a knotty point for possibilities to turn new needs into new jobs. As Scharpf (1985) has demonstrated by a thorough analysis, there are still possibilities for additional jobs through a further expansion of personal services. Market-oriented solutions (which he calls the "US-american" solution), but also state-oriented strategies (symbolized in his arguing as the "Swedish way") have both achieved considerable employment effects in the area of personal services. But they did so within a specific historical setting and balance. While the high differentiation of incomes and the low wages in personal service areas stirred additional personal service employment in the United States, the accommodation to high taxes and a social service-oriented social budget are by-products of the Swedish type of job creation. Given the fact that there is only a loose connection between modernization in the industrial sector and production-oriented services on the one hand and progress in employment on the other, the question of the limits, possibilities, by-effects and conflicts when trying to transform needs for personal and social services into jobs is quite a prominent one in countries with high unemployment. And insofar as many social services, especially care, are tasks shared by the formal service system and the informal (care) systems, the question of shifts in this mix is tightly linked with choices of work and employment. In countries with a planned economy the link between the issue of work and shifts in the welfare mix is however different. Here, the nexus between the future of personal services and employment seems to be a looser one. Beyond the question of a 'second' or 'black' economy, which we have left out in our debates, the link is here mainly with the future role of the household economy. When employment creates only relatively low income, the household economy is an important sphere for compensation, use of time and efforts be it in search for consumer goods ('consume-work') or in informal self-production.

As can be seen, the issue of *social services* is already a central one through its tight links with questions of work and (un)employment. While some recommend a widening of public employment in the social service sector (trying at the same time to moderate the aspects of follow-up-effects for state finances and/or tax payers), others make an appraisal of the multiplicity of possibilities for additional jobs in the market economy, in a 'fourth' or 'fifth' sector of new needs for personal services of all kinds, reaching from care and therapy to a breakfast-at-home service. Apart from these concepts of a shift in personal and social service provision towards state or market, there are proponents of strengthening the elements of self-help and community in the third sector. Besides the differences between those, which want to introduce thereby savings in public services and those, which want to strengthen a collective basis for claiming different kinds of professional services, the common purpose is in both cases one of social policy. What we detect is a tight link between the issues of work/employment and social services or between labour market and social policy. Either one promotes new ways and needs in the area of personal and social services through social policy, ending up with questions of employment and its effects, or social services and social policy are considered as a genuine ground for labour market policies and job creation. In the highly industrialized countries with a planned economy such kind of link does however not exist. Since a system of personal services is historically less developed here and access to social services even tighter bound to participation in work, there remains the problem of how to build up social services (especially care services) and to grant the right of access to them. Such a problem is increasingly pressing, the more people are to be found at the margins of the employment system and the lesser family systems and especially women are willing or able to compensate this low level of care services.

To sum up, our research started from the observation that the sphere around households, the social and economic activities to be found there, as well as working time spent in this connection, represent a strategic variable of high impact for the quality of welfare and related policies. Household work and household economies seem to be of special importance with respect to social services like care services, while the latter are at the same time tigthly linked with questions of (un)employment and job creation.[3]

From the Economics of a Shifting Welfare Mix towards a Debate on Welfare Policies

We have already touched upon some direct implications of a shifting welfare mix for work, social services and social policies in that field. There are, however, some additional sociological and policy-related facts which hardly can be treated adequately in economic terms. Altogether they structured the discussions in the common research meetings. In the following, we present those five major issues, which where most influential for the research design.

Between Economic Interests, State-action and Household Behaviours – Introducing Collective Actors and Social Innovations

In a French presentation (1986) of his main thoughts on "Social innovation and the division of labour", Gershuny himself states that concerning the way he puts inter-relations between formal economies, state and household "one might object to the extreme individualism and economism of the concept". He admits that in his work "the optimization of material production and of a series of services looks as if they would be the highest goal of mankind" and that his argumentation is suggesting "that individuals or households choose in a certain sense" while they are in fact objects of diverse pressures (1986: 62; translation by the author of this article). Gershuny has yet no problems to concede that his arguments follow the tracks of a more narrow economic reasoning; he helps himself by underlining that one can "manoeuvre" these economic trends through societal policies (1986: 82). It is indeed problematic that economic reasoning does not know *collective* actors except in the case where they are introduced as 'rational' actors in the same way, individual behaviour is described in utilitaristic thinking. Yet we know that such collective actors, like consumer movements, self-organized clients, traditional and new corporatist interests are decisive. Not only that they shape the surrounding of economic action through politics; they are also themselves *producers* of welfare as voluntary organizations, self-help groups, social cooperatives in the field of social services. Besides, Gershuny states himself, that "closely associated with the household production system and encouraged by the same social and technical developments, is what might be called the 'communal' production system. Included in this sector are 'voluntary' or religious organizations, baby sitting circles, transport cooperatives, housing improvement cooperatives" (1983: 34). In his research concept, however, he does not refer to this 'communal system', maybe because its introduction would either have spoilt the elegance of his economic reasoning or been mistreated within his concept of the 'economic man'. Rose also in his concept of the welfare mix introduces the notion of 'barter', but says, that he is able to resign on treating this issue further "given the limits of barter" (1985: 7). In contrast to these restrictions on individuals and households as 'rational' economic actors, research should, the nearer it comes to a reasoning on welfare policies, widen its view on society. Most chapters in this book argue with reference to *collective actors* and collective *strategies*, whose rationale, impossible to be defined in mere economic terms, entails yet the dimension of *economic production*. Traditional and especially new forms of association at the local level were therefore a major focus of research work and discussion collected in this book.

Gershuny, at the very end of his book, reintroduces the "communal system", when outlining a future for *"social innovation"*. This concept is considered here in a wider sense going beyond the traditional understanding of 'social innovation' where it is used as the outcome of interaction between individuals/households,

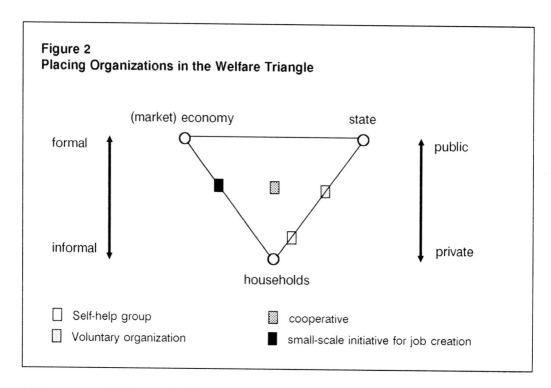

Figure 2
Placing Organizations in the Welfare Triangle

(market) economy ‧ ‧ ‧ ‧ state

formal ‧ ‧ ‧ public

informal ‧ ‧ ‧ private

households

☐ Self-help group ▦ cooperative

▦ Voluntary organization ■ small-scale initiative for job creation

state and market. Introducing what he calls "public service sector innovations", he states, that they have "a technological component as well as organizational", claiming that "the ground rules for innovation here are the same as for private innovations" (1983: 172 and 171). Taking up Gershuny's own labels, one might say that except for the Hungarian chapter, the research contributions in this book concentrate on such public social innovations and their potential role. (see: Blanke/Evers/Wollmann 1985; Informations sociales 1986) And it is exactly "public service innovation" as reorganization between state, market and households, what Gershuny himself presents at the end of his book, when he deals with questions of social policies. As an example for public service innovation, he discusses a crèche, where, by reducing the paid staff and introducing volunteers, much more can be done with less money.

It is, however, easy to imagine that in reality such type of social innovation presupposes something beyond the economic: motives and rationales like solidarity, maybe a common utopia and – if such experiments want to spread – a *culture of innovation.* Half-way in between state action and household behaviours and beyond the 'private innovations' there are such things as initiatives for work and training, changes in voluntary action, self-help groups and many more similar types of movements and institutions. They represent interests, which certainly have an economic dimension but cannot be reduced to it. Questioning the traditional strict separation of the economic, the social and the political, or, to put it in other terms, of the 'private' and the 'public', they are located at different points of the field of tension represented by the 'welfare triangle' as shown in figure 2. Some are more influenced by state action than others; some are more market- than state-oriented; and there are others, which in themselves represent a special compromise between elements and values of market, state and community.

Summing up, one can simply state that our research endeavour was marked by a special interest in those dimensions of the social sphere and its informal economies, which are represented by collective actors and their organizations. A considerable part of them, by changing the relationships between the role of (market)economy, state welfare performances and the contributions of households and individuals, represent that type of social innovations which most of the research teams dealt with.

Why Should We Care? A New Look on Peoples' Work and Involvement in Social Service Provision

Thinking in terms of a 'welfare mix', it might be quite informative to learn – like e. g. through Rose's study (1985) – something about the relative proportions of the contributions of the state, (market) economy and households with respect to food, care, education, etc. Yet the question remains, why unpaid work should at all persist, especially if it does not pay off in economic terms, nor gets refunded through reciprocal relationships of mutual help or as a direct exchange of commodities without the intervention of money. The difference between total service work and professional work in social services might tell some stories both about work and services, which cannot be told in economic terms but have also not been part of the more socio-political debates on welfare.

As far as *work* is concerned, its notion is especially hard to define the more it is opened up to social and informal fields. No clear-cut difference between 'work' and 'action' exists here. Volunteers, members of self-help groups, or a local protest movement engaged in a 'public service innovation' are guided in their 'action' and 'work' by a combination of different motivations. Some of the chapters in this book start from the notion of 'unpaid work', where the latter is just a residual category, asking – like e. g. Pinker (1985) – how 'egoistic' and 'altruistic' motives mix in care giving and under which conditions 'solidarity' as a motive can mix with a private or public interest. From that point of view the welfare triangle could as well serve as a representation of different rationales and values which guide action.

Thereby the argumentation goes definitively beyond economic thinking, based, as Bell (1984: 89) has shown, on the double assumption that "the idea of maximizing benefits is the motivational basis for all action and that markets are the structural places for such transactions". The 'welfare mix' then, might be adopted also as an expression for the specific mix of rationales, guiding different types of individual and collective action, which are often more than 'doing a job', but also

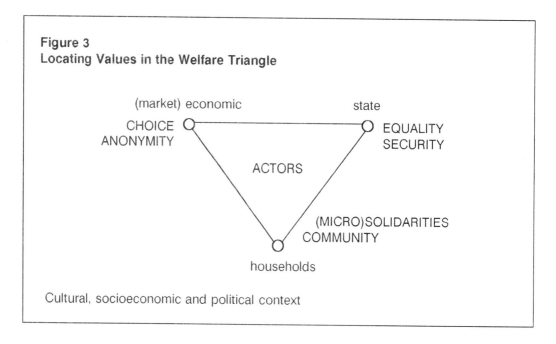

Figure 3
Locating Values in the Welfare Triangle

(market) economic   state

CHOICE   EQUALITY
ANONYMITY   SECURITY

ACTORS

(MICRO)SOLIDARITIES
COMMUNITY

households

Cultural, socioeconomic and political context

different from pure 'solidaristic action', which represent a specific 'mix' of social and private logics. The mix might also be revealed in different types of intermediary organizations, trying to link choice and community, equality and special solutions, anonymity and micro-solidarities. (for more details see Offe and Heinze 1986; Evers 1988).

Leaving thereby the narrow concept of the 'economic man', one can in *social services* overcome approaches which argue only in terms of cost comparative advantages, i. e. in terms of (saving) time or money. In his conclusions Gershuny states deliberately that "a mode of production, which does not use the most cost-saving resources might be preferable to others, if it favours the viability or personal autonomy" (1986: 62). With respect to that, we may find diverse examples: the elderly person, which prefers to go to a home for the elderly because such a choice allows him/her distance, even if that is more costly than to stay with the family of the daughter; a household which spends its money 'irrationally' for some special services because they are fashionable. But before trivializing further this argument about individual preferences for less 'economic' alternatives, we should remember that this also holds true in collective action. When public social services are attacked or rejected by the attempt to build up private or organized self-production as an alternative, this is often not due to a lack of quantity but to a loss of certain qualities, which can hardly be reached by the total equation of 'service', 'public' and 'professional'. While – due to the productivity gap – rationalization efforts still expand in main social service areas like the health system, one should take the arguments about a further dehumanization of such rationalized services not as a matter of taste but as an invitation for analytical reflection. Roustang (1987) has developed an argumentation showing, that in certain economies one of the predominant reasons for shifts in the welfare mix, – substituting work and time through goods or instruments and serializing the work done – makes no sense. This holds true for all *care* services, where the emotional and communicative aspects set limits to every strategy trying to make them less personal or time intensive, or to professionalize them. Beside care work itself, this is also true in other areas of professional services, where a certain enlargement of the number of pupils per teacher leads to counterproductive effects. Roustang speaks of an "economy of care" (1987: 67) and conducts further reflections on the diverse consequences for economic thinking as well as for social policy concepts in case one admits the existence of such a different economy. While this is going far beyond the research framework to be presented here, one might state nevertheless that such ideas had an impact on the style and sensitivity of our research work. It has to be accepted that reflections on personal services, especially care services, entail more than a specification of ordinary reasoning on work and production. Increasing 'productivity' according to the industrial models as well as further professionalization can be seen as serious threats to 'life worlds' through a further 'colonization' by markets and state institutions, money and law. This reinforces the issue about the future impact of 'time to care' in concepts of everyday life. And it also raises questions about 'how to care', especially when it comes to the third, informal area, to social networks, household, family life and their inherent economies.

Summing up, it may be said that the notion of the welfare mix led to two specific considerations as far as the social and household sphere is concerned:

● How to deal with the manifold types of activities, performances and *work* to be found there, guided by different mixes of motivations between individual utilitarism and solidarity, egoism and altruism?

● What difference does it make, if such activities are performed in the field of *social services,* where lots of them have a specific economy with respect to time, quality and productivity?

Therefore, the second common research question was: how to make social services run better in terms of costs and quality if we accept that 'informal work' and personal social services are specific types of action to which the inherited market or state type of rationality cannot be applied?

The Historical and Cultural Framework of a Shifting Welfare Mix: From Traditional to New Representations of Welfare and Well-being

Concepts for a restructuring of welfare and their viability are only conceivable in a concrete historical and cultural framework. By placing the welfare triangle into such a framework, as in figure 4, the reader might first of all realize how much traditions, past circumstances and trends, will inevitably shape the future. In addition, Eastern and Western European societies have shown enormous ability to create, change, reflect and modernize, especially in the last two decades. However, such a statement is only half-true or it might even be misleading if no differentiation is made between the social and the political and institutional levels. While major institutional arrangements and concepts of social policy and welfare as they are held by parties and administrations have shown a relative high degree of erratic stability, much more developments have become visible in the social and cultural sphere, on the local level and at the peripheries of economies and state institutions (see Jouvenel 1986).

When it comes to general values and visions, it could be said in accordance with a recent survey on international trends (Evers 1987) that *individualization* might be the most central fact when describing these processes of socio-cultural changes. Naturally, this is a manyfaced label, which includes defensive notions (the search for a privacy not disturbed by public institutions and policies which seem to be unchangeable and hostile to one's own interests) as well as offensive ones (trying to fight and change external rules and to adapt them to one's desire for more autonomy). This already shows, how much the often discussed 'value changes' in their concrete forms are dependent on the power relations wherein they grow and take shape. Insofar as the recompositions in the respective 'welfare mixes' are shaped by social policies, the question arises whether the traditional social values and the policies based upon them just vanish, lose importance or change. With the economic restructuring in Western and Eastern European countries and the predominance of a discourse on technological modernization, it should not be too surprising that those values which are linked to the market and the household angles of the welfare triangle have a growing impact.

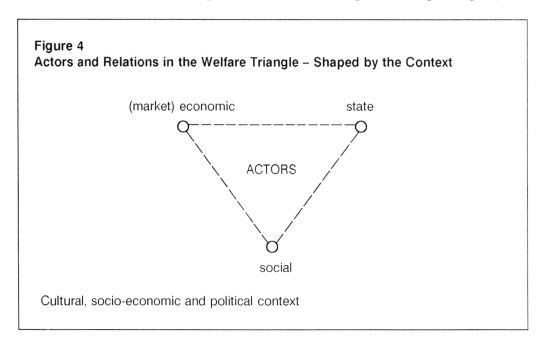

Figure 4
Actors and Relations in the Welfare Triangle – Shaped by the Context

(market) economic   state

ACTORS

social

Cultural, socio-economic and political context

'Choice' e. g. matters today more, when it comes to freedom and complementary to that 'security' seems to matter more; also the meaning of 'solidarity' seems to shift today from the traditional macro- to micro-solidarities, while other state-linked egalitarian values are seen to lose their impact. Social innovations, as represented through the different forms of collective action, social projects and self-management in the no-man's-land between the individuals and the macro-institutions of economy and state express such changes in people's value systems and their attempt to make better compromises between freedom of choice, equality and security (see figure 3). According to our concentration on the issues 'work' and 'social' services, it appears that both are in a quite central position within these social and cultural reorientations.

With respect to *work*, "we can speak of a crisis of the labour-centered society insofar as there are increasing indicators that formalised paid work loses the subjective quality to be the organising centre of life activities, of social judgements towards oneself, the social surrounding and the moral orientations. The ability of the institutions representing the system of paid work to absorb and tie in the people sinks below a level which was judged up until today as stable" (Offe 1984: 7). Concerning people's aspirations this becomes visible through the emergence of new images, how to insert work, especially labour, into their life plans. Sichtermann (1987) has tried to read – not accidentally – from women's biographies, what she calls a "patchwork model", defined through the attempt to balance different activities in a different mix over a life cycle. While there are phases, when the professional career stands in the foreground, there are others, where children and the family have priority. Such patchworks marked both by individualism and social pressures do not only break through the traditionally clear-cut lines of division towards 'youth' and 'old age', between 'work' and 'leisure', learning and practising. These patchworks also reflect the questioning of the basic concept of a 'full work place'. Market, state institutions and household may play here different roles at different times for the people. Much more configurations of their interplay are conceivable now than this was the case in times, when youth, adult male full employment and old age formed clear-cut sequences and emancipation of women was defined as an adaption to such a model. Seeing – like in the patchwork model quoted above – women in advance with respect to men makes, however, only sense in terms of a cultural concept or a vision but not in terms of a snapshot of today's reality. Here, women's patchworks are largely dictated by external powers; and they are discriminated by a type of welfare regulation, which is still nearly exclusively built around the male model of a non-interrupted working career taking 'patchworking' as a gender-related exception. Our example (concerning changing and pluralist conceptions of use of time – see Hinrichs and Wiesenthal 1982) is yet showing, how much more flexible a future-oriented welfare mix ought to be if it wants to keep up with changing orientations and values (see also Groupe Long Terme 1983).

Similar aspects emerge in the *social and care services.* Many discussions have centred around the question, how far new self-help initiatives are self-defensive measures against the dismantling of welfare state services and grants and how much they are constituted by the will to take over more self-responsibility in service and care issues. In fact, it is easy to see, that taken as social innovations, they represent both: the more defensive attitude, so visible in the flourishing second economy, all kinds of barter and similar which especially mark the reality in lots of countries with a planned economy. But at the same time, self-help is also a middle-class phenomenon, characterized by the search for more autonomy in those social strata, which are well off in traditional terms of measuring welfare. Self-organized crèches, as a type of social innovation already quoted, are linked to changing patterns and possibilities to use one's own time, given the background of a secular reduction of total working time in both, the labour market and the informal area. The whole 'culture of services' shows more than just signs of impoverishments and rising inequality: a changing role of people, who do not want to be seen anymore as mere clients but as co-producers, not in terms of standardized service offers, but of a service which is designed according to their highly individualized needs and potentials. Shifts in the welfare mix concerning "time to care" (Swedish Secretariat for Futures Studies 1984), be it towards paid professionalism and markets or towards more lay care, household work and self-help groups may therefore well be a loss of welfare and a sign of increasing self-exploitation. But sometimes they also indicate a new space for individualism, autonomy and choice.

It can be said in short that in work and social services issues like flexibility, the right 'package' of measures at the right time, competitivity and creativity have a more prominent role in tomorrow's welfare concepts than they had in yesterday's welfare states. While this conviction was shared by a solid majority of the research teams, it resulted in two questions, which shaped considerably our discussions and research efforts:

● With respect to what kind of future concept of *work* does one analyze the increasing dissolution of the inherited role of employment as a key element for welfare and people's well-being?

● What kind of future concept of *social service* provision is guiding one's analysis of new patterns of interaction between formal services and people's involvement?

Defend and Change. Deregulation and New Regulations in Work and Social Services

Turning from models and images of people, scientists and individuals to the level of collective strategies, actors and policies, one might say that actually the question of work is still spelt as a question of employment, or, to be more precise, as the regaining of *full employment*. In the meetings of the whole research group most of the debates crystallized around this issue.

On the one hand, there was a position insisting on the possibility of defending or regaining full employment. This perspective might be best characterized by a study of government policies in a couple of OECD countries, asking "why some peoples are more unemployed than others". Under this title, its author Therborn states that "mass unemployment occurs in some countries and not in others". He insists on the possibility of regaining full employment by "the wide range of policy options" available (1986: 162). Quite contrary to this position, another perspective has been outlined, which we also want to introduce here by making reference to a recent publication. Keane and Owens (1986) have undertaken a study on employment policies in the United States and the United Kingdom. Whithin this approach, they deny that there is any possibility to return to full employment, which they judge as "nostalgia". In the centre of such opposed statements is the definition of employment itself. Keane and Owens, like a variety of researchers in our group, insisted on the fact that the traditional "full employment" was a "special historical type of employment". It was full male employment, and based on one centring normality, a mostly well-regulated 'full' participation of each individual in the labour market. Instead of defending, trying to regain or even to widen such a historical model, one might ask, around what future type of employment it might be possible to safeguard the option of participating in the labour market as a basic right of people. Rethinking the employment society in such a way means that "it is essential and urgent that new political ideas and strategies for reducing and equitably redistributing paid work . . . become a central theme of contemporary politics" (Keane and Owens 1986: 8). The issues which became therefore controversial in the research meetings are easy to enumerate: part-time work, job sharing, the individualization of working contracts, etc. For some, these issues express nearly exclusively a "recapitalization of capitalism" (Miller 1978), which leads inevitably to a decreasing role of the working people and classes. Others, however, underlined that these issues, to a certain degree, also reflect a pluralization of people's interests in a new division of work, time, and income (see Hinrichs and Wiesenthal 1982). Their organizations should take them up as a point of departure for new social conflicts and new regulations. Instead of merely complaining that new types of (partial) integration into the labour market cause a multiplicity of disadvantages with respect to social rights, the construction principles for these rights should be revised. New social rights and securities ought to respond to a new multiplicity of forms to participate in the labour market.

A similar debate took shape around the issue of *social services*, and more specifically around the question whether we have to dismiss the former socio-political model of a 'full service' society. Here, dissimilar to 'full employment', the historical goals of transforming care and other social concerns into a fully professional task have been far less achieved. Concepts trying to develop new instead of just reducing old types of informal (care) work through an upgrading of volunteering, self-help and semi-formal organizations (see e. g. the famous 'Time to

Care' Study of the Swedish Secretariat for Futures Studies 1984), are, however, often still seen as a restaurative 'way back'. Similar to the conflict about employment, the core of the controversy about the future of care and social services is an issue on definitions. It makes a decisive difference whether one sees self-help as part of a *new* relationship between the individuals, their networks and state action, or merely as a substitutive strategy, helping the state to do less and putting on the people the pressure to do more. How far can we go in the direction of a "mixed welfare economy in which the state is an enabler and private participation is possible through . . . the contractual provision of services" like Friedman puts it in a summary of another comparative study on "Welfare states and their development" (1987: 289)? This question is not connected any longer with the defence of traditional responsibilities of a welfare state, but it concerns changing definitions of responsibilities to be shared between state, market actors, individuals and 'intermediate' service institutions.

The position one takes with respect to the future of 'full employment' and 'full service' concepts also structures the way one perceives *social innovations*, which often link the two issues together: the creation of new or additional services and the creation of work, occupation and jobs. New types of personal services with a strong self-help flavour and the types of work and labour to be found there offer more complementary options in terms of free time and training, but considerably less security and money. They differ from what could be seen as 'normal' in employment and social services. How to design therefore the future of such deviant but flourishing experiments? Should a critical analysis conceptualize them above all as an element of deregulation and of additional exploitation of the people involved there? Or might they also figure as an entry point to a different future normality of work and services still to be shaped and bargained? As different as the general options and views on employment, work and social services are, as different will be the interpretations of today's social innovations in the welfare mix.

But even if one argues for new designs of work, employment, social services and self-help, the dilemma hidden in the slogan "defend and change", formulated by Miller in the course of our debate, lingers on. While it makes well sense to construct better futures, where, through a social compromise, *all* sides move in a better situation, one knows that actually in reality, power, costs and advantages are divided quite unequally when it comes to new regulations in work and social services. Therefore the question how to link 'defence' and 'change' is extremely difficult to answer. This holds especially true with respect to social innovations and the bodies and institutions by which they are represented: new forms of community care, mixing diverse types of work and employment, new job creation programmes in the sphere of social services or environmental tasks, etc. (see e. g. Sharman 1983). Insofar as they represent a complicated mixture of costs and opportunities, wins and losses for society, the consumers and the employees it is impossible neither simply to reject them in the name of a defence of the former traditional service or employment system, nor simply to acclaim their spreading in the name of change. We would like to quote here a working document of the former Greater London Council, "The London Industrial Strategy" (1985: 138). With respect to a better future of work it takes up in practical perspective what puzzled our debates as a theoretical challenge: "The solution to this quite basic human problem would require absolutely fundamental root and branch changes throughout society, in how work is divided and rewarded, in the how of paid employment, in how skills are valued and passed on . . . In creating new relations of waged work and domestic care *the more humanising elements of both could be combined and the oppressive aspects of both reduced*. Perhaps we might make a future in which the meanings of work, creativity and care are transformed, so work was not onerous toil, creativity not for the favoured few and care the responsibility of a single sex." (italics by the author of the article)

Summing up, we can say that a fourth fundamental question for our debates and research designs concerned the possibilities of coping with the bads and goods, the losses and newly opened up choices linked with deregulation in employment and social services. The differences in the research reports can easily be detected: while some are underlining the new options and challenges to be found in deregulation and provisional, often case-limited new regulations, others concentrated on the deficits and losses of welfare they represent. For some, so to say, the glass they looked at was half-full whereas for the others, it was half-empty.

Welfare and Democracy. Which Regulation of Conflicts Between State, Society and Individuals?

If there are some links between shifts in the welfare mix and the problems of democracy, the most basic one may be found in the fact that, over time, the links between formal economy, state institutions and individual households have multiplied. Each cornerstone of today's welfare triangle is constituted through the other: e. g. families' reproduction through markets and state legislation and vice versa markets through the texture of their socio-economic and political context. As we have already stated in the beginning, there is not only the mutual reinforcement of an expansion of markets and state regulations but at the same time an increasing number of relationships towards the individuals, the households and social groups. While this process has – both in countries with market and planned economies – enlarged the space of public policies, it has yet done so in forms, which are today criticized as inflexible, patriarchal, bureaucratic, or even authoritarian. Despite the considerable differences between countries which see themselves as 'socialist' and others, often circumscribed as 'Western democracies', there exist today conflicts between collective actors and state institutions, and conflicts between the individual on the one hand and collective representations on the other – be they social or state institutions.

With respect to the links and contradictions between state and society, including those within society itself, the most stirring fact is the *multiplication* of collective actors, conflicts and social movements (Touraine 1985). The relationship which is constituted through collective bargaining, the conflict and contract between employers and employees is still quite a central one in welfare states with market economies. And the notion of the interests of people as 'the working people' in socialist countries is putting it in similar terms. In reality, however, these contracts and terms do everless cover the multiplicity of conflicts articulated through new movements and actors, in women's, ecological, consumer, regionalist and minority movements of all kinds. As Laclau and Mouffe (1985: 167) have put it, they represent different points of a complex system of social and power relationships which are as well but not anymore predominantly visible in labour relations. "The plurality of these relations cannot be magically erased to constitute a *single* working class." Through the organizational expression of a plurality of movements, society has somehow conquered new space for articulation which counteracts bureaucratization and commodification.

In this context, new collective actors as represented in 'communal' (local or regional) social movements and innovations have won a political impact. In the socialist countries, such bodies are today the representatives of a 'civil society' taking *distance* from the state and its organizations. In Western countries, they often represent innovations in the way of *mutual exchange* between societal and state institutions. Many of these new innovative groups and projects are visibly state dependent, but not part of the state; they are part of the social sphere, but at points, where state regulations play a more intensive role for its functioning. Instead of representing civil society vis-à-vis the state, they are kind of 'intermediate' bodies. With respect to the economy, such an intermediate role can be found both in the countries with centrally-planned and market economies. Once a co-operative or association is founded, it represents in itself a special compromise between social and economic goals to be acknowledged and stabilized by special legislation and other state guarantees. Consequently, this leads to a questioning of the inherited concept of 'civil society'. First of all, it becomes clearer that it is not only constituted through political, cultural and social protest organizations and their discourses, but also through organizations representing work, production and economies beyond markets and formal economies. Secondly, 'civil society' is envisaged here not only in terms of freedom from the state but freedom to be guaranteed by the state, not as a question of distance but of functioning types of more and better intermediation (see Donati 1984) between state and social actors.

Another observation concerns the links of state policies and societal organizations with the individual. For both, state institutions and social organizations, it is not self-evident to conceive the individuals as *actors*. Traditional planning concepts have constructed them mainly as objects or as potential factors of delegitimation to be persuaded or even forced into central state plans. And they were seen as receivers of protective legislation and recompensation; this explains why in some countries the welfare state is called 'état providence'. Yet, people's articulation in Western, as well as in Eastern European countries takes today the form not only of reaction but of *strategies*. Thereby they qualify as counterparts of state or economic planning institutions, not as mere 'consumers' but as 'producers' of their life circumstances. At once, new spheres and new terrains for societal and social policies become visible:

• New limits are perceived as tighter limits of state decisionism and the need for a "sensitive bureaucracy" (see Clode 1987): the more people and collective actors insist on their capability to develop strategies and concepts of their own, the more the state is not viewed anymore as the centre but as a kind of moderator of a plurality of societal projects.

• New spheres emerge, first of all, because public interventions for welfare might be needed, which offer beyond mere protection and compensation investments of a 'help for self-help' type, the more the addressee can be conceived as a person to develop strategies.

Another dimension of welfare and democracy is concerning the links between individual and collective interests, their rationalities and behaviours. We have already touched before the 'opaque' character of an individualism which, as Rosanvallon underlines, "accompanies all the phenomena of social retreat, of a search for individual alternatives in the labyrinth of social sectors, status and reglementations: a growing number of individuals think that it is the better solution to take one's own critical way through the big social map . . . than to better one's condition within the limits of a collective action . . . This marks in every case a crisis of the *form of the social*, the way individuals become composed in a social system." (1981: 133) This statement is, from our point of view, of some importance both vis-à-vis the consumerist way individualism is being exploited in market economies and vis-à-vis the rhetorics on deviation, anomaly and decadence which accompany the search for individualisms in countries with planned economies.

Since in both social systems the increasing multiplicity of links between the individuals and public institutions are not only of a restricting, one-sided nature, but also representing struggles and achievements (which gives the right to speak of a *welfare* mix), the individual has become today, through the "politicization of the private", a citizen with much more *social rights* than at the beginnings of social welfare (see Balbo 1987). Taking this notion of individual social rights seriously, negotiations about the future of welfare have today a quite different basis than in the early days of the 'Great Transformation' at the beginning of modern industrial societies. Since privacy and individual social rights are strongly mediated through public policies, it is a central problem of how to conceive the individual or the single human being in concepts of welfare. The classical confrontation here has been the one between market liberals, conceiving it as an autonomous person, 'free to choose', and their socialist counterparts, judging a system of state-guaranteed protection as the most basic step towards making them free as citizens. Yet, if one acknowledges today that in nearly every highly industrialized state education, skills, competence and security of an individual arc on a much higher level than at the time when this traditional controversy began, one might ask where we stand today. Even socialists do not deny today that state regulations have sometimes become 'overprotective' in a sense that making people more 'free from need' has in fact not always resulted in making them more free as actors and citizens, free in choice and decision. This observation concerns the actual dilemma to guarantee both in a way: security, equal norms and guarantees and a right to personal freedom and to difference. 'Individualization' in future welfare seems to be needed as a response to the actually distorted links between individuals and collective representations. It is a theoretical and practical challenge, which reminds us of the fact that the final goal of welfare policies is to make the individual less an object to be protected but more a self-confident actor to be further enabled.

From here, it is easy to sum up our fifth common guideline for research and discussions: What kind of links might there exist between concepts of freedom and democracy and the more central role attached to individuals, self-managed and non-state organizations through shifts in the welfare mix? Under what circumstances might an upgrading of the role of 'households' and the 'social sphere' within the welfare mix also result in more 'civil' society?

A Cross-national Attempt in Comparative Perspective – Some Methodological Remarks

Since it was the whole group of researchers which contributed to the development of the background of perspectives, ideas and challenges presented here, this publication gives evidence of the influence of cross-national ideas and concepts. Its perspective is comparative, insofar the group as a whole tried to reach a certain level of integration concerning basic assumptions while at the same time respecting the different interests of the national teams. All research contributions discuss the links between the triangle of formal economy, state and households, the shifts of balances and relationships between its three cornerstones and their impact on work and social services. But they all introduce the specific socio-economic, cultural and political context in which such shifts take a different meaning and impact for the people and social policy-makers concerned, reaching from the "Scandinavian Model" (see Erikson 1987) to Italian realities, from "state welfare" in the socialist countries to the type of "residual welfare" which shapes the reality in the United States from where Miller participates in the European debate. Therefore it might be oversimplifying but certainly stimulating to relate like in figure 5 the welfare triangle to the four cardinal points in order to highlight some of the most basic differences with respect to the realities of the eastern and western, northern and southern countries involved in this research project.

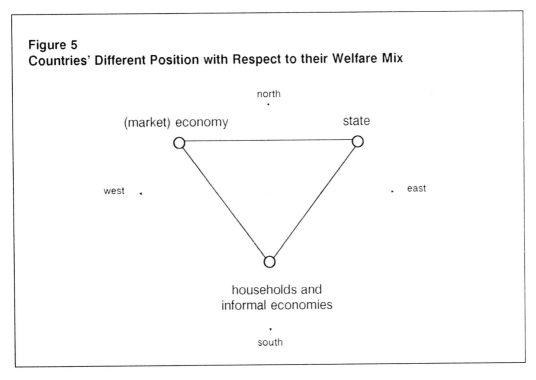

Figure 5
Countries' Different Position with Respect to their Welfare Mix

A plurality of dimensions of a shifting welfare mix has been introduced here, reaching from the description of socio-economic shifts to repercussions as changing representations of social welfare and to the political dimension of democracy. Even if every study is different with respect to the status it gives to one or the other of the dimensions introduced here, they all have in common that they try to transform a limited argumentation in socio-economic terms into a social policy debate which consciously integrates values and political concepts. Being in such a sense 'colourful' but with different 'spectra', the contributions also try to establish a link between attempts and orientations often separated, especially:

• Comprehensive and case-study orientation: they try to give a picture of the general situation to allow a better understanding of a special example.

• General trends and specific social innovations: a majority of the contributions concentrated on social innovations in the fields of work and social services, yet by relating them to the respective national context.

• The issues of 'work' and 'social services': only a few papers have elaborated on one of the two issues disregarding the other; to a different degree, they link a reasoning on both topics, showing how much solutions and problems in these two fields are dependent on each other.

Besides those choices, which were linked with the orientation of the single research team, the specific profile of each national study was constructed according to a common goal: to represent the most *significant* features of the overall 'shifts' in a country. Also in this respect, this project differs from the traditions of quantitative comparative studies. While giving less in terms of quantitative comparability, it might provide more in terms of information concerning the national specificities of shifts in the welfare mix shaped through actors and strategies in social policy. Yet it is also distinct from qualitative cross-national studies of the 'one desk/one person' type, where different national situations and policies are discussed with reference to a single system of values and basic assumptions (as a recent example see Therborn 1986). The difference to such type of qualitative cross-national research is the clear-cut plurality of 'styles' but also of values and options; they become visible, when going through the national contributions.

In a paper on methods in cross-national research, Przeworski (1983: 25) notes that "where the difficulty appears is in our relation to political power. Even those cross-national studies which satisfy all the methodological canons are likely to be based on theoretical assumptions that are not universally shared among competent scholars. There are probably rather few policy recommendations that would enjoy an anonymous support of the scholarly community . . . if we are to perform our responsibility to the society as a scholarly community, we should make such disagreements public and intelligible." Hopefully our research work has also something to offer in this respect.

Notes

1) Nine research teams from the following countries participated in the project: Austria: R. Pohoryles, D. M. Hoffmann, B. Rauscher, H. Wintersberger; France: G. Martin, G. Roustang, F. Sellier; Germany (Federal Republic of): A. Evers, I. Ostner, H. Wiesenthal; Hungary: E. Sik; Italy (B): P. Donati, I. Colozzi (University of Bologna); Italy (T): M. Bianchi, Ch. Saraceno (University of Trento); Poland: M. Ksiezopolski, I. Sienko; Sweden: I. Nilsson, A. Wadeskog; United Kingdom: St. Humble, A. Walker; Yugoslavia: I. Svetlik. S. M. Miller (USA) participated in the function of a senior adviser to the research group (see list of contributors).

2) While this introduction owes a lot to the four plenary meetings of the research groups, where, starting from an initial paper (see: *Evers/Wintersberger* 1985), the general concept evolved, it has not been discussed there. The author bears full responsibility, trying to rely on what has been collectively raised, yet being at the same time conscious that there are gaps and changes caused by the limits of his capabilities and viewpoints.

3) The research reports have addressed this complex problem field in different ways. While only the Hungarian contribution is concentrating on the socio-economics of shifts in the welfare mix, the contributions from Austria, FRG, Italy (B), Sweden and Yugoslavia reflect such shifting mixes mainly in terms of challenges and conflicts for social policy. In this context, *work* is the main focus in the contributions from Italy (T) and France; *social services* are the focus of the reflections in the contributions from Italy (B) and Poland while the contributions from Austria, the FRG, Sweden, the UK, and Yugoslavia deal with work *and* social services as an integrated key question for a restructuring of welfare policies.

Bibliography

Aglietta, M., Brender, A., 1984, Les métamorphoses de la société salariale, Paris.
Balbo, L. (ed.), 1987, Time to Care, Milano.

Bell, D., 1984, Modelle und Realität im wirtschaftlichen Denken, in Bell, D., Kristol, I. (eds.), Die Krise in der Wirtschaftstheorie, Berlin, Heidelberg, New York.

Blanke, B., Evers, A., Wollmann, H. (eds.), 1985, Die zweite Stadt. Unkonventionelle Initiativen zur kommunalen Politik im Bereich von Arbeit und sozialen Diensten, Leviathan-Sonderband, Opladen.

Clode, D., Parker, C., Etherington, St. (eds.), 1987, Towards the Sensitive Bureaucracy: Consumers, Welfare and the New Pluralism, Gower, Aldershot.

Donati, P. P., 1984, Risposte alla crisi dello stato sociale, Milano.

Erikson, R. et al. (eds.), 1987, The Scandinavian Model. Welfare States and Welfare Research, International Journal of Sociology No. 3–4.

Evers, A., Wintersberger, H., 1984, Can there Be a New Welfare State? Research Paper R 120/26, European Centre, Vienna.

Evers, A., Nowotny, H., Wintersberger, H. (eds.), 1986, The Changing Face of Welfare, Gower, Aldershot.

Evers, A., 1988, Kein Ort, nirgends? Zur Stabilisierung von sozialer Innovation, Arbeit und Engagement zwischen Haushalt, Staat und Markt in Offe, C., Heinze, R. G. (eds.), Organisierte Eigenarbeit Frankfurt a. M. (forthcoming)

Ferge, Zs., 1979, A Society in the Making. Hungarian Societal and Social Policy 1945–1975, New York.

Friedmann, R. R., 1987, Welfare States: A Summary of Trends in Friedmann, R. R., Gilbert, N., Sherer, M. (eds.), Modern Welfare States. A Comparative View of Trends and Prospects, Brighton.

Gershuny, J., 1983, Social Innovation and the Division of Labour, Oxford.

Gershuny, J., 1986, L'innovation sociale. Nouveaux modes de prestations de services in Futuribles, February.

Greater London Council (ed.), 1985, The London Industrial Strategy, London.

Groupe Long Terme 'Changements des modes de vie', 1983, Comment vivrons nous demain? La Documentation Française, Paris.

Hinrichs, K., Wiesenthal, H., 1982, Arbeitswerte und Arbeitszeit. Zur Pluralisierung von Wertmustern und Zeitverwendungswünschen in der modernen Industriegesellschaft in Offe, C., Hinrichs, K., Wiesenthal, H. (eds.), Arbeitszeitpolitik. Formen und Folgen einer Neuverteilung der Arbeitszeit, Frankfurt a. M.

Informations Sociales, 1980, Innovation dans le champ social.

Jouvenel, H. de, 1986, Les grandes tendances du changement social in Futuribles No. 100.

Keane, J., Owens, J., 1986, After Full Employment, London.

Laclau, E., Mouffe, Ch., 1985, Hegemony and Socialist Strategy. Towards a Radical Democratic Politics, Norfolk.

Matzner, E., 1980, The Future of the Welfare State: Towards a New Pattern of State Intervention, Papers of the International Institute for Management (IIM/dp/8-74) Berlin (West).

Miller, S. M., 1978, The Recapitalisation of Capitalism in Social Policy Nov./Dec.

Muysker, I., Wagener, H. J., 1986, The Welfare State: From Stabilizer to Destabilizer? in Albeda, W. (ed.), The Future of the Welfare State, Maastricht.

Offe, C., 1984, Arbeitsgesellschaft, Strukturprobleme und Zukunftsperspektiven, Frankfurt a. M.

Offe, C., Heinze, R. G., 1986, Am Arbeitsmarkt vorbei. Überlegungen zur Neubestimmung ‚haushaltlicher' Wohlfahrtsproduktion in ihrem Verhältnis zu Markt und Staat in Leviathan No. 4.

Oyen, E. (ed.), 1986, Comparing Welfare States and Their Futures, Gower, Aldershot.

Pahl, R. E., 1984, Divisions of Labour, Oxford.

Pinker, R., 1985, Social Policy and Social Care: Divisions of Responsibility in Yoder, L. A. (ed.), Support Networks in a Caring Community, Dordrecht, Boston, Lancaster.

Polanyi, K., 1944 (reed. 1978), The Great Transformation, Frankfurt a. M.

Przeworski, A., 1983, Methods of Cross-national Research 1970–1980: An Overview; Paper given at WZB-Forum 1983 "Cross National Policy Research" organized by Science Centre Berlin and Stanford University.

Rosanvallon, P., 1981, La crise de l'état-providence, Paris.

Rose, R., 1985, The State's Contribution to the Welfare Mix, University of Strathclyde, Studies in Public Policy No. 140.

Roustang, G., 1987, L'emploi: un choix de société, Paris.

Scharpf, F. W., 1985, Strukturen der postindustriellen Gesellschaft oder: Verschwindet die Massenarbeitslosigkeit in der Dienstleistungs- und Informations-Ökonomie? in Wirtschaft und Gesellschaft Heft 1.

Sharman, N., 1983, Appraisal of Local Government Employment Initiatives: The Experience of the Greater London Council in Bekemans, C. (ed.), Local Employment Initiatives, Assen, Netherlands.

Sichtermann, B., 1987, FrauenArbeit. Über wechselnde Tätigkeiten und die Ökonomie der Emanzipation, Berlin (West).

Swedish Secretariat for Futures Studies, 1984, Time to Care, New York.

Therborn, G., 1986, Why Some People are more Unemployed than Others. The Strange Paradox of Growth and Unemployment, Thetford.

Touraine, A., 1985, An Introduction to the Study of Social Movements in Social Research No. 4.

Whittaker, J., Garbarino, J., 1983, Social Support Networks, New York.

Shifts in the Welfare Mix:
Significant Features in Countries with Market Economy

Local Initiatives in a New Welfare State — A Fourth Sector Approach

Ingvar Nilsson and Anders Wadeskog

An Agenda for a New Welfare State

Introduction

The purpose of this chapter is to discuss the present situation of the modern welfare state, analyze the structural background to the present situation and present an alternative approach to solving some of its problems.

By choosing this approach we reveal some of our basic values. Let us make them more explicit. First, we consider ourselves as living in a welfare state. Secondly, we consider it valuable to live in a welfare state. Thirdly, we consider it even more valuable for our children to be able to do this. So this contribution is from an ideological point of view an argument for the continuation of the welfare society in its Western, modern form.

But this is not the same as arguing that the forms, the operationalization, the institutions and the policy instruments of the present welfare state are the best in the world. On the contrary, we will argue that some of these outer forms of the welfare state are in a certain sense obsolete and out of date, that they have served well for the major part of the post-war period but that they should sometimes be relieved and supplemented by other instruments.

The welfare state is more or less instituted in order to give ordinary people jobs, incomes, consumption possibilities and quality of life in a very broad sense. But it is also constructed to give the citizens social service and care, security and to create some kind of social context in everyday life.

In most countries this has been solved by a high growth rate of the industrial sector creating an overwhelming amount of goods and services to be consumed and a surplus to be taxed. This surplus has been used partly for public consumption in areas such as schools, medical care and social service and partly for transfer systems and redistributing consumption possibilities to single households, preferably those groups situated on the lower levels of the income ladder. This production system has been supported by a structural economic policy stimulating structural change, external trade, research and development – all leading to higher growth rates. But it has also been stimulated by an active, and on the whole successful, Keynesian short-run policy, leading to high levels of employment.

In many countries this era seems to have come to an end. The growth rates are decreasing, inflation is high and sometimes unpredictable, redistributing wealth in an uncontrolled way. The public sector is struggling with large deficits and high tax rates. The labour market does not seem to work in its historically smooth and harmonious way, causing extremely high rates of unemployment. The external markets are challenged by new industrial powers, most of them from the Far East and a dominant part of the Western world is troubled by trade deficit and external debts. In the European field the battle of the post-industrial society seems to be lost even before it began.

This is of course not a comprehensive and objective picture of the present situation. It is an impressionistic sketch drawn in order to define our field of interest for the study which follows.

The Swedish Model

Here we are discussing the future of the welfare state from a Swedish perspective. This implies a heavy bias towards the so-called Swedish model, defined by full employment, the solidaric wage principle, a strong public sector, a restrictive general macro-policy, a selective labour market policy, a general welfare policy and large transfer systems, to mention a few factors.

The major instrument for carrying out the tasks of the Swedish version of the welfare state is of course the public sector. So the balance between the private and the public sectors is a crucial factor for the viability of the welfare model. This balance is also based on a foundation of industrial and socio-cultural structures which must in some way survive and develop in order to make the model work. But this structure must, in order to survive as a traditionally defined welfare state, produce two basic results: full employment and social service. In this chapter, we will question whether this is possible or not. Let us also remark that this description is in no way objective. It is rather a subjective and personal view of the threats we can see.[1] It is subjective in two ways. First, it is our view, second, we are not trying to see the other side of the coin – the possibilities; our ambition is limited to describing the long-term structural threats.

The Hexagon of National Threat

On the macro-economic level, the state of the crisis could be described in several different ways depending on whether you have a short- or a long-run perspective, if you have a strictly neo-classical, economistic perspective, or if you have broadened your view. In the following section we will try to describe the crisis in an eclectic perspective where long-run phenomena and structural changes will be of more importance than short-run cyclical changes.

The first element is the *introduction of new technology for production*. Most model simulations and quantitative predictions of this process give similar results, although the degree of problems might vary slightly. Unless we are facing a period of extreme growth for the next 10 to 20 years, the technological unemployment rate in Sweden could be expected to vary from anywhere between 6 or 7 per cent up to 24 per cent (compared to the present 3 per cent). The local variations are even more troublesome, where the typical industrial area of Sweden could be facing double digit unemployment rates, even in scenarios of extreme growth.

The second element, further emphasizing the first, is the *situation on the world market.* Most signs seem to stress that in the medium-run perspective disturbing elements are the dominating factors. The debt burden in the Third World, the paralysis of the Common Market, not being able to raise a counter-force to the American and Japanese challenge, the energy and dollar markets, the pacification of the world economy, the neverlasting problems with the GATT negotiations (General Agreement on Trade and Tariffs), the tide of new protectionism, the some 30 million unemployed in the area of the Organization for Economic Cooperation and Development (OECD) – all these are factors indicating that the European share of the world economy cannot certainly expect a period of high and stable growth. This is of course serious for a high-export country like Sweden, which partially bases the development of its welfare model on a high-growth export scenario.

The third element, which underlines the first two, is the *development of the public sector*. This sector, now running into heavy financial problems, has been the employment engine of the Swedish economy for the past 10 years. Now this pattern has changed and is one of the basic reasons for the unemployment situation in the country. The private and public sectors are linked together through taxes, the solidaric wage principle and their productivity. It is very easy to see that, as the productivity in the private sector grows with 3–5 per cent every year, with 0 or –2 per cent in the public sector, the costs, in terms of taxes, for a given volume of the public sector will be continually rising. This could be solved either by increasing taxes – which is politically impossible for the next 10 years, by relinquishing the solidaric wage principle which is also politically impossible, or by giving up the service ambitions of the public sector. This solution would permit a financial balance of the public sector in a 20-year perspective but would also create unemployment rates of approximately 14 per cent and heavy cuts in the standard of the public service. To this problem there is no simple solution within the present welfare system.

These three problems are all structural in terms of being unsolvable within the next 10 to 20 years, unless something very dramatic occurs either with the institutions of the welfare state or in outside conditions like the world market. They are even worse if we consider the next three problems.

The *tax burden* is the fourth problem. Taking all transfer systems into account, the total marginal tax effects of the present welfare system are rather higher than 80 per cent for most income groups in Sweden. Considering this and the position within all the major political parties, it is easy to see that the problems mentioned above could not be solved by tax increases.

The *public debt burden* imparts this conclusion with an even stronger emphasis. The cost for the public debt is already today the second largest cost of the state budget, indicating that an increase of the public debt in order to increase the public service and public employment to balance the labour market is out of the question. On the other hand, a quick decrease of this debt burden has the same financial effects as a restrictive fiscal policy, creating higher levels of unemployment and worsening the labour market conditions.

The sixth factor is the *wage negotiation system* which, for the last five years, seems to systematically produce higher wages, costs and price levels in the Swedish economy than within the trading partners, stressing the problems of raising export volumes high enough to finance our public sector.

The results of these six underlying phenomena are that:

• We cannot expect world trade expansion to solve the Swedish welfare state problems (factor 2).

• We cannot hope that increased market shares will be a permanent solution (factor 6).

• Even if we can, technological development will deteriorate the labour market problems (factor 1).

• The expansion of the public sector is not possible as a solution for financial reasons (factor 4 & 5).

• Moreover, the public sector is struggling with structural problems of which the solution either increases the financial problems of the sector or increases the rate of unemployment (factor 3).

Overall, this creates a situation where the welfare state in the long run will not be able to produce its basic products: social service and full employment.

The Square of Local Conflicts

These structural problems are even more serious on the national level if you take into consideration what is happening on the local level. We can then distinguish four different groups of threats.

First, we have the *breakdown of the nuclear family* as a broad social phenomenon, causing social and psychological problems, but also, which is our focus of interest, creates high costs for the public sector. This is partly due to direct social costs for divorced parents with children and partly due to a reduction in incomes for the public sector. This effect contributes to a structural cost of several billions in all (perhaps tens of billions) for the public sector.

Secondly, we have the problem of the *so-called new poverty*. Being one of the most advanced welfare countries in the world, there are still some 500,000 people (out of a population of 8,000,000) receiving a direct financial support from the social security systems. This is in economic terms a rather marginal phenomenon (the total cost is not higher than some billions SEK every year). But in social and political terms it is quite serious, causing, on one hand, a large group being constantly dissatisfied for not being able to support themselves, and on the other hand, a much larger group being constantly frustrated because they feel obliged to support the minor group.

The third phenomenon is the *growth of the informal sector* of the economy. Caused partially by the tax system, partially by new sets of values, both the criminal part of the informal sector (the black economy) and the less criminal part (the white and the grey economy) seem to have grown very quickly during the last 5 to 10 years. Cautious calculations seem to indicate that the structural costs for this development rise for the public sector to several tens of billions SEK every year in terms of incomes lost.

The fourth factor is the *deteriorated health*, defined in a broad way, causing both lower quality of life and higher cost for society. This threat could be divided into three major parts. First, we have the general health costs, and heavy socio-medical costs. Second, we have the growing costs for alcoholism (not necessarily meaning that alcoholism in itself has grown but the social costs for taking care of it). Calculations seem to indicate that the annual cost for alcoholism is as high as 50 billion SEK. And finally, we have the rising cost for drug addiction (being further stressed by the growing epidemic of AIDS). Being socially a rather limited phenomenon in the early 1960s it is today a serious social problem causing annual costs of billions, perhaps tens of billions.

Taken altogether, these four local social phenomena, the changed family pattern, the new poverty, the growing informal sector and the health problems, have great financial effects on the welfare state. It is easy to see that they represent structural costs for the public sector of several tens of billions. So what we conclude is that the welfare state is not only threatened on the national level by structural problems, but also by the way of life of its citizens, causing to some extent heavy social costs. Moreover, these local phenomena seem to develop in some kind of relation to the national threats. Oversimplifying, one could say that the national efforts to solve the economic problems seem to develop local social problems that create, in the long run, heavy structural costs for the public sector. Let us demonstrate this statement with a few examples:

• When the structural change forces people to move, grandmother can no longer take care of the grandchildren. So the public sector produces day care centres.
• When the informal social control diminishes, the public sector expands the police force.

- When people increase their drug addiction (alcohol and narcotics), the public sector expands its medical and social-medical services.
- When there is a demand for high export, it creates demand for a high-quality labour force, segmenting the labour market into two parts – the able ones and those unable to participate in the world market competitive production. The latter groups, however, will still be supported by the welfare systems, causing ever rising social costs – the vicious circle of growth.[2]

The Agenda of Hidden Challenges

But these threats are also stressed by some more subtle aspects of the modern welfare society reaching down to its ideological and socio-cultural roots. Let us look at some of these threats, without going too deeply into an analysis of them. First, we have on the individual level some interesting phenomena. One is how more and more people feel that their lives are fragmented into a great number of split episodes. Their job, family life, leisure time activities, etc. are not coordinated into a unity. There is no holistic dimension in most people's lives. This is partly that they feel alienated in relation to society, not being included in their own welfare system. But moreover, and even worse, many people have no social and cultural identity, making them quite lost in an existential sense. This erodes the basis for a society with a living morale and ethic.

On the political level or, more generally, on the system level, these effects are visible. The alienation and lack of roots creates a legitimation crisis for the welfare system on the whole. The lack of participation reaches down to the roots of democracy itself.

So, given these very shallow descriptions of the hidden challenges, we can see that the welfare state is also threatened for value reasons. And we are *not* claiming that the principal threats come from the neo-liberals striving for a privatization of the welfare state, but rather from the ordinary everyday citizens in the welfare society.

The effects of this, if our description is correct, are rather overwhelming. First, we have the social, psychological and financial costs of having a lot of citizens not being comfortable living in their own society. Second, this erodes the basic values underlying the concept of the welfare state, such as solidarity, equity, justice, etc. You simply can't be in solidarity with a society which you don't feel that you belong to. You don't vote for a welfare system which you don't understand and you don't feel a part of. And finally this affects the very basis for democracy in its traditional occidental sense.

So, to conclude this section, we can see that the welfare state, as it is defined in Sweden, with the task of giving full employment and creating an adequate social service, is threatened from three directions: First, there is the structural, more economic problems occurring on the national level, making it difficult to achieve this task. Second, we have seen how people in their everyday life, as much for social reasons as for economic reasons, have changed their behaviour stressing the national economic problems. Third, we have seen how some more subtle aspects of the welfare state seem to be threatened by changed social, cultural and existential conditions.

The Emerging Fourth Sector

Local Reactions

From the description in the previous section it can be concluded that the Swedish welfare state no longer produces the social service demanded or manages to reach the full employment target. Moreover, many people can no longer support themselves in terms of high enough real income. The welfare state is also threatened by the legitimation crisis and the fact that many people lack basic social and cultural identity. These signs are emerging slowly, but they are clearly visible if you just care to look for them. We will describe here some of the reactions and the measures taken to cope with the situation, and we will distinguish between what we call local initiatives from above (FAIs) and local initiatives from below (FBIs).

The From Below Initiative (FBI)

Introduction - The Case of Övertorneå

Let us first stress that when we make the distinction between FAIs and FBIs this is from a strictly local perspective. We are profiling the distinction between local initiatives grown out of the local establishment and initiatives created by local grass-roots. Then it is important to see that there is no self-evident and clear-cut borderline between the FAI and the FBI we describe here. The division is primarily for analytical reasons. And furthermore, there is an important and sometimes rather subtle interaction between the different initiatives. We will return to this question at the end of this section so let us now only illustrate it with an example. The municipality of Övertorneå is situated in the very North of Sweden, close to the Polar circle. It has 6,000 inhabitants in an area of 2,367 km^2 - a very sparsely populated area with 3 inhabitants per km^2.

The major problems are emigration to central Sweden, an aging population, a nonviable, close to non-existent industrial sector, a general negative trend in the local economy and a very negative attitude towards the future. In order to cope with this, the municipality has initiated a local development process within the analytical framework of the future study, carried out by the Secretariat for Futures Studies. The starting point was a number of public debates, initiatives to create many study circles and quite a few meetings in all the small villages all over the municipality. This resulted in a number of local initiatives where small groups of people decided to take the future into their own hands. In one village a worker cooperative was started, in another village a local wildlife tourist cooperative was initiated. On a small island a small ecological gardening project was started.

In the town hall, the idea of an ecological community began to take root, and a number of local growers were inspired and have now changed their method of producing vegetables. Encouraged by this, the local authorities have now managed to raise central funds (4 million SEK for 1986 – 87) in order to stimulate further initiatives. The local cooperative projects started to affect the political debate. One of the animators is now definitely having an impact on the local political agenda by raising questions emanating from the small cooperative initiatives. This could then be described as a very dialectic process with the starting point being without any doubt a FAI where the local politicians tried to inspire and mobilize people. The success of the initiative has on the other hand been due to the FBIs that have stimulated the local establishment to take further steps forward – a kind of self-reinforcing 'positive circle'. And all this has been achieved in an environment whose main purpose is to defend the local community, the local lifestyle and most of whose activities have been of the sector-transcending kind with a strong emphasis on informal work.

The Local Problems

When you describe the problems and the solutions in the local society it is important to remember that people normally never act or try to change their perceived reality from ideological motives only (although this also happens). The normal pattern is to act in order to solve perceived problems or threats as they affect everyday life. In this section we will try to paint a broad picture of the problems we believe people act on and the types of local initiatives this results in. Our discussion is centred on the following five problem areas:
- Problems with social services.
- Social and cultural problems.
- Ecological problems and health problems.
- Problems concerning real incomes.
- Lack of jobs.

Lacking Social Services

This problem is either due to quantitative or qualitative deficiencies. The first arises when some service normally provided by society is lacking in supply. The typical Swedish problem today is lack of day care centres for children up to the age of seven. The typical local solution to this problem is for the parents to start themselves a cooperative day centre.

An example of the second type of deficiency, the qualitative aspect of social service, is when parents are dissatisfied with what the traditional education system has to offer. A rather popular solution today is that people with this common experience try to establish their own school according to some alternative ideology or pedagogical approach.

A problem that also has its root in the qualitative deficiencies is that elderly people increasingly refuse to be regarded as an intermediate good in the production system of the welfare state. One typical solution to this problem is for the elderly to build their own network for mutual help.

None of these examples are very large in number of participants or number of employed. Today there are about 150 cooperative day care centres run by parents. This is not so many. But on the other hand, three years ago there was only one. The number of alternative primary and secondary schools is also rather small, but in this field as well, the rate of growth is impressive, being today between 15 and 20. A few years ago it was less than five.

All these initiatives have different faces, and offer different solutions to everyday problems. In some of the cooperative day care centres, parents play largely the role of employers and the service is carried out by employed professionals. But in the dominating number of cases there is a mixture of informal labour from parents and paid labour from professionals.

The solutions and ventures described in this section have certain characteristics in common. First, to some extent, they create work opportunities. Second, they contribute to, or produce social networks and a culture of self-reliance, including major or minor changes in basic values. With this they also demonstrate that perceived problems can also be solved locally, even though social services or employment are lacking. Third, they create effects both on the tax system and on the demand for services through the public sector.

Social and Cultural Problems

This group of problems and activities concerns the social fragmentation and isolation in the modern welfare state. It is not only a problem of socially marginalized groups, recreation facilities and cultural poverty. It is often everything at once or a little bit of everything.

The reaction to this type of problem can take many forms. In a very modest way those small committees that exist in many tenement buildings fulfil the function of expressing the general opinion of the tenants when dealing with environmental or social problems, be it a pollution problem or a care centre for drug abusers.

This is a modest start, but a potential platform for a group of wider social initiatives and local networking.

In areas with a more advanced social structure or with heavier problems, a more elaborate form has developed; a form that is sometimes called experience workshop, utility workshop, cultural and handicraft club or perhaps a local multi-purpose cooperative.

They all share one ambition and that is trying to break down social isolation and fragmentation by stimulating some kind of grass-roots movement – combining cultural activities, social contacts, handicraft and recreation facilities. Let us illustrate this by describing the culture and handicraft club in the community of Järna, South of Stockholm. The club is situated in an old factory where they used to manufacture skates. On these premises there are today some 8 or 10 small companies, producing or selling mostly high-quality handicrafts made from natural materials under socially and environmentally acceptable conditions. One of the primary ambitions of the club is to stimulate an active cultural life in the community. They do this by staging art exhibitions, giving lectures, music evenings, etc. Another ambition is to stimulate people to start working with their hands, in order to experience their own possibilities of creating and producing.

Many of the activities taking place in the club do so in a very unclear grey zone between the small functioning handicraft companies and people just working on a do-it-yourself basis. This highlights the club's role as a greenhouse for new commercial ventures. In the everyday running of the skate factory, as it is called, it is never easy to distinguish clearly what is wage labour and what is informal labour.

This description, which is also valid for other places like 'Nyttoverkstaden' in Gothenburg or 'Erfarenhetsverkstaden' in Sätra, is an example of a rather new feature in the local economy and society. They serve as both preventive and rehabilitative institutions and try to get hold of youngsters and other marginal groups before they slip into the marginalized society. They play an active, but often informal role in the rehabilitation of some of the already marginalized groups in the local community and seem to create self-confidence and self-respect for people involved. But they also contribute to society in a more concrete way by stimulating small enterprises, employment opportunities both in cooperative companies and in more conventional businesses in the local economy.

From a more economistic perspective the results could be described in a slightly different way. First, activities aimed at alleviating social problems create human capital and social networks, thereby increasing the local aggregate production function. Second, this leads to businesses and jobs in trades that ordinary development agencies, banks or authorities never even consider, increasing the gross local resource base, potential markets and a flow of information that, on the one hand, affect local demand, and, on the other decrease the costs for information and thereby increase efficiency of the local economy by reducing uncertainty and risk.

This group includes many different areas but the common denominator for all of them is that people in one way or another are aware of problems with the ecological environment or their own personal health (or the health of their family – specifically children). People react in several different ways, depending on how strongly they perceive this threat and on their personal ideology.

The strongest reaction comes from those groups of young people (the so-called green wave) that move out from the cities and create their own ecological community in the countryside. Sometimes this is done in a sectarian way whereby the participants say goodbye to all kinds of modern technology such as tractors, chain saws and motocars. A much larger group, including about a hundred different collectives, has a more moderate attitude to modern society and its technology. A third group, perhaps the fastest growing today, are the people trying to create their own ecological community on a spiritual platform. They combine their exodus out of ordinary life with a strong striving for a holistic life in harmony with a certain set of spiritual principles. A few dozen of these groups now exist throughout Sweden, quite a few of which are inspired by Eastern religions such as the Krishna movement, and by Findhorn.

Another group of people are those coming together in order to discuss and change the role that food plays in their lives. The first step in this process is the formation of study circles on food, health and the global situation. The second step is the joint production of food. In a simple form it is perhaps just a question of baking bread together in an organized way or starting to grow vegetables together. Both activities could prove to be very profitable when translated into increases in purchasing power.

In a later phase they could begin to organize their activities in a more formal way. They may create an association for purchases and start to buy their own food directly from biological or organic growers, thereby saving money, acquiring better food and developing a social relationship to the farmer and to each other. It has been reported that a few hundred groups of this kind are in existence today. In the most advanced phase, this process develops into a more or less traditional consumer cooperative with a small grocery shop. Three or four years ago there were just two 'new' consumer cooperative shops in Sweden. Today they number about 20.

Solutions to ecological and health problems affect the local economy in several ways. On a wide scale they create better health, thereby lessening the burden of the public health systems. On a narrower scale they very often create local markets for food, hence affecting the local production systems. In a more dynamic perspective it can very often be seen that what first started out as a pure ecological project turned out to be a business idea well worth exploring commercially. This is the case, for example, with many of the solar cell companies that began in the late 1970s and early 1980s. One such organization, Solsam, which was started out of local ecological considerations, is now a commercially sound business in at least half a dozen municipalities all over Sweden.

Real Income Problems

Another type of problem is that which people have in balancing income and the cost of living. This problem has increased in intensity due to the long stagnation of the Swedish economy and the decline in real wages that has taken place over the last decade. The reactions to this can take several forms.

Those initiatives mentioned above where people try to get a better quality of food and save money represent one type of reaction. Another type of solution is when people are trying to utilize their resources better. This often means that people organize themselves in formal or informal associations for the exchange of advanced tools. 'I've got a chainsaw and you've got a welding kit'. By using each other's things we can all save money. A more advanced initiative is when people come together in a consumer organization owning their private cars but utilizing them in a collective form. This has been done in few places in Sweden (for example Vivalla bil in Örebro). Apparently this helps people to save up to between 5 – 10 per cent of their monthly expenditures, still having up to 95 per cent accessibility to transportation facilities.

Another type of solution is utilized when people who are unable to pay for different services in their house or in their household create associations for work exchange. In one of them bills are issued, each worth one day's work. Each member of the association is given a specific number of bills, and whenever he wants help with anything (from painting the house to cleaning the windows or perhaps building a new roof) he pays with those bills. A local currency (the bills) is created, valid only within a small group or community, for exchange of work and services. Actually what has transpired is the invention of money – but for a very specific socio-economic purpose.

In all these initiatives a lot of production is taking place. The majority of this is carried out through informal or cooperative work, mostly with the help of capital goods from the formal economy. So here we see an example of what Gershuny calls the self-service economy.[3]) But it is important to realize that work in most of these initiatives is not only functional in the sense of producing goods or services, but that it also has a very important social function.

These types of initiatives have two major impacts on the economy. One is that they alter the balance between the sectors in the economy through the self-service effect. The other is that they can function as an informal testing ground for new businesses in the service sector.

Lack of Jobs

A very obvious reason for starting grass-roots projects is that people do not get a job at all or the job they want through the usual institutions. The lack of jobs has a qualitative as well as a quantitative aspect, as does the lack of social services discussed earlier.

People can start initiatives aimed at providing a job in many ways. One group with special problems is of course youngsters not being able to establish themselves on the ordinary labour market. In many cases, during the last two years, young unemployed have been enrolled in initiatives called youth cooperatives. This type of initiative could be described as FAI with a mixed social and economic purpose. In some cases these youth cooperatives function as ordinary small-scale companies, sometimes as cooperatives with a substantial financial support from the local government, and sometimes as advanced socio-therapeutic institutions for marginalized groups.[4]

Another type of initiative are those used as a testing ground for a new social or economic venture. Here we find handicraft cooperatives for young artists who are not completely able to support themselves in a traditional way. We also find people who take a part-time leave from their ordinary job in order to experiment with something new or something they always wanted to try.

Still another type of initiative is when people want to support their local community with public services, revitalize local social networks and create viable job opportunities for themselves and others. This type of initiative may well be cast in a form called community cooperative.[5] One example of this is the island of Torsö in the municipality of Mariestad where 500 local inhabitants have come together in a kind of community cooperative, creating formal as well as informal jobs. In the process, they demonstrate how to save resources within the social services, by reducing unnecessary transportation costs, something that is all too common in remote areas.

Some Conclusions

To conclude this section and pave the way for the following discussion on the initiatives taken from the preceding paragraphs on some aspects of these FBIs' interaction with each other and with the FAIs. First of all, we can see that of all those initiatives described in this section, very few can be strictly categorized. They all seem to be a mixture of different motives. A cooperative day care centre could be regarded both as a way of solving problems with social service and of decreasing costs for child care. Growing your own vegetables could be seen both as a way of getting better food and of saving money, etc.

Second, we can assume that there is a tendency for one initiative to lead to another. People start cooking together, they continue by growing together and they inspire other people to start a new cooperative consumer organization. In other words, the successful local initiative seems to be contagious. It creates positive self-reinforcing circles. So, although they may start out with what seem to be trivial activities, they can generate projects with a real impact on the local economy. Thirdly, we must see that the 'from below initiatives' are related to the 'from above initiatives' in a very complex way. One description of this is that when there are a great number of successful grass-roots initiatives they create a cultural climate that makes it possible for the local decision-makers to take on new initiatives. This is perhaps what is going on in the municipality of Södertälje today.

We should also consider the reversed process, i. e. how FAIs can create a climate that stimulates grass-roots initiatives. This is perhaps the case of Övertorneå. It seems as if the relation to the established institutions in the welfare society could be described like a process of growing wine. If you give it too much nourishment, you get a flat and uninteresting wine, and if you give too little, the plant will die.

The From Above Initiative (FAI)

Introduction to the Concept

In this description of initiatives taken from above, we choose the Swedish municipality of Norberg as an illustration.[6] But before we go deeper into the case of Norberg, we shall make a cursory description of some of the other above-mentioned local initiatives, primarily to show that the case of Norberg is not just a very odd phenomenon in the welfare state, but rather a representative of something quite new.

Let us then first distinguish between initiatives taken in rural areas and those taken in more populated areas. Then, we should distinguish between initiatives taken as a reaction to an acute and present crisis and those, taken as a response to a slowly emerging or latent crisis. Given these two pairs we get a typology as shown in figure 1.

In the case of Norberg, a small industrial town, we have the typical situation for local and broad mobilization. In Bräcke, we have the small scale and a serious crisis on a long-term perspective. So the local projects in Bräcke still have a very

	rural	urban
Figure 1		
acute/quick	Norberg	Landskrona
latent/slow	Bräcke	Södertälje

long mobilization perspective, but lack the dynamics and anarchistic patterns which are so visible in Norberg.

Hence many of the initiatives taken in Bräcke are the result of small groups creating themselves in a very informal way, quite close to the established society. The results have been quite diverse: a small-scale cooperative fishing and exporting pikes to Paris, a large number of study circles, studying the local history, a local energy company, a youth cooperative, just to give a few examples of what could happen in a very small municipality, when new and sector-transcending strategies are used to create jobs and local development.

The case of Södertälje is completely different. Here we have a medium-sized industrial town in the middle of the industrial heartland of Sweden. No obvious crisis is present. But it is also clearly understood from the local level, that in the post-industrial society the winners are not the typical industrial towns. As a result of this, a lot of future-oriented work is being carried out in Södertälje. Coalitions have been created between local politicians and local representatives of centralized public authorities, between the formal and informal sector and between politicians in different parties. Support is created for new and unconventional projects in the nowhere-land between the formal and informal sector. Slowly there is a growing support from the local government for the very strong advocates of the Steiner movement located in the municipality, inventing a unique coalition between the established society and the alternative movement.

The case of Landskrona is still completely different. Landskrona used to be one of the leading shipbuilding towns in Sweden. But within just a few years the entire shipbuilding industry and all its supporting industry was wiped away. The solution was a strange combination of massive industrial policy, local mobilization and regional fund raising, carried out by new and unexpected coalitions of actors in the local arena.

Norberg – Some Background

Norberg, a small municipality of about 6,500 inhabitants takes its name from the densely built-up centrally located town of Norberg itself, with a population of about 5,500. The town has an industrial tradition which goes far back in time. Mining and the manufacture of iron and steel have served since the middle ages as the hub around which other economic activities have developed. Like other mill towns, Norberg has a rich association life, often with strong ties to the labour movement. The past few decades have been marked by continuous closures of iron and steel plants. One of these, Spännarhyttan, was shut down in 1981, an event which can be seen as the end of Norberg's history as an ore-based mill town.

The Play and the Model

In Norberg one can speak of two separate but connected schemes of experiments, the Norberg play and the Norberg model. The plays sprang from a lively theatrical ensemble based in the neighbouring municipality of Fagersta, which in the mid 1970s wanted to try out new forms of drama and to make people conscious of their roots and their own history. A number of associations and both local governments were successfully brought into the drama project, which was a precursor of the "Dig Where You Strand" movement that got underway a year or so later in Sweden. Each year about 400 persons take part in this theater festival, and performances have been put on every summer since the premiere in 1977.

The plays managed to get the Norberg residents involved in their own history, to give them self-esteem and to demonstrate the toughness and fighting spirit which are inalienably associated with Norberg, and were most notably manifested in the strike of 1981 – 82 – the theme of the first play. To simplify a bit, we can say that the Norberg play introduced a special Norberg spirit, a sense of pride and a readiness for battle.

The Norberg model, initiated in 1981, is an attempt to create employment in a municipality that has been hit hard by structural change in the iron and steel industry. Its aims were defined as: "to bring in all sections of the community to forge a united front *against* unemployment and *for* more permanent jobs locally and the development of Norberg in as many areas as possible".[7]

The birth of the Norberg model is intimately tied to the closure of Spännarhyttan and can be seen as a result of, first, an insight into the necessity for Norberg to create its own employment pattern; and second, a commitment by ASEA, the National Development Foundation and a consultant for Spännarhyttan who had worked earlier on the closure of another foundry, Vikmanshyttan. The consultant drew up guidelines for a local development project and won over the local authorities. After some preliminary meetings between the municipality and interest groups, a public meeting was held, attended by some 200 Norberg residents. The idea was presented on this occasion, and a number of study groups were formed, consisting of hand-picked group leaders and interested locals. Quality was put before quantity: the leaders of the various groups serve as private persons and not as representatives of different organizations, associations and institutions. The cooperation of key figures in business, labour and local government has been successful, a configuration the project leaders considered essential for the model to work properly. In this way the model symbolized a team effort that cuts across all party and interest-group lines, with a firm base in local government. Such teamwork was no doubt rendered smoother by the favourable experiences gained at the drama festival.

The Norberg model has done well by the locality. Some 110 jobs have been created in Norberg. Local unemployment would thus have been something like

50 per cent higher without the project (ceteris paribus). If we include the spread effects of the jobs created by the project, e. g. in the service sector, another 100 jobs can be ascribed to the Norberg model.[8] Efforts are made wherever possible to transmit the tradition of enterprise and craftsmanship that is to be found locally. An atmosphere of optimism has no doubt spread in Norberg as the model has developed successfully. Some of this atmosphere must be ascribed to the plays that gave the first boost to local morale, something the model has been able to build on and develop.

Objectives – Jobs or Visions?

The precipitating factor for the Norberg model and the striving it embodies was the closure of the foundry. It is also no exaggeration to say that the closure decision was like the explosion of a bomb in the community. Efforts were mobilized to save jobs, i. e. work through the formal system (sending a group to Stockholm to discuss with the Minister of Industry and others within the government), but that failed. With the shut-down of the foundry, the ones that lost most faith were the local councillors: it was evident that the usual political and administrative channels would not come to the rescue, as the local authorities assumed. The realization dawned on them that they would have to do their own job creation, and that this had to be done in new ways, as the ordinary way of doing it pre-supposed governmental financing.

The germ of a self-reliance idea took shape within local government. Support for the development of this idea was forthcoming from a cooperative consulting group, which, in the project's first phase, accounted for many of the intersectoral analyses and specific inputs that were made in the study groups and new firms. There is much evidence to suggest that a large part of the credit for the Norberg model goes to one man, the part-time employed project leader Egon Gröning (also vice chairman of the municipal council). Gröning is the project's prime mover and front man. It is no exaggeration to say that a majority of the ventures in the Norberg model have developed in his office or kitchen.

On one plane the Norberg model can be said to lack a vision, i. e. no official objective has been formulated to change the community in a specific direction. Instead there is a very concrete objective – to create as many permanent jobs as possible. But underlying this prime objective and the work that has been done is a vision of self-reliance, a thrust aimed at small-scale production, etc. It is hard to judge how important this vision is compared to the pragmatic objective of creating employment. We feel that this is a strength as well as a weakness in the Norberg model and other similar job-oriented projects. The objective to create as many employment opportunities as possible is easy to understand and rally to. It is also very easy to follow the fulfilment of specific targets in terms of the number of employed people. However, in the long run, this might turn out to be a weakness. As time goes by and jobs are created, it must be difficult to keep people enthusiastic. Once we have created 100 or 200 jobs, then what? It is then that the vision of a change on another plane in the community becomes important. The project must incorporate some ideals to strive for. They may be cultural, social, ecological, ideological or whatever, the point is that one needs something besides the crude objective of creating more employment opportunities. Maybe the weariness that seems to be spreading in the Norberg model today is a sign that this wider/deeper objective was missing. Maybe the plays gave this wider objective in an indirect way during the first two years of the model. It is possible.

A Fourth Sector Approach to the Cases Described

All the cases described in this chapter have something in common. They meet the eye in an unknown land between the formal and informal economy. They are neither really a part of the private first sector, nor the public second sector, nor even the informal third sector. From our point of view, they represent something completely new within the framework of the Swedish welfare society – a fourth sector. This sector is trying to cope with some of the deficiencies of the traditional welfare state; it is not primarily a substitute for the welfare state, but a complement making it marginally better. Looking upon the local initiatives presented here and others not mentioned,[9] this fourth sector could be defined as initiatives that are:

Local in the sense that the initiative and the main actors appear in the local arena with the specific purpose of strengthening the local economy. The local aspect also stresses the importance of local control over the developing process.

Self-reliant insofar as this is one dominating aspect of the initiative taken. This could be seen as a major break with the ideology of the welfare state, where it is always assumed that 'somebody else' (the government, the unions or the technostructure) is responsible for the solution of local problems. The traditional definition of self-reliance stresses both the physical access to resources, the organizational skill and the mental attitude.[10] And all three of them are important features in the development of the fourth sector. This aspect of the fourth sector rules out all initiatives taken from outsiders believing that they can solve local problems (in other words a requiem for the Florence Nightingale solution).

Cooperative in a broad sense, i. e. with organizations, individuals and institutions cooperating to reach a goal. This rules out any unilateral initiative, both personal (i. e. a single entrepreneur trying to start a business) and organizational/institutional (i. e. a big corporation making 'social investment' or a municipal council engaging in an employment scheme for young unemployed). The "sole actor model"[11] is therefore ruled out.

Sector transcending in that both the public and the private sector participate in many initiatives. Another frequent element can be the participation of organizations from the voluntary or non-profit sector.

The initiative often *includes informal elements that are important for the success of the project.* We regard the informal networks, work groups, study circles, etc. as a vital ingredient in fourth sector initiatives. They may play a more or less prominent role in each and every project.

The initiatives often have to *apply new evaluation criteria* in the sense that formal profitability is not enough to judge a project worthwhile or not. This is not to say that the people involved do not want commercial ventures to be economically profitable, of course they do. It is more a reflexion of the fact that the ventures undertaken stem in many cases, from a public, mixed public/private or a mixed initiative explicitly involving the informal sector in terms of employment or goods/services produced.

The majority of fourth sector initiatives have additional/other objectives than merely creating jobs. As we see it, the most important objective, at least in a commercial business, is to *produce and sell something one believes in,* be it a pizza, a piece of small-scale machinery, an environmentally sound paper mill, biologically grown grains, a better social environment for immigrants, etc.

Countervailing powers is another aspect of the fourth sector. Most, not to say all, fourth sector initiatives grow out of the conviction that many forces from the outer world, be it a locally dominating mining company, governmental labour market measures or local effects from events on the world market, affect the local economy and the local social life in a more or less devastating way. Hence the fourth sector initiatives could be regarded as a counter-force with the specific purpose of creating a less vulnerable local culture and economy.

Cultural and social aspects are important and sometimes dominating in fourth sector initiatives. In most cases there is a local understanding of the fact that they can't compete with the Silicon Valleys of this world. Instead they have to identify, investigate and stimulate the specific local culture in order to create a local economic and social development process based on their own abilities and advantages.

To summarize the characteristics of the fourth sector initiatives one could say that they are initiatives that grow out of the local community as a reaction to forces from the outside world. These reactions are very often cooperative, socially biased and are often cast in an informal and sector-transcending form. They have as a main objective the creation of a viable local culture based on a sound, self-reliant and not so vulnerable economy, producing things that people believe in, the majority of which, in the long run, are marketable both internally and externally.

With this delimitation in initiatives qualifying for the fourth sector title, we can easily see that the 'usual' entrepreneur or the 'usual' governmental (at whatever level) employment scheme is ruled out. This may appear strict, but we feel it is necessary in order to capture what we believe is a new and promising feature in economic development and labour markets locally in the entire industrialized world. We have to rule out the business-as-usual initiatives in order to crystallize the genuine features of this new and exciting type of project.

What Might Come Out of the Fourth Sector?

Introduction

The first section of this chapter presented a very gloomy picture of the state of the Swedish economy in general and the welfare state in particular. Against this gloomy picture we then described many interesting initiatives taken at the local level, directed at alleviating personal problems or problems in the local community.

The natural thing to ask at this point is of course: 'how do these initiatives affect the gloomy picture of the present status of the welfare state?' To say that we could answer that question would of course be a great exaggeration. Nevertheless we will discuss the possible positive effects of the emerging fourth sector initiatives in this section.

Let us begin by stating that we do not envisage everything in the Swedish economy and the Swedish welfare state to be run as fourth sector initiatives. They will

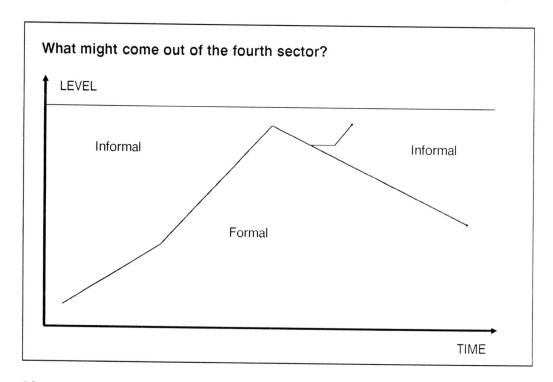

What might come out of the fourth sector?

LEVEL

Informal

Formal

Informal

TIME

remain a complement to the usual workings of the economy and the welfare state. The fourth sector will not emerge as a quantitatively huge economic sector as the public sector once did. In statistical terms, fourth sector initiatives become private, public, informal or mixed activities just as before. Fourth sector expansion is more of a qualitative nature than a quantitative one.

Fourth Sector Initiatives and the Public Sector

The problems of the public sector are multi-faceted. We have pure financial problems, problems with productivity decreases and decreasing legitimacy, etc. What can fourth sector initiatives do against this background?

The crucial point here is the fourth sector mixture of informal/formal activities. It may not seem like much to say that we can envisage more informal elements in the production of social service, medical service, education, maintenance, etc. Technically speaking, however, this means a lot. It means that employees in the public sector become more and more productive as their duties are shared by informal workers. Tax payers get more service out of every SEK they pay. From the production side we can see it as a new mode of social service provision.

In this diagram we illustrate a development in which provision of social service first becomes formalized and institutionalized. This is the development up to the early 1980s when growth rates began falling short of the 2-3 per cent needed to counteract the negative productivity development. We envisage social service production becoming more and more informalized over the coming years. This informalization of social services can take on many shapes. In some countries it is just a fine way of making drastic cuts in public expenditures, which is not what we are after here. The end result may well be reduced public outlays (as a result of a reduced need for them), but it must not be the starting point.

The diagram illustrates another important point to make. We should never fool ourselves into believing that the services today performed by the formal economy in general and the public sector in particular were created by them. Many, not to say most, tasks performed by the public sector today, were previously performed within the informal economy, by households and groups in the local economy. So the level of services does not have to be affected by a reinformalization of social services (the main objective with the present mode of welfare provision has of course been distributive, something we return to in the following section).

So, we assume that the mode of welfare provision changes. How will this affect the gloomy picture of the welfare state? In several possible ways:

(a) The financial strain for a given level of services can decrease, i. e. it *costs less* to produce the same amount.

(b) It is possible to *expand the level of services* provided at constant or less than proportionally increased costs.

(c) The *quality of the services improve,* as there is a more direct contact between users and producers.

(d) As a consequence of (a)-(c), *legitimacy* of the public sector and the welfare state in general is improved.

Fourth Sector Initiatives and Employment

If provision of welfare services is one basic tenet of the welfare state, full employment is the other and just as hard to live up to today. Many fourth sector initiatives are geared to creating employment in different ways as we saw for instance in the case of Norberg previously. What will happen if the emerging fourth sector type of employment initiatives becomes *the* normal way of influencing employment opportunities?

Let us first of all state that fourth sector employment initiatives, like the one described in Norberg, have been very successful in their local context.

• They work with *local resources* and are primarily aimed at utilizing local resources, thus i. e. stealing businesses from a neighbouring community is rare in these circumstances.

• They explicitly develop a *unique local economic culture,* with its own profile of branches, entrepreneurs and skills. This culture does not develop overnight, but on the other hand, it is persistent.

• They primarily go for small-scale businesses, thereby increasing the *flexibility of the local economy.* As more and more businesses are created through the local initiatives, a firmer social and economic network will emerge between these businesses. This network will be productive on its own and promote further development.

• They create *informal and formal networks* between important actors on the local and regional level. This may well lead to a looser attitude towards those rigid decision rules that otherwise block development projects. In general, decision-makers will have better understanding of each other's problems and possibilities and of how they can be useful to each other.

Bearing this in mind, we can envisage local economies working more smoothly and creating more employment than the faltering and rigid economy of today. This is not to say that every municipality should make it on its own and that national policies and support systems should be abandoned. Not every municipality or intermediary organization has the capacity or stamina to turn a declining labour market on its own. They must have help.

The rigidity of the labour market of today can very well be influenced in a positive way. The most crucial aspect of this transformation is of course the realization that employment, or work, does not have to be synonymous to 8 hours a day, five days a week, with full pay and security benefits. Alternative work patterns can and should be explored.

54

Having said this, we fully realize that it could be seen as a way to ruin everything the labour movement has strived for and accomplished. This is not the case. On the contrary, we see it as one necessary ingredient in the development of the employment component in a functional welfare state.

Fourth Sector Initiatives and Social Relations

One of the serious problems of the modern welfare state is its deteriorating social relations. Many people find their lives totally fragmented. This causes a lot of strain and mental as well as physical illness, which in turn strikes back at the welfare state in terms of medical bills, increasing social costs, etc. It is a never-ending vicious circle.

We argue that social networking in general and increased social contacts between people are the core of fourth sector initiatives. Thus, fourth sector initiatives represent a break with the trend towards further individualization and fragmentation. Whether this will be sufficient enough to turn this dismal development in its entirety, we cannot say. It will certainly not add to it.

The social benefits of fourth sector initiatives will in themselves generate economic effects. In our description of Norberg earlier, we tried to present two connected events – the play and the model. After having studied several local development projects, we feel it is safe to say that such an initiative as the play, formally unconnected to the economic or social initiative is a key factor for its success. This brings us to an interesting observation. Although social, cultural, or other non-economic effects may be seen as less worthwhile in the short run, they may be crucial for the long-run development of the economy and a welfare state. Fourth sector initiatives then create social by-products that lay the foundation for a further development of the welfare state. The present development in the Swedish welfare state does just the opposite.

Problems of Fourth Sector Initiatives

Introduction

Fourth sector initiatives can alleviate many of the problems in the Swedish welfare state. This is the positive message from the previous section. But there are also problematic features of fourth sector initiatives. In this section we look into some of these problems.

As before, we will only be able to hint at some results and the necessary analysis.[12] Let us look at the questions one by one.

Allocative Effects of Fourth Sector Initiatives

Judging allocative effects may be the most common trait of the traditional economist. Armed with general equilibrium analysis and a belief in Paretian efficiency, the economist looks first of all for disturbances in the information system, i. e. market prices in most cases. Fourth sector initiatives, as we have described them in earlier sections, are taken in many areas, some of which have repercussions on the market and some have not. Let us dwell on two types of fourth sector initiatives that may affect the market.

Our first example is Norberg, described earlier, which fits the role of a local development agency. Have we any cause to assume that this development agency will act in concordance with the usual efficiency criteria applied by development agencies elsewhere? Maybe.

In a region struck by economic crisis, previously dependent on a single manufacturer, with a one-sided profile on labour competence, etc. the likelihood of finding ripe business ideas and entrepreneurs is small. In this situation, it is natural to assume that the development agency in question will apply less strict criteria for helping out with seed money, consultants, permits, etc.

It is, however, impossible to say that this will lead to inefficiency. On the one hand, the end result may prove it to be efficient in a way no one could envisage in the first place, and on the other hand, the resources utilized in the venture (labour, land, premises, etc.) may be over-valued, seen from a societal perspective.[13]

So, by simply stating that an agency applies more accommodating criteria, we don't have a case for inefficiency; at least not when viewed from a profitablility perspective alone. We can, however, pursue the effects one step further and ask what impact it will have on the entrepreneurs' incentives to strive for profitability. Will they foster a new economic culture where goals other than economic success are seen as important?

This is also a question that is hopeless to answer in advance. And even if the agency did contribute to a less jungle-like economic culture, will this be detrimental to the economy and efficiency? We do not believe that this has to be. Cooperative firms and economic systems (Yugoslavia, Mondragon in Spain, etc.) seem to be doing just as well as or better than their private capitalistic counterparts. Mixing social with economic goals does not have to be at the expense of economic efficiency.[14]

This brings us over to the ventures themselves, cooperative or otherwise. In employment initiatives we must assume that most ventures are initiated to be economically viable. So, even if there are other types of goals present, profitability or breaking even surely must be on the agenda. And, if this is the case, we should not have to worry too much about whether they are efficient or not. Maximum private profits after tax don't tell the whole story.

So, when looking at the local employment and development type of initiative and the ventures they create, we should not be pessimistic as to their allocative effects. They may be seen as somewhat unusual compared to ordinary business development agencies, banks, big corporations, etc. but that does not mean that they are inefficient.

Looking at other types of activities, mainly non-market, directed at social service provision, the market is not the point of reference. In most welfare states, social services are provided by a public sector and by a non-market allocation process, something which many economists are critical of in itself.

Fourth sector initiatives should be attractive to all those who believe that a closer coupling between producer and user is beneficial to efficiency in resource use and quality of the service produced. Certain services, such as highly specialized medical services, are out of the question, as they require resources impossible to create in a fourth sector initiative. But, apart from these few scale-dependent services, most social services surely could be produced (more?) efficiently in fourth sector initiatives. On the other hand, efficiency has not been the leading star in the growth of the social services provided by the public sector.

Distributive Effects of Fourth Sector Initiatives

In introducing fourth sector initiatives in the provision of social services otherwise provided by the public sector, we find ourselves on the controversial terrain of distribution policies.

Equal treatment and possibilities have long been regarded as the prime characteristic of the Swedish welfare state. You should be expecting the same medical care, social care, etc. regardless of income, age or geographical location. This is also the first criterion against which all changes are measured. One for all and all for one.

The introduction of fourth sector initiatives does not fill this requirement. By necessity, the service provided will be different depending on the people participating. They will find different solutions in different types of regions, demographically different groups, economically and socially different groups, etc. The degree of informality in the provision of the service will determine what chances there are of redistributing resources between different groups and regions.

As long as part of it is informal, most politicians and interest groups will be sceptical, and quite rightly so, about their distributive effects. Many investigations have shown that the resourceful also have a tendency to come out on the winning side when it comes to informal economic activities.[15]

But this is not the same as saying that it is impossible to make informal economic activities more acceptable from a distributive point of view. We believe that it is possible to do so.[16]

Although many would claim that the welfare state of today is an equal society and use this view of the welfare state as a comparison, we feel this is a completely incorrect approach. As we argued previously, the welfare state is heading for inequalities, with the so-called new poverty being only the first sign. The effects of our present tax and transfer system are impossible to evaluate and we just keep on patching it up at the edges. The financial problems of the public sector will lead to less equal treatment and low quality services, etc.

Thus, the picture to compare with is instead one of an economy moving towards inequality and increased difficulties in upholding the equality, once it has been gained. In this perspective fourth sector initiatives may be seen as a possibility rather than a problem, a possibility well worth exploring once we can show that the negative distributive effects are possible to overcome or to minimize.

Stability and Fourth Sector Initiatives

In the ILE programme of the Organization for Economic Cooperation and Development (OECD)[17], the following properties concerning local employment initiatives are put forth.

● They create supply and demand with minimal substitution effects on existing markets, i. e. it is not a question of stealing employment opportunities from the neighbouring municipality.

● They generate investment and employment with small inflationary impact and comparatively low requirements for capital and energy.

● They contribute, at a very low cost, to investments in human capital through job experience, training, etc.

● Overall, they demand very little government support and accomplish a great deal with the little support they receive.

This gives us a very promising picture of how fourth sector initiatives can contribute to the overall macro-economic development. No inflationary pressure, no disruptions, no zero-sum games, less pressure on the state budget, etc. But will the Minister of Finance be happy? How will local economies with abundant initiatives react to fiscal policies?

(a) They create *information problems* by utilizing the informal economy to a large extent. And as economic decision-makers base their decisions on economic accounts of different sorts, they will miss part of the picture.

(b) In the *short run,* they will *lower* the *taxbase* and thereby contribute to the deficit in the state budget. In the long run this will be offset by a reduction in expenditures.

(c) Macro-economic *policies* will become *less potent.* The multipliers decrease as the leakages between the formal and the informal economy increase. On the other hand, this also increases the stabilizers in the economy, i. e. it will tend to fluctuate less and therefore require less intervention.

(d) Most likely, fourth sector initiatives will contribute to a decrease in imports. This will *decrease the leakages* through imports and thereby make macro-economic policies more forceful, i. e. it will counteract the effects of increased leakage between the informal and the formal economy.

It is impossible to say whether this list of pros and cons will seem attractive to economic decision-makers. We find these macro-economic characteristics appealing in light of the economic problems we are facing today. To lose some macro-economic control (did we ever have it?) seems a small price to pay.

The Fourth Sector and the Welfare State

Introduction

We have discussed the threats to the present welfare state. We have also discussed some local solutions to the problems. Local initiatives, or what we call the fourth sector, is certainly not the complete solution to the present predicament. On the contrary, it must and should be seen as a complement to conventional macro-policies, investments in R&D, reshaping the infrastructure, etc.

But by stressing the local perspective and putting the fourth sector into focus, we are pointing at an under-utilized instrument and field of interest in the revitalization of the welfare state.[18]

The emerging fourth sector could be regarded both as a threat to the present welfare state and as a unique possibility to revitalize it. But it could also be completely neglected as just a minor phenomenon on the outskirts of the welfare society. However, as far as we can tell, the latter is not the case.

Given the fact that the fourth sector in the economy exists and assuming a further expansion of it, how could it be related to and integrated with the present welfare state?

Some Effects

First, we can see how the growth of the fourth sector affects the minds of established politicians. We can actually speak about some kind of *mental infiltration* on several different levels; local politicians considering cooperatives like the cases of Övertorneå and Orebro; the growing ambitions within the political establishment support all kinds of different local initiatives, be it biologically grown vegetables or social networking. This phenomenon comes from the political periphery and is now slowly reaching the political centre, at least on an intellectual level.

Secondly, we have the *institutional effects*, the fact that the emerging fourth sector is altering the institutional balance of society. The most obvious field is the labour market where the mix of formal and informal work is now slowly redefining the concept of work itself. Another interesting field is within the public sector where fourth sector initiatives, parents participating in school with their children, relatives contributing in medical care, etc. seem to loosen the boundaries of the public sector and increase its formal productivity at the same time. If this institutional fragmentation accelerates, some of the traditional policy instruments of the welfare state will decline in value and power.

The third phenomenon is the creation of *new coalitions* as a result of an emerging fourth sector. As this new economic sector by definition is sector-transcending, an effective use of it will presuppose new coalitions of actors; between local authorities and the local branches of state authorities, as in the case of Södertälje, between the established society and different social and cultural movements, as in the case of Norberg. These coalitions are not only changing but also improving the performance of the present welfare state.[19]

One should not misjudge the concept of the fourth sector. First of all, it is not an economic sector in the traditional sense. It could not be measured by conventional statistics. Rather it is a very subtle, qualitatively new phenomenon transcending the normal economic sector boundaries. Sometimes private, sometimes public, sometimes informal, but most of the time a little bit of everything. Furthermore, the size of this phenomenon should be neither over- nor underestimated; not overestimated because it is, when it comes to numbers, rather small; not underestimated because, when it comes to effect, it seems to have a non-negligible power.

Some Policy Implications

The emerging fourth sector indicates a number of potential policy implications. Let us very briefly indicate some of them.[20]
- The emerging fourth sector points out the need for a new entrepreneurial theory for local development, being able to define those entrepreneurs missed by conventional thinking.
- The emerging fourth sector indicates that local development is primarily a social and cultural phenomenon, not an economic pattern. There is a need for a local socio-cultural development theory.
- The emerging fourth sector as a phenomenon is primarily linked with the phenomenon of creativity. Nobody has defined the concept of local creativity in such a way that it is useful for local development policies.
- The emerging fourth sector builds on sector-transcending phenomena. Yet, at present no theory nor policy instruments have been formulated for facilitating this. Altogether, it is quite clear that if the fourth sector, is to be a contributing factor in vitalizing the welfare state, an urgent need exists for a completely new local industrial and development policy. To explore this field will be a task for our future research.

Notes

1) A detailed analysis is presented in Nilsson, I., Wadeskog, A., 1986, The fourth sector, OECD/SEE.
2) See also paper with the same title by Nilsson,I., Wadeskog, A., 1982.
3) Cf. Gershuny, J., 1978, After Industrial Society, Macmillan; Gershuny, J., 1983, Social Innovations and the Division of Labour, Oxford University Press.
4) Nilsson, Wadeskog, Höök, 1984, 'Ju mer vi är tillsammans. . - en analys av fyra ungdomskooperativ' (The more we are together – an analysis of youth cooperatives), The Cooperative Institute/SEE.
5) Cf. Stettner, 1980, 'Community Cooperatives in the British Isles', Journal of Rural Cooperation, No. 1-2.
6) Norberg is part of the Bergslagen region which is studied in the OECD/ILE programme (cf. OECD/ILE SME/ILE/85.07); we base part of this description of the Norberg model on Nilsson, I., and Wadeskog, A., 1983, 'Role of Culture in Local Development Process', National Council for Cultural Affairs/SEE.
7) Taken from the information sheet about the model.
8) OECD/ILESME/ILE/85.07
9) A full description is to be found in 'Hur såg Heffaklumpen egentligen ut?', Nilsson, I., Wadeskog, A., 1986, SEE & Sekretariatet för framtidsstudier.
10) Cf Dahlgren, Mártensson, 1983, 'Sårbarhet och självtillit' (Vulnerability and Self-reliance), nordREFO.
11) Cf Watzke 'Large company involvement in local employment initiatives' OECD SME/ILE/84.11.
12) For a more thorough description, see: Nilsson, I., Wadeskog, A., 1986, 'A Fourth Sector Approach to Local Development and Employment Initiatives', SEE/OECD, SME/ILE/(86.01.).
13) By this we mean as measured in conventional cost-benefit analysis, by the scarcity value.
14) For formal and empirical proof see: Stephen, 1984, 'The Economic Analysis of Producers Cooperatives', Macmillan.
15) Cf Redclift, Migione (eds.), 1985, 'Beyond Employment', Blackwell.
16) We develop this in Nilsson, I., Wadeskog, A., 1986, 'Kooperation och informell ekonomi' (Cooperation and the Informal Economy), Brevskolan.
17) See: OECD/ILE (84)2 (1st revision) 'Clarifying Report on the Economic and Social Role of Social Level Employment Initiatives'.
18) It should be mentioned that our empirical base for the statements to follow is a rather thorough experience from our work as consultants, lecturers and seminar leaders for some hundreds of local and regional politicians during the last three years. See also Nilsson,I., Wadeskog, A., 1986, Hur såg egentligen Heffaklumpen ut? (A Study About Local Change) SEE/Sekretariatet för framtidsstudier.
19) It has for example been clearly shown that this kind of coalitions in the case of Södertälje has managed to get some 300 young people into jobs on the conventional labour market in less than one year.
20) These policy implications are discussed at length in Nilsson, I., Wadeskog, A., 1986, 'A Fourth Sector Approach to Local Development and Employment Initiatives', SEE/OECD, SME/ILE/(86.01.).

Institutional Reorganization and New Shifts in the Welfare Mix in Italy During the 1980s

Pierpaolo Donati and Ivo Colozzi

Premises: Our General Framework

This is a general report on the Italian welfare state. It is based on a theoretical framework which conceives of the welfare state as a societal sub-system (see figure 1) which regulates the economic sub-system *via* a corporatist compromise between the government, political parties and unions. Outside this institutional structure, which rules the whole society, there are welfare organizations and networks clearly inter-related to the other 'side' of society (and constrained by it), but at the same time free to take initiatives, run services and enact different (i. e. non-economic and non-political) exchanges.

The main assumption is that the present crisis of the post-war welfare state can be interpreted as a major inability and/or impossibility of the state as 'institutional structure' to produce its own civil society, which it has been trying to do at least to some extent during the late 1960s and the 1970s[1]).

Aside from many practical reasons[2]), such an impossibility is fundamentally linked to two macro-structural trends:

• After the 1970s the Italian society has been undergoing a large-scale process of *deep social differentiation,* whereby new social spheres and actors tend to emerge, particularly in relation to a new welfare society.

• Such a societal process of differentiation is basically understandable as *an increase of complexity* at whose core there is an opposition between the 'formal welfare state', built up on the 'state-market complex', and the 'third and fourth sectors', shaped mainly by social-private agencies (e. g. non-profit and voluntary organizations) and infomal networks arranged by families, friends, neighbours and other informal actors. Of course the formal and informal sides are not separate, but strongly interlinked and interdependent; their 'opposition' can be conceived of in terms of an increasing distance and difference in their needs, symbolic codes, and ways of functioning and coping with social change.

The present societal change is characterized by the emergence of 'new rules' in

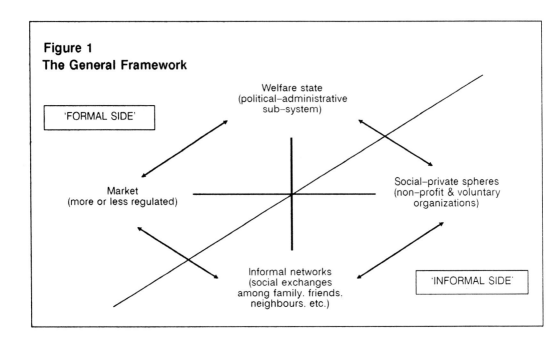

Figure 1
The General Framework

'FORMAL SIDE'

Welfare state
(political–administrative
sub–system)

Market
(more or less regulated)

Social–private spheres
(non–profit & voluntary
organizations)

Informal networks
(social exchanges
among family. friends.
neighbours. etc.)

'INFORMAL SIDE'

all the sub-systems (figure 1) in such a way that each sphere of specific social relations needs its own 'symbolic and material code' in order to be able to answer
to 'meaning and practical imperatives' embodied in that relational sphere[3]).

As research has shown, the Italian welfare state cannot solve its problems by rationalizing the 'state-market complex' alone[4]). Certainly, it can try to externalize
its financial, social and political costs from the institutional side to the informal
one. To a certain degree this is true for the more recent state budget laws ('financial laws' for 1985 and 1986). But also in this way the Italian welfare state seems
unable to cope with its most important problems, such as the public financial debt
and the inefficiencies of the public (esp. welfare) administration. In the end, it
must resort to the 'informal side'. The issue is *how* it happens and/or *can* be
done in such a way as to enrich, and not to dismantle, basic welfare rights.

In order to make all this clear, we will examine first of all the failure of the 'great
plan' of the 1970s, aimed at setting up a quasi-total welfare state. By relying upon
empirical data, we will then describe the structural features and trends to which
the Italian welfare security system has to react. At this point we will give a general
outlook of the new orientations among policy-makers, and finally we will discuss
the role of the voluntary sector in Italy. Other issues, in particular those linked to
the labour market and the delivery of social services at the local level, will be
presented in the other Italian chapter by M. Bianchi and C. Saraceno. In our conclusions, we try to offer a fresh image of the changes being effected in the Italian
cultural and political approach to welfare.

The 'Great Plan' of the 1970s and Its Failure

The reorganization of the Italian welfare state cannot be fully understood without starting from the crisis of institutional arrangements, both legal and actual, which began to take shape in the 1970s.

These arrangements have been largely set up by the body of laws dating from 1970, when regions under ordinary statute were created, to 1978, when law no. 833, establishing the national health care service, was passed. Law no. 382/1975 and the Decree by the President of the Republic (DPR) no. 616/1977 deserve particular mention, having decentralized most social relief functions and services (social and health care services) to local administrations, with the exception of social security which is still managed by the national system. From 1970 to 1978 a new public offer of welfare by the state was made, through tasks and functions delegated to regions. The idea was to enhance the institutional pattern of the welfare state towards a 'quasi-total' pattern (Donati 1983). According to this pattern, public bodies were in principle expected to guarantee the satisfaction of all social needs to the population through a wide network of universalistic decentralized welfare services under nationwide uniform standards, with chiefly preventive orientation, and with broad participation by the population. Within the social and health care services, the private sector and the third sector (i. e. non-profit-making or solidaristic associations) should have been potentially configurated as 'residual' interventions.

After 1978, especially with the beginning of the health care reform, the difficulties of implementing such a pattern became increasingly self-evident. In fact, a very severe crisis hit the institutional pattern of the welfare state in the early 1980s. In our opinion the indications of this crisis can be summarized as follows:

• First of all, it became evident that the public administration was unable to change from a mainly welfare-oriented and social control layout to an up-dated organization 'promoting well-being' in character. In actual fact, the 1970 laws resulted chiefly in disclosing a very high degree of ineffectiveness, inefficiency and lack of equity in services rendered by the state administration. This body was basically unable to use local intervention for solving the major and material social problems.

• On the other hand, the revenue crisis of the state was largely a consequence of economic stagflation, imposed to curb social expenditures, and accordingly expenses for services were cut in some sectors.

• Social intervention patterns appeared to be incapable of being coordinated and supplemented amongst the major welfare sectors, namely employment, revenue, and (general and personal) social services sectors. Policies for the labour market, low-income support categories, and social relief and health care sectors remained very fragmentated and confined to sectors.

• In particular, the failed integration between health care and social services is ascribed to the fact that the national implementation act for social services has not yet been passed. Bills relating to this have failed because the government and political parties had little motivation and were immobilized by internal conflicts. In this connection it appears today that regions are taking measures by passing their own laws about reorganizing the social services and relating plans.

In conclusion, the Italian welfare state in the 1970s showed its will to offer well-being through public channels which have been largely neglected.

In the mid 1980s the overall political aura seemed favourable to a restriction of public welfare interventions. Parties' and trade unions' attitudes can be summarized along three main lines.

The defence of the institutional welfare state was supported by parties of the left (by the Italian Communist Party in particular) and by workers' trade unions. Their programme is to get rid of waste and inefficiency, but not to revise the philosophy underlying the laws of the 1970s. In other words, this attitude expresses the need to rationalize redistribution.

An attitude for *stronger selectivity* in social welfare actions was maintained by centre parties and Christian Democrats (DC) in particular. Their programme is to make the welfare system more effective and efficient by means of a more managerial administration of services as well as through a more accentuated selectivity of benefits to the poorest and more marginalized social classes. Catholic lobbies in particular proposed an enhancement of the third sector, the non-profit-making sector. However it is not clear if such enhancement of primary and secondary solidarity represents a superior form of guarantees and life quality, or if it represents only the discharge of public responsibilities.

The attitude for *resorting to the market proper* was supported by *lib-lab* currents which include some liberals and some socialists – the most 'modern' ones – in addition to minor components from other centre parties. They were backed by entrepreneurial unions, the independent workers' union and other professional categories. Their programme is to confine direct state action by entrusting market agencies with production and distribution of welfare interventions. The main objective is the *deregulation* in each sector.

We shall observe later on in this chapter the quantitative consistency and articulation of these different attitudes.

There is an evident re-emergence – *at the ideological level* – of a sharp polarization between public and private facilities as solutions and practices of action for the well-being of the population.

Our thesis is that such polarization does not grasp factuality, since the situation appears to be characterized by interaction between public and private welfare interventions. In other words, the set of solutions offered by the three above-mentioned attitudes is not viable, either in theory or in practice.

With this contribution we intend to demonstrate that in Italy:

• There is an extreme regional variability in the welfare system and this raises formidable problems of social equity and territorial redistribution.

• Social political guidelines are quite favourable to a compromise between public and private interventions, as a compensatory system of local intervention. This makes plausible the hypothesis that the Italian welfare system cannot be conceived of as either entirely public or entirely private.

Actually the Italian welfare state is largely public and still highly 'relief-based' (in the conventional sense of the term). As a consequence, a disengagement of the state would mean a disaster for the collective well-being. However, the requirement for a more modern and adequate competence of the service machinery is increasingly evident. This updating can be pursued either trusting in a change within public administration or it can be made by means of a strong competition between private and public systems. Today the latter seems to be the most effective and productive method. However, this does not imply the disruption of the welfare state in favour of a renewed capitalistic market, which could produce new inequalities and poverties. The private branch must be prompted in those non-profit actions which are typical in the third sector (referred to as 'social-private' sector) acting in collaboration – although having external and independent management – with local administrations (communes and regions) to which the direction, planning, and coordination of public and mixed welfare pertain.

Basic Structural Features and Trends of the Italian 'Formal Welfare State'

Analysis of the Italian Welfare Structure Broken Down by Regions.

Since post-war years, Italian expenditures have been growing more rapidly than production capacity[5]). Despite many attempts to reduce social expenditures – particularly by means of financial laws after 1980 – these expenses kept on increasing at a rate exceeding Gross National Product (GNP) growth (table 1). On the whole social expenditures increased from 1980 to 1983 by 89.4 per cent against a GNP increase of 58.2 per cent (ISTAT 1985).

Table 1
Annual Increases of Social Expenditure and GNP in Italy 1979 – 1983*) (%)

	1980/79	1981/80	1982/81	1983/82
Social expenditure	+ 22.7	+ 31.7	+ 19.4	+ 20.5
GNP	+ 25.4	+ 18.5	+ 17.4	+ 13.7

*) Social expenditure include all fields of social protection (viz. health care. social relief. social security including interventions for the labour market).

Source: Our elaboration on ISTAT data.

Within social expenditures, the highest percentage increase concerns social security, while social relief is almost steady and health care expenses fluctuate around a mean figure (percentage of GNP) which is lower than the European average[6].

We describe here the Italian welfare structure by means of two tables. The first one (table 2) shows the values of some social demographic indicators, the labour market, some health care services, the seats of political parties in regional councils and social expenditures per region in 1980. The second table (table 3) shows correlation coefficients (Pearson's r) between some of the previous variables, again for 1980. First of all these data prove the extreme territorial variability (by region) of the Italian welfare state. This variability corresponds to an inner differentiation which cannot be attributed superficially to North-South dualism, even if this polarity keeps a dramatic consistency.

These data also indicate that generally social expenditures grow with the increase in people's ages (and death rate), employment percentage rate (on the total resident population), offered services (hospital beds availability and other services), trade union conflicts, and left parties prevalence[7].

In general, the welfare state grows in tandem with the index of social, cultural and economic 'modernization' of the population[8]. The general analysis carried out within our research confirms the theory that social expenditures increase more considerably in the presence of economic, social and cultural modernization processes. But the Italian case departs somewhat from the empiric generalization prevailing on the international scene, where welfare state growth is always positively correlated with economic development (Flora and Heidenheimer 1981). In actual fact, the Italian welfare state has grown from 1974 to date despite the recurring dramatic economic crises of the last decade.

The main incentive for social expenditures in Italy seems to be the weakening of primary solidarities (starting from the family), while there is a high female employment rate, low birth rate and high population aging rate. In Italy the correlation coefficient of overall social expenditures to the modernization index was 0.85 (with $R^2 = 0.72$) in 1977 and 0.81 (with $R^2 = 0.66$) in 1980. In any case the results of our statistical elaborations (table 3) confirm that the Italian welfare state (on the whole and in the course of time) gave higher priority to economic considerations than to social services. It is curious to note that this trend is positively correlated to pressure by one trade union for an increase in social expenditures by means of strikes. A rather disconcerting result (see again table 3) is that within the Italian welfare state, social expenditures by regions are in negative correlation with the proportion of poor families in each region.

Distribution of Some Meaningful Variables of the Italian Welfare State among Regions (Year 1980)

Variable	Piemonte	Val d'Aosta	Lombardia	Trent. A. A.	Veneto	Friuli V. G.	Liguria	Emilia Romagna	Toscana	Umbria	Marche	Lazio	Abruzzi	Molise	Campania	Puglia	Basilicata	Calabria	Sicilia	Sardegna
People over 65 years of age (% of total population)	15.8	13.6	12.9	15.3	12.8	17.7	18.5	16.1	17.0	15.4	15.1	11.5	14.4	15.3	9.9	10.7	12.6	11.9	12.3	11.2
Birth rate (newborns out of 1000 inhabitants)	8.7	8.0	9.7	11.2	10.0	8.3	6.7	7.7	8.5	9.7	10.2	11.3	10.9	10.3	16.7	15.2	12.9	14.2	14.6	13.9
People registered in employment exchange lists (% of total number of employed people)	5.5	5.2	4.5	4.2	4.9	3.7	7.3	6.2	4.7	8.0	4.8	11.7	10.3	12.9	24.0	10.2	17.8	13.8	15.8	15.7
Ratio: non labour force/labour force	125	135	131	142	141	153	160	118	144	141	119	171	153	140	174	171	154	199	198	176
Employed people (% of total resident population)	42.4	44.9	40.4	39.0	36.1	37.8	39.0	42.3	38.4	36.5	38.1	35.1	33.6	37.2	30.2	32.6	35.4	27.8	28.7	29.8
Strikers (% of total number of people employed)	48.4	32.0	50.1	20.2	26.0	74.9	18.9	70.9	74.0	12.8	18.8	5.2	15.3	10.8	11.3	14.7	9.4	10.2	14.4	22.8
Beds available in public hospitals (per 1000 inhabitants)	8.6	5.3	7.6	9.1	12.0	12.5	10.3	9.7	9.6	8.6	12.2	6.9	9.0	5.3	5.9	7.7	5.3	5.4	6.7	6.6
Beds available in private hospitals (per 1000 inhabitants)	1.2	1.1	1.2	1.3	0.9	0.7	0.8	1.5	0.9	0.4	1.4	2.7	1.8	0.6	1.5	2.0	2.5	1.5	0.8	
Number of doctors per 1000 inhabitants	2.4	2.1	2.7	2.4	2.6	2.7	4.1	3.7	3.6	3.6	3.0	4.5	3.2	2.5	3.3	2.5	2.0	2.9	3.1	2.7
% of DC seats in Regional Councils	33.3	20.0	42.5	31.4	53.3	42.6	32.5	26.0	30.0	30.0	40.0	36.7	50.0	56.7	41.7	44.0	46.7	45.0	43.3	40.0
% of PSI seats in Regional Councils	15.0	2.9	13.8	5.7	11.7	8.2	12.7	8.0	10.0	13.3	10.0	10.0	10.0	10.0	11.7	12.0	13.3	17.5	11.1	11.3
% of PCI seats in Regional Councils	33.3	20.0	28.8	10.0	21.7	23.0	37.5	52.0	50.0	46.7	37.5	31.7	30.0	16.7	25.0	26.0	26.7	25.0	26.7	27.5
% of social per capita expenditure of per capita GNP	16.9	16.3	15.4	19.4	18.2	21.6	20.5	18.4	21.1	21.9	21.6	24.2	25.0	26.0	25.1	23.2	24.2	29.5	26.3	24.6
% of collective consumption of private (family) consumption	22.2	17.8	23.1	25.7	24.9	26.1	22.4	24.6	25.3	30.3	28.6	26.9	29.4	34.8	33.8	35.6	39.5	37.7	31.6	35.3
Per capita social security expenditure (in 1000 Liras)	1056	1304	995	925	826	1174	1251	1044	1061	994	925	1017	806	800	692	673	732	703	739	779
Per capita health care expenditure (in 1000 Liras)	289	296	306	424	331	406	411	371	367	349	347	452	336	263	321	301	276	309	300	314
Per capita social relief expenditure (in 1000 Liras)	105	113	100	116	97	117	124	101	106	109	104	110	100	90	93	79	79	84	110	89

Source: Elaborations on ISTAT data.

Table 3

Correlations (Pearson's r) Among Some of the Italian Society's Characteristics and Regional Social Expenditure 1977 – 1980

(in brackets significance degree p of r coefficient)

	Per capita expenditure for social services		% of services in kind of the total of services in cash		Total per capita social expenditure	
	1977	1980	1977	1980	1977	1980
Old age index	.78 (1)	.79 (1)	−.54 (1)	−.69 (1)	.74 (1)	.76 (1)
Birth rate	−.83 (1)	−.83 (1)	.74 (1)	.83 (1)	−.81 (1)	−.81 (1)
Death rate	.90 (1)	.87 (1)	−.67 (1)	−.72 (1)	.85 (1)	−.84 (1)
% of people registered in employment exchange lists	−.59 (1)	−.68 (1)	.68 (1)	.73 (1)	−.55 (1)	−.66 (1)
% of non–labour force	−.55 (1)	−.44 (3)	.62 (1)	.76 (1)	−.52 (1)	−.41 (4)
Employed people (% of total resident population)	.67 (1)	.72 (1)	−.77 (1)	−.85 (1)	.65 (1)	.70 (1)
% of strikers due to ind. conflicts	.74 (1)	.51 (2)	−.58 (1)	−.50 (1)	.69 (1)	.47 (2)
Public hospital beds available per 1000 inhabitants	.55 (1)	.47 (2)	n. s.	−.38 (5)	.50 (2)	.44 (3)
Private hospital beds available per 1000 inhabitants	n. s.	n. s.	.61 (1)	.43 (4)	n. s.	n. s.
Number of doctors per 1000 inhabitants	.33 (6)	.32 (6)	n. s.	.33 (6)	.37 (6)	.37 (6)
% of seats to centre–left coalition (DC + PSI + PRI + PSDI + PLI)	−.53 (1)	−.68 (1)	.28 (5)	39. (5)	−.53 (1)	−.67 (1)
% of DC seats (Regional Council)	−.63 (1)	−.70 (1)	.29 (5)	.35 (5)	−.63 (1)	−.68 (1)
% of PCI seats (Regional Council)	.25 (5)	.28 (2)	n. s.	n. s.	.25 (5)	.27 (2)
% of PSI seats (Regional Council)	−.12 (5)	−.49 (2)	n. s.	n. s.	n. s.	.28 (2)
% of social per capita expenditure on per capita GNP	−.50 (2)	−.58 (1)	.60 (4)	−.67 (1)	−.46 (3)	−.55 (1)
Ratio: collective consumption/ private consumption	−.82 (1)	−.82 (1)	.62 (1)	.61 (1)	−.81 (1)	−.81 (1)
Per capita social security expenditure	.96 (1)	.97 (1)	−.63 (1)	−.72 (1)	.97 (1)	.97 (1)
Per capita health care expenditure	.83 (1)	.63 (1)	n. s.	n. s.	.84 (1)	.66 (1)
Per capita social relief expenditure	.56 (1)	.86 (1)	−.51 (2)	−.46 (3)	.55 (1)	.86 (1)
% of poor families	n. s.		−.66 (1)		−.74 (1)	

(1) p = .00
(2) p = .01
(3) p = .02
(4) p = .03
(5) p = .04
(6) p = .05

n. s. = non significant

Source: Elaborations on ISTAT data.

Table 4
Spheres of Action and Group Tendency

Factor Analysis	Eigenvalue	% of variance	cum %
Factor 1 = welfare state for marginal people	4.60185	64.0	64.0
Factor 2 = social security state	1.80695	25.1	89.1
Factor 3 = self–referential service state	.78102	10.9	100.0

Variables	Factor 1	Factor 2	Factor 3
1. Per cent of people registered in Employment Exchange lists from the total number of unemployed people	.63563	−.49610	.12451
2. Per cent of non–labour force from the total labour force	.90467	−.16084	.03542
3. Per cent of employed people from the resident population	−.82465	.47163	−.02139
4. Total expenditure for services per inhabitant	−.32198	.94750	−.00072
5. Total social expenditure per inhabitant	−.29169	.95329	.08511
6. Per cent of expenses for wages and salaries of total social expenditure	.31779	.00770	.91512
7. Per cent of expenses for wages and salaries of total services in kind	−.26544	.26677	.89102
8. Per cent of services in kind of total services in money	.80794	−.43520	.06443
9. Per cent of social services of total number of services	.01856	−.04423	.22477

Table 5
Matrix of correlation coefficients (Pearson's r) for variables 1 − 9 of Table 4

Variables	1	2	3	4	5	6	7	8	9
1. Per cent of people registered in Employment Exchange lists from the total number of unemployed people	—								
2. Per cent of non-labour force from the total labour force	.67	—							
3. Per cent of employed people from the resident population	−.74	−.87	—						
4. Total expenditure for services per inhabitant	−.68	−.44	.72	—					
5. Total social expenditure per inhabitant	−.66	−.41	.70	.99	—				
6. Per cent of expenses for wages and salaries of total social expenditure	.32	.29	−.24	−.09	−.00	—			
7. Per cent of expenses for wages and salaries of total services in kind	−.15	−.22	.31	.33	.40	.72	—		
8. Per cent of services in kind of total services in money	.73	.76	−.85	−.66	−.63	.37	−.35	—	
9. Per cent of social services of total number of services	−.12	.01	−.15	−.05	−.04	.20	.21	.10	—

71

The Three Structural Factors of the Italian Welfare State

By using the same basic statistics it is possible to identify the main structural features of the Italian welfare state through factor analysis procedures (see tables 4 and 5).

Our analyses clearly show three basic structural factors of the Italian welfare state (table 4):

Factor 1: This is the welfare state for marginal people (i. e., non-manpower or unemployed people registered on Employment Exchange Lists, women and young people in particular) whose needs are satisfied by the welfare state mainly through services in kind.

Factor 2: This is the social security state which gives guarantees to employed people. There is no doubt that this is the 'strongest' factor, which means the factor using most revenue funds to protect and reward medium-low income labour.

Factor 3: This is the bureaucracy welfare state which we referred to as self-referential service state. It is represented by the expenditure share for wages and salaries to civil servants, employees and operators giving priority to welfare aid dispensing in terms of services rather than through income support.

The results show that the *regional variability* of the Italian welfare state is linked to three very clear and positively inter-related factors which in order of importance are:

● *The weakness of the labour market,* i. e. the scanty labour demand; the lower this demand the less developed is the welfare state.

● The fact that social security is dispensed *in proportion to wage contributions* from the employment system; in other words, the Italian welfare state recompenses better those people who are regularly employed.

● *The large number of civil servants,* i. e. the public regional machinery dispensing services; the greater the modernization of the region involved the larger this welfare state factor.

This consideration, after all, is proportionate to two additional features of the Italian welfare state:

First, to the fact that so far it gave priority to economic methods rather than social services, and in general services in kind; second, to the fact that Italy ranks among those countries which allocate the highest proportion of GNP to private and family consumption rather than to community consumption, although in recent years the latter had higher relative per cent increases than did private consumption.

Groups of Regions 'kindred' by Way of Welfare Expenditures

By means of cluster analysis, we shall attempt to show the most significant groups of Italian regions having adopted similar patterns of social policy. By 'social policy' here we mean – operatively – the methods of welfare expenditures. Table 6 gives a *general pattern* based on some general indicators (see the 8 variables used) for 1980. Clusters are differentiated as follows:

First group with maximum social expenditures Cluster 1):

including Val d'Aosta, Friuli-Venezia, Giulia and Liguria (mean social expenditures per capita = 1,539,000 Liras).

Second group with medium-high social expenditures (Cluster 4):

including Trentino – Alto Adige, Emilia Romagna, Tuscany, Umbria, Latium (mean social expenditures per capita = 1,319,000 Liras).

Table 6
General Model of Cluster Analysis on the Regional Subdivision of Social Protection Expenditure in Italy, 1980

A. Cluster Analysis: General Model

Variables used:

1. population older than 65
2. legal separations (between spouses)
3. hospital beds × 1000 inhabitants
4. collective consumption/family consumption

5. number of workers participating in strikes
6. % regional counselors of the PCI
7. % regional counselors of the PSI
8. social expenditure per capita

Cluster 1	Distance	Variable	1	2	3	4	5	6	7	8
Valle D'Aosta	18.3	Center	16.6	82.7	9.3	22.1	41.9	26.8	7.8	1572.8
Friuli V. G.	49.3	St. dev.	2.6	11.6	3.6	4.1	29.3	9.3	4.8	37.9
Liguria	48.9									
average distance	38.8									

Cluster 2	Distance	Variable	1	2	3	4	5	6	7	8
Lombardia	26.7									
Veneto	80.3	Center	14.2	43.8	9.9	25.6	31.7	30.3	12.1	1199.7
Marche	58.2									
Abruzzi	62.7	St. dev.	1.3	26.8	2.1	3.2	16.4	5.8	2.2	65.8
Piemonte	83.7									
average distance	62.3									

Cluster 3	Distance	Variable	1	2	3	4	5	6	7	8
Molise	40.3									
Campania	22.3									
Puglia	64.8	Center	12.0	12.3	6.1	35.4	13.3	24.8	12.4	1022.2
Basilicata	28.4	St. dev.	1.7	9.0	.9	2.5	4.6	3.7	2.4	43.8
Calabria	18.1									
Sicilia	28.6									
Sardegna	63.3									
average distance	38.0									

Cluster 4	Distance	Variable	1	2	3	4	5	6	7	8
Trentino A. A.	42.6									
Emilia Romagna	39.4									
Toscana	43.7	Center	14.6	56.9	8.8	26.5	36.6	38.1	9.4	1265.9
Umbria	62.1	St. dev.	2.2	23.9	1.1	2.2	33.1	17.6	2.8	41.0
Lazio	74.7									
average distance	52.5									

Table 7
Specific Model of Cluster Analysis on the Regional Subdivision of Social Protection Expenditure in Italy, 1980

B. Cluster Analysis: Specific Model (including variables relative to: labour market, political power, and social expenses)

Variables used:

1. % people looking for a job from total number of regular employees
2. % of labour force from total number of labour force
3. % employed people from the total resident population
4. % of regional seats of DC
5. % of regional seats of PCI
6. Total per capita social expenditure (for services)

7. % of expenses for wages and salaries from the total social expenditure
8. % of expenses for wages and salaries from total expenditure for services in kind. wages and salaries, intermediate consumption
9. % of expenditure for services in kind from total expenditure for services in cash
10. % of expenditure for social services from total expenditure for services
11. total per capita social expenditure

Cluster 1	Dist.	Var.	1	2	3	4	5	6	7	8	9	10	11
Valle D'Aosta	23.9												
Friuli V. G.	50.4	Center	5.4	149.2	40.4	31.7	26.8	1513.3	2.2	23.5	8.5	19.4	1572.8
Liguria	62.2	St. dev.	1.8	12.4	3.8	11.3	9.3	40.3	.0	2.0	1.7	5.9	37.9
average distance	45.5												

Cluster 2	Dist.	Var.	1	2	3	4	5	6	7	8	9	10	11
Lombardia	20.3	Center	6.0	133.7	38.1	43.8	30.2	1156.6	2.3	20.4	11.2	21.9	1199.6
Veneto	110.6	St. dev.	2.4	13.3	3.4	7.9	5.8	65.2	.3	1.9	1.4	2.9	65.8
Marche	70.5												
Abruzzi	83.7												
Piemonte	104.5												
average distance	77.9												

Cluster 3	Dist.	Var.	1	2	3	4	5	6	7	8	9	10	11
Molise	60.1												
Campania	30.7	Center	15.7	173.0	31.6	45.3	24.8	979.0	2.8	20.7	14.5	20.9	1022.1
Puglia	88.2	St. dev.	4.3	21.7	3.5	5.4	3.6	40.1	.3	4.9	3.1	2.1	43.7
Basilicata	39.7												
Calabria	33.2												
Sicilia	46.5												
Sardegna	86.3												
average distance	55.0												

Cluster 4	Dist.	Var.	1	2	3	4	5	6	7	8	9	10	11
Trentino A. A.	39.9												
Emilia Romagna	32.0	Center	6.9	143.1	38.2	30.8	38.0	1298.0	3.2	24.6	11.7	24.1	1365.9
Toscana	41.1	St. dev.	3.0	18.8	2.7	3.8	17.6	23.5	1.7	5.3	2.3	5.8	41.0
Umbria	56.0												
Lazio	67.6												
average distance	47.3												

Table 8
Accounts of Social Protection by Juridical Status of Institutions 1980 – 1982
(billions of Liras)

		1980	1981	1982	1982/80
Public administrations	Revenue	71,474	89,007	111,340	+ 55.8%
	Expenses	71,566	94,064	112,942	+ 57.8%
	Total	− 92	− 5,057	− 1,602	
Non–public social institutions and undertakings	Income	11,228	13,339	15,285	+ 36.1%
	Expenses	5,769	7,738	8,690	+ 50.6%
	Total	+ 5,459	+ 5,601	+ 6,595	

Source: Our elaboration on ISTAT data.

Table 9
Orientation of Policy–makers

Orientations on	Left parties	Lay centre parties	Christian centre party
1. Future of welfare state	Institutional pattern with integrations from social– private spheres	Neo–residual pattern	Competition/comparison between public and so- cial–private actions
2. Social security	Establishment of a single social security fund	3–category system with plurality of social se- curity funds	3–category system with plurality of social se- curity funds
3. Social relief	Larger decentralization of public services with in- tegrations from volun- teer associations	Adoption of more adequ- ate informative methods on persons entitled	More voluntarism and self–determination
4. Selective measures	Little favourable	Favourable	Favourable. but with reservations
5. Expenditure budget controls	Critical	Favourable	Extremely favourable
6. Relationships be- tween volunteer asso- ciations and reduc- tion of employment	Pattern of "functional de- pendence"	Pattern of weak "partner- ship"	Pattern of strong "partnership"
7. Enhancement of vol- unteer associations and reduction of em- ployment	The problem does exist but it can be overcome by means of clear–cut laws.	The problem does not exist (extreme flexibility in laws).	The problem does not exist (possible transition of volunteers to the em- ployed status).
8. Development of self– managed coopera- tives	Favourable. but attentive to risks of exploitation	Favourable. but attentive to risks of relief–type support and patron–to– client connections	Favourable. but attentive to risks of relief–type support and patron–to– client connections
9. Development of non– market mutual aids	Favourable. if intended as supplements	Symbolically important but practically ineffective	Symbolically important but practically ineffective

Third group with medium social expenditures (Cluster 2):
including Lombardy, Veneto, Marches, Abruzzi, Piedmont (mean social expenditures per capita = 1,121,000 Liras).
Fourth group with low social expenditures (Cluster 3):
including Molise, Campania, Apulia, Basilicata, Calabria, Sicily, Sardinia (mean social expenditures per capita = 957,000 Liras).
Table 7 offers a more specific pattern of cluster analyses which focuses on relationships between social expenditures and labour market conditions. We elaborated it in view of the particular characteristics of the research project coordinated by the European Centre for Social Welfare Training and Research in Vienna.
The sub-division into four clusters gives a result which is parallel to the previous general pattern. The clusters which are thus identified are the following (table 7):
First group with maximum social expenditures (Cluster 1):
It has the smallest number of persons looking for a job, a non-manpower proportion which is quite large when compared with other regions, a small difference between Christian Democratic (DC) seats and Communist Party (PCI) seats in the regional council, the lowest expenditures for services in general and in kind.
Second group with medium-high social expenditures (Cluster 4):
There is a small number of both people looking for a job and non-manpower, a high employment rate, a strong position of PCI and a scarce importance of DC (with the exception of Trentino – Alto Adige), a considerable welfare bureaucracy corresponding to a higher level of social services dispensed.
Third group with medium social expenditures (Cluster 2):
This presents few people looking for a job, and the smallest share of non-manpower, high employment rates; a strong consistency of DC but also a fairly large presence of PCI, a smaller welfare bureaucracy with a low proportion of services in kind and – relatively – of services in general.
Fourth group with low social expenditures (Cluster 3):
It has a very high proportion of people looking for a job, the highest non-manpower number, an extremely strong DC with minor incidence of PCI and, although it has no broad welfare bureaucracy, there are maximum expenditures for services in kind (not for social services).
Going back to the problem of public-to-private relationship, we can analyze social expenditures in Italy from 1980 to 1982 and draw a distinction between those bodies dispensing them, mainly through public governmental channels (public administrations), and those dispensing them through other channels (quasi-public or private) (see table 8).
Many comments can be made about this. In brief, however, it is important to note that:
• Social protection directly via public administration (governor) is about six times greater than that of other institutions (including undertakings).
• While public administration shows a deficit, the other institutions have a positive balance.

• Eighty per cent variations in 1982 indicate that expenses grew more than incomes for both public administrations and other institutions; the difference, however, is greater for the latter.

In short, this means that against public administrations' financial deficit and inability to rationalize expenses, there is a tendency to shift social protection onto non-governmental institutions which, however, remain controlled by the political administrative system.

To put it briefly, these figures indicate that Italian welfare state structures and features are strongly based on what we can call the 'industrial citizenship'. In other words, social expenditures privilege regular workers, prefer money aids and use social services only as marginal services. The latter are increasingly identified as pathological needs of the population rather than physiological ones. In any case, services in kind and other services cannot compete with money benefits by importance and are granted to the weakest and most marginal people.

In dispensing social expenditures, the public administration shows a much larger deficit than other non-governmental institutions, which seems to lead to social protection functions being increasingly shifted onto the latter. Generally speaking, the stronger the Communist Party within regions, the larger the social protection expenditures increase. However this does not appear to substantially modify the above-mentioned social policy pattern.

What emerges therefore is a *'nearly jammed-up'* welfare system, which seems to be characterized by the following aspects:

• There is a 'political blockade', that is to say the prevailing social protection pattern does not change considerably among regions as a consequence of the different weight of political parties as such (in other words, welfare interventions are relatively homogeneous among parties when the same degree of modernization exists in regions).

• Social expenditures cannot be decoupled from their close connection with the labour market, since they tend to protect those who have a 'regular' post.

• Public administrations show a remarkable inability or impossibility to manage the social protection network and in particular to expand services in kind and services proper. Among other things this seems to entail a greater reliance on non-governmental institutions (social institutions and undertakings).

• While being extremely variable and not steadfast, the regional distribution of social expenditures shows an increasing territorial gap between Central and Northern Italy on the one side and Southern Italy on the other. This *gap* basically mirrors a labour market polarization and evidences the severe structural inability of the Italian welfare state to pursue objectives of social equalization between determined territories.

These are the ground hypotheses on which we conducted the second part of the research. In this section of the chapter we want to verify the extent to which policy-makers match or react against these conditions and boundaries of the Italian social state. In particular, in view of the *jammed-up* character of the structural situation just considered, we are interested in knowing whether, how, and why policy-makers intend to resort to new types of mixed (public and private) interventions as well as new types of *exiting* from the public system, considered as alternatives to restrictions and dysfunctions of the welfare system.

New Orientations Among Policy-makers: An Empirical Assessment

The Crisis of the Welfare State and How to Overcome It

The evaluation of the crisis of the welfare state given by the representatives of different political parties and unions is well articulated. It appears, however, that some basic lines with specific features can be drawn (table 9).

We can define the first line as 'change in continuity'. It is particularly strong among the *left parties*. It stems from two fundamental observations: a) the decrease of funds available for expenditures; b) the start of a social change resulting in the emergence of different needs and new problems. According to this line, it becomes necessary to change social policy guidelines in depth, but in a direction which does not impair the steps which the welfare state has taken forward. Within this framework the first problem is to identify the socially weaker groups or particularly exposed categories which in this period have partially changed and probably widened (e. g., young unemployed). The second problem is to modify dispensing criteria of service organization patterns. As a matter of fact, their validity does not lie in their total deregulation, but rather in their capacity to make effective responses to real needs and requirements.

Therefore, for the left there is much room for transformation and rationalization which may enable the institutional welfare system to reproduce itself and overcome both its revenue crisis and its partial crisis of legitimation.

The second tendency, which is expressed by *centre non-religious parties*, could be referred to as 'neo-residual pattern of welfare state'. They ascribe the crisis to the fact that our present welfare state pretends to respond to all citizens and needs in terms of free social relief, thus preventing the market from working properly. Therefore, what is demanded today is the economic upswing which is to be made possible by granting larger freedom to private branches. This does not mean embracing the 'laissez-faire' idea of an extreme 'deregulation' or disordered development, but rather a demand to the state to conceive of new rules which are to be far more flexible than those currently in force. This line can be defined as neo-residualism because some vested interests, especially the right to health care, are regarded by now as well-established rights, to be guaranteed to everybody, though with differences from the viewpoint of contribution by individuals.

The third opinion is held by the *centre party of Christian inspiration*. Its criticism is not against the principles and the spirit of the social state, but against the implementation guidelines, particularly at the local level. According to the DC, public services, despite their pretension to comprehensiveness, actually became rigid frames incapable of satisfying adequately the needs of citizens, especially new and emerging needs. For this party, the degradation of social and health services cannot be solved by putting them under strict private control, but rather by creating the conditions for competitiveness and comparison between public and private interventions, the latter being meant as a private market with social features recognized and legitimized by the government.

As to the three major trade unions, their attitudes basically overlap with the position of left parties though with different nuances. In particular, they emphasize the need for better productivity and efficiency in public provisions. Therefore, the suggested line is for continuity with all those changes, i. e. technical adjustments and rationalizations, which are deemed necessary and suitable according to experience.

Selective Measures

The attitude of the left is on the whole against selective measures and means tests, though acknowledging the inevitability of their adoption.

In any case contributions should be linked to a determined level of free services classified on the basis of a real income assessment which, in the present state of affairs and despite recent revenue reform measures, seems hardly feasible.

Non-Christian centre parties, on the contrary, consider selective criteria to be fully positive and stress their worth as an educative means to awaken responsibility among citizens. However, there are perplexities about capacities to ascertain the real economic situation of beneficiaries owing above all to the inadequacy of empiric instruments for assessment used by public administration.

The idea that services are not to be indiscriminately free is shared in principle by the centre Christian party. Nevertheless there is radical disagreement with the irrational way this image and related plans have been carried out in practice, since they produced further discomfort and complication to citizens. For instance, they are forced to queue up first to get their blood sample taken and again to pay their ticket.

The position of trade unions on these matters is very close to the left parties. But, regarding the previous issues, it tends to stress different problems, such as higher productivity of administration, more correct management, and high reliability of revenue assessments.

Effectiveness and Equity of Expenditure Control Instruments

Among left administrators and politicians, the prevailing attitude vis-à-vis budget controls introduced by financial plans of the last years is definitely critical. It is especially so because these controls can only determine top limits, or partial limits for health care expenditures, but cannot give rise to quality controls such as cost/benefit controls or correspondence between income and expense. In any case the prevailing proposals from the left appear to be more corrective measures of the present state of affairs than complete alternatives. As a matter of fact, two hypotheses have been put forward: either to give an independent tax levying capacity back to local administrations so that they must be held directly responsible to citizens; or to save money by effective management and reutilize it within the same block of the budget.

On the contrary, the judgement of lay parties is entirely positive. At most they claim a heavier transfer of resources from state to local administrations, but again within previously established limits, and after further updating of assessment methods so as not to privilege always 'historical expenses' against needs and situations which are continually changing.

The Christian Democratic Party, not only believes that controls are indispensable, but that those introduced so far are not strong enough. Moreover, it believes that they are anomalous insofar as there is an overlapping between controllers and controlled people. The relating proposals, therefore, suggest the appointment of authorities really independent from political parties and not linked in any way with the applicants.

Also on this subject we find that trade unions are basically lined up with the left in their criticism of the expenditure control policies. They think that such policies eluded a definition of service standards and objectives to be pursued, and that they cannot make real controls, it being impossible for control commissions to operate adequately within the present rules.

However, at variance with previous viewpoints, trade unions, while insisting on connecting control to planning, question the proposal of an independent levying by local administrations. They see the risk of increasing discriminations and inequalities among citizens.

Voluntary Associations and New Welfare Mixes

Regarding the organic fitting of voluntary associations into social policies, thereby giving rise to a new welfare mix, left representatives consider this as a sound hypothesis but stress the following risks and difficulties:
• Indefiniteness of roles and tasks of voluntary associations.
• Possibility of hidden financing and relief-type action to phenomena which start as voluntarism but necessarily end up as entrepreneurial activities.

• Hazard of 'lebanonization', i. e. every region and/or commune making its network of collaborations on the basis of criteria differing from those of public services, depending on the political orientation of the council.

• Severe social consequences stemming from bringing complete sections of welfare or organized activities outside public services.

In any case, the emerging image is that voluntary associations do not 'replace' public services, but 'support' and 'supplement' them.

All centre parties have totally different concerns. They imagine a type of voluntary associations which – respecting their own independence – engage themselves in planning and managing services and guarantee an adequate level of professionalism and the capacity of satisfying general social needs. It is evident therefore that there are two patterns of relationships which are quite different from one another. We can call the first one 'functional dependence' and the second one 'partnership'. After all, they are both already present and can be identified within the body of regional laws issued on this matter.

The Enhancement of Volunteers and the Employment Question

A further problem raised by the enhancement of volunteers and their use within the framework of social welfare services is the possibility that this produces a reduction of employment posts. Trade unions have expressed this concern particularly in the past years, but it seems to have faded in recent times. Both trade union representatives and the spokesmen for all political directions agree on the following points:

• The enlargement of public posts is not always the most realistic and effective way to solve the problem of unemployment – especially for young people.

• A positive use of volunteers within the framework of services does not determine a zero outcome, but rather a positive addition. This means that public positions are not withdrawn, but that new work opportunities are created by finding new sectors for intervention and response methods.

• The risk, if any, can be avoided, however, by means of a correct relationship between public administrations and voluntary organizations, secured by a proper framework of laws enabling sharp distinctions to be made between:

– *voluntary services* which are and must remain gratis, even in the expectation of financing voluntary organizations for covering services' running costs and

– *intermediate types of businesses, such as service cooperative societies* and social solidarity cooperatives[9]. Despite stemming from forms of voluntary action, they can be located in an area between the market and the third sector and as such, represent socially useful and effective employment outlets.

Needless to say, in this case, while left parties and trade unions insist an accurate regulations, all centre parties favour flexibility.

Voluntarism, Cooperatives, Mutual Aid

In the previous section we mentioned the necessity of defining accurately the third sector which cannot be identified only with voluntary associations. Though voluntary groups are perhaps the most consistent portion of this sector, it is worth mentioning other types of self-organized social groups which respond to both old and new needs. We refer to cooperative societies and mutual aid.

Many of the Italian policy-makers we interviewed stated the need to make an analytical distinction between voluntary associations and services and/or social solidarity cooperatives which operate within the welfare sector and may enter into special arrangements with public administrations. As a matter of fact, in spite of their originating from motivations of social engagement, cooperatives act according to entrepreneurial and professional schemes which as such must have no part in voluntarism. The development of these cooperatives is well regarded because they may represent a real work opportunity for young people. Left parties, however, and trade unions in particular, fear the possibility that within these cooperatives kinds of labour exploitation are produced. This is why they urge for control and as much clarity as possible of the inner situation whenever they use public money. In opposition to this, centre parties fear that arrangements with public authorities may hide a sort of creeping assistance and political patron-and-client system. They urge the public authorities to evaluate the services of these cooperatives in terms of cost-benefit ratio, i. e. cost-effectiveness.

New types of mutual aids, different from private insurances, which have recently developed in our country, are receiving various comments. The left judges them positively insofar as they are characterized as additions to services guaranteed by the state. This comment would not be true if they showed up as alternatives or replacements. After all, the worth lies more in being an alternative to private schemes rather than in the experience itself, which is necessarily limited to confined frameworks and, accordingly, is virtually corporative.

For all centre parties, on the contrary, mutual aids chiefly symbolize the citizens' mistrust in the welfare state, and in particular the failure of the health care reform which activated the National Health Care Scheme. However, within the present economic and social situation, mutual aids are condemned to remain very limited and confined initiatives, which are entirely unable to become alternatives to the supplementary insurance market.

The Role of Voluntary Associations and Their Composition

From previous sections it is already clear that we consider the third sector as a wider social framework than mere voluntarism. It cannot be reduced to voluntarism since it also includes new or renewed types of mutual aid and self-determined production of goods and services for collective use (service and social solidarity cooperatives).

The latter component certainly deserves further investigation in view of an attitude which gives priority to finding possible solutions to the unemployment question. Such solutions would be different from the by now obsolete arrangement of promoting the growth of civil service job opportunities, especially in the service branch.

Unfortunately, we do not have sufficient information on the quantity or type of these self-determined cooperatives. However, we do have information on voluntarism. Therefore, we thought fit to use this information not only because of its intrinsic value but mainly because in many instances collective goods and service cooperatives or self-determined businesses which originated from voluntarism, are deep-rooted in the culture they express and are almost an evolution of this culture. A quite detailed picture of voluntary organizations, their composition, and their relationships with public authorities, can suggest at least in part which changes and orientations are in progress.

Voluntary Associations in Italy: A Classification Based on Fields of Action

The following data and information are derived from the first national investigation on local voluntary groups in Italy which has been promoted by the Italian Ministry of Labour and Social Security in collaboration with the Ministry of the Interior. This investigation has been led by Ivo Colozzi and Giovanna Rossi.

Conducted in 1983 on 7,024 local voluntary groups, this research does not constitute a census of voluntary associations, but rather the first approach to the understanding of such phenomena on a nationwide scale.

Thanks to the number of groups interviewed and to the wide scope of the questionnaire (107 variables), this investigation was able to collect a large body of information which has been organized on the basis of different classifications by the authors. We shall confine our report here to data based on a scheme which classifies the local groups according to their field of activity.

Fields of Action: A Brief Outline

The most widespread field of action is the social relief sector to which 56.2 per cent of the groups devote themselves. In decreasing order follow the sector of cultural, educational and entertainment activities (52.7 per cent) and the health care sector (33 per cent). The total of the above-mentioned percentages exceeds 100 per cent because about half of the groups (50.6 per cent) operate within one sector only, and the rest within one or more fields. Therefore we can point out the existence of a strong *inclination to multivalence.*

These results evidence that voluntarism performs functions to fill absent public services – as the massive presence in the social relief sector shows – as well as innovative functions through responsive services such as therapeutic communities or family centres. However, it performs also alternative and supplementary functions as witnessed by the significant presence in cultural and health care services which are already largely covered by the public social security system. Furthermore, about half the groups which are operative within two or more sectors at the same time show that such twofold functions often exist within one group.

The Social Relief Sector

With reference to univalent groups – that is those operating within one sector only – the highest percentage of them (16.2 per cent) operates within the social relief sector. The majority of these groups (67.5 per cent) join federations and/or associations which are wider in scope, but this tendency is lower than that of the health care field.

Concerning the legal status of groups, the structure is kept to a minimum. Here in fact is the strongest concentration of informal groups (32.9 per cent) and proportionally, the lowest concentration of legally recognized associations (21.9%). An important datum deserving mention relates to cooperative societies, which is not widespread in voluntarism, representing just 3.4 per cent of the total. However, it appears to be expanding, especially in this sector. 5.1 per cent of the groups dealing exclusively with social relief in fact are incorporated under a cooperative status and they represent 24.2 per cent of the total number of cooperative societies.

Another feature of this sector is that in most cases voluntary groups involved have a small or very small membership: 32.0 per cent of them have 2 to 10 members, and 32.2 per cent of them have 11 to 20 members. They also feature a prevailing tendency to stability concerning the number of member volunteers and amount of time they spend for the group. With regard to composition, here the presence of women is overwhelming (49.1 per cent of groups consist only or mainly of women) and old people also rank at the top (15 per cent of the groups have elderly people in the majority). Young people to the contrary show a very peculiar distribution pattern. Their presence is generally quite significant, but rather than being distributed among all associations, they tend to be concentrated in groups with members of the same age. So, on the one hand, 41 per cent of the groups declared that they do not have young members at all, and on the other, almost the entire membership (80 per cent to 100 per cent) of 12.5 per cent of groups is formed by young people.

These volunteers operate for the most part with no insurance coverage: 86 per cent of the groups declared that they do not provide for insurance in any way.

The social relief sector also presents peculiarities as far as group management types are concerned, and this deserves some explanation. On the one hand, the highest per cent value (20.4 per cent) of groups make a practice of direct democracy with no leadership. This could mean that in the social relief sector the level of democracy – in its proper meaning of diffusion of power – is maximum. At the same time, however, there is also the highest percentage of non-elective leadership (17.3 per cent). The apparent self-contradiction can be accounted for by the large diffusion of both informal groups and brotherhoods. As to the latter, especially those founded long ago, in many cases by-laws of associations envisage non-elective management structures which are renewed by cooperation or appointment by some authority outside the group. But, owing to their very characteristic absence of structures, informal groups may have either participating management and decision-making patterns featuring strong symmetry between members, or types of charismatic leadership which render any formal democratic backing unnecessary.

This explanation seems to be actually corroborated by data. In fact, if we substract the percentage of groups in this sector which declared they are brotherhoods (5.4 per cent) from the overall per cent value of the two above-mentioned management types (37.7 per cent), we obtain 32.2 per cent, which is extremely near to the informal group proportion (32.9 per cent).

39.9 per cent of other groups engaged in social relief declared they have a complete democratic structure (general meeting, board of elective managers, council and president) while 22.3 per cent have an incomplete democratic structure where one or more of said management elements are missing.

Periodical training of volunteers is performed by 65.9 per cent of the groups, with a sharp preference for self-determined training (54.3 per cent). 34.1 per cent of the groups do not arrange training. This can be certainly referred to groups who perform activities such as food purchase and meal preparation, reading, walking, etc.

An important detail is that this sector has the largest proportion of groups (7.4 per cent) whose volunteer members are trained by other voluntary groups who are clearly more organized or have easier access to experiences available within the territory; also by virtue of longer life and activity in the field. This could lead to the hypothesis that training is becoming a link for horizontal coordination between social relief groups.

With reference to relationships of groups with public authorities (table 10), the emerging characteristic is a remarkable isolation or – if preferred – an accentuated separation. Over half the groups (57.9 per cent) do not have any relationship, while just 8.2 per cent of the associations have some arrangement with public authorities – this is the most stable and organized mode of connection. The picture derived from this shows that an aura of mutual distrust continues to exist between voluntarism in this sector and public institutions. This feeling originated from the events following the unity of Italy which unfortunately led to forced nationalization of most social relief organizations owned by the Roman Catholic Church.

Given the situation described above, it is no wonder that more than one-third (33.3 per cent) of groups working in this sector pay all their own expenses for their activities, that is group members and volunteers pay out of their own pockets (table 11). 56.7 per cent of the remaining organizations declare a mixed form (self-financing and external financing) and 6.0 per cent receive only external financing.

Only a few responses to the question on public contributions to groups were received. Therefore, it is impossible to compare this with data on modes of financing. However, responses received confirm that public contributions are given to a minority of groups in an occasional fashion and not on a regular basis (table 12).

This sector also incorporates the largest number of religious organizations which are the absolute majority of social relief associations (69.8 per cent – table 13). Accordingly lay humanitarian and socialist solidaristic components have the smallest proportions with 26.7 per cent and 3.4 per cent respectively.

The conclusion which may be drawn is that the characteristics of social relief voluntarism are to some extent also the characteristics of Catholic voluntarism, partly portrayed in this section.

The Health Care Sector

This is definitely the most structured and coordinated sector. Not only are almost all groups (92 per cent) associated or federated, but their absolute majority (62.1 per cent) selected the legally recognized association as their juridical status. Their tendency to be thoroughly organized seems to be confirmed also by the data relating to employees and volunteers who do not come in contact with the

Table 10
Spheres of Action and Relationships with Public Authorities

Relationships with public authorities	Only social relief type	Only health care type	Only cultural type
NONE	57.9	21.4	49.8
Special contracts	3.0	3.0	5.1
Agreements	20.7	15.8	22.4
Recognition of qualification	10.1	10.2	11.5
Arrangements	8.2	49.7	11.2
% TOTAL	100.0	100.0	100.0
A. V.	1129	805	847

Source: Italian Ministry of Labour and Social Security. National Investigation on Local Volunteers Groups in Italy. Rome. 1984. Mimeo.

Table 11
Spheres of Action and Economic Support Sources

Economic support sources	Only social relief type	Only health care type	Only cultural type
Self–financing	37.3	22.4	41.9
Self–financing + external financing	56.7	56.6	52.5
External financing only	6.0	21.0	5.6
% TOTAL	100.0	100.0	100.0
A. V.	1127	804	853

Source:: Italian Ministry of Labour and Social Security. National Investigation on Local Volunteers Groups in Italy. Rome. 1984. Mimeo.

Table 12
Spheres of Action and Type of Public Financing

Type of public financing	Only social relief type	Only health care type	Only cultural type
None (private financing only)	58.5	17.5	19.8
Occasional	28.8	32.9	59.9
Fixed	12.6	49.6	20.4
% TOTAL	100.0	100.0	100.0
A. V.	697	623	491

Source: Italian Ministry of Labour and Social Security. National Investigation on Local Volunteers Groups in Italy. Rome. 1984. Mimeo.

Table 13
Spheres of Action and Group Tendency

Group Tendency	Only social relief type	Only health care type	Only cultural type
Religious	69.8	14.2	47.1
Socialist solidaristic	3.4	5.6	8.6
Lay humanitarian non–sectarian	26.7	80.2	44.3
% TOTAL	100.0	100.0	100.0
A. V.	1134	804	839

Source: Italian Ministry of Labour and Social Security. National Investigation on Local Volunteers Groups in Italy. Rome. 1984. Mimeo.

public. In both cases this sector shows the highest proportions (12.4 per cent and 56.2 per cent respectively) which probably means that the majority of groups have complex structures requiring considerable efforts within the group to function. 44.5 per cent of organizations declare a small number of volunteers (2 to 20), but on the other hand, this sector possesses the highest number of large groups (17.5 per cent have more than 200 volunteers).

As far as volunteers are concerned, there is a sharp predominance of men over women – groups solely or mainly made up of women are 7.6 per cent – as well as adults over young or elderly people. The health care sector shows the highest level of insurance coverage for volunteers (58.2 per cent). An analysis of management forms confirms the characterization as a thoroughly organized and formalized sector. 83.7 per cent of groups adopted a complete representative and participative structure, while only 3.6 per cent make a practice of direct democracy which is typical for a portion of informal groups.

This sector shows the largest number of groups who do not carry out training activities (51.3 per cent). This datum may be surprising as the typical field of action within health care seems to require a level of training and skill which on the average is higher than those required in the social relief sector, for instance.

This apparent contradiction can be explained, however, by the fact that many local groups associated with AVIS, AIDO, and similar blood donor organizations are covered by this sector. Their particular targets do not usually call for their volunteers or blood or organ donors to have any special training. As compared with the social relief sector, here there is a larger number of groups who cooperate with public authorities. This might indicate that any training activity is performed at quite high levels, which frequently require experiences, structures or training means available only to public organizations.

Furthermore, the connection of these groups with local public authorities shows a symmetrically opposed trend to that of the social relief sector. In fact, here 78.6 per cent of the groups declare their interaction, and 49.7 per cent operate under arrangements with public bodies, the last percentage figure being absolutely the highest value within sectors involved in this report. There is a significant relationship between this value and 49.6 per cent of the groups who receive regular financing. Therefore, the health care sector represents a privileged circle within the experimentation of a new transaction between public and private-social institutions. This already merits further consideration and detailed study with particular reference to quality aspects, which have been ignored by this investigation. We believe that the development of such a strong interaction has been prompted by the existence of the Medical Care Reform Act expressly stipulating – under art. 45 – cooperation between the National Health Care Scheme and voluntary organizations.

From the aspect of financing, the peculiar feature of the health care sector is a high proportion of groups relying exclusively on external financial support (21.0 per cent). This value, on the average, exceeds the percentage of other sectors by almost four times and it is almost equivalent to the number of self-financed health care groups (22.4 per cent).

This strange phenomenon can be accounted for by the number of arrangements with public authorities, which show the highest percentage (49.7 per cent), as already mentioned. In our opinion, about one half of the groups with such arrangements support organizational and running expenses only by means of public financing granted by virtue of these arrangements, and ask their volunteers only for their services.

If this interpretation is right, it reveals an element which cuts both ways and deserves further consideration. On the one hand, it is evident that public financing for voluntarism is a real investment, since it permits a variety of services to be offered which could only exist otherwise at a far higher cost. Suffice it to think about the implications of making a business of blood donation. On the other hand, the complete dependence of many groups on public financing is evidence of their structural weakness and precariousness. In the event that such financing is no longer available, it is unlikely that these groups will be able to survive. In the end, the absolute majority of voluntary groups engaged in health care are lay or non-sectarian (80.2 per cent).

The Cultural Sector

This is the second sector in order of diffusion and width. The special feature of cultural groups seems to be their stronger local character. This is proven by the fact that this sector has the smallest number of adhesions to larger associations or federations (60.4 per cent). The association is de facto the most widespread juridical status adopted by 43.3 per cent of the groups. Here also the status of cooperative societies begins to take root (4.6 per cent).

The small number of conscientious objectors (4.8 per cent of groups have 1 or more of them), employees (6.7 per cent) as well as volunteers who are not in contact with the public (73.5 per cent of groups have non at all) confirms the low level of the groups' inner complexity, especially when they are small (55.2 per cent have 2 to 20 volunteers). As opposed to this, religious people, of whom there is a differing number in 45.7 per cent of groups, are quite widespread. As in the social relief sector, here the prevailing trend is towards stability which, however, is more remarkable in terms of availability of time (54.3) than number of volunteers (47.0 per cent). A further similarity with the social relief sector is the composition of volunteers. Although in lower proportions, here as well there is a fairly large presence of women and old people who prevail in 16.3 per cent and 4.9 per cent of the groups respectively.

The element of marked difference is the massive presence of young people (they are the only or principal presence in 43.2 per cent of the groups). Volunteers have no insurance coverage in 71.8 per cent of the groups.

Most associations operating within the cultural sector adopt either complete (57.5 per cent) or incomplete (18.3 per cent) democratic forms of management. The other two forms – i. e. direct democracy and non-elective representation – cut the remaining number of groups almost in two, with 12.5 per cent and 11.6 per cent respectively.

The cultural sector presents a large proportion of groups who perform training activities (71.7 per cent)[10]. This is not surprising in view of the service they offer. Regarding the implementation of training activities, the majority of groups (61.3 per cent) determine their own training, as in the social relief sector. There is also some inclination to coordinate with other groups, and although it still concerns a clear minority of associations (5.0 per cent), it is, however, more widespread than cooperation with or delegation to public authorities.

Also, with reference to connections with public authorities, the cultural and free-time entertainment sector has strong similarities to the social relief field. Here, the proportion of groups which do not have relations is about one half (49.8 per cent) and all the forms of relationship provided for – special agreements, contracts, arrangements, recognition of qualifications – follow the trend of the social relief sector.

However, there might be different reasons for this policy of relative separation which appears in this sector as well. Rather than deep-rooted distrust it might be an indication of the fact that here group activities are described as alternative to those managed by public authorities. There are some Italian institutions, i. e. alternative or full-time schools, where children may study and also play after school hours. The same holds true with respect to free-time activities, alternative to those offered by multivalent centres managed by districts or communes.

With reference to financing, most groups declare a mixed form (52.5 per cent) while the rest rely almost completely on self-financing (41.9 per cent). This latter figure seems to be in contradiction to the number (19.8 per cent only) of groups who do not enjoy public financing. It must be mentioned, however, that there are fewer answers to the question of public financing than to financing in general. Therefore the two data cannot be compared. In this sector, however, we might remark the phenomenon of a variety of groups receiving considerable amounts of public money. As a matter of fact, many regions provide small contributions to cultural groups who can evidence their past activities through documents: this does not imply any form of cooperation or control.

In the end, the cultural sector basically presents a balance between lay operators (44.3 per cent) and Catholic operators (47.1 per cent), with a slight supremacy of the latter. Groups with a socialist solidaristic tendency are a minority within this sector as well, although they have a larger proportion (8.6 per cent) than within the social relief and health care sectors.

Emerging Orientations in Voluntary Associations

Our research evidenced that empirically there are different systems of relationship between local administrations and voluntary associations.

• In some sectors – health care above all – there are strong mutual connections which entail both continual exchanges and mutual support. We refer to the fact that public administrations offer voluntary groups training opportunities, various supplies (e. g. premises and/or equipment) and financing in return for the services which the groups perform, thus supplementing, substituting or anticipating the public provision of commodities and services. In some instances these relationships take the form of clear dependence, since any break in public financing might imply the practical impossibility for the groups to continue operating.

• On the other hand, in other sectors – the social relief sector in particular – such relationships are basically non-existent. Groups are self-financed or receive private financing, use their own equipment or offices, and perform training for their members in complete self-determination.

But, beyond mere facts, what are the attitudes emerging from voluntary groups towards the welfare state and its changes?

By using an ideal-typical pattern (Donati 1984: 197) it is possible to derive two strong lines.

The first one is to intend voluntarism as an *alternative exit* to the welfare state, with which it shares neither targets nor methods. In such cases, a demand for a considerable reduction of public interventions and services should emerge or, somehow, the choice for 'different' strategies in terms of productivity and distribution of commodities and services should appear.

The second line, which we refer to as *collaborative exit,* is supported by those who leave the welfare state scheme and nevertheless share its purposes, but who have the intention of enriching them with other operative instruments and methods identified and managed independently. In this case, a demand for guaranteed possibilities of social private interventions within the framework of the welfare state pattern should emerge, together with a willingness to accept controls by public administrations on the use of resources and service standards.

In our research it has not been possible to verify the above-mentioned hypotheses empirically by means of interviews with people responsible for voluntary groups or their members. Therefore, for the time being we shall consider only the declarations made by some persons responsible for voluntary associations or federations which have a fairly large local group membership. In particular we refer to MOVI (Movimento Volontari Italiani), a non-sectarian federation of groups with a Christian tendency, and to APAS (Associazione Pubbliche Assistenze) which gathers groups with a lay socialist background.

The president of MOVI, based on the premise that volunteers have a culture of solidarity which inspires both public and private spheres, maintains that conscious voluntarism cannot give its full contribution for the functioning of the public framework. Voluntarism can perform its original and different function, which is not adverse or merely collaborative but also anticipating, designing, and utopian, only if the state is efficient. Otherwise, there is the steady risk of role confusion. The main idea, therefore, is collaboration with independence and mutual respect, and with no confusion of roles – volunteers cannot be used as an excuse to postpone what institutions must do – within a juridical framework recognizing voluntary associations as fully-fledged service institutions.

On the lay socialist side, declarations received indicate that a profound change of mind has begun.

Until recently, lay volunteer organizations remained linked with the simple idea of service. This means that voluntarism was thought of as an instrument to awaken needs but mainly as a supplier of services backing up public action, in the expectation that the latter would fully assume its responsibilities. Today, this image of voluntarism as being divided into sectors, and as functional to the maintenance or improvement of services is no longer sufficient. Indeed, it ends up by justifying the maintenance of a predetermined order, that is the capitalist order.

To the contrary, the question is changing this order by means of two major tools, which are also the basic values of voluntarism: solidarity and gratuitousness. Collective solidarity may represent an important feature for constructing the bases of a more advanced society, in that it expresses a strong basic democracy, new types of self-management and self-determination, and real decision-making decentralization without interference from state institutions in this perspective, they may be seen as new types of self-guidance and self-government rather than merely self-managed groups.

Therefore, voluntarism is not to be seen as a 'stop gap' or as a supplementary or additional instrument. It is a collective project and a way for people to have the major role in changing the state.

As we can see, the two hypothetical lines tend to be confirmed. Christian voluntary associations have an attitude of collaborative exit which does not question the institutional welfare state pattern as being a compromise between capitalism and democracy. They tend rather to enrich and organize this by means of a greater institutional enhancement of solidaristic initiatives which stem directly from the civil society and are self-determined.

The emerging directions in Marxist voluntary associations, on the contrary, show an attitude of alternative exit. They refuse the present compromise of capitalism and democracy. In their opinion the state enhancement not only of voluntarism but of the whole third sector is the start of a general social change around the hubs of self-management and solidarism. This can affect the process of accumulation which increasingly tends to confine investments of resources to technological rearrangement, financial speculations, and safe sectors, while being close to any investment aiming at the formation of greater job opportunities. In view of the current balance of powers, however, the first direction should be the most widespread.

92

Conclusions

Around the mid 1980s, collective objectives of the Italian social policy pursued through new public regulations and interventions appeared to be 'jammed-up', mainly because of the bounds of social expenditures (for health care, social relief, social security) and also due to the failure of the integration between social services and the labour market. As a matter of fact, the laws of the 1970s aiming at protecting weak categories of people as well as at reorganizing health care services were unsuccessful.

This 'jammed-up' situation causes the awakening of new orientations which we can summarize as follows:

• First of all, there is a *new 'democratic individualism'*, aiming at releasing the creative and entrepreneurial capacities of the population by eliminating social constraints and dependences within a framework of social equity. This enhances, increases, and improves life conditions and *changes* for the largest possible number of individuals, starting from those who rank in the worst positions. The struggle here is chiefly against the over-emphasis of ideology, governmentalism, and egalitarianism of the 1970s, in order to set up a social 'package' of guarantees equal for everybody. This basis shall serve to organize the widest possible variety of opportunities and demands, within a framework of convertibility and selection. The target is to ensure 'a possible rise as well as a protected fall'.

• In the second place, a *new resorting to 'social-private' actions* emerges. This is defined as a sphere with management independence in both labour and services. Though having to be accountable, these actions should move freely for social non-profit-making purposes with the aim of creating new flexible work opportunities and new services that are not administered directly by public administrations. It is a fact that public administrations increasingly resort to social-private interventions.

• The last emerging tendency is for a *collective mobilization* in form of *self-management*. This line represents a way towards political change of the state and the entire social organization, setting apart the old project of 'taking the power to the state'. This cooperative and self-management method is regarded as a solution to most antitheses between civil society and the state, between private and public.

These three orientations are not isolated and contrasting, but largely *inter-related and mixed*. In fact, they represent *three compromises* with a common motivation, that is to say, enhancing individual action within a collective system which is politically ruled but not managed directly by the welfare state itself. The first one is an ideological compromise *(lib-lab* convergence); the second one is an institutional compromise (between public and private), the third one is a compromise between particular and general interests which gives up universalistic participation. Obviously, each of them has special problems. The first line must make clear which are the 'minimum' social guarantees forming the 'package' of equality on which equity is to be erected. The second line must make clear to what extent society has an advantage by resorting to social-private actions. It is also to verify if this is not a means of discharging public responsibilities and tasks, which can be seen from the results anyway, at least theoretically. The third line must make clear how a 'collective mobilization' is possible in a historical time when there is a deep crisis of collective identity as well as a decreasing justification of 'social' projects and institutions.

In any case, it is easy to see that currently the fundamental knotty problem of social policy is *the interweaving between private initiative/self-management and public regulation/support.* Experimentation is open on this interlacing. The main traditional doers of the welfare state today act by reaction to the crisis rather than in a really innovative manner. This, however, does not mean that nothing changes:

• Central and local administrations tackle the crisis of welfare plans by decentralizing tasks and organizations to the periphery of the political-administrative system, in order to activate more open and local exchanges between public operators and private people (both beneficiaries and service or employment agencies).

• Workers' unions attempt to fight this crisis by appealing again to the contractual mentality which accepts new instances only to renegotiate them with public and private powers. But they realize that not everything can be negotiated.

• Political parties seek contingent solutions by using the public-private mix insofar as this is favourable to them and always as a mere procedure, whereby they lose their ideological borders.

In brief, our analysis tries to demonstrate that in Italy a ground *pattern* is emerging which is very widespread and shared by the different actors as a means for understanding and implementing social policies. On the basis of this *pattern* the identity of doers and deeds, their otherness and relational nature are increasingly determined in the crucial time of interactions, exchanges, and social practices. They are not predetermined actors any longer and their actions are not accomplishments of – or even mere attempts to implement – already coded demands and projects. Welfare interventions rely increasingly on the magic moment of 'micro-relationships'. Action plans fail even before being formulated, because the above-mentioned joint cultural code thwarts them and proves them wrong *ex ante.* And this symbolic code governs more and more the mentality which is emerging among policy-makers, operators and beneficiaries.

Notes

This research report is fruit of a joint work. As to its compilation, P. Donati wrote the sections: Premises, the Great Plan of the 1970s, Basic Structural Features and the Conclusions, while I. Colozzi drew up the sections: New Orientations among Policy-makers and the Role of Voluntary Associations.

1) This statement can be fully understood by reading Rossi, G., and Donati, P., 1983; Donati 1984.
2) Such an analysis is developed in Ferrera M. 1985 as a part of the international research led in the European countries by Peter Flora.
3) We are clearly referring to N. Luhmann's theory as interpreted and applied to the Italian context in Donati P. (ed) 1986.
4) For a general discussion of this topic see Donati P. 1984.
5) See several reports on the country's social situation by CENSIS, as well as data by ISTAT. For an appraisal see Donati P. 1984.
6) For a more detailed analysis of social expenditures and its dynamics 1977 to 1980 see Di Nicola P. 1984, ch. 3.
7) The latter correlation however is not very strong even if significant.
8) Regarding this modernization index see Di Nicola P. op. cit.: 200 ff. It has been constructed with four highly and positively inter-related indicators: employment rate (employed people proportion of the total population), union conflictuality rate, aging rate and rate of legal separations (virtually identical to divorce rate).
9) Social solidarity cooperatives are a juridical status which is not envisaged by the Civil Code of our country. Their recognition is welcomed by a bill presented by Salvi and other Christian Democrats to the Chamber of Deputies entitled 'Regulation of Social Solidarity Cooperatives'. In actual practice, these are cooperatives established on a voluntary basis which dispense services to the benefit of third parties (not their partners) and in the ultimate analysis to the community.
10) Also in this case we mean training by groups for their members. As a matter of fact and despite the special sphere of action, vocational training intended as preparation to introduce non-members into the labour market is rarely made by voluntary groups. Only 10.1 per cent of these do so with some continuity. This is due to the fact that vocational training in Italy is managed by regions either directly through their centres or indirectly through arrangements with a particular business of the cooperation sector. This sector is well structured and institutional. It avails itself of regularly employed and paid personnel to perform such training activities. Demand for vocational training, however, is increasing (+ 1.7 per cent enrolled people in the 1982–83 school year, compared with the previous school year) in spite of the difficulties of training supplied to keep up with the ongoing development of professional types and new qualifications required by the labour market. Presently, 45 per cent of the pupils in the regional vocational training scheme are enrolled in agriculture and industry courses, while only 9.3 per cent attend courses in the service sector.

Bibliography

Di Nicola, P., 1984, 'Il welfare state italiano come sistema di protezione sociale', in Donati, P. (ed), Le frontiere della politica sociale. Redistribuzione e nuova cittadinanza, Angeli, Milano.
Donati, P., 1983, 'Natura, problemi e limiti del welfare state: un'interpretazione', in Rossi G., Donati P. (eds), 1983.
Donati, P., 1984, Risposte alla crisi dello Stato sociale, Angeli, Milano.
Donati, P. (ed), 1986, Le politiche sociali nella società complessa, Angeli, Milano.
Ferrera, M., 1985, Il welfare state in Italia, Il Mulino, Bologna.
Flora, P., Heidenheimer, A. J. (eds), 1981, The Development of Welfare States in Europe and America, Transaction Books, New Brunswick, N. J.
ISTAT, 1985, Annuario statistico italiano,Edizione 1984, Roma.
Rossi, G., Donati, P. (eds), 1983, Welfare state: problemi e alternative, Angeli, Milano.

Changes in Labour Market Regulations
Three Italian Case Studies

Marina Bianchi and Chiara Saraceno

Introduction

Research on the crisis of the welfare state must address itself to the different processes and phenomena which are changing the labour market, both from the point of view of the characteristics of the labour force and from that of the strategies and actions of the different social actors involved. These phenomena are relevant to at least three levels: methods for dealing with mass unemployment and its effects on the living conditions and perspectives of different social groups; ways in which the working status is being redefined and the work life cycle of individuals and groups is being redesigned, also with reference to the social security system; the new balances and relationships which are developing among the different social actors involved: the state, local governments, workers and employers unions, political parties, etc.

On one hand, therefore, it is interesting to see how the balance among the traditional or new forces operating in and around the labour market is affected by the crisis and changes within it. On the other hand, it is relevant to understand how the different measures taken to regulate unemployment or to protect particular groups (e. g. measures for the young, or the old, of for the *cassintegrati*[1]) can affect not only their position in the labour market today, but the concept of a working life itself, as well as the question of traditional forms of social security.

It is impossible, however, to delineate a general picture of the Italian situation. The differentiation among the various contexts in which the above-mentioned phenomena are occurring is too great, not only in terms of economic resources, but of past history of industrialization, of local union history and traditions, of local political history and set-up (in terms of local government coalitions), etc. On top of this, there are the specific features of the Italian state, which is characterized both by a high degree of legislative and regulative intervention at the central level, and by a fragmented and somewhat erratic approach to social policies. These fragmented and uncoordinated measures must be implemented at the local level, where they interact with, and become the outcome of, the interplay in the local labour market situation, the balance of powers among the political parties as well as among and with the unions, and the political and union local traditions and history.

Given this complexity and fragmentation, we have chosen to study two specific local situations, which are different with respect to the kind of labour market, the trade union tradition and the balance among the three main unions, and finally with respect to the local political history and balances. In addition, we present a case study of the implementation of a law instituting a particular kind of work contract. Within each case we had to choose only a few of the different issues which constitute the focus of the international research project, neglecting others. In particular, it would have been useful to study informal activities, unpaid work, volunteer activities, etc. Adequate research data on these phenomena are lacking, however, and to collect them anew would have required more time and resources than we could command.

The first case is Turin, where we analyze the answers given to the occupational crisis at the level of public labour policy measures and of social welfare policies. The second case is Brescia, where we study the labour policy measures developed by the local government and negotiated with the unions in order to face the employment crisis. Finally, we present an analysis of a particular kind of part-time work contracts – *contratti di solidarietà* – which are meant to avoid lay-offs and also to favour the creation of new job positions. We analyze their implementation in a specific regional context (Lombardy) and with regard to a specific productive sector (textile).

All three cases are located in the most industrialized area of the country, the North-West. However, they represent distinctive experiences both in the history of industrialization and unionization and in the reaction to the current processes of restructuring and of mass unemployment. Moreover, the two territorial cases studied present the specific features respectively of an area of central economy (Turin) and of an area of peripheral economy (Brescia), according to the analytical categories developed in the political economic studies conducted in Italy since the 1970s (Bagnasco 1977). Breaking the traditional dichotomous division between the developed and industrialized North and the backward and underdeveloped South, Bagnasco presents evidence of the social and economic relevance of the development model – *de facto* a social economic formation – of the so-called Third Italy. This is geographically identified in the North-Eastern and Central regions of Italy. It is characterized by urban and industrial diffusion (decentralization), and by a prevalence of small and family managed manufacturing enterprises. The main political feature of this formation is the stability of the voting behaviour of its population, therefore the political continuity of local governments, which are single or strongly dominant party ones: Christian Democratic in the Veneto area, Communist in the regions of Central Italy.

Brescia and its province, although it is increasingly gravitating towards the region city of Milan, and, in some respects, tends to be incorporated into the Milan me tropolitan area (with many workers commuting to Milan), presents however all the above-mentioned features of a peripheral area.

Turin represents an example of central economy, which is characterized by a high urban, productive and residential concentration, with the unique peculiarity (for Italy) of a monocultural kind of industrialization in the automobile sector. As it happens in all large Italian cities, the voting behaviour of the population is not linear, and the local government is increasingly unstable.

We aim at comparing the impact of the economic and occupational crisis, as well as of its social effects, on these two kinds of territorial contexts, which correspond to two different models of development and of social and economic organization. In order to do this, we have looked at some collective actors who are central in these phenomena, trying to detect their actions, reactions and strategies in the period from the early to the mid 1980s.

Turin: A Case Study of a City under Stress[2])

Premise

Our focus is on the early 1980s, since 1980–81 is really a turning point in the economic and political situation of this city: long and costly strikes were not able to prevent mass lay-offs and the insertion of large numbers of workers of FIAT into Cassa Integrazione Guadagni (CIG)[1]. Of course, the economic crisis and the relative inability of trade unions to forestall the shrinking of labour are not a unique Turin phenomenon. The particular social, economic and political history of this town, however, gave to the Turin crisis specific features in terms of the resources and limitations with which the different actors involved entered it and developed strategies to face it. We will very briefly sketch those which are most relevant to our analysis.

Up to the late 1970s we could observe not only a high productive specialization of the Turin labour market and economy (in the automobile sector), due to the dominant role af FIAT, but also a high degree of concentration in the city and in its metropolitan area of the main labour market resources as well as of the management problems of the whole province, if not of the region.

It must also be remembered that immigration to this area continued up to 1973–74, involving mostly unqualified workers coming from the South. The economic growth continued until 1977–78, providing new jobs especially inside the so-called *indotto* (the many small and medium factories and workshops around the automobile industry). However, this growth was not supported by any planning, especially concerning its consequences on the urban structure and everyday life conditions. This lack of planning and of a strong and autonomous government of the city as a whole, was a peculiar feature of the economic growth of Turin in the post-war years, with its costs for the immigrant workers and for the overall quality of life in the city and in the metropolitan area (IRES 1984).

This period – especially the first half of the 1970s – was also characterized by a growing strength and presence of the workers movement and its organizations, mainly the trade unions (particularly the Communist inspired CGIL, which traditionally had a monopoly on workers' representation in this area, and particularly at FIAT plants) and the Italian Communist Party (PCI). This process started with the so-called *autunno caldo* in 1969 and culminated with the victory of the left at the local government elections in 1975. The left coalition (the so-called *giunta rossa,* with the Italian Communist Party (PCI), the Italian Socialist Party (PSI), the Italian Social Democratic Party (PSDI) and the Italian Republican Party (PRI) was faced with the problems of governing a city which up to then had merely accepted the economic changes and moves dictated mainly by FIAT and by the most important economic groups. For the first time, the city government defined itself as an important actor in the decision-making processes involving the city and its inhabitants, negotiating with the other social actors: trade unions, employers unions, FIAT, the banks, etc. As a matter of fact, the left coalition entered the local government explicitly stating the goal, as well as the value, of an active government of the city, through the definition of a platform, the transparency of its acts, the participation and consent of the different actors involved. While it tried to involve the other relevant forces (FIAT, the main banks and enterprises) in a project of global restructuring of the urban and metropolitan area in order to solve pressing problems – transportation, pollution, housing – the *giunta rossa* paid attention also to the needs which were being voiced by rank and file movements, such as the neighbourhood groups and associations, and also to some of the new social movements.

The political and cultural model which was implicit in this attitude implied not only that the government should be a crucial force in mediating different interests and in guiding economic development, but that it should promote citizenship rights, the content and boundaries of which were perceived as changing and expanding, as it was indicated by the focus on the quality of life.

But the left coalition, and particularly the PCI within it, looked at these problems from the perspective of a growing economic expansion (in fact, they were concerned with the question of counteracting the devastating effects of the economic growth), of a still growing strength of the workers movement and of its continuing centrality in the political and economic situation within the Turin context (Negri 1985). The unions, and particularly the CGIL, shared this vision as well. They were unable to foresee both the severe economic crisis and the restructuring of the labour market which the technological changes were already bringing about, with their consequences also on the traditional forms of social and political representation. They also had an idea of social integration and of the working class which did not account for the differentiation promoted by migratory processes and by changing working conditions (Negri 1982). They were planning for a dif-

100

ferent relationship among the social actors, but they were counting on the 'old' (political, as well as economic) resources to do it. And while they were envisioning a partially different citizenship mode, from the point of view of social rights, one of the most important traditional bases for citizenship, membership in the labour force, was being weakened and changed, and the trade unions were having difficulty in even achieving one of their most traditional goals: the defence of jobs and job security.

The left coalition was eventually disrupted by disagreements among its constituent parties and particularly between the PCI and the PSI, therefore further weakening the labour movement and the left. Also the strategy aiming at persuading the relevant 'private' social forces to cooperate was not successful, given the resistance of the big economic groups to collaborate with a left coalition. All this, however, cannot conceal the wider, and as important, gap which opened between expectations (and the culture which supported them, based on the idea of a continuous growth) on one hand, and the changing economy on the other.

These phenomena started to become more apparent at the turn of the decade. First of all, the traditionally high industrial specialization of the Turin area started to decrease. FIAT increasingly diversified its productive sectors and became a holding. This meant that it had diversified personnel and industrial policies, which had to be met by an equally diversified approach by the trade unions, which therefore lost the strength coming from a tendentially unified basis. At the same time, the overall weight of the industrial sector started to decrease in the city, in favour of a still timid, but continuous, tertiarization. This too contributed to a fragmentation of the work force – a phenomenon for which the unions were not prepared and which reached also the basis of the consent given to the left coalition. All this was compounded by a rate of economic growth which touched its historical minimum, and in some sectors was even lower than the national rates. Starting in 1980, the occupational crisis became increasingly severe, as shown both by the number of workers covered by the Cassa Integrazione Guadagni (CIG)[1]) and by the number of unemployed (IRES 1983; ORML 1984). At the same time, the cost of living in Turin increased (inflation), being among the highest in Italy, resulting in the impoverishment of the weaker social groups. In this same period the number of people temporarily or continually on welfare increased dramatically. The crisis in the official labour market is doubled by that in the grey and black ones, which until then had functioned as a safety valve both for the labour market and for the family economy.

There have also been changes in the geographic distribution of the population. The migration process has inverted its direction, from the city to other areas: to the surrounding towns and villages, to other parts of the region or to other parts of Italy, although a mass return to the South is not occurring. The old immigrants who have settled here cannot go back where the situation appears to be even worse.

Notwithstanding these population shifts, Turin and its metropolitan area remain the central locus both of the economic crisis, with a large number of unemployed and of *cassintegrati,* as well as of the restructuring processes due to technological innovations.

Given this background, let us now turn to the specific focus of our research:

The situation in the labour market and the labour policy measures developed to counteract it; and

the welfare measures and models developed to meet the impoverishment of large numbers of people and families.

Labour Policy Measures Vis-à-vis the Occupational Crisis

Some Data on the Labour Market Situation

The negative trend in economic growth began in 1976, though slowly and somewhat contradictorily. In 1978–80 a fleeting recovery was made. It was only in 1980, as stated above, that the crisis became dramatically apparent, first of all in its effects on the labour market. Given the crucial role of FIAT in this area, the industrial sector was the most affected by the phenomenon. FIAT eliminated a large surplus of manpower within its plants, while, changing its demands, it also modified the labour force composition and structure of the *indotto.*

The total number of hours worked decreased by 10 per cent from 1978 to 1983.[3]

But the most interesting, as well as most dramatic, indicators of the width and seriousness of the phenomenon are the data on the *Cassa Integrazione Straordinaria*[1] and on unemployment.

As shown in table 1, in the Piedmont region, and particularly in the province of Turin, the number of people covered by the Cassa Integrazione Guadagni (CIG) increased disproportionally starting in 1980. With the (numerically as well as socially relevant) exception of FIAT, the firms involved are mostly small or medium ones (with 100–499 employees).

By the end of 1983, it is estimated that there were 27,000 workers which had been covered by (extraordinary) CIG at no hours (that is, totally out of work) for more than two years. The workers most heavily affected by this experience were the weakest quotas of the labour force: un- or dequalified workers, women, handicapped and disabled workers, people who were highly politicized and had been particularly active in the industrial conflicts of the preceding years (which were also dramatically marked by terrorism). They had also more difficulty not only in being recalled by their firm, but in finding another job. Not all those who exit the CIG, do so by going back to their previous job. There are no systematic studies on the different paths by which people exit CIG, but from empirical data it appears that while a few (the better qualified) find a different job, many resign, in exchange for a lump payment (many new self-employed belong to this category). Still

Table 1
Ordinary and Extraordinary Cassa Integrazione
Number of hours provided for in Piedmont and in the Torino Province, by productive sector: 1977–1984 (thousands)

| | 1977 | | 1980 | | 1981 | |
	Region	P.Torino	Region	P.Torino	Region	P.Torino
Ordinary CIG	**18,855**	6,870	**16,443**	6,497	**45,756**	29,254
● industry	**12,212**	5,623	**13,288**	5,787	**42,513**	27,894
● building	**4,643**	1,247	**3,155**	710	**2,975**	1,124
● services	–		–		–	
Extraord. CIG	**12,354**	5,538	**11,398**	3,758	**130,054**	117,784

| | 1982 | | 1983 | | 1984 | |
	Region	P.Torino	Region	P.Torino	Region	P.Torino
Ordinary CIG	**45,671**	28,633	**58,626**	39,610	**75,644**	–
● industry	**40,607**	25,922	**54,887**	37,965	–	–
● building	**3,908**	1,582	**3,511**	1,446	–	–
● services	**1,155**	1,128	**227**	199	–	–
Extraord. CIG	**126,386**	109,745	**131,351**	104,089	**135,019**	–

Source:
Regione Piemonte. Osservatorio sul mercato del lavoro. Rapporto sul mercato del lavoro. Bolletino n. 5. Giugno 1985. p. 196.

others (the older) accept early retirement. Others eventually get fired (especially in the smaller industries); some get sick and become *de facto* disabled workers; and some also commit suicide (see also Comitato di Lotta 1984).
While the *Cassa Integrazione* became a mass phenomenon starting in 1980, a dramatic increase in the unemployment rate occurred three years later, in 1983, when the 'persons looking for a job' increased by 17.8 per cent (equal to 172,000 persons) with respect to the preceding year. In the same year, the unemployment rate in the city reached 8.3 per cent. If we add to this figure those who have been covered by CIG at no hours and for many months, we have an unemployment rate of 10 per cent in Turin. The rate is higher in the metropolitan area (11 per cent), and still higher in the province (20.3 per cent).
In this situation, the institutional agency for job placement, the employment agency *(agenzia di collocamento)* appears totally inadequate. On one side, the informal recruiting channel, which has always existed, regains strength as employers can more easily choose their own workers in a situation of offer surplus; on the other side, those enrolled in the agency appear to be the weakest members of the labour force: they are mostly youth and women, with a low degree of education (middle school, or short professional high schools), who expect to work in low qualified, generic white-collar jobs. The presence of people coming from the South is high especially among the youngest and less qualified. They can remain on the agency list for a long time (more than a year). And studies

show that those most in need, since they have been unemployed longer, find it more difficult to obtain a job (ORML 1984: 95–106).

Labour Policy Measures Coordinated and Implemented by Local Governments

When speaking of local governments, we should keep in mind that there are differences by institutional status, range and area of influence, among the city, province and regional governments. Moreover, the coalitions which govern at the three levels might be different or enjoy a different consensus. The left coalition was always weaker at the regional level (where it broke up earlier) and stronger at the city level. Finally, although *de facto* we must speak of a metropolitan area concerning Turin, there is not such a thing as a metropolitan government, but at best an effort at coordination. The 26 municipalities of the area plus that of Turin have therefore elaborated and administered different strategies and policies, in the face of processes which affected the metropolitan area as a whole.

At the same time, some of the restructuring and crisis processes (such as FIAT lay-offs and *Cassa Integrazione,* but also mass youth unemployment) were of such scale and social and political relevance that they were faced and negotiated at the national level, among the national unions, the national government, the central secretariats of the political parties, the Parliament, and the employers. This weakened the power of local forces, be it the local government or local trade unions, while they had to bear the brunt of the everyday consequences of the crisis and of the demands of people under stress. Again and again this feeling of having been robbed of direct negotiating power through the nationalization and centralization of the negotiating process comes up in the interviews with trade unionists and *cassintegrati.*

A final warning concerns the fact that, in collecting the material for this research we realized that the difficulty the local governments have continued to experience in reacting promptly to such a severe, complex and widespread crisis, derives not only from their cultural and political unpreparedness. It derives also from the inability of the administrative apparatus to systematically keep records of even less extraordinary events. Only very recently has a Regional Observatory of the labour market been instituted, to systematically monitor the tendencies in the offer as well as in the demand.

Given this situation, it appears that the policies are thought out on the basis of opinions and impressions, more than on reliable and verified data. On top of all this, there exists a lack of coordination among the different sectors: the welfare services have no power or influence on the workings of the employment agency or of the various job creating projects which are being developed.

We can, therefore, look at some of the measures taken in the field of occupation yet without searching for a unifying logic or rationale. The rationales might be diverse and cannot be forced on a homogeneous plan. Moreover, the fragmen tation, and at times very small scale, of the different interventions and measures, would require some effort at tracing multiple strategies and courses of action.

Three kinds of interventions appear to be interesting, from the point of view of the potential workers they address, as well as of the model of work career they suggest: the *contratti di formazione-lavoro* (training and work contracts), the *cooperatives* and the *cantieri di lavoro* (public work yards).

These measures, which in part are an implementation at the local level of national policies and laws, on one side select and define particular groups at risk, from the point of view of labour market participation; on the other side, they define a status of worker which is different, usually less protected, than that of 'regular', or 'strong' workers. It is through these measures that a revision of the system of guarantees in hiring and firing was initiated as well as of rigidities in the labour market. This revision developed in the past twenty years and especially after the so-called *autunno caldo,* through the process of industrial conflicts and negotiations, and culminated in the *Statuto dei Lavoratori.* It is true that not even all the workers who participate in the official or formal labour market are equally covered, not only because of the varying strengths of the trade unions in the different sectors and in large or small firms, but because many social security measures are addressed only to workers in large firms. This is true in particular of the measures concerning lay-offs. The coverage granted by the *Cassa Integrazione,* for instance, is much greater for workers of large industries. But even larger differences exist between those who in some way participate in the so-called system of guarantees and those who are altogether out of it, because they are in the grey or black labour market (among whom women, little qualified young people and Southerners are disproportionally present). These differences become dramatically evident in the case of an occupational crisis, when, on one extreme, the *cassintegrati* have a right to 60 up to 90 per cent of their pay for an indefinite period, while at the other extreme, those who have been laid off by a small firm can count on approximately 800 liras a day, if they care at all to collect their unemployment subsidy. In September 1985 there were public demonstrations in Turin by unemployed workers and people registered at the employment agency against the *cassintegrati* and the unions. It was the first time such a conflict came out in the open. The unions were ill at ease in facing it, also because at the same time they were facing the negative reactions of the *cassintegrati* themselves to the proposals advanced by a national union leader in order to revise the use of the *Cassa Integrazione.* The position of the *cassintegrati* within the trade unions is not an easy one. Sometimes they organize within the unions, both in order to make themselves visible and to maintain some kind of collective identity. But sometimes they organize outside the unions, since they perceive themselves as abandoned and forgotten, as one of their informal leaders in Turin told us.

In this situation, it is interesting to observe that workers and unions are moved (or compelled) to revise the format of the job contract, to introduce rules or paces of flexibility concerning not only hiring and firing, but the whole work career, in a situation of weakness, where the losing of security mechanisms is immediately more evident than the eventual advantages a more flexible and differentiated system may have for the workers themselves – also because not all the workers have the same resources to take advantage of it. It is not surprising, therefore, that while the protective system for the strongest workers continues to be defended, the labour market flexibility measures affect first of all the weakest workers – unemployed people or long-term *cassintegrati*.

Let us now turn to the three above-mentioned measures.

Contratti di Formazione-Lavoro

These contracts – literally "training and work contracts" (somewhat similar to the French Travaux d'Utilité Collective – TUC – community employment schemes) were first instituted by national law in January 1983 (law no. 79), which was partially changed in December 1984 (law no. 863). They are intended to encourage enterprises to hire young people for a two-year period within a training project. The target group is 18–29-year olds. This law in part overlaps with the law on apprenticeship, since the latter concerns 14–18-year olds. In a way we might say that, in the face of a growing percentage of people above 25 having difficulty in finding a job[4]), this measure prolongs the status of apprenticeship, that is of not full adulthood from the point of view of labour market participation and of the access to the full (adult) guarantees of a wage working status.

This kind of contract offers two kinds of advantages from the employers' point of view. On one side, differently from other regular contracts, they allow the direct hiring of workers on a personal basis *(chiamata nominativa),* without having to pick them from a list, according to their position in it *(chiamata numerica).* A second advantage is the possibility of terminating the job contract after two years. Therefore, it permits both the selection and testing of one's own employees (the usual trial period is much shorter), and the enlarging or reducing of one's own work force according to the needs of the enterprise – which is something very valuable to small and medium-sized enterprises, artisan workshops and the like. In addition, as it happens for apprentices, workers under this kind of contract are not included in an enterprise's labour force, from the fiscal point of view. Moreover, again as for apprentices, the employers must pay less social security contributions.

In order to be able to make these contracts, the firm has to submit a training project which must be approved by a regional office. In some cases, they can also obtain funds from the European Economic Community (EEC).

The impact of these contracts on youth employment is somewhat mixed in Turin as in the rest of Italy. On one side, they seem to substitute the apprenticeship contracts (with unfavourable consequences for those under 19 – see ORML 1984). On the other side, it appears that these contracts involve situations which previously belonged to the grey or black labour market (ISFOL 1985). Rather than increasing the total youth employment, they seem to allow a part of the formerly clandestine and unprotected workers to become visible and at least partially protected. It must be added that in the Piedmont region the employers have been more willing to use the law and to put up with its many bureaucratic requirements than in other Centre-North regions such as Lombardy and Emilia-Romagna. They have also set up some kind of consultant services to help prospective employers with all the paper work needed. As a consequence, in this region comparatively more *contratti di formazione-lavoro* were offered and more young people involved than in other areas since the law has existed (Bugarelli, Dutto and Giovine 1985). As for Turin specifically, around 15,000 young people were hired in this way during the period January 1983 – December 1984. And by the end of January 1985, 4,312 other training projects involving 15,715 young people were approved by the competent local offices. Approximately 65 per cent of these contracts involved males, 35 per cent females (a slightly higher percentage than in apprenticeship contracts where the girls are 33 per cent). They were concentrated mostly in the 19–24 age bracket. Most of these youth had only the compulsory middle school degree. More recent national data, however, indicate that both the age and the schooling of the youth involved in these contracts are increasing.

The size of the enterprises also seems to be increasing: less artisan enterprises are now availing themselves of these contracts than in the past, while more medium and large ones are proposing projects (ISFOL 1985). Notwithstanding the legal request that a specific training project be incorporated in the contract, in Turin, as in other parts of the country, the training offered is poor. Although experience with these contracts is only in its initial stage, the risk is already apparent that these young workers, and especially the less qualified among them, just go from one contract to another, without being really trained for anything, until they become too old for this kind of opportunity, and become unemployable 'adults' (ISFOL 1985).

Cooperatives

The cooperatives have a long-standing tradition in Italy. Historically they found support both within the Catholic political culture and with the left. Recently, they are (with some exaggeration) being looked at as a possible solution to many different problems: as a work relationship less alienating that that of wage work, as a suitable and humane way of providing services as against the impersonal bureaucratized mode of public services, as protective work environments for people suffering from some social or individual weakness, such as drug users, handicapped people, etc. In Piedmont, however, differently from less heavily industrialized and more politically homogeneous areas, such as the 'Catholic' Veneto or the 'Communist' Emilia-Romagna, there is no such strong cooperative tradition. For this reason, the role of the local government appears to be more crucial in the setting up of cooperatives, while the lack of a 'cooperative culture' and know-how may be a difficulty.

Both, the national and local government support cooperatives under two different sets of conditions, or aiming at two different groups of workers. On one side, they fund and facilitate cooperatives set up by young people (within the same age range as the *contratti di formazione-lavoro*). The *Progetto giovani* was launched by the left coalition in 1977, aiming at encouraging young people to set up some kind of economic, and in the long run self-supporting, enterprises. This project was funded anew each fiscal year, providing for the first financing of youth co-operatives, for a total of one billion ninety million liras: a small amount of money, considering the period involved (seven years). Also the number of youth who were thus employed seems to be quite reduced (although there is no general rec-ord of these enterprises and of the number of people involved over the years but only of the amount of expenditures); moreover, not all the cooperatives so funded become really self-supporting. Rather, they appear to offer a sort of transitional status between unemployment and a stable employment.

A second target group of the public funding of cooperative endeavours is a mixed one. As the regional law of June 1984 (law no. 28) stipulates, funds are provided "for the qualified insertion of unemployed youth and of workers covered by Cassa Integrazione Guadagni (CIG) or of workers who have been laid off by firms in economic difficulty, into already existing cooperatives or in new ones". In this case, there is no need to set up a cooperative, or to be young. It must be noted that with this law the Piedmont region anticipated the national law of February 1985. In this case too, however, the amount of funding indicates that the number of people involved is small (here too data are lacking): 807 million liras for one year in the whole region.

Both of these kinds of cooperatives may be in agriculture (but this is not the case in Turin), either in the secondary or in the service sector. It is difficult to evaluate their impact and their success. There is no specific office and formal process delegated to approve, control and follow up these cooperatives. The danger of clientelism is particularly apparent, since these cooperatives are de-pendent on public money to get started and to survive, not only in the form of a first funding, but also insofar public agencies become the buyers of the co-operative products. Many problems of transparency, control as well as of general planning are involved here, although they are rarely spelled out when discussing and financing this kind of cooperative, in which the main official ob-jective is to support employment rather than to provide specific goods or ser-vices. Notwithstanding this serious criticism, or warning, and the small numbers involved, once again the fact must not be overlooked that in any case the fin-ancing of these cooperatives cannot be reduced to just another way of handing out public welfare money, insofar as they encourage entrepreneurial behaviour and working habits.

Cantieri di Lavoro

A third measure is the public work yards, on the basis of the regional law no. 55, 1984, which provided funding for the "temporary and extraordinary employment of unemployed people in local government administered work yards". This is not a new measure as far as relief labour policy goes. Many such public works are routinely organized in rural Southern Italy. What is new is their application in an advanced industrialized context and in the heart of one of the most economically advanced Italian regions. Differently from the first two measures, this one has neither a training aim nor a self-supporting one. Rather, it aims at giving some kind of temporary (six months or 140 working days) relief, both in economic and in social terms, to those who are unemployed. The target group are the long-term unemployed. We might say that the main target are the hardly employable while poverty is not necessarily a criterion. The social welfare department of Turin has tried to insert some kind of quota for these jobs, for those who are below the poverty line, but this has not been accepted by the agency and unions since it goes against the principle of the *chiamata numerica*. While specific rules – or exceptions – are made to face youth unemployment, this is not accepted for those – mostly adults and their families – who are in poverty. This is due not so much to an overlooking of the experience of poverty[5]), as to the problems which would arise from the point of view of the definition of the workers' status if special provisions were made for particular adults. Traditionally, protective legislation was developed by defining specific groups – children, handicapped, women and now also youth – as not fully adult.

The *cantieri di lavoro* were first set up in Turin in May 1985, through the approval of five different projects employing a total of 598 people: a very small number compared to the number of unemployed in the city. They are funded partially by the city, partially (18.7 per cent) by the province, for a total expense of a little over three billion two hundred million liras. Notwithstanding the reduced number of people involved and the short period of time they will be employed, the five projects are however interesting insofar as they address problem areas, or community needs, which had to be addressed anyway; that is, they do not appear to be just made up jobs. The first project, which employs 205 persons having some very generic clerical qualification, concerns the updating of the register of housing property, a much needed job in view of a more efficient taxation. The second project – which is the only one to employ both high school graduates and college graduates (12 people in all) – concerns putting the historic archive of the University of Turin in order. The third project is directed to the strengthening of the social and health services. However, it is not clear what exactly this means since all the 76 people so employed have no professional qualifications whatsoever. It is therefore probable that they are used as cleaning people or the like (with no opportunity for receiving some kind of on-the-job training). Also the fourth project, aimed at taking care of the city parks, employs mostly people with non specific training (230 persons), but also 50 graduates from professional high schools. The fifth project, which employs only 24, mostly unskilled, persons, aims at the maintenance and restructuring of one of the largest and most important parks in Turin (Parco di Stupinigi).

Changes in the Social Welfare Sector

We indicated above that the left coalition had entered local government with the intention of making an impact on the quality of life through a different distribution and use of resources which were perceived as abundant and increasing. There was the idea – quite widespread not only in Italy – that the time had come to think not only of a quantitative expansion of goods and services, but of a restructuring of their basis and content in order to move from work and citizenship rights to fully realized social ones. There was a particular effort made in Turin to trace the linkages and interdependencies among different kinds and sources of social difficulty, aiming at developing preventive, rather than curing, measures (see also the series of research projects sponsored by the local government under the heading *Progetto Torino*[6])). The decentralization of social services and their focusing on integrated and homogeneous situations was the nucleus of the social services reform of the late 1970s, which was thought to allow both a greater efficacity and greater citizen participation in the planning and managing of services (Savi 1976; Città di Torino 1978). As we already pointed out, this ambitious project was based on the idea of the persisting centrality of the working class and of the homogeneity of its needs, motivations, behaviours. Both these ideas were being severely questioned by the restructuring of the social fabric of the city (see also Negri 1985). The shrinking of economic resources with the loss of rights attached to work and the new visibility of "old needs" (poverty, social marginalization – see Barbano 1982) further complicated the situation.
Notwithstanding these cultural shortcomings, this process of rethinking the organization and delivery of social services left its mark, especially in the social welfare sector, which is perhaps the most crucial for detecting tendencies in the definition of social citizenship, since it addresses the weakest members of the community. It is also the sector which has been more dramatically affected by the economic crisis: in 1979, 2,734 income subsidies were granted, but in 1981 they jumped to 4,238 and in 1982 to 5,373. In the same period, the number of families who received continuous economic assistance went from 284 to 1,043. And the total expenditure for the vital minimum and other income subsidies went from 406 million to 1 billion 339 million liras.
From 1978 onward, the deliberations and activities of the town government showed a constant effort at coordinating the different projects, services and measures which affect the lives of the groups at risk of falling into poverty, while setting up a preventive rather than merely a relief system. Also the vital minimum

system was revised and enlarged, both to include different groups at risk and to provide an integrated approach to poverty, without discriminating among the poor, but also providing more concrete and focused measures. All this was underscored by the attention for granting the welfare recipients their dignity and rights as citizens. Also, a preoccupation is shown (and spelled out again and again in the forewords and declarations which accompany the successive deliberations) that the economic assistance must not substitute for, but only integrate, the offer of services in the fields of health, education and housing.

Differently from the labour policy measures, the welfare measures and projects appear to be the outcome of some kind of investigation of the needs, of an attempt at foreseeing their possible impact, as well as of a discussion and systematic checking with the *circoscrizioni* (neighbourhood governments) which must implement the measures. These were partially modified in 1983 and then in 1984 as a result of this debate and checking. It is all the more paradoxical that the inertia of the bureaucratic know-how and rules still prevents the collecting of systematic information on the kind of individuals and families who receive this kind of help, since the information is collected and stored on an itemized basis.

It appears, therefore, that even under the pressure of an increasing demand for welfare, the left government tried to uphold its goal of enriching its conception of needs and rights, although the implementation of these rules and measures require a fair amount of control. It is as yet not clear if the new, quite fragile, centre-left coalition will continue this policy or change its criteria.

Brescia: A Peripheral Economic Area in Crisis[7]

Type of Territorial Context

As we mentioned the typical features of a local economy (Bagnasco 1977) prevail in this province:

Lack of major urban centres (communities of more than 10,000 are rare), but with many small towns.

General movement away from agricultural labour, but without an accompanying depopulation of the rural communities.

Very high levels of industrialization scattered on the territory; few tertiary activities.

Endogenous industrial development; external industries present on a small scale.

Prevalence of small and medium-sized enterprises and craft industries, as an expression of widespread local entrepreneurship which has concentrated its energies on traditional sectors utilizing local mineral and chemical resources: metallurgical, mechanical and other manufacturing industries.

This peripheral economic area contains monocultural situations and 'system areas' showing the most typical features of a local economy: a deep-rooted industrial culture, a consensus over the production model which diminishes industrial conflicts, labour and community solidarity. As is typical of the model of peripheral economy, industrial incomes are often supplemented by earnings from agricultural labour.

Features of the Labour Market

At the beginning of the 1980s, levels of male employment in Brescia were high, and female employment levels were rising with respect to the regional (Lombardy) average. Unemployment rates and the number of people in search of their first job were among the lowest in Lombardy.

The expansion of the labour market during the 1970s was largely the result of the increased supply of female labour. Employment levels continued to rise until 1983, when the level of employment in industry, which so far had been relatively stable, began to decline. However the warning signals of an imminent crisis in the industry of the Brescia area were already discernible in 1981 (see table 2).

Compared with the rest of the region, the employment situation in the Brescia area had been relatively healthy but from 1983 it deteriorated rapidly. Companies cut back on personnel either by resorting to the *Cassa Integrazione Guadagn*. with increasing frequency or by dismissals (see diagram 1). Thus, the numbers of those seeking employment were swelled by the 'unemployed', in the strict sense of the word, who joined the large numbers of young people in search of their first job. Added to these were those workers who had been affected by the

Table 2
Official Unemployment Rates by Sex: the Provinces of Lombardy,
October–December 1983 and October–December 1984

	Oct.–Dec. 1983			Oct.–Dec. 1984		
	m	f	m/f	m	f	m/
Bergamo	5.1	12.5	7.9	5.4	14.7	8.
Brescia	7.2	13.6	9.6	7.4	14.6	10.
Como	4.3	11.1	6.9	4.4	11.5	7.
Cremona	5.6	14.4	8.9	5.6	15.2	9.
Mantova	5.2	10.2	7.2	6.1	11.5	8.
Milano	4.9	12.6	8.0	5.3	13.2	8.
Pavia	6.3	14.3	9.4	6.9	15.9	10.
Sondrio	11.0	13.2	11.7	11.1	13.0	11.
Varese	5.6	13.4	8.9	5.7	14.7	9.
Lombardia	5.4	12.8	8.3	5.8	13.6	8

Cassa Integrazione Straordinaria. These workers had little hope of re-employment, even in the event of a recovery in production, and were further at a disadvantage because of their relatively advanced age. Thrown out of work, their only alternative was to resort to the illegal labour market.

Furthermore, the technical and professional skills required by the tertiary and industrial sectors in the process of restructuring made the reabsorption of industrial workers difficult because of their low educational and professional qualifica-

Diagram 1
Cassa Integrazione Guadagni (CIG) in the Province of Brescia 1980 – 1984

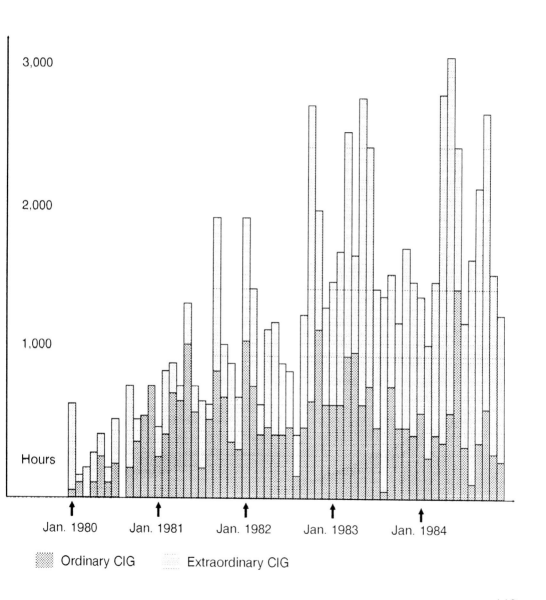

tions. Generally, both major components in the labour supply – unemployed workers of both sexes and the new intake of middle-aged women – are markedly underqualified with respect to the present and foreseeable future demand on the labour market.

We can predict the future evolution of the labour market along the following lines:
• There will be further increases in the activity rate of women (an increase in the active female population to at least 20,000).
• The laying off of redundant personnel in industry will have increasingly severe effects: the 13,000 workers now covered by the *Cassa Integrazione Guadagni* are equivalent to half the number of people explicitly looking for employment.
• On the other hand, there will be demographic changes, particularly in the age structure of the resident population. Studies of the labour market predict that in the 1990s population increase will cease to be a significant factor in the supply of labour and that the pressure on the labour market will therefore diminish.
• Employment prospects in industry are and will remain gloomy, while the present underdevelopment of the tertiary sector will presumably lead to an increasing demand for labour in this sector. This will favour the new, more highly-educated entrants into the labour market – sought after for reasons of industrial renewal, where technological innovation will lead to profound qualitative changes in the nature of labour demand.

The Economic Crisis and Unemployment: Causes and Patterns of Development

The crisis has most seriously affected the industrial sector in an area where unemployment is concentrated in industry and in the public and private services sector, and in an area that is among the least developed in Lombardy. The factors that have contributed to this crisis are several: the international crisis in the steel industry, which reached Italy some years after the Federal Republic of Germany and France; the crisis in the textile, metallurgical and food industries – a sector comprising the major industries (medium to large-sized) in the Brescia area, belonging to the most important local industrial families. The crisis made its presence felt in the 'Bresciano' some years later than in Milan and Turin because of the marginal nature of the area and also because of delayed technical innovation, which the unions blamed on the local entrepreneurs. The effects of the industrial crisis on employment may be summed up by the following statistics:
• The hours of ordinary CIG rose from 3 million in 1980 to 7 and a half million in 1983.
• The hours of extraordinary CIG rose from 1.7 million hours in 1980 to 17.2 million in 1984 (almost a tenfold increase).
When these figures are translated into terms of the total numbers of people receiving CIG, we may make the following estimates: from 1981 to 1983 almost

5,000 workers were permanently out of work; those receiving CIG for reduced working hours came to a total of more than 20,000 for the three years; approximately 18,000 workers were affected by 'extraordinary' CIG. From a total working population of approximately 450,000, in 1984 almost 40,000 workers in Brescia were receiving CIG, with almost half of them on 'extraordinary' CIG – that is, in disguised employment and suffering economically due to the 12-month delay before the redundancy pay finally reaches the unemployed worker.

The Welfare Model

The resources available to the population of the Province of Brescia are typically those of a peripheral area as described by the interpretative model of Italian development known as the "Three Italies Model" (Bagnasco 1977).
• Incomes from the labour market: these comprise the principal source of family income, thanks to high levels of employment, mainly of male workers in small to medium-sized industries and in crafts industries. This source of income is supplemented by earnings from illegal labour (lavoro nero or 'black work') involving adolescents, women of all ages, unemployed or temporarily redundant men and women, old people. This form of decentralized industrial labour has played an important role in the productive structure of every part of the province – even before the crisis of the 1980s.
• State-subsidized incomes are of secondary importance in the area, and this is true of the whole of the Lombardy region. The various forms of Cassa Integrazione of the 1980s represent the local population's first experience of mass social assistance and have led to serious contradictions and subjective conflicts within a deeply-rooted culture of industrial labour.
• The public social services are not as well-developed as they are in the other provinces of Lombardy and are certainly unable to cope with high levels of industrial development. This, however, is one of the various features of industrial development which characterize 'the peripheral model' – decentralization, the role of women in society, their limited presence on the explicit labour market (female activity and employment rates are lower than the Lombardy average), and household duties combined with informal work.
The local government has behaved in a similar fashion to those of other ‚classic' peripheral areas in Italy (Marche and Veneto, for example) and has sought to reinforce this model of development. The managerial class of the Brescia area is well-known for being the most conservative wing of Confindustria (the Italian confederation of industry). The local government is Christian Democrat. Within this political context, characterized by the electoral stability of the majority party and by a traditional industrial labour culture, the role of the family – and the role of women's work within it – has been decisive for the formulation and maintenance of a family and kin-based welfare system in order to cope with the crisis.

• Another important local resource is the high percentage of owner-occupied property and, in many cases, of second holiday homes: a feature that may be explained by special territorial characteristics and by the pattern of urban settlement. Housing, therefore, is not the explosive issue that it is in other Italian industrial areas. Also, given the strong local tradition of saving and investment, most families have bank deposits to fall back on. Finally, as in the case in all peripheral areas, incomes from industrial work are supplemented by activities for personal consumption, i. e. the cultivation of a family plot of land or the raising of animals, made possible by the diffused and decentralized pattern of urban and industrial settlement.

Social Actors and the Crisis: Ideologies and Strategies

The Entrepreneurs

The leadership of the Brescian entrepreneurial class belongs to industrialists in the mechanical and metallurgical sectors. The present President of Confindustria, Lucchini, is one of these.

The two guiding principles of AIB (Brescian Industrial Association) are:
• The defence of the Brescian model of development based on small, scattered companies and supported by the traditional investment of the local entrepreneurial class and by order and consensus in the factories; and,
• an interpretation of the crisis according to which the companies are "dying of trade unionism". The onset of the crisis, is seen as being directly related to the rapid increase of trade unionism in the 1970s. The intractable attitude of AIB has led to increasingly localized, single-company bargaining, in the face of AIB hostility, with the result that negotiations between trade unions and companies only become possible by decentralizing them. An example of the intransigent behaviour of AIB is its wholesale refusal to apply the law regulating the *contratti di solidarietà* (solidarity contracts stipulating reduced and redistributed work schedules with eventual compensation for lost earnings).

The public utterances and behaviour of Brescian entrepreneurs in the 1980s have shown a resistance to technological innovation of products, to research development, and a reluctance to abandon a separate, individualistic entrepreneurial model. The launching of the 'Brescian Model for the 1980s' showed a strategy based on productive decentralization and on cheap local manpower, relying at the same time on state aid in the form of the CIG and subsidies for the steel industry.

The Trade Unions

The Brescian trade unions have adopted complex and in some respects contra-dictory positions and strategies. The official ideology of the three trade union con-federations is often at odds with choices and strategies at a local level and in dif-ferent productive sectors. Thus, for example, while at a national level the CISL (the Catholic trade union) advocates *contratti di solidarietà* as an instrument for the defence of workers' interests during a period of crisis, in Brescia it is the CGIL (the Communist trade union) alone which resorts to this form of contract as a bar-gaining counter. This is in contrast with trade union bargaining practices else-where (Turin, Milan, etc.), even if *contratti di solidarietà* are still comparatively few in number (the numbers of workers covered by these contracts amount only to a few hundred). Likewise, while 'solidarity' continues to be a value of prime import-ance for the Catholic trade union, the 'centrality of the factory' is equally so for the CGIL, who has taken a number of steps to assist the unemployed and young people in search of their first job. In recent months, the deterioration of the situ-ation in medium-sized companies has seriously weakened the CGIL, a trade union that has been traditionally active in the larger factories of the mechanical and metallurgical sectors, where it will be more difficult to utilize the system of ro-tating redundancy and the *contratti di solidarietà*. This is because trade union cul-ture on the one hand, and the extremely high percentage of male manpower on the other, have so far been hostile to measures designed to redistribute work schedules and wages among workers.

The trade union movement has spoken out in favour of technological innovation and the modernization of productive processes during the crisis of the 1980s. In doing so, it has won support from the more enlightened political sections in the area and in the universities; a class which has relatively deep roots in the local social-productive context.

As far as the unemployment crisis is concerned, the objective is therefore to open up opportunities for employment by means of contractual bargaining over work schedules (reductions in working hours, *contratti di solidarietà),* over plant utiliza-tion and shifts. Priority is given to increased employment rather than to wage de-mands.

Local Government

We will utilize the 'Social-economic Provincial Plan' to provide a description of the strategies adopted by local government to cope with the crisis. According to this plan, each province must set its own objectives and priorities of action for econ-omic growth and define its social aims and the steps required to fulfil them. For obvious reasons, the data and research findings on which these plans are based have been provided by specialists, university lecturers and research workers, but the final form of the plan may be regarded as being an expression of the local political class, at least as far as its overall objectives and the image that it seeks to project of itself are concerned.

The plan is quadriennial and foresees the adoption of the following measures in an attempt to find a solution to the economic crisis and high local unemployment: the creation of a technological infrastructure; fiscal incentives for innovative enterprises; the promotion of initiatives that 'emphasize human capital' by means of professional retraining programmes for dismissed and redundant workers; a well-organized career advisory service for school leavers; specific measures designed to synchronize labour supply and demand at a local level.

It is anticipated that these measures will reduce the qualitative imbalance between labour supply and demand, although the quantitative imbalance will persist until the 1990s.

As far as health and social services are concerned, it is to be expected that a 'redimensioning' and redistribution of public resources from one social group to another will take place (in particular, in favour of old people).

Two Examples of Reaction to the Crisis: The Contratti di Solidarietà and the Centro Informazione Disoccupati (Unemployment Advisory Centre)

Contratti di Solidarietà have been signed in the Brescia area mainly in small-sized manufacturing and garment factories, which have been among those hardest hit by the crisis. Since there is no general consensus as to how exactly to apply this form of contract, and since the crisis has made the situation extremely fluid, we will refer primarily to estimates rather than statistics. It appears on the basis of these, that in April 1985, according to CGIL Brescia, there were 13 companies in which work had been redistributed on a part-time basis or by *contratti di solidarietà* and involving approximately 300 workers.

As the following section emphasizes, this form of contract was introduced primarily in small companies. We wish to add here how a scant emphasis on ,solidaristic' values is particulary evident from interviews with trade union leaders, and even with the female workers involved, despite the fact that these measures would seem to entail disinterested, even altruistic behaviour on the part of those concerned. In contrast, the *contratti di solidarietà* are regarded as a bargaining counter like any other, to be adopted in certain circumstances and under certain conditions. This, however, does not significantly alter the fact that this phenomenon – albeit in a limited fashion – has been able to grow and consolidate in the small textile companies of the Brescia area (regarding the reasons for this, see the following section).

The *Centro Informazione Disoccupati* (CID) (Unemployment Advisory Centre) is an initiative promoted by the CGIL, originating from a survey conducted on 'Brescia and Unemployment' during the winter of 1984–85. Questionnaires were compiled by trade unionists and unemployed workers in the employment exchanges of Brescia and two other towns of the province. The 670 replies provided a picture of unemployment that more or less coincided with official statistics: two out of three unemployed workers were women; unemployment mostly affected young people. There was a lower incidence of unemployment among people of 40 years or more. Only 4 out of 10 informants had previous experience of permanent employment. Moreover, half of the informants had been out of work for more than a year, a third for three months to a year, and only 17 per cent for less than three months.

On the basis of their findings and direct contact with the ranks of unemployed, the researchers involved in the survey set up a CID on the premises of the Brescia Employment Exchange, open in the afternoons and staffed by a group of unemployed workers. Its aim was the notification of job opportunities in the public administration, with all relevant information concerning job competitions, training courses authorized by the regional government, and how to cope with the bureaucracy and unemployment legislation. The CID also provided legal assistance and distributed information on how to set up labour cooperatives. A 'Guide to Getting a Job' was printed and circulated.

Concurrently (and analogously to an initiative promoted by the Milan CGIL), a campaign for special enrolments in the trade union was launched, for a symbolic fee of 1,000 Liras. Membership in the union authorized the workers to utilize all the services of the Brescia Union Office: the 'Ufficio Vertenze' (labour disputes), the 'Ufficio Legale' (legal aid), 'Sindacato Inquilini' (advice to tenants). Results of survey show that the CID has catered mainly to young people. Enrolments, after some months, are a few hundred. The publicizing of CID activities has so far been limited to the CGIL: the press and the local media have until now 'censored' both the CID unemployment survey and reports of its activities.

Contratti di Solidarietà in the Textile and Garment Industry

We present here the results of an investigation[8]) into the various forms of application of the *contratto di solidarietà,* as understood as a possible answer to the unemployment crisis; a solution influenced not only by altruistic considerations, but also by diversified constraints and conditions.

The law no. 863 of 19. 12. 84, entitled 'Urgent Measures for Maintaining and Increasing Levels of Employment', regulates *contratti di formazione-lavoro* (training and work contracts) (article 3), part-time work (article 5), and the establishment of Regional Commissions for Employment. It also provides for *contratti di solidarietà* (solidarity contracts), which can be applied in two forms, both based on the stipulation of company contracts.

The first of these (article 1) seeks to avoid totally or partially, and by means of reductions in working hours, the cutting back of personnel or the declaration of redundancies. According to a decree issued by the Ministry of Labour, up to 50 per cent of the consequent loss of earnings are to be compensated for by INPS (the Italian social security) for not more than two years, subject to authorization by the National and Local Labour Offices. Beneficiaries of this legislation are workers in industrial enterprises, in agricultural firms with major contracts to supply canteens and restaurants, in business concerns with more than 1,000 employees, and in newspaper publishing companies and press agencies with national circulation.

The second application of the *contratti di solidarietà* seeks to encourage the hiring on a permanent basis of new personnel – after reduction in work hours and with consequent cuts in wages. Those workers who are already in employment do not receive compensation for their loss in earnings, but employers are offered incentives to take on new labour: they are allowed to choose and recruit new personnel themselves and grants are made available to them (out of the anti-redundancy insurance fund) in decreasing measure for the first three years. Incentives are offered, in particular, for the hiring of workers aged from 15 to 25.

We have limited our field of investigation to one particular industrial sector: the textile and garment industry in Lombardy. The reasons for this are twofold:
• The strong development of bargaining policies in this sector (in advance of tendencies that would become generalized in other sectors in subsequent years), which have concentrated on both reductions in work hours and on the organization of daily, weekly and annual work schedules to absorb excess (or otherwise redundant) personnel. Here the *contratti di solidarietà* have played an important role (CESOS 1984).
• The predominance of women among the workers in this sector – and consequently among those who risk losing their jobs. (According to trade union data 74 per cent of textile workers who were in extraordinary CIG in Lombardy in the first three months in 1985 were women).

These considerations lend special importance to the examination of possible solutions to the unemployment crisis and of the directions in which they lead, bearing in mind that those persons who are directly affected do not only find their job opportunities reduced, but also – because of the crisis in welfare policies – have to conduct a profound reappraisal of their general life prospects.

Strictly speaking, the *contratti di solidarietà* concern only the provisions of law 863/84, but we will include previous agreements concerning the redistribution of work among the employees of a company (with accompanying pay cuts), intended to avoid recourse to the zero-hour CIG, or to the laying off of workers. It should be emphasized, however, that these cases often concern only small groups of workers of minor companies, which manage to avoid trade union control. 1984 and 1985 saw a significant increase in part-time work: a fact that would lead one to suppose (although, clearly, some part-time work is opted for voluntarily) that pessimism over future job prospects has led to an increase in job-sharing.

Types of Implementation and their Effects on Labour

Even if accurate statistics are hard to come by, we may estimate that between 1983 and the first six months of 1985 approximately 40 *contratti di solidarietà* were negotiated, 7 of them in 1985.

With the exception of a single case, where a reduction in working hours led to the taking-on of a correspondingly limited number of workers (as under article 2 of law 863/84, the *contratti di solidarietà* have been drawn up with the intention of limiting – in situations of crisis or restructuring – the total loss of jobs (as provided for by article 1 of the law).

Even if it is too early to give precise statistics, many of these agreements regulate situations where it is improbable – for reasons related to the company framework – that there will be a return to full work schedules in the foreseeable future. Accordingly, it appears that these *contratti di solidarietà* have been adopted as extreme defence measures; to be used, not as an alternative to, but in conjunction with other measures designed to combat unemployment: ordinary and extraordinary recourse to the *Cassa Integrazione Guadagni* (CIG), early retirement, part-time work, the increase of plant utilization by the introduction of new shifts, the use of flexible work schedule, and the reduction of nationally contracted work hours. Examination of the effects of the *contratti di solidarietà* on the workers involved reveals a wide variety of situations. This is not only a question of the costs incurred by the workers because of the reduction in their hours of work, but also, and above all, of the access these workers have to the various forms of supplementary benefit provided for by law 863 to compensate for their loss of earnings. Alongside situations where the contract provides for a covering contribution from INPS of 50 per cent of lost earnings, there are, however, numerous cases where workers are provided with no supplementary benefit at all and must bear the financial burden themselves.

Between 1983 and the first six months of 1984, approximately twenty of these agreements were signed, providing for a drastic reduction in working hours for the majority of the workers involved, or for part-time work, without recourse to the *Cassa Integrazione* (CIG) or the provision of any form of 'solidarity' funds. These are cases of companies with an almost exclusively female work force, where, after an initial phase of threatened wholesale dismissal or of the declaration of permanent redundancy, this solution has been resorted to thanks to the willingness of those workers whose jobs are not directly threatened to halve their working hours. Although this situation has mostly concerned small companies, we estimate the numbers of those affected by the agreements at about 340 (FULTA – Lombardia 1984).

Only three cases have been reported of companies that have undertaken to provide contributions to compensate for the salary losses incurred. The responsibility for those contractual situations where the workers have had to carry the full financial burden must be assigned to the weakness of the trade union organization in small companies, but delays in legislation are also to blame: the absence of regulations governing the legal obligations of those concerned, and the means and procedures for obtaining the granting of supplementary benefits has created a situation where companies have refused to adopt these measures.

It should also be pointed out that workers in small or medium-sized companies – in contrast with those employed in large-sized companies – find it much more difficult to obtain the issue of decrees assigning them to the *Cassa Integrazione* (CIG). In some companies – mostly medium or large-sized – where there is a more solid tradition of trade union activity, and where the *Cassa Integrazione* was already being applied, the setting in motion of legislation for the *contratti di solidarietà* (dating from law by decree no. 12/84), cleared the way for bargaining over working hours, a rotating CIG, and the commitment – on termination of the CIG period – to the signing of *contratti di solidarietà*. It is estimated that 416 workers on zero-hour CIG could return to work on the basis of these agreements (FULTA – Lombardia 1984).

Other large-sized companies, however, which for years have been involved in comprehensive restructuring, whith the resultant loss of a great number of jobs (e. g. Cantoni), have continued to resort to zero-hour CIG. They are reluctant to adopt *contratti di solidarietà,* both because the aim of the company is to reduce manpower radically, and also because the existence of rosters listing workers who are in *Cassa Integrazione* and those who are not has created a deep division between the workers who remain in their job, and therefore feel safe, and those who have been excluded, with consequent diminishing hopes of finding another job. In the majority of cases, the new work schedules introduced by the *contratti di solidarietà* provide for an overall reduction in working hours. With the exception of small companies, where there has been a general trend towards part time employment, these work schedules have mostly ranged from between 28 to 32 – 33 hours per week, and, in some cases from 20 to 23 hours per week. The tendency would seem not to be towards making any substantial changes in existing schedules, but, where there is shift work, towards the rotation of workers temporarily not employed on a weekly or monthly basis, or else shortening the length of the work shift.

The cases of the garment and shoe industries are different: these are subject to seasonal variations in work flow and normally apply work schedules by the day. This provides wider scope for the organization of work on a yearly basis, but makes it more difficult for the workers' council to keep check on the observation of the rotation system and on supplementary and overtime hours.

Inside the factory, the *contratti di solidarietà* do not affect *all* the personnel to the same extent, but apply almost exclusively to production workers, a high percentage of whom are women. More highly-skilled workers such as cutters, foremen and section heads, store keepers and dispatch clerks usually work full-time. Overall, there seems to be a tendency towards preserving already existing organizational practices and effecting a change-over system among workers with th same functions; a tendency, therefore, towards keeping the factory functioning as before, but on a reduced scale.

This might be the limit of possibilities, if one bears in mind that restructuring does not always affect every production department of a company. On the other hand by means of innovative organizational ideas, more closely applied to internal mobility and to the drawing up of new schedules, it should be possible to involve a greater number of workers (thus apportioning the obligations of the contract more evenly), to create more homogeneous work conditions, and to avoid the formation of groups of those workers destined to lose their jobs.

A completely innovative approach to the application of the *contratto di solidarietà* is to be found in two contracts signed in 1985. These agreed upon a general reorganization of schedules and extended work to Saturdays, Sundays and night shifts. In these cases, by means of a slight cut back in working hours, it was possible to reduce average weekly work schedules to below the threshold of 32 – 33 hours, and to introduce a fourth or fifth shift. This has had a tangible effect on manning levels (as under articles 1 and 2 of law 863/84). The main feature here has been the favourable reception given to the new schedules; but this new application of the *contratto di solidarietà,* with its limited economic cost to the work force, has given an entirely new perspective to the organization of working hours.

The Contratti di Solidarietà:Restrictions and Resistance

Any evaluation of reactions to the *contratto di solidarietà* will be difficult to accomplish if we ignore the fact that, at this stage, the behaviour of both parties to the contract is strongly conditioned by the progress of negotiations over labour costs, the revision of the index-linking of salaries, and the regulation of the labour market.

Nevertheless we would argue that the limited spread of the *contratto di solidarietà* – despite the existence of the law – is also due (for several reasons) to the attitudes adopted by industry on the one hand, and by the work force on the other.

Resistance from Industry

It would seem that there is still a widespread resistance to the adoption of *contratti di solidarietà* among companies belonging to Confindustria (the confederation of Italian regional industrial associations). This is due to the fear that these measures will lead to a reduction in working hours, and thus to demands for the payment by the companies concerned of the supplementary benefit, once the INPS contributions have ceased (after 24 months).

Since future developments in industry are unpredictable, companies feel compelled to prepare themselves for every eventuality by setting strict limits to their personnel. This practice leads automatically to the selection of those who can 'stay' and those who must be 'let go', and to measures designed to avoid the build up of pressure towards collective 'solidarity' by, for example, posting the CIG rosters. At best, the *contratto di solidarietà* is perceived as a useful means of reducing tension – like the rotating CIG.

A further reason for company resistance arises from the fact that law 863/84 provides new scope for company contract bargaining and creates room for experimentation in work schedules and the organization of work.

Finally, it should not be forgotten (especially in certain sectors like the garment industry and toy manufacturing) that a tendency towards drastically reducing manpower goes hand in hand with an accompanying tendency towards resorting to productive decentralization, which enables companies to draw on the pool of those many workers who have lost their jobs and are willing to accept unfavourable working conditions and wages.

This resistance by employers has led to bitter conflicts for which the trade unions and the workers as well as the local government officials, had to be called in to mediate. This occurred in two Brescia companies, where the female workers waged struggles in order to obtain *contratti di solidarietà*.

Workers' Attitudes Towards the Contratti Solidarietà

According to trade union officials, workers are still largely unaware of law 863 and its applications. Thus it is principally the trade unions who, through their local representatives, bring the law to the attention of the factory councils. From what has been possible to deduce from our findings, when the work force is informed of the provisions of law 863 they often require its application. But 'solidarity' requires a special environment within which to develop, and is conditioned by relations among workers in the factory between them and the factory workers' council, and by the way in which the onset of the crisis has been handled by the company – as we shall see later. For the moment the *contratti di solidarietà* are much more popular among female workers, and are rarely agreed to in companies with a predominantly male work force. The only exceptions so far reported have been dyeing and printing works (where, at the time of this survey, the contract still had not been ratified) and a small shoe factory.

In the opinion of union officials, this favourable reception among female workers is due to the fact that they regard their wages as merely a supplement to the family income and accept a reduction in working hours if this enables them to coordinate their work and household duties better. The officials emphasize, however, that, when their jobs are threatened, women tend to show greater solidarity than men. Conversations with female delegates from various factories in which this situation has arisen have revealed a strong determination to fight to protect jobs and to accept reduced hours, rather than become unemployed.

In general the willingness among workers to accept *contratti di solidarietà* seems to depend on various factors: from the workers' seniority in the company and their sense of fellowship, to their shared experience of trade union conflict; from the workers' experience of studying together in the '150-Hour Courses' (workers' extension courses) to their unity in presenting their demands and grievances. Whether or not the work force of a company is willing to accept a *contratto di solidarietà* would therefore seem to depend more on a sense of 'togetherness', than on the militancy or the political or trade union affiliations of its members. It should be pointed out, however, that this willing attitude among workers is extremely vulnerable: it depends very much on the general cultural climate, on the external life values of the local context and, above all, on how the initial stages of the crisis are handled by the company. It will weaken – with a non-appreciable difference between men and women – if redundancy lists are posted, if workers are assigned to zero-hour CIG, or if, despite rotating CIG, the management calls some workers rather than others to report to work, thereby indicating its preferences. In other words, material and symbolic resources are crucial in this case, just as are the constraints on the situation and the concrete social actors.

Concluding Remarks

Our research shows that the answers of social actors to the crisis, at the practical and behaviour level, if not at the ideological one, are not yet clearly defined. The impact of the crisis itself, its seriousness, its effects, have developed rather quickly, at least in some respects. Therefore, one's strategies must be continually redefined and these same redefinitions contribute to changing the feature of the crisis and its effects. Moreover, the national and international political and economic framework conditions and reshapes the cases we have considered in a way which is difficult to isolate. On the other hand, the overall transformation of the welfare state, its criteria and its organization, has a different and more delayed timing: the timing of the decision-making processes of the political parties, the legislative apparatus, and public institutions; although in Italy, during the period considered, there was a concentration of legislative measures aiming at increasing the fiscal revenues, on the one hand, and reducing the public expenditure in the health, welfare and social security sectors, on the other.

Given this premise on the dynamic features of the situation, we see first of all that the strategies of the social actors in the two territorial cases examined present a degree of coherence with the specific features, respectively, of both a central and a peripheral economy area (in table 3 we attempt to visually plot them).

The higher productive diversification, the availability of financial capital, the technological patrimony, the access to new, important international markets, oriented the Turin industry towards a restructuring process based on a reduction of its workers and on technological innovation besides an international decentralization of

Table 3
Strategies of Social Actors in Two Italian Social-economic Formations

	Central economy area (Turin)	Peripheral area (Brescia)
Enterprises	• Technological innovation • Discharging of the social costs on the state (CIG) and on local government (welfare, job creation, etc.)	• Decentralization • Discharging of economic costs on the state (CIG)
Trade Unions	• Defence of 'strong' and 'guaranteed' labour force (little is done for either the unemployed or for the cassintegrati)	• Single company negotiation • Reduction of working hours in order to avoid lay-offs and to increase employment
Unemployment and 'Cassintegrati'	• Conflicts with unions • Recourse to tribunals	• There are signs of union-solidarity
Local administration (government)	At the Province level: • Development of infrastructures (transportation and the like) as a service to industries) • Partial job creation measures • In the social welfare sector there are attempts to develop measures adequate to face unemployment and its effects.	At the Province level: • Employment agency services • In the social welfare sector there is a redistribution of scarce resources, giving priority to elderly people.

work. The social costs of the occupational crisis, at the local level, have been discharged on the structures of a large municipality which had been culturally and institutionally equipping itself to function as a social container of FIAT.

In Brescia, less technological and capital resources, the reduced size of enterprises, and the lack of expanding sectors have provoked an answer by enterprises which is based on labour intensive productive decentralization at the local level, with the diffusion of work at home (cottage industry) and of underpaid black work.

In both cases, the state financed the restructuring processes – or even the mere survival of enterprises – through the device of the CIG.

The trade unions strategies may be interpreted as a consequence of both the two

126

different development models and of local trade union cultures, and of the different policies of the three major trade unions and of the various productive sectors. The implementation of the *contratti di solidarietà,* for instance, has been strongly opposed both by the Piedmont CGIL and by FIAT metal workers; while the same metal workers asked for this kind of contract in their single company negotiations in Brescia. In both cases, however, unions appear to be concerned more with defending and representing the interests of the most guaranteed workers, than with striving to obtain new jobs for the young and the unemployed.

In Turin, the size and concentration of the occupational crisis make the conflicts sharper, often setting unions, *cassintegrati* and the organized unemployed against each other. In the Brescia area, on the contrary, the workers involved in the crisis do not organize outside and against the trade unions. In both cases, of course, the search for a new job – even a black and unprotected one – is the most widespread individual strategy among the unemployed and the *cassintegrati.* From this point of view, the Unemployment Advisory Centre in Brescia constitutes a quite rare and interesting experience of self-organization by the unemployed within the CGIL: it was created 'from below'; the trade union leadership certainly did not initiate it; but it somehow accepted and incorporated it into the structures of the CGIL.

The initiative of local administrations can be only a part, albeit a crucial one, of the reshaping of the welfare state *vis-à-vis* the crisis. This initiative is, moreover, conditioned by the central government, which in Italy is virtually the only receiver of direct and indirect revenues, while it redistributes the public financial resources to the regions with long delays, and not always following adequate criteria. The action of local governments in Italy, however, is determined more by the social policies developed by the local administrations than by the amount of available financial resources. The Piedmont region, which tends to give priority to Turin as its industrial pole, directs its major efforts to improving its transportation system, developing its infrastructures and services to industries and encouraging the advanced tertiary sector. It also strives to create jobs for the youth, using the law concerning the *contratti di formazione-lavoro.* At the same time, it creates a welfare assistance system which takes account of the increasing long-term poverty. In Brescia, on the contrary, which is a small town still maintaining a certain exchange with its surrounding countryside and with the resources of a mixed economy, social difficulties appear diluted and welfare policies tend to concentrate on old people without financial and family assistance. Labour policies are limited to a development of services for the measurement of labour market flows, which can be used both by unions and by enterprises.

A few recent exemplary events can lead us in reviewing this dynamic situation some months after the conclusion of our research. From the perspective of these new events, the cases we have analyzed above from the point of view of the strategies and behaviours of social actors, can also be looked at from the point of view of the ideologies they express.

• In March 1986 an agreement was signed between FIAT and the trade unions concerning the return to work (albeit not all of them to FIAT or to the automobile industry) of 5,500 *cassintegrati* who, put in extraordinary CIG in 1980, have not yet succeeded either in being recalled or in finding another job.

• In its 1986 annual speech to the Italian entrepreneurs the president of Confindustria (the industrial entrepreneurs' union), Lucchini, who well exemplifies the Brescia entrepreneurs, expressed his satisfaction for the recovery of the Italian industry, due to increased productivity and decreased absenteeism and conflicts. Few lines are devoted to the question of the relationship with the trade unions, which in the past years had been the focus of denounciations and complaints. The fact that the question of occupation is still unsolved – Lucchini maintains – is due to the trade unions' exclusive concern for guaranteed workers.

• Recent research reports (see especially ISFOL 1985) start to show the effects of the legislative measures aimed at linking flexibility in time schedules and in hiring and firing procedures, with the creation of new jobs. The *contratti di formazione-lavoro*, in particular seem to encourage the legalization of quotas of youth work, until recently unprotected and submerged. On the other hand, they are used by employers as new forms of selection processes and short-term employment, making it convenient and legal to employ young people who can be dismissed after two years, instead of hiring adults under normal contracts. The result, therefore, is not that intended of creating new jobs for the youth while offering them on-the-job training, but of subsidizing the employers for job places which already exist, but which now risk to become less stable.

These events point to three different, albeit integrated, ideologies which are widely used both by employers and by politicians and influential opinion makers. First there is the 'ideology of the crisis'. In Turin, FIAT suddenly recalled thousands of people. The emphasis on the seriousness and irreversibility of the crisis served as an ideological weapon with respect to trade unions, the state, and public opinion. Now one can turn to the ideology of the 'healthy enterprise', which succeeded in overcoming the crisis against the image of the 'sickly' Italian enterprise. There is a double neglect of the importance of public intervention in overcoming the crisis: of the state income transferrals to FIAT – as to other companies – under the CIG, and of the local governments' paying the costs of the restructuring of FIAT through an action of containing and supporting the labour force during the whole period. Finally there is the 'ideology of flexibility'. The economic analyses have proved that flexible time schedules allow for the creation of new job opportunities only in the expanding sectors, while in the contracting or stable ones, in the long run they permit a reduction of job positions. Through the *contratti di solidarietà,* implemented in the sectors which are facing a crisis or are being restructured, the wider flexibility of time schedules has permitted, as a matter of fact, an increased productivity reducing or partially substituting for the recourse to CIG and to lay-offs. No new job positions have been created, while the aspiration of the workers involved, women included, remains that of working full ime, full year, at full pay, with a normal time schedule. Viewed in light of these effects, the diffident attitude of the Italian trade unions towards flexibility (even when they use it as a means of negotiation), as a new solution to the question of occupation, appears quite realistic; although concrete alternatives are still far from being developed and thought out.

Notes

In the collection and analysis of the material for this study we were helped by Piergiorgio Ceresa and Anna Tempia. In particular P. Ceresa collected the material on Turin, A. Tempia collected the material on Brescia and the solidarity contracts. She also wrote the Italian draft of the section on the latter. Altough this study is the product of a joint authorship, Marina Bianchi wrote the section on Brescia, Chiara Saraceno that on Turin.

We are grateful to the following persons who gave us the information and the data about the three case studies:

Turin: Dr. Aragno and Dr. Barotto, Assessorato al Lavoro, Provincia di Torino; Alberto Canale, Assessorato al Lavoro, Comune di Torino; Mario Dell'Acqua, "Coordinamento Operai in C. I. G."; Dr. Ferero, Ufficio Regionale del Lavoro e della Massima Occupazione – Ministero del Lavoro e della Previdenza Sociale; Mr. Gancerro, Assessore al Lavoro, Comune di Torino; Roberto Genovese, Assessore all'Industria, Lavoro, Occupazione, Immigrazione, Regione Piemonte; Epifanio Guarcello, "Coordinamento Operai in C. I. G." (FIM-FIOM-UILM); Dr. Masiello, Assessorato Assistenza Regionale Mercato del Lavoro; Concetto Maugeri, Osservatorio Regionale Mercato del Lavoro; Roberto Salmasi, Assessorato al Lavoro, Provincia di Torino; Mr. Scollica, Ufficio Regionale del Lavoro e della Massima Occupazione, Ministero del Lavoro e della Previdenza Sociale; Giorgio Valesano, Assessorato Industria, Lavoro, Occupazione, Immigrazione, Regione Piemonte; Luigi Varbella, Istituto Ricerche Economico-Sociali, Regione Piemonte; Mr. Zoccola, Assessorato al Lavoro, Comune di Torino.

Brescia: Piero Greotti, Ufficio Studi, Camera del Lavoro; Mr. Filippini, Comprensorio Brescia; Mrs. Morelli and Mrs. Zanotti, Centro Informazione Disoccupati.

Contratti di Solidarietà': Mario Agostinelli, FILTEA CGIL, Regione Lombardia; Mr. Asoni, FILTEA CGIL, Bergamo; Marisa Beretta, union official "Milord" Company; Beppe Cacopardo, FILTA CISL, Milano; Adriana Cassinerio, FILTEA CGIL; trade union officials of "DYANA" Company and of "CRONERT" Company; Mr. Filippini, trade union official, Brescia; S. Mele, FILTEA CGIL; Dora Maffezzoli, FILTA CISL, Milano; Agostino Megale, Segretario Nazionale FILTEA.

) The Cassa Integrazione Guadagni (CIG) is a measure originally intended to cover workers who are temporarily redundant, due to restructuring processes within a plant. For a fixed length of time they work reduced hours, or no hours at all, while maintaining their job and their seniority and receiving up to 80 cent of their forfeited pay. When the crisis became severe in the late 1970s, the Cassa Integrazione found new application in the form of the Cassa Integrazione Straordinaria (extraordinary CIG), now extended to cover also those workers who are structurally redundant and who otherwise would be laid off. In this application, it is de facto both a form of masked subsidy to enterprises which have to face the costs of restructuring processes and/or shrinking markets and a form of masked unemployment benefit. Differently, however, from the special unemployment benefit introduced in 1968, which covers 80 per cent of the former pay for only a limited amount of time, money spent by the extraordinary CIG has virtually no time limit, can be renewed and grants the workers the continuitiy of their job relationship. That is, the CIG workers officially expect to be recalled to work. On the basis of this expectation some of FIAT cassintegrati in Turin have sued FIAT in order to be recalled to work. Up to now. this kind of legal action has yielded mixed results and does not appear to give strong chances to those involved. See also Comitato di Lotta 1984.

2) The sources and material used here were collected over a three-month period in the spring of 1985. They comprise the following: a) the available published and written material on the social and economic situation of Turin, the province, and the region; b) interviews whith three kinds of privileged witnesses: 15 civil servants in different administrative offices, 2 leaders of organizations of CIG workers, one of which is supported by the union, and a local expert of the CIG question and situation.
3) These data refer to the official labour market. They should be completed with data on the black and grey markets as well quite important in the area (see Gallino 1984).
4) In the 1977–83 period, while in the 14–24 age bracket the number of those looking for a job had a less than average increase (61 per cent as opposed to 63.8 per cent), in the 25–29 age bracket the increase was above average (72.7 per cent). As for the time spent people had been looking for a job for over a year, as opposed to 27.6 per cent in 1980. Those who had been looking for over two years went from 8 per cent to 14.5 per cent (ORML 1984).
5) In October 1984 the Catholic Metal Workers Union (FIM-CISL) organized a conference on the experience of poverty (see FIM-CISL 1984).
6) Three of the seven projects are now completed and published: Barbano, F. (ed.) 1982; Martinotti, G. (ed.) 1982; Belloni, C. 1983.
7) All the documentary material was collected during the period May – September 1985, including an interview with the trade union official who is responsable for the Centro Informazioni Disoccupati and with three people working there. The written sources used are the 1982–85 issues of the bulletins by the Osservatorio del Mercato del Lavoro of the Regione Lombardia and of Brescia, the 1985 issues of Sindacato oggi and trade union leaflets.
8) This survey draws upon texts of the implementation agreements and interviews conducted with trade union officials from Italian regions and districts containing important textile industries. Interviews were also conducted with delegates from various factory councils where attempts had been made to introduce contratti di solidarietà.

Bibliography

Amministrazione provinciale di Brescia, 1985, Presentazione degli studi per il piano socio-economico provinciale, Brescia, June.
Barbano, F., 1977, Sanità, salute e servizi soziali, Stampatori, Torino.
Barbano, F. (ed.), 1982, Le frontiere della città, F. Angeli, Milano.
Bagnasco, A., 1977, Le tre Italie, Il Mulino, Bologna.
Belloni, C., 1983, Il tempo della città,F. Angeli, Milano.
Bulgarelli, A., Dutto A., Giovine M., 1985, 'I contratti di formazione e lavoro', ISFOL in Osservatorio sul mercato del lavoro e sulle professioni, 2, pp. 8–18.
CESOS, 1984, Contrattazione e contratti di solidarietà, Edizioni del lavoro, Roma.
CGIL – Camara del lavoro di Brescia, Sindacato Oggi, issues 1985.
Città di Torino, 1978, Progetto per la sperimentazione di un modello partecipato di unità locale dei servizi nella zona 6, S. Donato – Campidoglio, mimeo, Torino.
Comitato di Lotta degli operai FIAT in Cassa Integrazione, 1984, FIAT: Cassa Integrazione e 'Giustizia', Torino.
FIM-CISL Piemonte, 1984, Lavoro e non lavoro. Vecchie e nuove emarginazioni a Torino, Cooperativa di cultura Lorenzo Milano, Torino.
FULTA-Lombardia, 1984, Analisi della contrattazione in Lombardia. 1980 – 1 semestre 1984, November, Milano.
Gallino, L. (ed.), Occupati e bioccupati, Il Mulino, Bologna.
IRES, 1983, 'Il ricorso alla cassa integrazione straordinaria in Piemonte nel 1981' in Quaderni di ricerca, No. 14.
IRES, 1984, Trasformazioni della società piemontese negli anni settantà in Quaderni di ricerca No. 21.

ISFOL, 1985, Rapporto ISFOL 1985, F. Angeli, Milano.

Martinotti, G. (ed.), 1982, La città difficile, F. Angeli, Milano.

Negri, N., 'I nuovi torinesi: immigrazione, mobilità, struttura sociale' in Martinotti 1982.

Negri, N., 1985, 'Problemi di prospettiva nelle politiche sociali' in Sisifo, 6, December.

Osservatorio Regionale sul Mercato del Lavoro (ORML), Regione Piemonte, 1984, Rapporto sul mercato del lavoro, bulletin No. 5, June.

Osservatorio Mercato del Lavoro di Brescia, Telegramma sulla disoccupazione, issues 1983 – 84.

Politica ed Economia del lavoro, 1984, No. 1 and 2.

Osservatorio Mercato del Lavoro di Brescia, Telegramma sulla crisi occupazionale, issues 1983 – 85.

Regione Lombardia, Osservatorio Mercato del Lavoro, Telegramma sulla disoccupazione, issues 1982 – 85.

Regione Piemonte, Notizie, various issues in the 1980 – 85 period.

Savi, E., 1976, 'Il ruolo dell'ente locale per il superamento dell'assistenza-beneficienza' in Prospettive sociali e sanitarie, 5.

A Challenge
Under Conditions of a Changing
Reality of Work

Gérard Martin, Guy Roustang, François Sellier

Introduction

The purpose of this chapter is to examine some of the changes currently taking place in social policy, although is is still too early to foresee the exact form that the new system of regulation will take. The crisis in our social security system has two main causes. The first is the slowing down of economic growth and the rise in unemployment. The second is in some ways a crisis of legitimacy: although French people are very attached to their social security system, it must also be acknowledged that the system is no longer sustained by the collective movements that gave rise to it: people have become used to it. The system has become much more complex, and by taking over responsibility for individuals and recognizing their rights, it has thus discharged them of their responsibilities and their duties.

It is for these reasons that we have decided to analyze both *community employment schemes* (travaux d'utilité collective), which are a response to the employment crisis and involve some 200,000 young people, and the *decentralization* of *social policy to département level,* which may help to relaunch the debate on social security and help bring the system closer to the people.

Before discussing the community employment schemes, we shall give a summary of the main youth employment schemes introduced in France. It was the failure of these traditional measures to create jobs that made it necessary to experiment with the community employment schemes, which have been surprisingly successful.

Similarly, before examining the decentralization of social policy to département level, we shall summarize the main characteristics of the French social security system.

Although we have singled out two main causes for the crisis of the social security system (others could be mentioned, such as the increasing number of single-parent families), it is the analysis of the community employment schemes and the decentralization to département level which raises similar issues. In particular we shall focus on those connected with new interactions between economic and social policy and which open the way to the reconstruction of the economic and social system.

Measures for Job Creation or Reduction of Labour Supply

During the period 1975–1984, a series of measures were edicted in order to enhance employment by private firms through subsidizing investment or reducing work hours. At the same time, the propensity of workers to retire early was favoured by compensating a proportion of the loss of earnings. In 1982, the socialist government enacted a law permitting retirement at age 60 with full pension.

Active Employment Policy: Measures Aiming at a Creation of Jobs

Apart from some rapidly reversed measures of increasing public employment as in 1981-82, manpower policies were effected through the reduction of working time, the inducement for workers to retire early or for the unemployed to create new firms.

Effective weekly working time has decreased regularly from 1968 (46 hours) to 1975 (42.7 hours), 1986 (39 hours). The 39-hour legal working week, as well as a fifth week holiday, were enacted in January 1982. Only a small amount of new employment is due to legal reductions of working time. More important is the spread of multiple shifts, flexible and part-time or weekend work, linked to an increased utilization of fixed capital. A law of February 1986 allows employers to pay only a part of the weekly overtime by fixing a reduced working time for the whole year of 37.5 to 38 hours. By this arrangement the employees receive a fixed salary per hour, regardless of the amount of hours they work. This must not, however, exceed the fixed total working hours per year. As early as 1963, the National Employment Fund could help enterprises or industries to finance redundancy plans by allowing employees to retire before they had acquired full pension rights: these are known as pre-retirement schemes. Such schemes developed rapidly until 1982 for 56- and even 55-year-old workers with a 70 per cent wage compensation until retirement age and with 60 per cent to 65 per cent thereafter. In 1982–1983 the government offered financial inducement to employers for such schemes if they maintained their manpower by hiring new employees: 200,000 employees received such benefit during these two years (contrat solidarité – pré-retraite). The scheme was cancelled in June 1984 and its cost was partially transferred to the state.

Income maintenance schemes (garantie de ressource) were introduced in 1972 for 60-year-old employees who were dismissed or retired voluntarily (1977): they received 70 per cent wage compensation until age 65. Such schemes became obsolete with the fixation of 60 as the age at which employees get full pension (1982). However, the scheme will 'live' until about the year 2000 for those who have already benefited: they number around 425,000 (April 1984).

The Raymond Barre government issued an award in 1979 allowing unemployed to get six months of capitalized unemployment compensation as a financial aid to create or maintain a firm. Free contributions to the social security and retirement schemes were provided during six months. The socialist government has maintained and increased such aid (ordinance 21. 3. 1984) which has so far been successful: from 1979 to 1983, 135,000 unemployed received such benefits (middle management: 33 per cent; workers: 36 per cent). Fifteen months after their take-over or creation, 85 per cent of the firms were in operation.

The cost of unemployment insurance, solidarity schemes and restructuration plans is so high that governments insisted increasingly on subsidizing the creation of jobs instead. Another objective was to reduce the length of unemployment insurance full compensation: from 1983 to 1984, about 600,000 were transferred from insurance to mere 'solidarity', a form of assistance.

The Special Problem of Young People

The 1984 employment sample survey gives a classification of young unemployed by level of education. According to this source, more than one million were unemployed: 58.7 per cent had either no diploma or the diploma of final primary schooling. As apprenticeship only concerns small craft and commerce firms or vocational schools, and few young people get a professional or technical diploma. This could explain the relatively low activity rate of young people in France as compared with the Federal Republic of Germany. However, new schemes for dual training in industry are in progress (formation alternée).

Since 1975, the different governements have experienced a number of continuously protracted and improved measures to enhance the hiring or training of

Table 1
Activity Rates of Young People: France, Federal Republic of Germany

Countries	Men		Women	
	15–19	20–24	15–19	20–24
France	22.4	69.1	16.7	67.2
Federal Republic of Germany	35.2	77.2	31.4	69.8

Source: Enquête 1982 d'après OCDE. Comité de la main d'oeuvre et des affaires sociales. Examen des politiques d'emploi des jeunes en France. 1983. p. 38.

young people, by subsidizing employers. Reduction or exemption of social security contributions during a period are allowed for employers who hire or take young people in apprenticeship. Wages are subsidized.

For normal employment or apprenticeship, social contributions as well as wages are subsidized. For special contracts which combine normal employment and training (employment training contract – ETC), employers are subsidized according to the number of training hours given. Different types of contract take into account the different skill level of the young. Another type of measure specially open to young people without any qualification provides training periods (stages) for which employers or associations are subsidized.

In October 1984, unions and management associations concluded an agreement for a new type of short-period subsidized contract for 'initiation to professional life' (CIVP – three months of 'training') transformed in a law by the government at the end of the year.

However, most employment training contracts (ETC) are concluded by small firms (less than 50 employees) who hire mainly men (60 per cent). Contracts are generally concluded for the lowest qualification type of contract (insertion: 80 per cent). 'Stages' (training periods) are themselves sub-divided into two, then three and four levels (initiation, orientation, insertion, qualification). Young people who benefit from these types of stages (around 100,000) are on the average younger and less qualified than those who are hired in ETC: they often come from underprivileged families. Most of them (60 per cent) have no other formation than that acquired up to the age of compulsory schooling (16 years). 75 per cent of the firms contracting for this type of training have less than 50 employees and were for the most part in the commerce or tertiary sector. At the end of the training period, 45 per cent remained unemployed, women being employed less than men (50 per cent unemployed compared to 40 per cent.)

Table 2
Occupational Distribution of Young People (16–25)

Military service	235,00
Schools and universities	2,652,00
Apprenticeship	218,00
In 'stages'	154,00
ETC	83,00
Employed*)	3,393,00
Unemployed*)	1,033,00
Non active*)	371,00
Balance*)	46,00
	8,584,00

*) Adjusted according to the estimated number of young people in the 1982 census: 8.584.000.

Source: INSEE. Premiers résultats. n° 36. avril 1985. p. 3.

Table 2 shows the occupational distribution of young people (16-25) in March 1984, according to the employment sample survey:

It not only appeared that many young people remained out of work or training, but also that contracting employers as well as associations selected the better skilled, and that those who remained out of the system were the less educated and more underprivileged. Hence the stress put progressively on 'insertion' and 'initiation', and at the same time, on the necessity to find outlets for young people 'in difficulty'; a criterion which gathered together handicapped people, people coming out of prisons,. . . and the permanently unemployed. In 1984, the gouvernement launched another type of subsidized employment for young people, known as the community employment scheme (travaux d'utilité collective – TUC).

Community Youth Worker Programmes in France

The TUC Scheme and Youth Policy

This scheme was inaugurated in France in late 1984; an examination of it will cast some light on the changes that are taking place in the socio-economic system. Those changes which we detect as a result of the TUC scheme are not linked to a clearly defined policy. Rather, it is as if these measures were taken (independent of any ideology), under the pressure of events, to respond to the risk of social breakdown due to massive youth unemployment. The confusion about the objectives of the TUC scheme mirrors the confusion about the causes of current unemployment. What is involved? Is it compensation for the lack of training tailored to the needs of the production-oriented system, which narrows the gap between the educational system and the work environment, and keeps the youth busy until the economy takes an up-turn with return to full employment? Or, is it meeting needs (not taken into consideration before by the market place or by governments), which might later lead to job creation? If such an ambitious youth employment scheme programme has taken shape in France, it is no doubt because youth unemployment is particularly high; the lessons we can try to learn from it, however, go beyond that age group and open up perspectives to the new socio-economic balance we are seeking.

Since 1977, a multitude of youth employment-focused programmes have taken shape in France; essentially these were attempting to remedy two types of difficulties which must be clearly differentiated:

● The shortcomings of general or occupational training. In France, the school system operates by 'survival of the brightest' and one-fourth of the students leave school with no diploma.

● The lack of any relationship between the academic institutions and those offering jobs (or in other words between the educational system and the production system). In the Federal Republic of Germany and Japan, there is a much closer relationship, although each country has a totally different mechanism for this.[1])

In comparison with the Federal Republic of Germany, France's young people are proportionally much more affected by unemployment than the rest of the population. In 1982, of the 6.7 per cent unemployed in the Federal Republic of Germany, 9.6 per cent were between the ages of 15 and 24, while in France, 20.2 per cent of the total 8 per cent unemployed were in that age group [2]).

In order to provide young people with better training, to attempt to close the gap between the schools and the work place, and to encourage businesses to hire young people, many steps have been taken to decrease the cost of employing them. The most important measure has been state assumption of part of the salary costs or employee benefits[3]). These measures, while not ineffective, have been insufficient, as the figures quoted for 1982 show.

With the advent of the TUC scheme there has been a change in the nature of the interventions for young people; this is what justifies examinations of the experiment as we address 'planning the welfare mix'. What is involved is not the greater facility that businesses have for hiring young people, but rather the creation of specific jobs, a *production space* between school and work. Of course there are loud protests that this arrangement is only provisional – the young people cannot spend more than a year in this transitional stage, as the government wishes it to look as if there were hope of returning to full employment 'soon'. After taking steps to facilitate the hiring of young people by employers, as well as their passage from the educational system to the production system, a transitional space is created between the two systems. But there is a clear message that this is just a temporary bridge, while waiting for a drop in unemployment. Today, after more than a year of the programme, this temporary bridge is taking on an increasingly permanent look.

Who Benefits from the Community Work Programme?

The main characteristics of the TUCs organized as a result of the orders-in-council of October 16 and 17 were as follows:
- A young participant in the programme receives 1,200 FF per month for 20 hours of work a week.
- Local communities, associations and public institutions may sign agreement with the state to employ young TUC participants.
- This programme is open to youth aged 16 to 21 who are looking for work.
- The activities performed by these young people must contribute to the social life of the community, without competing with the local economy.
- The contract can be between 3 and 12 months in length.

Since the programme's beginnings, there has been a gradual consolidation or ex

138

pansion: now it has been extended to the 21 to 25 age group, provided they have been unemployed for more than a year; the contract may also last more than 12 months; work place committees, social security organizations and the 'mutuelles' can also hire TUC participants and enter into agreements with the state.

As of 25. 10. 1985 there were 168,368 people in the TUC programme. From the programme's beginnings at the end of 1984 until 25. 10. 1985, the total had been 263,364 (in other words 94,936 are no longer in the programme, either because their agreements ended of because they dropped out).

On that same date of October 1985, 82,583 agreements had been signed relating to the hiring of one or more young people. As of the end of July 1985, the breakdown of the host organizations who had signed agreements with the state was the following: communes (municipalities), 33 per cent; associations, 40 per cent; and public institutions, 18 per cent. In 43 per cent of the cases, the projects lasted 3 to 6 months and in 49 per cent, 6 to 12 months.

The government and the administration have made great efforts to promote the programme's success; at times the public institutions felt almost forced to accept participants. The success surprised even the promoters, however, as they had counted on 70,000 participants. The TUC participants were well accepted, since they filled a need. In early February 1985, a survey asked the following question: do you want to see TUC schemes organized in your area? Eighty per cent of those questioned answered in the affirmative. The second question, which was asked to a sample of youth aged 16 to 21, representing all socio-economic levels, yielded 91 per cent positive responses.[4]

The 'Overnight' Success of the TUCs

Agreements were signed all over France, in all regions and in all sizes of municipalities. By May 1985, more that 16,000 communities had signed an agreement, or 45 per cent of all communes in the country.[5] By August, fifty départements (regions) had exceeded the goal of the national plan, which was "to have the number of requests for TUCs equal 37 per cent of applications for employment registered in the local offices of the "Agence Nationale pour l'Emploi" (the national employment agency)[6]. In four rural regions, the number of places to be filled equalled or exceeded the number of young people who were unemployed. In highly urbanized areas, however, particularly Lyon and Paris, the number of contracts was proportionally lower as fewer young people were interested in the positions offered. Surveys should be made to discover the reason for this. Political opposition in areas represented by the opposition of the Communist Party had no real effects on the overall results. A measure that ten years ago no one would have dared to propose has therefore been accepted wholeheartedly. This is an indication that all those involved recognize that the return to full employment will not come tomorrow.

There are two major explanations possible for the success of the TUCs: that participation is highly decentralized and that the young people need work only half-time. The state frees up the funding (3.6 billion francs for 1986, which corresponds to 220,000 jobs for 12 months, or more than 300,000 participants)[7]) but it is the communes, the associations, the public facilities which decide what activities they will offer to the young participants, what needs they wish to meet in their community, as a function of a wide diversity of experiences. An approximate evaluation showed that the TUC participants represented 10 per cent of the salaried staff of local communities and 17 per cent of the staff of associations[8]). Of course, the TUCs work only half-time, but they still represent a market increase in the activity potential of their host organizations.

According to the promoters of the TUC programmes, many of the young people seem to like the part-time nature of the arrangement, in light of their past experience with full-time schooling and their future plans for military service (the boys) or full-time employment. It was commented that this was the first time they had had the opportunity to gain both social recognition, through their activities in the TUC programme, and 'time to live' (i. e. recreation, increase their general knowledge, continue to look for work, take further training). The low pay does not seem to be much of a problem, at least for the 16-21-year-olds, who are often still living at home and have no dependants. One of the founders of the TUC scheme spoke of the success of the programme "based on a strong acceptance by the young people of the division of work, time and income"[9]).

Both sexes participate equally but there are many more young women than men in the administrative and social-educational activities and the reverse in the environmental protection and maintenance activities.

The host organization is allowed to pay a maximum of 500 FF supplement to the 1,200 FF from the government: in February 1985, half had paid such a supplement, averaging 300 FF.

TUC participants could be offered additional training, and 40 per cent of the host organizations did indeed offer such training. It is interesting to note, also, that in conformity with the possibility set out in the order-in-council of October 16, 27 pe

Table 3
TUC Activities at the End of February 1985

Categories	
Administrative	20.
Social or social-educational	17.
Cultural animation (facilitation)	9.
Protection of nature or the environment	9.
Maintenance of community facilities	20.
Manufacturing or assembly	1.
Other	21.

cent of the host organizations used people approaching retirement age to give such training.

The TUC Policy Doesn't Fit Into a Single Category

The TUC scheme is a highly original creation; it defies easy classification. It is not a classical economic measure to create an overall rise in employment by encouraging investment or consumption, nor is it a selective programme offering aid to specific sectors. The TUCs do, however, create jobs; the young people are doing something and are no longer part of the unemployment statistics.

Neither is the programme a traditional welfare measure; the young participants must work for the 1,200 FF they receive. Nor is it part of a traditional unemployment insurance programme.

The measures are not simply a new method facilitating the entry of young people into a given occupation, by increasing their training; or of making it cheaper for employers to hire them, because their activities take place in a production space that is different from that of regular employment.

The TUC scheme is a hybrid; its economic and social objectives are interwoven and any attempt at labelling is impossible. The objective of the 'Beat the heat' programme run for young people in the most deprived areas for several weeks each summer,and which offers recreational activities, was to stop them from wrecking everything in sight. The TUC programme, on the other hand, while concerned with keeping many young people from being idle, does so by offering more long-lasting occupations and by making them part of society. Most of the TUC participants are aware of their social role and do not see themselves as merely welfare recipients. Their monthly stipend is not a wage, but neither is it a welfare or unemployment insurance payment, because they provide goods or services in return for it. Considering the poverty of the welfare state at the present time, the public would have looked askance at young people being given something for nothing. Entry into traditional employment afterwards may be facilitated by the fact that the TUC participants receive supplemental training (in the most ideal arrangements) and familiarize themselves with working life by learning about work schedules, working relationships and so on. It is, therefore, impossible to differentiate between the multiple objectives of the TUC programme: to decrease the number of unemployed (employment objective), avoid demoralizing idleness (social), facilitate subsequent employment, etc.

The TUC Scheme: Change without Change

This scheme is probably the least costly way for our society to respond to certain needs, to face the challenge of massive youth unemployment, while not changing the main thrust of its policies, institutions or attitudes. By 'less costly' we mean, in this instance, in terms of change, and change is something that we would like to avoid. The TUC programme is an important innovation (and thus unclassifiable according to any prior system of categorization), but it is a localized innovation. If the young people involved in the TUC programme are agreeable to the division of time, work and income, then public opinion and the large majority of wage earners, as well as most occupational associations, employers and labour unions, could envisage such an arrangement as well. Essentially, the institutions continue to live in the hidden hope of a return to the 'good old days', to the methods of social regulation that were in effect when there was full employment growth and a strong welfare state. Return to full employment remains the major hypothesis. If this is the case, there will be no problem in gradually doing away with the TUC scheme: each institution will be able to function again according to its previous standards. The TUC programme will have been only a provisional arrangement, a temporary and one-time detour from the main path.

The Relationship Between the TUC Scheme and the Rest of Economic and Social Life

No one hopes to return to full employment, at least in the medium term. Therefore, it is unlikely that the TUC is only a temporary detour from the main path. Is not the TUC scheme rather one of the responses to the permanent changes our industrialized societies are undergoing? Will it not have a certain impact on the structure of the labour market, on income distribution, and on the supply and demand of goods and services?

The TUC programme is still on its honeymoon – the technical advisers have good reasons to be euphoric, to rejoice over the brilliant idea that led to this "miraculous" operation.[10]) But many of the TUC agreements are coming to an end and many participants are again unemployed, or have found another TUC programme, since the employment situation is still very bad. The manifold objectives of the TUC scheme must settle a bit; in the months to come we must look into the successes and failures in meeting those objectives, the impact of social and occupational rehabilitation, the activities of host organizations and the production of goods and services resulting from the TUC programme. A number of studies commissioned by various departments, along with the detailed statistics which are reported regularly, will provide answers to these questions.

Addressing these questions leads to decompartmentalization of the TUCs, since estimates are that in 1986 the TUC participants will represent 1 per cent of the labour force and 10 per cent of the unemployed.

In 1986, 3.6 billion FF were allocated to the TUC programme. If we can look at it rather cynically, the 'yield' from such an investment is excellent, as it allows the unemployment rolls to be decreased by 220,000. Without the 'brain-storm' part-time work, the cut would have been only 110,000. If the decision had been made to pay the minimum hourly wage (26 FF), the figures would have been still lower. In other words, if many TUC participants are content with 1,200 FF (or 1,700 FF if the host organization pays the maximum supplement allowed), many more would consider being a TUC participant tantamount to being a pariah of society. The trick of the TUC scheme is not only to decrease artificially the unemployment figures but also to precipitate France by this devious method into a dual society: on the one hand, the elite, the people with stable jobs, and on the other, the legion of those with precarious employment.[11]) This radically critical point of view is based on the Communists' conviction that it is possible to create 'real jobs' with normal pay. We cannot share this point of view, but it is still abnormal to see young people saddled with the main burden of the costs of changes in our industrial society. Eventually the decision-makers, the employers and the unions must take a stand on this.

The TUC programme should be better tolerated because it was stated at the outset that it would not offer any competition to existing economic activities. The first surveys available[12) 13]) show the diversity of situations. We shall concentrate here on two contrasting situations. First, there are the associations, the hospitals, the schools, etc, which depend on public financing and whose resources cannot meet the demand for patient care, services to the elderly, assistance to children with problems. For all of these institutions the TUCs are life-savers; they make it possible to meet essential needs which could not otherwise be met without budgets being allocated to them. In November 1985, Laurent Fabius, the head of the French government, indicated that it would be possible to assign 20,000 TUC participants to serve the elderly.

In such services, which are financed by public funds, those with stable employment do not see the participants as competition, but as help. This is not the case with our second example; in other activities, particularly the construction industry, workers feel that the participants are in direct competition with them. The head of the construction trade union at Romans sent a letter to the mayors of the major municipalities in the département of Drôme, warning them of the potential harm of the TUC programme. He saw this as a particularly underhanded competition; by placing the TUC participants in jobs involving finishing or maintaining buildings, the risk was taken that workers in the construction and building trades would be laid off.

In the latter case, the competition between TUC participants and tradesmen or salaried workers is obvious. In the case of the publicly-funded institutions, which can meet certain needs because of the TUC programme's help, the question still exists: why two kinds of jobs, one for the TUC participants and one for the others? Why not create permanent jobs for all? The answer is obvious: this would be too costly, but why then do young people have to be the principal victims of such a system?

Another question will also be examined in depth in the coming months in several studies that are currently underway: the contribution of the TUC scheme to the general system of social and occupational training for this age group.[14][15] Which young people are in the TUC programme; what education do they have, what previous training and to what extent does their on-the-job experience add to that training; how many participants find a job after the programme? All of these questions can already be answered, at least in part, via the existing monitoring systems. There is a problem relating to the overall cohesion of the programme, as sometimes it has an 'anti-training effect'[16]. Counsellors finally succeed in convincing a young person to enter another training programme but he/she drops out when the family pressures him/her to take advantage of the 1,200 FF from the TUC scheme, which is often better than what training programmes pay.

In April 1985, one of the responsible for the TUC programme wrote that in the short term (i. e. four to five years), he could not see the TUC programme being done away with, although he was aware that "an upswing in hiring will sound the death knell for the TUC programme"[17]. Believing that there will be a rise in employment all those involved in the social sector cannot simply save money by using TUCs. But, when confronting a future marked by maintained or even higher unemployment, it will become increasingly necessary to link the issues of social change and savings in a more elaborated way. Our hypothesis is that the present TUC scheme has made it possible, through local innovations, to avoid facing the full scope of the problems posed by a new organization of the production of goods and services and a new system for distribution and redistribution of goods and services. But how long can these young people continue to accept the situation they are being placed in? They will continue to get older and eventually our society will be forced to look at an overall restructuring. Social security is only one element of the social system but nevertheless it has become an essential piece of it.

Evolution and Structure of Social Benefits

The main characteristic of the welfare system lies in its administrative fragmentation. It is fragmented at first acording to the economic status of insured people secondly according to the types of risks, thirdly according to the source or righ (contributory or non-contributory, legal or voluntary) and finally according to the locus of their administration (decision-making and management).

Economic Status of Insured People

A complete social security plan (excluding unemployment insurance) was enacted just after World War II. The first project intended to cover all active people and their families according to professions, whether they were dependent or not

However, it encountered strong opposition from non-salaried professionals who refused to pay heavy contributions as the project assumed they should pay the total sum, which normally would be divided between employees *and* employers. Their own schemes were legally organized.

Consequently the French social security system is composed of a 'general' scheme for employees in industry and commerce, autonomous schemes for farmers and independent professionals, and other 'special' schemes which have long been in existence for wage earners, such as schemes for miners, railway workers, etc. . . . Each of these schemes is administered by one or several funds: e. g., one fund for each 'risk' in the 'régime général', one general fund for agriculture: agricultural mutual societies (MSA).

As a consequence of this fragmentation, only the active population (and their families) was covered, as well as retired people having contributed to pension schemes; the benefits granted by each scheme were different.

Benefits became steadily more equalized and measures were edicted to grant the benefits to the whole population or special benefits to those not covered, for example handicapped adults. The generalization of social security rights was enacted by a series of laws (1974–1978) especially by the law of 1975, and progressively put into effect in 1978. For instance, from 1978 onwards, family benefits became the right of all people without any condition of activity. By 1984, 92.2 per cent of the population was covered by a social security scheme. Table 4 presents a picture of the whole system.

Table 4

RISKS	WAGE & SALARY PEOPLE	SELF EMPLOYED Outside Agriculture	Agriculture	Non active
Health Expenses				2)
Loss of Earnings				
Maternity Expenses				2)
Loss of Earnings				
Disability				
Old age				3)
Widowhood				
Work injuries and disease				
Unemployment	1)			4)
Family benefits				

1) either insurance or assistance:
2) laws on 'generalization'.
3) Every elderly person is entitled to a minimum pension without a means test.
4) For certain categories of young people or women. without any condition of activity.

Source: J. J. Dupeyroux. 1986. p. 318.

The generalization laws have enlarged the population covered, this coverage was obtained by the addition of new categories (mothers, students, handicapped adults,. . .). For family benefits, the generalization is quite complete. As a consequence, some people (4 per cent) remain outside the system. In order to offer everyone the possibility of entering, a 1978 law enacted a 'personal insurance' scheme. The contributions, calculated as a percentage of income or as a fixed amount, may be paid by a social security fund or by local funds in case of poverty.

Types of Risks

Besides the usual insured risks (health, old age, disability, unemployment, children) specific allowances are provided, either with or without a means test, for housing, one-parent families, handicapped adults, training and vocational education. Many special benefits are related to problems of family life: parental leave, first child, third child, yearly entrance at school, children attendance. . .

Source of Rights

Benefits may be legal or contractual, but also voluntarily granted by social funds pertaining to the state, the social security funds, local goverments or municipalities. Most benefits are enacted by law or state decrees. Unemployment insurance is however a contractual scheme between unions and management (1958). Since 1984, unemployment benefits for certain categories (young people aged 16-25, the unemployed who were over 50 and no longer have a right to insurance benefits, single-parent or widowed women, etc.) are paid by the state on an assistance scheme. Another contractual scheme – although generalized by law since 1962 – relates to supplementary pensions (contributory).
The source or rights may either be contributory or non-contributory. However, most of them are contributory. For the social security schemes, contributions are about 90 per cent of expenses, but the funding of schemes for independently active people, especially in agriculture, is made with a greater participation from the state. The general social security scheme (régime général) contributes a lot to the financing of other schemes.

Types and Locus of Administration and Management

Social welfare is sub-divided between social security and social aid, a form of assistance.
Social security is administered by three categories of national, regional and local

funds according to the three major types of risks (health, old age, family). Unemployment insurance is managed by a special fund, created on a bilateral basis by the collective bargaining of 1958. National social security funds, whose director is nominated by the governement, have power of control over all financial decisions concerning local funds. The boards of all social security funds are composed of elected union members and management members. The Direction of Social Security, a state agency with regional agencies – and since 1986, the political representive of the state at the local level (Préfet – Commissaire de la République) have power of control over the decisions concerning local funds. The control of health expenses has recently been enhanced by the fixation of 'global ex ante budgeting' for hospitals.

Outside the administration of legal social security rights, regional and local social security funds have at their disposal a certain percentage of their budget (social and socio-medical action fund), which may be distributed according to their own criteria for special benefits based on particular needs, or to associations devoted to social activities. These are the fields of 'social aid' and 'social action'.

Social aid was substituted for traditional assistance by a 1953 decree. Resources come from special state or local public funds and from the social funds of social security. 'Social aid' benefits are progressively transferred to social security. Instead of benefits in cash, social aid produces services rendered by establishments (e. g. educational) or social workers (e. g. housekeeping for the elderly). Legal services are given to people in need according to legal categories of definitions. Other non-legal aids may be granted on behalf of local authorities and social security boards. Wages are paid to the social workers employed. Categories of services and definitions of needs divide the whole of social aid into 'sectors': aid to children in need or in 'danger' (generally granted to parents but only for special cases of administrative or judiciary tutelage); coverage of all medical costs when they exceed the financial resources of the patients (but with no means test); coverage of expenses for mental illness, aids to the elderly for remaining at home rather than being in hospitals; aids to handicapped children or adults (although the major benefits and expenses have been transferred to social security or public education), especially the financing of special work centres; and generally aid to every form of 'social inadaptation' and prevention.

Social aid expenses are only a small share of all welfare expenditures (3.6 per cent in 1980); but, although benefits are progressively transferred to social security, on the whole expenses are growing at approximately the same rate as social welfare (twice from 1945 to 1980).

The administration and management of social aid is the field of the so-called 'social action', which has been organized by the laws of 30. 6. 1975 and fundamentally restructured by the 'decentralization laws' of 1982 – 1986.

'Social action' is managed by public and private establishments or institutions (associations) in the medical, educational or social fields. Since the first decentralization law (22. 7. 1983), the financial responsibility for social action in certain fields (handicapped, health in school, mental health, pregnancy interruption) no longer pertains to the state but mainly to the 'département' (Conseil Général). According to this regulation, one-third of the total expenditure, pertains to the state. Coordination and control is performed at the level of administrative regions and départements by the direction of health and social affairs (DRASS, DDASS).

In order to enhance coordination efforts, the decentralization law has created departmental councils for social development.

Two departmental directions exist instead of one since the decentralization laws, as a consequence of the two financial responsibilities pertaining to the field of action of the state and the département.

On the financial side, an important reform of the decentralization laws has been to unify the financial responsibility of either the state or the département for their decisions. Before the law of 22. 7. 1983, social aid expenditures, decided at the local level, were shared ex-post between the state and the different local communities according to legal norms (percentage of coverage differentiated according to the different forms of aid: crossed financing). There was then a propensity, at the local level (département, municipalities), to favour expenses for which the share of the state was the largest. From now on, the authority who decides would be the payer.

The different public authorities at the national, regional or local level, as well as the boards of social security, are responsible for the distribution of funds to the establishments or associations in charge of producing the services. A 1986 law has allowed the private associations to collect funds by issuing voluntary organization bonds (titres associatifs).

Conclusion

The welfare state was geared to a full-employment economy, especially in France, where unemployment insurance, organized apart from the social security plan of 1945, emerged from a special collective contract concluded in 1958 by unions and management confederation. The unemployment insurance was itself geared to a state of quasi-full employment, either frictional, cyclical or during short-term slumps. It worked perfectly until 1978, when the rate of unemployment never exceeded 6 per cent. During these 20 years contributions – paid by employers and employees in the private sector – were rather low and benefits grew. In 1978, the unemployed could obtain as much as 100 per cent of their net wage during one year, with an eventual continuation for one year at this rate if they entered a retraining scheme. But, by 1979, deficits were growing and the social partners decided to reduce the 100 per cent benefit to 3 months. From 1978 onwards, the financial crisis increasingly affected the system: contributions were raised, rates and length of benefits reduced. At the same time, the decreasing mass of contributions, a consequence of the decline of employment, affected a branches of social security. In 1984, a governmental reform reorganized the scheme, thereby dividing it between insurance (social partners) and 'solidarity' (state).

Social security benefits had two main functions: on the one hand, the classical function of redistribution according to the risks (health, old age, number of children) without any clear redistribution effect between rich and poor; but, on the other hand, an anti-poverty function, especially based on family allowances. This scheme has played an important role in the French social security plan, especially in the first years of the scheme, as family allowances increased less than the average wage during the period of economic prosperity. But, such a function always remained important for low-wage families. In 1980, family benefits for a worker's family with three children and only one bread-winner were as much as half the earned wage. Table 5 shows the impact of fiscal taxes and family on three types of households, classified according to the deciles of their initial income: numbers are positive or negative percentages of initial income.

Table 5
Anti-Poverty Effect of Family Benefits

Deciles according to initial income	Income tax	General Family Allowance	Family benefit with means test	Housing taxes	Total effect
1st decile	−0.2	27.2	20.3	−1.7	45.6
2nd decile	−0.5	8.6	7.7	−1.3	14.5
3rd decile	−3.1	1.9	0.7	−1.2	−1.7

Source: INSEE. Données Sociales. 1984. p.176.

A survey conducted in 1976–1977 among poor families in the city of Reims showed extraordinary results of this anti-poverty function. Seven per cent of the families (around 2,000) received a monthly income from work (or unemployment insurance) of less than the monthly legal minimum wage (SMIC): 70 per cent were wage earners working part-time. Half of the total income came from family benefits.

Such poverty was for the most part a marginal phenomenon until 1975. With growing unemployment and decreasing benefits, many individuals or families fell into a state of poverty, not only as they lost their income from work, but also as they had often contracted debts during the years of prosperity by buying durables, a car or a house. Economic and social causes of poverty were cumulative as unemployment increased the risk of divorce. At the same time, the change in social attitudes increased the number of one-parent families. Such poverty cases are more and more uneasy to tackle at the macro-social level. It has become necessary to decentralize decisions at the local and département levels.

The Transformation of the Social Policies at the Level of the Département

The changing of the social policies during the economic crisis and the transformation of the policies of the welfare state initiated since around 1977 are still in effect. Because they have not yet terminated, we should patiently decode them and analyze their characteristic tendencies and modalities, bearing in mind that there is no alternative model that would automatically and naturally impose itself as better or more effective than the previous one. In the same way, there is no theoretical and methodological answer to this long transformation that could satisfy the Cartesian mind of the French intellectuals. We are therefore confronted with mercurial matter, difficult to enclose and apprehend as a whole. That is why it is necessary to go out into the field (which offers, as we know, such a variety of situations) and look for signs of this transformation at work. The level of management of public policies chosen here is that of the département[18]) or, when they are the scene of new policies or innovation, smaller local authorities.

Indeed, there exists in France today a veritable *recomposition* of social and health policies expressing a fundamental crisis in the regulation of policies. This is a consequence of situations of poverty and precariousness, the growing pressure on the moneys made available by a limited budget and of the recent decentralization of the French administration. It is mainly occurring at the level of the département, level of decentralization chosen by the Acts of 3. 1. 1983, 22. 7. 1983 and 8. 1. 1986, and concerns a new central actor, the Conseil Général (county council), elected by universal suffrage.

In order to understand the modalities of this recomposition today and formulate hypotheses for the future, it is necessary to define briefly not only the system of policies we are dealing with, but also the way it has worked up to the 1980s.

Before 1980

Social protection in France (statutory benefits and others, health insurance, social aid and community services) was elaborated from central and national norms, but this was done by institutions of various legal natures at the level of the département and sometimes even the commune (municipality). These institutions comprised decentralized state administration, administration of local authorities (départements and communes), organizations of the Sécurité Sociale (national health insurance scheme) and voluntary bodies governed by the Act of 1901. The social sector employs approximately one million people (i. e. a little less than 5 per cent of the French total active population) of which 400,000 belong to the voluntary sector.

Up to the 1980s, the policies of social care and medico-social care which are in accordance with the state policies of social protection (health insurance, family allowances, old-age pensions, unemployment benefits) developed according to a pattern of sectoral policy or more exactly, an aggregate of sectoral policies. This, from the point of view of the analysis of public policy, constitutes in itself a remarkable achievement insofar as the French system for social protection is regulated by a mixture of different legitimate entities (national or local universal suffrage, corporative representation, advocacy of voluntary bodies) corresponding to different types of solidarity (solidarity at national or local level, solidarity within the professions and the voluntary sector and also solidarity within the family, through legal inter-generational maintenance).[19]

This aggregate of social policies started with the 1964 administrative reform which created the Directions Départementales des Affaires Sanitaires et Sociales (departmental authorities for social security and health) and culminated or, if one prefers, reached a 'fulcrum', in June 1975 with the passing of the Acts on the social and medico-social institutions and the handicapped.

These policies are truly sectoral and not, as many would have expected, global and transversal. Indeed, around the initial basis of social aid (state provision and norms), various sectors of activity, benefits and professions progressively emerged, following a vertical and not a territorial logic (special education for maladapted and disabled children, family policy, policy of aging, etc.). To each sector and each activity corresponded a specific mode of finance, specialized structures, facilities and services, not to mention specific professions.

The intervention of the central state was indispensable in holding all these elements together. This explains the 1964 administrative reform and the Acts of 1975. The purpose was to give the state the means to regulate all these different sectors which had a tendency to generate their own autonomous logic of reproduction.

There are six principal reasons why the system has so far worked relatively harmoniously:

First of all, there is the capacity of all the actors in social protection, and particularly the professionals and the state technocracy, to provide themselves with a system of reference common to all components (global, preventative and promotional action) which, while maintaining and even developing the status quo of the professions, relates with the global system of reference to the French society (modernity, economic rationality within a context of humanism and welfare).

In addition there is a professional corporatism associated with the dynamics of each of the sectors of social protection (e. g. in special education) and therefore progressively becoming a sectoral corporatism. The nature of this corporatism varies according to the sectors. It is to be found at its 'hardest' and strongest in the medical profession and among certain administrative staff who went to renowned academies such as the Ecole Nationale de la Santé Publique or the Centre National d'Etudes de la Sécurité Sociale. Inversely and despite the efforts of their representative organizations, corporatism within social workers (11 different professions) has remained relatively undeveloped.[20]

The third element is the mechanism of social inflation in periods of growth, a veritable lubricant balanced and regulated by state control over norms (respect of legislation) and over financial provision (economic circulars and control over the price of institutional care and services).

The legal counterpart to the economic instrument of regulation can be found in the 1975 legislation which can therefore be seen as a legislative model of regulation.

These structures were implemented and orchestrated in the field by one man, the Directeur Départemental des Affaires Sanitaires et Sociales, playing the role of a super-steersman, navigating between the national and global constraints, the supply system and the local specificities. His essential function, together with that of the departmental medical inspector, was precisely to ensure the coherence of all sectoral policies.

Finally, this set of policies related only slighty with the territory and the transversality of the social problems and phenomena. It was characterized by the relative failure of coordination procedures and appropriation mechanisms of the different territories, or by the sharing of areas to the benefit of certain institutional or professional sectors.

Since 1980

This 'balance' of social policies has been fundamentally challenged since the 1980s, for three reasons:

Firstly, sectorization has proved to be increasingly inefficient when confronted with social phenomena, the deepening of the economic crisis, and particularly the development of the process of pauperization and the increasing economic insecurity in French society.

Secondly, the pressure on financial provision has been growing particularly since June 1982, when the government introduced its austerity budget. Until then the government had been pursuing a policy of rationalization of the different activities sharing the same ideological system of reference (viz. May 1982 circular on social work) which redeveloped the ideals of a global transversal and promotional social policy.[21] The break of June 1982 materialized in a policy of compulsory redeployment whereby the previous system of reference was increasingly challenged and even abandoned. A new system of reference which is today being proposed and developed, i. e. the idea of local social development, emerged exterior to the Ministry for Social Affairs and particularly in the Commissariat Général du Plan (Ministry for Planning).

Finally the administrative reform of decentralization initiated by the Act of 2. 1982 fundamentally modified the interplay of power, the roles, the levels of competence and the financial provision, thus, the general economy of social policy France. In effect and in this particular area, decentralization was carried out in fo stages:

• Act of 22. 7. 1983: transfer of decision-making to the Conseils Généraux of the départements.
• 1. 1. 1984: financial transfers corresponding to the transfer of the decision-making seat.
• Spring 1985: partition of the Directions Départementales in application of the Act of 22. 7.
• 8. 1. 1986: so-called 'specific' Act adjusting the regulations and the norms of the legislation governing public health, social care and family care to the new powers exercised by the Conseils Généraux.

This process of decentralization redistributed a large portion of the powers which had so far been largely attributed to the state. The total amount of expenditure transferred can be estimated at 21 billion francs. They concern social care in general, social care for children, protection of mother and baby, social services, care for the elderly, institutional care and prevention. The state will still be responsible for health services in general and particularly medical care, statutory benefits, disabled children and adults, school health services and mental health. With respect to the allocation of expenditure between the Conseil Général and the state for the départements concerned, 70 per cent have been transferred to the département as a territorial collectivity, 30 per cent remaining with the state. This does not take into account the expenditure of the sécurité sociale. In order to give an idea of the number of people concerned, there are, for example, 2,800,000 people under social care in France, of which 600,000 are children. These are now placed directly under the responsibility of the departmental councillors.

Regulation Crisis and Future Trends

With such a process of decentralization as outlined above, we can see that the disintegration of the preceding policy would result in a regulation crisis. From then on, the question is therefore to know whether or not this crisis is being reabsorbed and if so, how, and what the future trends could be.
An empirical analysis carried out in the three départements chosen for this study allows us to formulate the following series of hypotheses:
Against a background of rationality and even fragmentation of the individual and the family, we are witnessing today in French society an increase in the importance of the modernist economistic system of reference, now tending towards neo-liberalism. In contradiction, a new system of reference (or new myth of liberation?) is trying to emerge and gain consistency, a system which is positive, humanistic, transectoral or territorial: social development and solidarity on a local scale.
The first one corresponds to a progressive shift away from incentives for the rationalization of public management towards the obligation of redeployment. It is in direct accordance with the austerity programme adopted at that time. The sec-

ond system of reference opens up new perspectives for and qualifies the social scene. On the one hand, social welfare should not be global any longer within its own field, but opens out towards and becomes part of other policies (professional training, employment). On the other hand, the local scene (i. e. the territory) becomes the place of experimentation and application of these new perspectives: in this respect we have a qualitative changing of the system of reference.

This leads us to ask a series of questions concerning the future of social policies: who will undertake the fashioning of the image of the new system to be regulated and from what concepts and through what mechanisms? Where are the discrepancies and inconsistencies between the politico-organizational level and the interaction of the social and economic relationships? Who are the negotiators and mediators who have to handle these discrepancies and how do they do it? What kind of policies are being set up: policies of adaptation or policies of anticipation?

These questions bring us to formulate the following hypotheses:

• There is no shift from the welfare state to a welfare commune or départemen (as might have been the case sometimes in periods of strong economic growth)

• There is no shift from sectoral policy to territorial policy (or at least not in such a simplistic way).

• There is in fact a paradoxical movement which is at one and the same time the reterritorialization of the sector and the sectoralization of the territory.[22]

• In this two-way movement the various actors and institutions participating in social protection find their place either in the economistic system of reference or in that of local social development. Actually all the actors are operating at the same time on both registers and cannot do otherwise. This results in a hybrid amalgam whose consequences, unfortunately, might be borne by the population.

The Modus Operandi of the Actors

In order to materialize the series of hypotheses which have just been formulated it is necessary to analyze the actors' behaviour, and to reflect as well on the consequences of and the problems posed by the current process of recomposition. Regarding the actors, we must take into account not only the Conseils Généraux the Préfet Commissaire de la République, the organizations of the sécurité sociale and the voluntary organizations managing social welfare services, which are all present at the local level, but also the central state which propels and pursue a certain form of decentralization management.

The State

The segment of the state apparatus treated here is the Ministry for Social Affair It is not certain that decentralization is viewed and carried out in the same way other parts of the state apparatus, such as the Ministry of the Interior, the Ministry for Finance or the Commissariat Général du Plan (Ministry for Planning).

Moreover the analysis cannot be instantaneous, as the decentralization of social policies is a continuing process, which began on 22. 7. 1983 and whose implementation is only beginning now in 1986. Furthermore we are not dealing with a linear movement, since it is the seat of divergences or even dissensions.

First of all, the Act of 22. 7. 1983 on the repartition of the power of decision was for the most part not prepared within the Ministry for Social Affairs but in the Ministry of the Interior and the Ministry for Finance. This has an effect on the general economy of the distribution of power. Indeed 'hard' sectors with strong corporatism (psychiatry, the school health service, special education for maladapted and handicapped children and adults), and those which demand much public financial investment (hospitals and institutional health care) are still under the responsibility of the state. 'Softer' sectors are devolved to the Conseil Général and shifted to local authorities in relative disorder. Furthermore, what is being transferred in terms of power of decision is defined according to services (e. g. service for the protection of mother and baby, social services), rather than a philosophy of the policy to be pursued. The département is thus inheriting a series of sectoral fragments. In addition, the state has not felt it necessary to provide administrative senior officials with the appropiate intellectual and technical means allowing them to adapt to this new situation.

This shift to the département has destabilized the whole system of social and health policies management. Let us take just one example: the coherence of the system used to be ensured by a single person, the Directeur Départemental. This function has been split, now having two directors and two distinct services. The actual partitioning of the services as studied in the three départements shows a schismatic situation and a split that the staff at the different hierarchical levels have found very hard to accept.

The second phase of the implementation of the decentralization is the preparation of the specific Act, finally passed, almost unanimously, by Parliament in December 1985 and published on 8. 1. 1986. This Act is very important as it sets the rules for procedures and institutions at the département level, as much for the Conseil Général as for the other actors when different authorities are involved locally. From this point of view it should provide an instrument of policy regulation similar to that of June 1975 on social and medico-social institutions, even more so than the Act of 22. 7. 1983. Without going into the details of the text, which is not our purpose here, it can be said that the Act partially gives back to the state the responsibility for ensuring policy coherence, requires real coordination among partners through the social development council of the département yet to be created, imposes the planning of activities and services through the departmental scheme, and specifies that economic balance and management stability should be respected and a more rigourous evaluation of needs be effected when judgements are made or decisions taken about increasing or reducing the number of services offered to the public. However, it does not preclude the possibility that the Commissaire de la République would intervene a posteriori to counterbalance possible irrational decisions of the Conseil Général and take alternative action if the latter proves deficient.

On the whole, the state has provided itself with legal means to control and contain the Conseil Général and the local partners within a collection of rules in order to avoid and minimize any possible deviation.

The Conseil Général

What is then in this context the attitude and strategy of the Conseils Généraux? At the beginning of 1984, many actors feared the politicization of local social policy. In fact, with a few exceptions, this did not occur. Furthermore trends are almost identical, whatever majority, right or left, prevails. It must be pointed out that at first, the Conseillers Généraux were panic-stricken when confronted with the extent (in terms of personnel and financial involvement) of the powers that had been devolved to them. This was emphasized by the fact that they had been almost completely ignorant until that time of what was happening in the social and health sector, which had been the jealous preserve of the professionals. They were therefore very naturally anxious from the start to give their future expenditure programmes a sound financial foundation. This is why the budget of 1983 (before financial transfer), which was to serve as a basis for the determination of the global dotation, provided by the central state for decentralization, had been in many cases artificially inflated! Afterwards, and often with the help of private auditing consultants, they set out to rationalize the running of the services, control more effectively the use of benefits and the activity of the professionals and develop techniques for a better management of the social sector, in one word raise the agents' productivity. This led to a significant increase in controls over benefits and agents, sometimes cuts in services that were considered useless and at times dismissals, especially within the agreed voluntary bodies contracting with the Conseil Général. The picture as described above is unmistakably earmarked by economistic rationality and shows that, as a consequence of this type of attitude, the Conseil Général, even if it claims to do so, is now in a position to putting into practice neither the transectorality in concrete policies nor a veritable territorialization of its action. The need for budgetary moderation is obviously intensified by the political necessity of not weighing too heavily on the local taxation of the département in view of the unfavourable electoral results which might ensue. Such attitudes have already produced concrete effects in terms of expenditure: a study conducted in 1985 by the Commissariat Général du Plan (Ministry for Planning) has shown amongst 50 sample départements in France that social and health expenditure managed by the Conseils Généraux had fallen by 4 per cent in one year.

Over and beyond such careful economistic conduct, one can also find in the sample départements the reproduction of traditional organizational models. Indeed, the administrative officials, although they have changed bosses, have not yet fundamentally changed their practices and, as with decentralization, entire services have been transferred. They naturally tend to reorganize themselves according to the former administrative and corporatist models.

Thus, the result may well be the survival and reproduction of the pattern of sectoral policies which we have identified above. These, however, do not serve the interests of another actor who, on the contrary, is increasingly developing innovation procedures and techniques with a transectoral dimension, i. e. the Préfet Commissaire de la République, with the obvious support of the central state (Department of Employment, Ministry for Planning, Secretary of State for Social Economy and the Ministry for Social Affairs in particular).

Thus, in a number of areas, often new ones, the state exercises control derived from the Conseil Général or implements new policies to work around the surviving sectoral practices. One or two examples will illustrate this mechanism: the state has imposed (according to an extensive interpretation of the Act of 22. 7. 1983) the maintenance of its own social service. It retains control over the financial engineering of the policies directed to the poor and the new poor and, as decided in October 1984, develops with the aid of voluntary organizations the implementation of the community employment scheme for young people called Travaux d'Utilité Collective (TUC), stimulates and finances innovation in social economy (intermediate companies or quasi-companies, partnership zones[23]), and maintains control over the gerontological sector. In short, the state is present and active in any new procedure which, through its innovative and transectoral nature, would be likely not only to annihilate previous sectoral practices but, above all, to find alternative methods of dealing with the social consequences of the economic crisis. It adamantly wishes to be the inductor and the actor of the new system of reference of local social development. This is the intention, but it is quite clear that the inadequacy of the tools of analysis and the technical instruments, as well as the weight of tradition and corporatism are a significant curb to mutation, however much it may be desired.

The Organizations of the Sécurite Sociale

The third important actor in the management of social policies consists of the organizations of the sécurité sociale, whose governing boards were modified in 1984 to give larger representation to the socio-economic representative bodies. In fact, so far this transformation does not seem to have fundamentally changed the social policies of these organizations. This is due first of all to their great responsibility in the management of social protection which requires careful husbandry and ever greater control at the time of implementation of the hospital reform and application of the global budget and of effective control over general practitioners[24]). Moreover, unlike the Directions Départementales, the organizations of the sécurité sociale are not subjected to the transformation of administrative management mentioned above, particularly as they are administered by directors trained in the Centre National d'Etudes de la Sécurité Sociale. This is a very tight-knit professional corps, well-versed in the techniques of management and often in new techniques using computer technology at a very high level. This means that the services of the sécurité sociale hold a strong position at the local level and, while acknowledging their secondary position in relation to the Conseil Général elected by universal suffrage, they make a point of showing both their presence in the field (thanks to their staff and the services solidly implanted there for some time) and their specificity in the general structures of social protection. Consequently, despite the financial pressure exerted upon them, as on all other social organizations, the services of the sécurité sociale will always necessarily remain partner with the Conseil Général and the Commissaire de la République. It is a partner which, due to its resources from the social welfare fund, carries great weight in the negotiations, due especially to its capacity to negotiate specific interventions directly with the communes or groups of communes.

Of course, this does not mean that the services of the sécurité sociale can do without the Conseil Général, but it shows that they will continue to be in a position to play quite a powerful arbitrating role in the current recomposition. They are all the more ready as, regarding the family, they are very anxious to achieve the territorialization of their activity. Thus they are relatively close to the system of reference of local social development.

Besides the actual organizations of the sécurité sociale, we shall examine two further actors which hold a particular position in the local debate, i. e. the Mutualité Sociale Agricole and the Associations pour l'Emploi dans l'Industrie et le Commerce.

The Mutualité Sociale Agricole

The Mutualité Sociale Agricole, a subsidiary branch of the sécurité sociale, covers inclusively three areas of risk: health, old age and the family. It is therefore already transectoral by definition. Moreover its administrative bodies at the national and local levels, based on a true network of active mutualists and agricultural organizations, took a turn in the early 1980s from the 'agricultural' to the 'rural', thus from the sector to the territory. This means that we have here, especially in the areas where its services are implanted on a large scale, an institution corresponding to the system of reference of local social development (viz. the programme for the regeneration of rural areas), which is in a position to negotiate directly with the local magistrates. Moreover, its action is not specifically social but extends far beyond this into the domain of employment in rural areas, as well as the present vation or even the development of the social fabric and neighbourhood communication, through its affiliated organizations which provide services and leisure activities.

The Associations pour l'Emploi dans l'Industrie et le Commerce (ASSEDIC) (the associations for employment in industry and commerce)

The ASSEDIC, an interprofessional federation of unemployment insurance bodies, is a relative newcomer to the local social policy as it is understood here. Set up in 1958 to deal with the unemployment risk, these insurance bodies are well and truly the expression of the legitimacy of socio-economic representations. They soon realized that with the growth of unemployment and lengthening of its duration, they could not limit their action to the mere compensation of job losses. Thus, since 1979 – 1980, a movement has emerged, taking momentum in 1983, instituting cooperation and collaboration with the other local social actors, first of all in the social management of unemployment and more recently in the development of local employment. This is particularly obvious in the use of social welfare funds allocated to the assistance of the long-term unemployed. We have here again a policy which is less sectoral, more transversal and territorial, less specifically social and more geared towards insertion into the local economic and social structures.

The Voluntary Organizations Managing Social Welfare Services

Voluntary organizations, managing welfare services according to the Act of 1901, could become a central element in the transversal policies and local development policy, if they have the capacity, desire or determination to do so. Among other reasons, this is due to their legal and financial flexibility. In the context of decentralization, they have a choice between two possible courses of action. The first, which unfortunately tends to persist all too often consists of holding on to traditional positions, advantages gained and sectoral corporatism, while hoping to obtain from the state and the Conseil Général the preservation of positions and activities implemented in the last thirty years. From this point of view, the assertion of organizational legitimacy is a strong enough argument to hope to safeguard the positions gained on the local scene. Nevertheless, should the Conseils Généraux in particular be in a position to introduce and develop their strategies, we might see (and the process has already started in certain départements) the closing-down of some establishments or services that were considered non-profitable, too costly or inadequate by the local magistrates: as a consequence dismissals can be foreseen. The national representatives of these organizations and particularly the UNIOPSS (Union Nationale des Institutions et Oeuvres Privées Sanitaires et Sociales, national union of voluntary bodies providing health and social services, which represents in France approximately 300,000 employees) were aware of the risk, since they themselves were operative in the design of the Act of 8. 1. 1986, the general economy of which we have dealt with above.

Thus we see that the sector of organizations managing social welfare services, whose economic role was affirmed during the parliamentary debate on the creation of the titre associatif (voluntary organization bond), is playing a significant role in the recomposition of social policies. This role will be all the more dynamic in that the organizations – this being the second possible course of action – must for their own sake assert their legitimacy, open their activities and services more widely to the local scene and participate in the struggle for employment. Supported in this by numerous governmental measures (financial aid to intermediate companies or quasi-companies, community employment schemes), the voluntary organizations are therefore an essential partner in the future image of social policies.

We have seen the dynamics of the institutional apparatus. It is now necessary to assess the first effects of the recomposition process on the public and the acute social problems that France has to face, and then to establish the orientations for further research and reflection on social policies today.

The Current Process of Recomposition

In the last five years there have been undeniably important innovations in the fields of health, social and employment policies in France. Evidence of this can be found in a certain number of figures given at the end of 1985; for example, the relative balance in the domain of social finance and the relative stabilization of unemployment. However, empirical studies and the analysis of the social and economic situation at the local level lead us to modify certain national global assessments which have been hastily presented as positive. It is indeed obvious[25] that poverty and economic insecurity are increasing, whether it be in the domain of family income, unpaid rents, long-term unemployment or unemployment of young people. In addition to this already alarming situation we must consider the adverse effect of decentralization and the process we have just analyzed, which may develop into regressive situations. In the context of recomposition which we have examined, the following mechanism is at work: the organizations instituting social protection at the local level will find themselves managing together individual functions and joint financing. Now, no matter what can be said about local social development, it seems that the necessity for each actor to cut down costs leads to a peculiar mechanism, not only of greater control resulting in the reduction of the total amount of the benefits that were granted, according to some, with laxity, but also of mutual pushing of the public from pillar to post, i. e. from one benefit to the other, from one service to the other, from one institution to the other. Indeed a kind of tennis game is being played whereby the Conseillers Généraux, reducing such or such benefits, tell the recipients to turn to other benefits or other kinds of assistance, particularly services funded by the state or the organizations of the sécurité sociale. A clear-cut tendency, now confirmed by statistics, shows a drift towards the provision of health, legal or psychiatric care instead of social support, and institutional care instead of domiciliary care and support. This can be observed in the areas concerning children, teenagers and the elderly. Finally the tutelage of families (a relatively compelling legal protection) is showing a definite increase. In one of the départements studied, it doubled in a year.

We are thus confronted with a paradoxical situation whereby, on the one hand, the new procedures and policies are trying to organize from a different approach the modes of social insertion or reinsertion (with some success, we must admit), but, on the other hand, there is an underlying and heavy-handed tendency towards an archaic type of policy which runs counter to the whole ideology of social protection developed in Europe since the 1960s; this strengthens social control, heavy and costly assistance and finally leads to an immobile state and society.

Orientations for Further Research and Reflection

Do there exist in this situation, however, possible barriers to prevent the drifts? Apart from waiting for a (hypothetical?) comprehensive reform of social protection in France, there are opportunities for development in three main areas of the decentralized management of policies: that of the functioning of institutions and planning, that of benefits and finally that of the interplay between the social and the economic.

• Where the functioning of the institutions is concerned, the Act of 8. 1. 1986 provides in our opinion a range of instruments well adapted to the situation. Indeed it sets up firstly a Departmental Council for Social Development where all institutions participating in social policy, professionals and users should be represented. It constitutes a real small local parliament for social affairs and can become the place for common objectives to be expressed and policies coordinated. Apart from this council, is the necessity for planning which is materialized through the departmental scheme for establishments and services in the social and health sectors. This document can be used to achieve coherence among policies and financing proper to each institution in the field. Finally, coherence at the regional level in operations carried out in the different départements should be achieved within the regional commission for social and health facilities.

The actual implementation of these new instruments presupposes political agreements in the field through which they are still fighting their way. Moreover, it supposes a certain apprenticeship of the decentralization process and the creation of methodological instruments to assess the resources, needs and impact of policies which for the moment are still largely lacking.

Another problem neglected by legislation which deserves to be mentioned is the level at which policies are managed. If indeed the département is the level chosen by the laws on decentralization for the coordination of policies, it must be emphasized that, for quite a number of activities, it is already too distant from the actual problems of the population, one could say too abstract. Even for medium-sized départements (250,000 to 350,000 inhabitants), the variety of the geographical territories, the social territories, the areas of economic activity and the local employment scene suppose the localized adaptation of policies, institutions and their resources. A kind of decentralization of decentralization could therefore be envisaged, whose axis would be the commune or groups of communes or areas. This would not imply the formalization a priori (and from this point of view the silence of the legislation shows prudence) of a new administrative division within the département. On the contrary, flexible structures should be envisaged which will be tailored to the local social and economic entities such as they now exist and operate. The condition, however, for a successful management at the local level is not only that means be provided but also that a pluralist political control be exerted.

• In order to handle the distressful social situations generated by ever increasing economic insecurity and more particularly long-term unemployment and unemployment of young people, the institutional response is certainly much more effective. But it is also important to consider carefully the actual orientation of the instruments for social protection (benefits) and its inadequacies, particularly as it was designed for a time of economic growth, and is thus not well-adapted to a long period of economic crisis and underemployment.

From this point of view, it is first necessary to achieve a real coordination between non-statutory assistance policies pursued by all the social institutions. A start was made in 1983 concerning practical help for unpaid rents (special fund for unpaid rents subsidized for 35 per cent by the state) and such integration of policies must be continued. Otherwise the present dispersion can only persist at the expense of families and individuals in serious financial difficulty. The plurality and political specificity of the institutions existing in the field go against this movement, because they are unwilling to give up the slightest portion of their autonomy of decision. However, positive experiments are currently being carried out in some départements which lead us to believe that the contradiction, again obvious, between the sectoral approach and the transversal approach, can be overcome.

Over and above non-statutory assistance, for some time in France a debate common to almost all Western countries has developed over the creation of a guaranteed minimum income. Certain countries, as we know, have already introduced it, with some degree of success. France has not made its choice yet, even if ce ain communes and recently one département (Territoire de Belfort) are experimenting with it at the moment. Without wishing to develop here a subject that would warrant a complete study, let us merely say that there is no sovereign solution to the problem of new poverty, or, rather, that the implementation of a guaranteed minimum income can only be a means of silencing it. On the contrary, the minimum income will only be justified if it is contractualized and provides not only temporary assistance, and if it is designed as a lever for the social reinsertion of people in difficulty (through professional training, employment and finally the recovery of a social status). It is also necessary, for the reasons mentioned above, that the minimum income be designed on a local scale (the département) to correspond to the manifestations of economic insecurity actually developing there.

• The minimum income solution is in itself necessary and yet it does not cover all the issues of the debate. Indeed the contradictions and problems raised in this section lead us to believe that the recomposition of the social policies can be significant only if they are associated with a fundamental reorientation of their strategies towards employment, work, areas of production and activity within which men and women can once more give their life meaning.

Conclusions

As the economic crisis persists and unemployment rises, the prevailing impression is that our social security system will undergo profound changes. It is still much too early to predict the values on which it will be based or the principles that will govern its operation. However, we have attempted to analyze two areas (the community employment schemes and the decentralization of social policy to département level) that to us seem to provide a basis for analysis of the issues of the future.

The slow-down of economic growth has reduced the financial resources available to the welfare state concurrently with increasing needs, particularly because of the rise in unemployment. In the face of this challenge, there are several possible lines of development. Some of these seem to be marked by the policy that characterized the period of rapid economic growth in the thirty years after the end of World War II. Others seem to be more innovatory and better suited to the new economic situation, i. e. to a slow-down in economic growth; this in no way excludes all types of social, human and cultural progress. Usually, however, the changes taking place and the measures implemented are not based on a clear ideological decision. The decision-makers and actors in question are as much influenced by the constraints and conflicts of interest and the need to find short-term solutions as by their ideological orientations. This is the reason why any attempt to analyze the changes currently taking place or being planned is necessarily a hazardous undertaking. It is nevertheless necessary to attempt such an analysis.

The guaranteed minimum social wage may be an interesting solution from the technical point of view, to the extent that it would bring together benefits from a variety of sources. But it does contain the following danger: our society would be wrong to assume that it is discharged of all responsibility once individuals o families have been given enough money to survive. In a market-oriented society it is essential to have a minimum level of income, but in all societies, including our own, it is equally important to be recognized by others and to have activities with social significance. Those dependent on social security are in the most dis credited position in society. It thus seems impossible nowadays to be satisfied simply with distributing money to individuals or families without resources. Tha was possible in periods of full employment in that the lack of resources was often temporary (given the relative ease with which jobs could be found) and affected only a very small proportion of the population. Today, with an unemployment rate of more than 10 per cent in France (rising to 25 per cent among the economically active members of the 15–24 age group), the relationships between the econ omic and social dimensions have changed. The economic growth of earlier peri ods made it possible for everyone to find a job and thus ensure their social inte gration. With direct deductions from wages paid for sickness and unemploymen benefits and also for pensions, the social security system came to the assistance of the small proportion of the population who remained outside the insurance sys tem.

Today, resources which could have been allocated directly to the social policy c assisting people in difficulty are being used to subsidize firms in order to encour age them to take on young people; the state, for example, pays part of the wages bill or the employers' social security contributions. Some people regard this as the channelling of resources away from social policy towards private firms. This is undoubtedly true. But this channelling of resources represents a widely held conviction that there is little point in a social policy which provides assistance fo individuals if those individuals cannot find employment. Instead of dreaming of a return to the past (when the resources allocated to social policy were spent on social policy and those allocated to economic policy were spent on economic policy), it seems to us preferable to assess the benefits and illusions which such interventions bring. The benefit is that they reduce the disadvantages experi enced by young people in the labour market, especially in France, as the unem ployment figures show. The illusion is that such measures can lead to significan increases in the total number of jobs available, whereas all that is actually achieved is the transferring of jobs to a different age group. This is why the com munity employment schemes seem much more innovatory. They guarantee a minimum level of income, provide jobs that are socially useful and, in the best cases, result in the social integration of those involved and the acquisition of skill as a result of the training provided by associations, local authorities and state in stitutions. The fact that the jobs are part-time means that the same financial re sources can be used to provide twice the number of opportunities. Finally, need hitherto neglected by the market economy, such as protection of the environment or care of the elderly, are met by those taking part in the schemes. Thus, the community employment schemes represent a reconstruction of the economic and social systems, and not simply a transfer of resources from social to economic policy.

However, there is a serious risk of dualism inherent in the community employment schemes, unless the innovations which characterize them (very considerable reduction in working hours, lack of relationship between work done and payment received, importance attached to social integration and proliferation of socially recognized activities) are the subject of debate between both sides of industry, particularly with respect to the distribution of jobs and income among the economically active population. It is not healthy for those employed on the community education schemes to be a category apart. If this were to be the case, the community employment schemes would remain a limited experiment, of which only the negative aspects would be remembered: low-paid, unskilled jobs whose only merit was to keep young people off the streets and to reduce delinquency. The community employment schemes are either a limited experiment or one of the elements in the reconstruction of the economic and social system.

Analysis of the decentralization of social policies to département level poses the same type of problems. There is tension between a purely financial response seeking to make savings and a model based on solidarity and social development at the local level. If the old, fragmented system of assistance for the individual or the family is maintained, diminishing resources and the piecemeal response of the institutions concerned will mean that the situation will continue to deteriorate. Unless it is accompanied by a process of desectoralization, more detailed analysis of needs in the context of the crisis and real social planning on the local level, the lack of resources will have perverse results: for example, a lack of resources and the absence of a coherent policy to enable psychiatric patients who are not too seriously ill to stay with their family, will, in fact, mean that even more money will have to be spent on providing care for such people in psychiatric hospitals. This is the effect that can now be observed and which was described above.

However, there are more encouraging prospects, although they are still only in the embryonic stage. On the one hand, the resources available are being distributed in accordance with a more global, more transversal system of planning, while, on the other hand, the distinction between economic and social policy is becoming blurred. Better coordination of resources between the various social institutions is essential, in view of the financial restrictions, in order to avoid the duplication of jobs and abandon certain schemes that are of little value. But this coordination is perhaps also essential for another more fundamental reason: the fragmentary nature of the assistance provided for the individual and the family and of their contact with a multiplicity of government departments may lead to a certain degree of irresponsibility on the part of both the claimants and the departments making the payments. The compartmentalization of the possible sources of social security payments may sometimes encourage people to remain dependent on social security; on the other hand, these various sources may sometimes be insufficient to help someone get out of a temporarily bad situation. It is only at the local level, and certainly at a more decentralized level than that of the département, that it is possible to imagine all the resources being coordinated and dialogue taking place with the individual or family in difficulty in order to seek the best solutions and the corresponding obligations. At the level of the département, it is to be hoped that the period of economic austerity will be accompanied by a period in which the departmental councils for social development which are being established will draw up coordinated policies and objectives suited to the different situations in which families and individuals find themselves. An alternative social policy based on a less fragmented view of the individual or the family and rights to this or that benefit, but rather on analysis of individual cases and an attempt to respond to individual situations, does run the risk of being paternalistic or of increasing the level of social control. It must be recognized that all social policies involve certain risks. These risks will be minimized if the main objective is the eventual autonomy of the individual or the family. However, if this is to be achieved in our market society, paid employment is essential. It is here that the community employment schemes, and many other initiatives as well, form the links between social policy and economic policy by encouraging employment and local development. It is symptomatic that not only the state, as indicated above, but also institutions with a social purpose, such as the Farmers' Mutual and the Associations for Employment in Industry and Commerce, have started to go down this path.

Notes

1) Maurice, M., Sellier, F., Silvestre, J. J., 1982, Politique d'éducation et organisation industrielle PUF, Paris; Nohara, H., Enseignement technique, qualification industrielle et marché du travail: le cas du Japon; Document LEST 83. 8.
2) OCDE, 1985, Politiques novatrices en faveur des jeunes, Paris.
3) Sellier, F., Responses to the Crisis of the Welfare State: The Case of Young People, LEST-CNRS Aix-en-Provence.
4) Lebouteux, F., 1985, 'Les TUC . . . et après?' Droit social, April.
5) J. L. D., Direction de la Prévision, Bureau Emploi et Salaires, 1985. 9. 6.
6) Le Monde, 1985. 8. 24.
7) Canal 127, 1985, La lettre du ministre. Ministère du Travail, de l'Emploi et de la Formation Professionnelle, No. 1, November.
8) J. L. D., Direction de la Prévision; Bureau Emploi et Salaires 1985 9. 6.
9) Lebouteux, F., 1985, 'Les TUC . . . et après?' Droit social, April.
10) Le Monde, 1985. 8. 24.
11) Perreux, J., 1985, Secrétaire du Mouvement de la Jeunesse Communiste, Le Monde, Octobe 22.
12) Galland, O., 1985, TUC-Pré-enquête qualitative auprès des organismes, Ministère du Travail, de L'Emploi et de la Formation Professionelle, Centres d'Etudes de l'Emploi, July.

166

3) Puel, H., Brachet, O., Dieppedalle, D., 1986, Signification du programme TUC par rapport au développement local, Economie et Humanisme, Ministère du Travail, de l'Emploi et de la Formation Professionnelle, January.

4) J. L. D., Direction de la Prévision. Bureau Emploi et Salaires, 1985. 9. 6.

5) Schalchli, D., 1985, 'Les mesures d'insertion des jeunes: juxtaposition ou cohérence', Droit Social, No. 4, April, pp. 217–320.

6) Puel, H., Brachet, O., Dieppedalle, D., 1986, Signification du programme TUC par rapport au développment local, Economie et Humanisme, Ministère du Travail, de l'Emploi et de la Formation Professionelle, January.

7) Perreux, J., 1985, Secrétaire du Mouvement de la Jeunesse Communiste, Le Monde, October 22.

8) This section is based on studies carried out by the author in three départements in the south-east of France: Drôme, Savoie and Haute-Savoie. The reader will understand that for obvious reasons of policital sensitivity, no precise reference will be made to the particular situation of each département.

9) Martin G. 1984, 'Les politiques sociales en France, crise ou mutation' in Nowotny H. (ed.), Social Concerns for the 1980s, European Centre for Social Welfare Training and Research, Vienna.

0) Despite the desire for unification of the social work professions according to an idea of polyvalence, the efforts to arrest the development of social work specialization in France proved unsuccessful. In the strict social domain, we have the following professions: generic social workers, specialized social workers for children, psychiatry and schools, industrial social workers, all categories of social workers involved in the educating of maladapted children, social workers involved in prevention, justice and education in social and family economy, tutelage for social benefits, help in the home. This situation is the consequence of a double mechanism which characterizes sectoral policies: on the one hand, the typical mechanism of the well-known professionalization of sociology and, on the other, the simultaneous tendency of each administrative service (or policy segment) to constitute its own units of specialized personnel.

1) This circular by Nicole Questiaux, then Minister of Social Affairs, was considered by all categories of social workers as the reassertion of the importance of their role and of their functions in the perspective of the renewal of global social policies. This 'new bible' was to become a testament only.

2) For example, sectors in which financing may be jeopardized (e. g. infant and adolescent psychiatry) will try to become closer to the territory through a larger participation in the field and an improved coordination with other professionals and services. Conversely, other activities, which had so far been enjoying a relative autonomy of decision and operation on their territory of activity, are subjected to a vertical re-centring (financial control, control over the opportunity of decisions) at the département level. This can be the case for special workers providing help in the home or non-statutory aid granted by the social services for child care.

3) These are limited territories (a valley, a town, an 'area') where, on the initiative and with the financial incentives of the Secretary of State for Social Economy, all the partners of the social and economic development meet within an organization governed by the Act of 1901 (Territorial collectivities, social and health services, training organizations, private companies, local committees for employment, etc.).

-) Through the TSAP: Tableau Statistique de l'Activité du Praticien Médecin, which serves as an evaluation standard.

-) Offredi, C., Martin, G., 1984, Formes de la précarité: repérage dans la Drôme; Martin, G., Offredi, C. (under the responsibility of), 1985, Pour une nouvelle politique sociale à l'égard des pauvres et des précaires dans la Drôme, Report of the Groupe Solidarité; Offredi, C., Depit, M., 1985, Les allocations mensuelles en Haute-Savoie: évaluation financière et regard sur les pratique sociales; Marron, P., Klebaner, P., 1985, Etude sur les travailleuses familiales en Haute-Savoie: évaluation financière, approche de fonctionnement et bilan; Martin, G., 1985, La politique à l'égard des personnes âgées en Savoie: repères; Martin, G., 1985, Evaluation de la psychiatrie infanto-juvénile en Savoie.

167

The Limits of Consensus and Continuity – A Challenge for the Austrian Welfare State?

Ronald Pohoryles, Dimiter Martin Hoffmann, Brigitte Rauscher, Helmut Wintersberger

Introduction: Programming Welfare Policies Within the Austrian Political Culture

The Austrian social security network is just as connected with labour market developments as that of most other Western industrial countries. Moreover, at first glance, it appears to be both 'over-centralized' and 'splintered'. The thesis of 'over-centralization' is due to the social security system's reacting somewhat slowly to practical experiences and is expanded through social partnership compromise and the consensus of the political parties. The thesis of 'splintering' of social security systems refers to the differing responsibilities of the different institutions which impede an integrated concept of social security and welfare.

The development of Austrian social policy during the last fifteen years shows a clear change in paradigm on the national level: a dominating tendency towards integrative social policy up to the mid 1970s, with the equalization of social disparities as the ultimate target. This objective was met by including a greater number of population groups in the compulsory social insurance scheme and by a labour market policy with the explicit aim of removing social and regional inequalties. The health insurance scheme now covers directly 64.6 per cent of the Austrian population; the addition of co-insured persons (dependants) leads to a grand total of 99.8 per cent of the Austrian population covered by health insurance.

This integrative formulation of policy was considerably helped by the traditional climate of consensus which has been the essential element of Austrian politics since the 1950s. This climate of consensus is not only limited to the national level: it exists also in the provinces (in fact, political cooperation is a fixed part of the provincial constitutions) as well as between the different (federal, provincial and local) levels.

There is also a steering instrument in social policy (particularly in incomes policy, but also in social security), which makes the Austrian system rather unique: the system of economic and social partnership with the representation of all relevant social groups as an instrument to balance social interests; it has created a broad basis of social consensus for the policies which have turned Austria into a welfare state.

The instruments of integrative social policy were still being expanded in the early 1970s; this is only superficially contrary to the fact that 1966 saw the end of the heretofore applied principle of shared government responsibility by way of a 'big coalition', moving Austria in the direction of a 'democracy by competition'. Central decisions in social and economic policy were still influenced and negotiated by way of social partnership.

The orientation on the model of integrative social policy has clearly diminished in the mid 1970s, with national social policy concentrating more and more on labour market policy. The fragmentation of the welfare state system, both with regard to supply and demand, has also increased in this context. This is due to labour market developments and to the fact that welfare state benefits were mainly seen as problems of financing. These problems had a negative impact as well on the climate of cooperation between the federal government and the provinces.

The shift in social policy towards labour market policy could be explained by the importance of a high level of employment for the functioning of the welfare state. The following diagram shows the interdependencies between labour market policies and the social security network; it could also be seen as a paradigm of an unemployed person who moves through different institutions and programmes offered by social policy, but finds him-/herself finally permanently excluded from the labour market. Unsuccessful reintegration of unemployed people leads ultimately to marginalization and to public assistance benefits just on the edge of the subsistence level.

The diagram also shows the distribution of responsibilities between state (Labour Market Support Act, General Social Insurance Act) and provinces (Public Assistance Acts) on the one hand, and between the different institutions of the labour market (labour exchange, social insurance, and social welfare offices) on the other.

In order to analyze the shift in the Austrian welfare mix three objectives must be met:

• A more detailed analysis of the contents of social policy requires a view of the development of labour and labour market policy over the course of time. The role played by state instruments in this development cannot be ignored, for unconventional initiatives in Austria are directly connected with state measures for promoting and supporting the labour market (section 1).

• Social action as well as the opinion of major social actors are important concerns of the study, which takes into consideration the reaction to the developments and innovative social projects with regard to 'networking' between traditional and new institutions of social welfare and employment initiatives. The view

Preliminary Problem Scheme

 scheme of
time
schediule

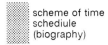 scheme of time
schediule
(biography)

Labour market policy (to prevent
or reduce unemployment or reduce unemployment. as opposed
to the previous aim of full employment) Labour Market Support Act

System of social security

Mainly
preventive
measures

Mainly
curative
measures

Provincial Public
Assistance (Public
Assistance Acts)

Social Insurance
(General Social
Insurance Act)

regular
labour market

experimental
labour market

problems in the economic structure

Reform (reductions)

of Public Assistance

Reform

of Social Insurance

general discus-
sion about re-
duction of
working hours

structural un-
employment

problem groups
on the labour
market

structural
crisis of nation-
alized industry

youth. women.
disabled

entitled

not entitled to
unempl. benefit

shuttling between

social welfare office
and labour exchange

Title unempl. ended:
emergency help

commuting between social welfare

office and labour exchange

— retraining measures
— experimental labour market
  policy*)
— so-called 'Project 8000'

connections with the provinces

(public assistance)

success in transferring to:

traditional
labour market

non-traditional
measures/projects etc.

*) New discussion about
professionalism: e. g. 'Labour Market Relief Wor-
kers' recruited from the
professional field of social
workers; youth leaders:
teachers.

'alternative' projects:
self–administrated en-
terprises etc.

without success

* invalidity pension.
* early retirement

trad. labour market

'alternative' labour market

public assistance

social insurance

171

and initiatives of traditional institutions are also analyzed as part of the basic conditions for the heterogeneous development of social initiatives.

Section 2 deals with both the views of traditional and newly emerging actors on the central level; section 3 continues with a more detailed description of some projects on the level of the Austrian provinces and a case study of an Austrian community. Whereas reports on social policy are usually primarily concerned with the national level, the provinces and communities play an important role in Austrian social policy. This study does not offer a representative cross-section of innovative social projects, but rather some illustrations, concentrating on projects exemplifying the new elements of the welfare mix.

• Finally, this chapter discusses the future of the welfare policy, bearing in mind the two most likely options:

– The 'conservative' one: Social policy would go on administering the constantly growing marginalization which cements segmentation in line with the decoupling of growth and employment.

– The 'innovative' one: Successful social integration would increase the options originating in innovative social projects and reacting against the traditional system. The redefinition of the concept of 'work', with an inclusion of moments of 'Lebenswelt' and qualitative aspects would be of major importance in this context.

The conclusions are drawn on the following basic assessments:

– The traditional industrial sector has no longer a great potential for growth o employment. There exists therefore a tendency towards isolation from the exter nal labour market and towards societal segmentation. Measures of rationalization – because of technological change and increasing competition in general – pro duce, however, a certain shift towards deregulation (the evasion of collective bar gaining agreements).

– The developments in the formal sector result in an increasing but restricted im portance of the so-called informal sector, a sector often financially supported by state and/or local authorities.

An Important Aspect of the Changing Reality of Work: The Rate and Structure of Unemployment

Development of Unemployment and the Labour Market

The Austrian employment situation has developed quite positively, with a growth of 3.3 per cent between 1970 and 1984. However, employment has dropped b about 1 per cent between 1982 and 1984.

1e development of employment has shown the secular trends common to all in-
Jstrialized nations: employment is still decreasing in agriculture and forestry,
⁄en though that development has levelled off somewhat since 1975; it is stag-
ating in production and increasing in the service sector (table 1).

1e structural changes are not only limited to the economy, but are just as ap-
arent in the social sector. Female employment has increased much more than
ale employment since 1970, but all employment (male and female) has de-
eased from 1982 on. The social structure of the gainfully employed has
1anged just as persistently, with a substantial growth of white-collar work at the
<pense of blue-collar work ever since 1970 (table 2).

1e Austrian unemployment rate was rather stable between 1970 and 1980
.round 2 per cent), but there has been a distinct deterioration from 1982 on: the
1employment rate in 1984 was more than twice that of 1980, and there is a very
efinite structure to unemployment (table 3). Men are more affected than women,
ue-collar workers more than white-collar workers. More women than men were
1employed in 1980, but that has changed in 1981. Blue-collar unemployment
as increased by 4.3 per cent in this period, white-collar unemployment by only
Dout 1 per cent.

owever, this picture is somewhat distorted: two-thirds of all unemployed blue-
ollar workers are men (1984), and in white-collar work there are twice as many
males unemployed as males (table 3).

1e age structure between 1978 and 1982 shows a distinct drop in unemploy-
ient in the age group '50 and older'. This seems to be due to a growth of early
tirement. The proportion of unemployed under the age of 20 is rather stable,
hile that of the other age groups is increasing (table 4).

1e last set of data used to show the changing structure of unemployment is that
f the duration of unemployment (table 5). Here, too, there is a decrease until
980, with an increase hereafter.

1e picture of labour market segmentation is intensified by the very evident
'owth of regional disparities. The less developed provinces in the Eastern part
f Austria were clearly more affected by the growing economic recession than the
rovinces in the Western part.

he Political Reactions to the Development of Unemployment

1e changed economic conditions have led to a mixture of labour market and
mployment policy with the top priority being the prevention of high unemploy-
1ent. The provinces and local communities are also active in this respect (e. g.
ith subsidies for new industrial ventures; by covering certain costs of such ven-
ires); they sometimes even compete with each other in order to attract certain
nterprises. But this development has also pushed somewhat in the background
1e promotion of economically underdeveloped regions (with the objective of

Table 1
Structure of Employment Levels

per cent of total number of employed	1970	1975	1982	Average 1971−75	Average 1976−82
I agriculture, forestry*)	2.7	1.8	1.4	− 6.0	− 2.6
II goods production	49.1	46.2	42.1	+ 0.8	− 0.6
III services	48.2	52.0	56.5	+ 3.6	+ 1.9
TOTAL in per cent	100.0	100.0	100.0	+ 2.0	+ 0.7
TOTAL in millions employed	(2,6)	(2,8)			

Source: Handbook of Economic and Social Statistics and calculations by the authors.
*) This table lists only the gainfully employed: this sector is therefore under-represented.

Table 2
Social Structure of the Gainfully Employed

per cent of gainfully employed	1970	1975	1982	1984	Average 71−75	Average 76−82	Average 82−8
blue−collar workers	58	52	48	47	− 2.3	− 0.6	− 1.3
white−collar workers	42	48	52	53	+ 2.2	+ 1.6	+ 0.4
males	63	61	59	59	− 0.8	+ 0.2	− 0.4
females	37	39	41	41	+ 0.8	+ 1.2	− 0.1
TOTAL in per cent	100	100	100	100	+ 2.0	+ 0.7	− 0.4
TOTAL in mill. empl.	(2,7)	(2,3)	(2,4)	(2,4)			

Source: Handbook of Economic and Social Statistics and calculations by the authors.

Table 3
Socio−demographic Structure of Unemployment

Unemployment rate	1975	1980	1982	1984
absolute (in 1,000)	55	53	105	130
unemloyment rate	2.0	1.9	3.7	4.8
blue−collar unemployment	3.1	2.8	5.7	7.2
white−collar unemployment	0.9	1.0	1.7	2.4
males	1.5	1.6	3.8	4.8
females	2.8	2.3	3.5	4.1

Source: Handbook of Economic and Social Statistics and calculations by the authors.

174

Table 4
Age Structure of the Unemployed

Age group	1978	1980	1982
17 – 19	8.8	6.8	8.1
(20 – 24)	–	–	(18.3)
20 – 29	28.0	27.2	32.0
30 – 49	41.6	45.4	44.5
over 50	21.6	20.6	15.1
Total in per cent	100.0	100.0	100.0
absolute in 1,000	36	30	69

Source: Official statistics.

Table 5
Average Period of Unemployment (in days)

average in days	1975	1980	1982
TOTAL	64.5	52.3	66.6
blue–collar workers	64.9	50.2	64.1
white–collar workers	63.0	59.2	76.4

Source: Handbook of Economic and Social Statistics.

Table 6
Acceptance of 'Project 8000'

	1984	1985	I/1986
number of persons supported	779	2,176	(897)
total sum of support (AS 1,000)	48,646	225,164	(97,916)
support sum/person (AS 1,000)	62,210	103,480	(109,160)

Source: Statistics of the labour market administration (unpublished).

avoiding unemployment, migration and/or large-scale commuting in these regions).

The objective of unemployment insurance is to bridge the gap in the case of short-term unemployment. This becomes increasingly precarious in view of the rise in long-term/permanent unemployment and the general unemployment structure. Thirty-five per cent of the 67,984 registered unemployed are already receiving emergency assistance. This shows a tendency which could not only lead to a shift of welfare benefits to alternative institutions of social welfare (public assistance by provinces and local communities), but also to a further reduction of services, along with an increase in contribution payments for those still included in the traditional social security network. The growing number of long-term unemployed should also provoke a new look at the traditional concept of 'marginal' groups.

Politicians seem to react generally faster than the social partners to these newly developing problems. 'Active labour market policy' is turning increasingly towards specific support programmes for this kind of problem. The 1970s have already known specific support for companies and projects which could be called 'socially innovative'. Several very new programmes are being developed in the form of 'subject support', such as 'preliminary vocational training for university graduates', or indirectly as in the case of the 'Project 8000' (employment programme for the target groups youth and long-term unemployed).

'Project 8000' was begun early in 1984 as a special employment programme by the labour market administration of the Federal Ministry for Social Administration in order to promote and support projects in the area of environmental protection, social services, urban renovation, culture and the arts, as well as individual activities in these areas. The labour market administration usually covers half of the wage costs (two-thirds since mid 1985) and up to 100 per cent of the wage costs in regions with special structural problems. The project was only haltingly accepted at first, but has become an entire balancing measure for the labour market from mid 1985 on, although there are distinct regional differences (table 6).

Even though this project concerns only a limited number of people, it is impossible to ignore its strong target-group orientation towards groups with increasing special problems in the labour market (unemployed youths, long-term unemployed). This project was particularly successful in the field of employment and social initiatives and will be referred to many times in this chapter.

Traditional Actors and New Actors: Perceptions and Perspectives

Ruptures and Axes: Traditional Social Policy Facing New Challenges

The introduction has already stated that Austria's traditional social policy system in its post-war development is very much oriented towards consensus between all socio-political actors. This consensus comprises the three most relevant levels of socio-political discussion:
- the political-administrative level (particularly parliament, but also central and provincial governments),
- the social and economic partners, and
- the self-administered social insurance system.

The interlinking of the three levels is a special Austrian characteristic. Almost all of the decision-makers interviewed for this study are officials in at least two of the three systems (e. g. the spokesman of the Federation of Austrian Industrialists is also a member of parliament for the Christian Conservative People's Party; the secretary of one of the trade unions here is also a member of parliament for the Socialist Party and an official of the Vienna Area Health Insurance; etc.).

This interlinking was considered not only to be unproblematic until the 1970s, but was even thought to guarantee socio-political progress by consensus. Central reform policies were negotiated by the social partners and afterwards passed by parliament. Many important social policy measures have therefore been passed unanimously, irrespective of existing government majorities. The strong interdependence of the different social policy systems has met with increased criticism and internal problems during the late 1970s and early 1980s. Public criticism began initially as discussion about 'getting rid of privileges' with regard to accumulation of high positions by the socio-political actors. The agenda setting of such a discussion in times of stagnating social policies and increasing problems is therefore not very surprising.

However, there are also very real material problems which question at least the traditional logic of each individual system. The consensual solutions of the 1970s stand essentially under the sign of distributing growth with the foil of continuous economic growth. It is not really surprising that consensus is endangered if redistribution rather than distribution of growth is the issue. It is, therefore, typical that socio-political decisions are transferred from the social partnership level to the political level.

Furthermore, the interviews show a psychological problem of social partnership: that of the 'succession of a younger generation'. There is general agreement within social partnership that the continuity of negotiators has contributed substantially to social partnership's stability. The young officials must first of all acquire that mixture of conflict and cooperation necessary to play the game of strategic negotiations.

A central problem with regard to the new 'welfare mix' is particularly difficult to grasp for social partnership: that of newly emerging parties and actors interested in social benefits, but also the newly emerging social and employment initiatives. Indeed, they are not represented in the traditional economic bodies. The political system is forced to react faster to these new developments, but the social partnership system – at least at the central level – is not very interested in this matter. It is characteristic that social initiatives are constructed in a legal form that excludes their adequate representation in the institutions of employers or employees.

The challenges of the changing reality of work for social policies are accepted very differently by politics, social partnership, and social insurance. A tendency exists towards innovation on the political level; as a result, new axes, but also new conflicts between the political parties and actors can be expected.

Government and Political Parties – Perspectives of a New Social Policy?

The Federal Ministry for Social Administration refers to two essential social policy issues: the reform of the pension system and active labour market policy.

Because of the great need for political consensus both issues cannot be pushed forward to the extent desired by the ministry. A basic reform of the pension insurance system seems unlikely. The recent reform in pension insurance consists mainly of minor changes with regard to benefits and contributions, with the tendency towards reducing certain benefits, on the one hand, and increasing the contributions of the insured, on the other.

Plans to find additional ways of financing the welfare system, such as the introduction of a *Wertschöpfungsabgabe* (tax with the objective of compensating the increased burden on the social affairs budget to the effects of rationalization) could not be realized because of social partners' opposition.

The reform of the pension insurance system was examplary and led not only to the relief of the pension insurance through a reduction of benefits, but also to changing distributive patterns among the recipients; prolonging assessment periods has a distributory effect, e. g. larger reductions for white-collar workers than blue-collar workers, since the salaries of the first group tend to increase at a continuous rate until retirement, which is usually not the case for blue-collar work. The ministry expects that the pension insurance system will show a positive development: the reforms of the 1970s (in particular the inclusion of new groups of self-employed and the opportunity to increase pensions by way of voluntary additional contributions) have led to a peak in benefits, but this effect will subside in the near future. Furthermore, the labour market is expected at least to stabilize, if not improve.

Expectations are therefore based on demographic trends and economic and labour market developments. Although there were no substantial changes in labour

178

market policy, new features, especially in the field of qualification, are emerging. Furthermore, vocational education has been left until now to the training institutions of social partners, and the ministry had only provided funding. Now the ministry is also closely involved in training contents. In addition, the introduction of the 35-hour week, the expansion of the service sector and general demographic developments will have a positive effect on labour market development.

Conflicts between the ministry and the social partners appear in the matter of 'experimental labour policy'. This instrument is the major tool for the support of self-managed enterprises (usually firms in crisis regions in danger of collapse; the objective is to have the employees run these firms themselves). The ministry feels that these measures have but little effect on the labour market, but this is also true for the financial resources available for this purpose (at present about AS 40 million). The ministry is of the opinion that socially innovative projects are rather more important than self-managed enterprises, for the emergence of long-term unemployment is one of the central labour market problems. The majority of the long-term unemployed comprises unqualified workers and it is highly unlikely that they could initiate and run self-managed enterprises.

New training programmes and employment subsidies are therefore considered to be of utmost importance for the long-term unemployed. These subsidies are not only paid to companies but also ('Project 8000' has already been mentioned) to political corporations, non-profit institutions, and social services. Socio-political support for employment in these sectors is considered to be particularly important, for regional political corporations and decentralized social services have run into increasing financial problems during the economic recession.

The ministry's view is shared by socialist members of parliament who usually also have a trade union background. This explains why they show a clearly more sceptical attitude towards experimental labour market policies and a much more positive assessment of the future perspectives and efficiency of social partnership.

A comparison of the social policy options of the ministry and the governing Socialist Party with the opinions of the opposition conservative People's Party shows accordance as well as differences. But, in any case, the emergence of new conflicts in social policy, at least on a medium-term level, seems to be likely. The social policy spokesman of the conservative opposition party agrees with the ministry's view on the opposition party's concessions in social policy matters due to forthcoming elections; this seems to be true for the extension of the groups entitled to receive pensions and to measures for pension increases with particular advantage to the middle classes that support the opposition party. Social insurance contributions, however, already had to be increased in the mid 1970s in order to finance this policy and further increases are now almost impossible, even though they are necessary.

The issue of social insurance is therefore more politically controversial now than in the past, which applies also to the fact that social partnership is less important in political decision-making at this time. Social policy must become more flexible and selective in order to change this situation. The legal fixation of social policy measures has the decisive disadvantage of not being able to react to new situations and of burdening the expenditure of social policy budgets in the long run. The social policy spokesman of the People's Party is strongly in favour of support for self-help initiatives. He agrees with the thesis that this form of service delivery is usually not only more economic, but also more efficient, as well as offering new employment. He feels that the problem of increased concessions during the economic boom is also apparent in labour market policies. New jobs which are available are almost never jobs for the unemployed because they are not well paid. Unemployed tend rather to live with the help of social benefits and to improve on these benefits by working illegally.

The spokesman on health matters of the People's Party (and head of the socio-political department of the Federation of Austrian Industrialists) agrees with these views. He also feels that changes in the system of need coverage are unavoidable because of a change of the classic task of social policy against the background of the conflict between capital and labour in connection with the new social question. There are new groups in need of additional social benefits (owners of small businesses/small farms, families with many children). Changes must, therefore, favour a more qualitative aspect in social policy, by taking into account such issues as self-initiative, neighbourhood and self-help, and subsidies, which would promote this aspect.

However, this would need a coordinated strategy between social insurance institutions, national bodies, the provinces, and local communities. It is the opinion of this spokesman that such a coordinated strategy is an essential prerequisite for the full development of support for self-help groups and social initiatives. Unconventional employment initiatives merit support in projects for the employment of unemployed youths in environmental protection, health, and the social welfare field, for not only do they promote vocational integration, but they also meet non-material aspirations to useful activity. However, it is clear that financial support can never become permanent.

Social Partnership in Crisis?

Officials in the political system emphasize the fact that the influence of social partnership seems to be declining and that this development had already begun during the 1970s. However, this thesis is not undisputed. Opinions differ, not only between the social partners, but also within the individual institutions.

The executive secretary of the Austrian Trade Union Federation agrees that finding a socio-political consensus between employers and employees has become more difficult. Furthermore, new officials must probe the negotiating range. Younger officials in the employers' organizations in particular have used the trends of recession since the late 1970s to question the social achievements of labour. This has provoked a sharp reaction from several younger trade union officials. However, one can expect on the whole that social partnership will overcome the newly arising problems of consensus finding.

The head of the socio-political department in the Federal Chamber of Commerce sees Austrian social policy as a quasi-unbroken continuity starting from the end of World War II. The consensus of social partnership has prevented sudden structural changes. He mentions the fact that all important social policies have been carried by consensus (even though there was a one-party socialist government during the 1970s), except for the adaptation of the social rights of blue-collar work to the position of white-collar work in 1979 and the extension of the minimum holiday to five weeks. From this standpoint, social partnership has shown its value in matters with highly ideological overtones. This is demonstrated by the regulations for codetermination in the Labour Constitution Act of 1975. Neither does he see any major problems for the social partners with regard to the provisions for old age. It is true that the early retirement scheme (which had socio-political motives) has also changed the ratio between the active working force and retired people, but this is not a fundamental challenge. Self-help groups could be useful in this respect but only in a subsidiary manner. One should not overestimate the value of individual provision through private insurances: the basic provisions have to be made by the traditional pension insurance system.

The situation in the labour market illustrates the advantages of the climate of social partnership. A good example of the Austrian method of dealing with social policy issues is the way which the social partners have handled the working time issue. The result is a respect for the needs of economic growth. The climate of consensus, the expected economic growth, and the demographic developments should eliminate the employment problem in a medium-term perspective. Most measures needed for coping with the present unemployment problem concern the sector of youth unemployment. He thinks that this applies in particular to vocational training. However, even today there are more offers to take on apprentices than people looking for apprenticeships. The lack of skilled workers is another indication of the fact that unemployment is also a consequence of unsatisfactory qualification and insufficient mobility.

He does not consider self-managed enterprises as a problem, as long as they do not distort competition by having too much financial support. This is the reason why the employers' organizations as well as the workers' representatives in the ministry's Labour Market Support Advisory Board have repeatedly voted against this support.

Regarding the future of social policy, he believes that problems can continue to be solved by way of social partnership consensus.

The opinions of the head of the socio-political department of the Federal Chamber of Commerce concur in essence with the opinions of top trade union officials. The secretary general of the Metalworkers, Miners, and Energy Industry Workers Union, for instance, stresses the good negotiating climate between the social partners in the different individual branches as well as on the level of general social policy questions.

This traditional official of the trade union is even less concerned with social and employment initiatives: he considers them as 'entrepreneurial activity', which cannot be included in trade unions' tasks.

The secretary of Austria's largest individual union, the Private Sector Employees Union takes a somewhat more detached view. He, too, stresses the need for social partnership consensus, but defines it within a less harmonious framework. The differing interests of employers and workers are plainly apparent in the question of financial social benefits. Social policy cannot be financed in a way which would shift the problems caused by rationalization exclusively to the public sector. The conflict over the *Wertschöpfungsabgabe* (tax which compensates for the increased burden on the social affairs budget due to the effect of rationalization) is therefore an essential socio-political task. He insists that growing unemployment must also be seen as an effect of rationalization. The Private Sector Employees Union, as the largest individual union, stresses its responsibility for the unemployed. This is, as already shown before, a rather controversial issue within the Austrian Trade Union Federation. The Private Sector Employees Union has in fact started its own unemployment welfare centre in cooperation with the labour market administration which intends to ease re-entry into working life.

The Private Sector Employees Union had once the function of forerunner in the reduction of working time. The Federation of Trade Unions has accepted a compromise which provides for a step-by-step reduction of working time, according to the requirements of the individual branches. Although the Private Sector Employees Union is the most progressive union, a general scepticism exists with regard to self-managed enterprises, for they cannot really relieve the labour market and represent also a high risk for all workers involved.

This almost official trade union line, ranging from the very traditional view of the secretary general of the Metalworkers, Miners, and Energy Industry Workers Union to the much more innovative view of the Private Sector Employees Union has met internal trade union opposition. This opposition, though, is in a minority in the individual unions as well as in the federation. They criticize the concealed manner in which decisions are made in the trade unions as well as their inflexible attitude towards the self-managed initiatives.

The head of the department concerned with basic questions in the Federal Ministry for Social Administration points out the criticism against expanding corporatism within the trade union movement. He considers this to be one of the major barriers for comprehensive structural reforms in social policy and connects it to the socio-structural differentiations within the group of the gainfully employed. These differing interests within the workers organizations lead to corporatism which weakens social partnership in general, for this partnership is based on centralization.

He thinks that the development of social partnership in general was abnormal. It was most powerful in the 1960s, during the coalition government of the two major political parties and has lost power since 1966, with the emergence of new forms of government. Moreover, the emergence of the new social movements has eliminated social partnership's claim to represent the society as a whole. The agreement of employers and workers organizations in questions of energy, armament, and environmental policies has somewhat united social partnership against new movements and initiatives.

The thesis of a diminishing influence of social partnership is also shared by the head of the socio-political department of the Federation of·Austrian Industrialists. The most important agreements in central social policy matters are now made between the political parties. This is partly due to the already mentioned succession of a new generation, but all social partnership organizations are now more concerned with the balancing of interests within their organizations. He also feels that, as far as the newly emerging problems are concerned, one should not overburden the social partners at a time when their organizations have reduced political effectiveness.

The Social Insurance Institutions

Austrian social insurance (health, accident, and pension insurance) is structured on general insurance principles. The system of social insurance has grown out of tradition. Begun as self-administered corporations organized on the principles of professional groups, there were originally 1,000 regional insurances in the area of present-day Austria a century ago. Because of the process of concentration ever since, there are now 24 independent social insurance institutions, incorporated in the Federation of Austrian Social Insurance Institutions.

The system of social insurance has gradually expanded from the 1950s on, in line with economic developments, and large groups of self-employed people have been included in the scheme during the 1970s.

The social insurance institutions' reaction to the economic recession in the early 1980s was to reduce benefits and increase different cost-sharing schemes.

The director general of the Federation of Austrian Social Insurance Institutions agrees fully with the principles of the social insurance system. The federation is by his definition the mouthpiece of the individual institutions. These turn their demands (in practice applications for amendments to the legal principles regulating benefits and contributions) over to the federation; the federation in turn sends the appropriate basic points for decision to the Federal Ministry for Social Administration. Societal and social concerns in social insurance are therefore negotiated bilaterally between the federation and the ministry.

Social insurance institutions are interested in maintaining the principle of insurance. This means that health and pension insurance benefits are limited by the income of the institutions with the modification that the differing share of the state's contribution towards the costs of the social network can protect social benefits over and above membership contributions. The social insurance institutions believe that this system has helped to keep rising costs under control.

The social insurance has a certain effect on the labour market policy: granting early retirement pensions, the pension insurance is responsible to relieve the labour market as well as the unemployment insurance system. Estimates calculate that official unemployment statistics would rise by about 1.5 to 2 per cent without early retirement.

The new social initiatives, social services, and self-help groups are seen as important supplements to the system. However, they are not viewed as a new movement: such services have always been offered by different charity organizations. Their use cannot be allowed to lead to cuts in benefits/services.

Innovative Social Projects: Development, Organization, Structure and Trends Compared with Specific Labour Market Policies for Problem Groups in Austria

Definition of Innovative Social Projects

From the mid 1970s on, state measures and instruments of labour market policy have not worked sufficiently against the growing tendency towards segmentation on the contrary, the development seems to promote the societal marginalization of demands due to the presence of specific groups.

Austrian innovative social projects define themselves as initiatives to reintegrate so-called problem groups into the labour market by offering them alternative training and work.

The Austrian discussion consists of two main topics:
• Is this a successful way of counteracting the tendency towards marginalization or do they create a new selection process within the marginalized groups?
• Do social projects actually reach problem groups (e. g. disadvantaged youth the disabled, long-term unemployed, women and migrants)?

Social projects would like to integrate into the primary and secondary labour market; however, they provide alternative jobs for their staff (social workers, skilled workers) and their clients in the so-called 'informal sectors'. Their political value is therefore, according to this point of view, somewhat ambivalent.

The alternative role of a project worker is tied to precarious working conditions (e. g. lacking capital, short-term contracts, unpaid overtime which leads to the well-known phenomenon of self-exploitation, etc.) which are usually not in compliance with the minimum standards required by the trade unions' collective agreements.

Despite the danger of deregulation, the virtually utopian demands for a redefin

tion of work, for education and qualification, for team work in self-management, and for new forms of community work and life, make many social projects interesting social experiments. But they are suspect as far as the traditional actors in social policy/labour market policy are concerned.

Austrian Social Projects: Development and Organization

Politicians and administrators respond to the problems of increasing regional disparities and the duration of unemployment by expanding the traditional instruments of labour market policy with new methods of so-called 'experimental labour market policies'.

There are specific youth employment programmes, employment initiatives based on self-help, counselling centres for this kind of initiative, and job-creation measures in the non-profit area. New forms of trial work-courses are also supported.

These improved means of support of new employment initiatives are part of the 9th amendment to the Labour Market Support Act (January 1983).

Provisions for employment initiatives based on self-help activities differ between:
• Self-managed (small) enterprises in order to create and retain jobs, and
• Non-profit initiatives with the objective of creating jobs for particularly disadvantaged unemployed people; these are called 'social projects' and are usually found in the social work field where they run employment initiatives for people difficult to place in the labour market.

Prior to this new legislation, some model projects in the form of trial work-courses and employment initiatives for long-term unemployed or problem youths, were run under the auspices of private (non-profit) and religious welfare organizations. These pilot projects were also supported mainly by the labour market administration.

Self-help groups of unemployed people in the strictest sense were comparatively infrequent. This changed in the early 1980s. Apart from already existing welfare organizations active in the field of training and youth unemployment, such as youth centres, probation help, social counselling for public assistance, self-help groups of unemployed people emerged.

Individual initiators of projects have very differing opportunities for receiving support. Projects have to guarantee employment for a number of years and usually advance staff salaries. These conditions are discriminatory to small institutions. Furthermore there are great differences between the provinces in giving financial and personnel support to the projects.

Crisis and even failure is therefore an often occurring event in social projects, for the project teams have only insufficient means and not enough practice in coping with the difficulties when initiating a project. The overload of work caused by economic and social-pedagogic crisis management may lead to extreme self-exploitation and

185

finally to the failure of some of the projects. A Federation for Social Projects in Austria was therefore established in November 1985 in order to protect certain minimum standards for personnel and material equipment of social projects.

Another problem which was not considered by the institutions responsible for project support is that social projects must cover the project costs with their income from production/services. This is extremely difficult if one wants to integrate the so-called 'less productive persons' (problem groups). Social projects have, therefore, a double function: to be productive and to fulfil social tasks. The social objectives are the losers in this conflict, because the social projects are forced to select from the problem groups one group of persons to be used 'productively' as soon as possible. The Federation for Social Projects is therefore trying to secure permanent support for employment initiatives with continuous programmes for new problem groups (transit jobs).

Prospects for New Developments in Social Projects

The question as to which of the two labour markets is the target of employment initiatives still remains unanswered. The efforts of many projects to use alternative vocational training in order to increase their clients' chances in the formal and informal sector of gainful employment can only be evaluated properly after these training programmes have been implemented for a longer period of time.

The alternative to the existing jungle of policies and supports often demanded in Western European countries – a combination of training and employment programmes in connection with local initiatives – exists in Austria only in a very rudimentary form.

Project workers with a socio-critical perspective of their project work and with a wish to define the political value of their activities from this perspective are confronted by a variety of inconsistencies.

The question of a continual integrative objective of labour market/social policy becomes particularly acute in youth unemployment. The working conditions in the innovative social projects tend to select between those accepted by potential employers, therefore being integrated into the primary labour market, and the others being pushed into the secondary, precarious labour market. Furthermore some still remain who only have the choice between so-called alternative roles and total marginalization at the end of this selection process.

And this is the context in which educational work with unemployed youths in social projets receives precisely that controversial importance voiced in the two above-quoted dilemmas:

Measures of improved qualification for problem youths will on the whole only increase the chance for some kind of job, but the jobs found are rarely training places and only some have any kind of long-term perspective.

Case Studies

Social Welfare Delivery: Some Examples of the Cooperation Between the Public and Voluntary Sectors in Austrian Provinces

Social policy is only in part the concern of the national level. The regional and local bodies also have important responsibilities in the welfare system. This leads to some different models of social benefits and service delivery, varying according to different political structures in the respective provinces, but also according to different needs to be met. Dealing with the Austrian welfare system, the study, therefore, describes some of the provincial programmes in the social policy area.

Vienna: The Different Forms of Cooperation Between City Authorities and Private/Voluntary Organizations

Vienna is a province as well as a local community and, of course, also the federal capital of Austria, with a population of about 1.5 million and a higher than average proportion of elderly and aged people. Cooperation between the public and private (non-profit) social welfare sector has been developed in Vienna after World War II and is now the fundamental component of the Vienna social welfare system. There are three different forms of cooperation in delivering social services:

Establishing private organizations for special projects. These organizations are usually established by the local authorities, and their boards consist of members of the Vienna municipal council. The president is either a council member or the city councillor responsible for the problem. Funding is also provided by the City of Vienna. Examples of such organizations in the social welfare field are:

- The Fund for Vienna Pensioners' Homes, established in the 1960s, whose purpose is planning, building and operating apartment-style residential homes for the elderly. There are at the moment 22 such homes with more than 5,500 places in apartments for singles or married couples and about 670 additional nursing ward quarters available.

- The Fund for Psycho-social Services in Vienna was established in 1980 as the backbone for the reform of Vienna's psychiatric system, decided upon in 1979. It operates a network of extra-mural psycho-social services. One of its objectives was the reduction of the very high number of patients in institutional psychiatric care. The success of the fund has been spectacular up to now, reducing the number of patients in Vienna's two psychiatric hospitals by about 50 per cent (from a total of about 3,700 beds at the start of the reform in 1979) and increasing the number of people voluntarily admitted to short-term institutional psychiatric care.

Services run by non-governmental organizations (NGOs) on behalf of the city of

Vienna. Most of the personal social services for the elderly/disabled are run on such a basis, usually with a full reimbursement for costs and in the form of a contract signed between the organization and the city. Home-help is a good example of this form of organization: Eight NGOs provide home-help services in Vienna on behalf of the municipality, with new clients being sent to the social welfare office's social stations. An average of 10,845 people received home-help services each month in 1985, and 2,655 home-helpers are employed by the 8 organizations.

• *Support and promotion of self-help groups.* The recent years have seen the development of a very active self-help sector in Vienna, and a special support system for this sector was introduced in 1985. An office within the municipal Health and Social Welfare Office has been established for this purpose, providing self-help groups with advice and information, and also offering financial help. The guidelines for this financial help are very strict in order to ensure that support is really limited to self-help groups. The guidelines define a self-help group as a group of people in need of help and coming together in order to provide this help for each other. Financial support is limited to a maximum sum of AS 25,000 per year and is granted either to aid in starting a group or to secure the continuous work of the group. However, the groups may not receive permanent financial support from other public sources.

Decentralized Personal Social Services in Lower Austria

Lower Austria is Austria's biggest province in terms of area; almost 1.5 million people live in this province, many of them in small towns and villages. It has therefore been necessary to find a very decentralized organizational system for personal social services. This highly decentralized form of organization makes use of 74 different service stations (at least one in every district) and an additional 32 contact offices for social services. The stations and services are run for the most part by the major private non-profit welfare organizations. The staff employed comprises 60 registered nurses, 35 family-helpers/helpers for the aged/nurses, 70 home-helpers, and about 720 voluntary helpers on a regular basis. There are about 1,500 to 3,000 clients per month, and the monthly average shows 30,000 man hours of work.

Burgenland's Model of 'Institutionalized Neighbourhood Help'

The province of Burgenland in the Eastern part of Austria still has the highest agricultural quota and the least industrial density of all Austrian provinces, so its commuting rate is three times higher than the Austrian national average. There are no large local communities, with 90 per cent of all the villages in this province having a total population of less than 2,000 inhabitants.

The organizing of flexible, extra-mural services is difficult in such an environment. The model introduced after some discussion was that of 'institutionalized neighbourhood help', which makes use of the still existing village/agricultural structure and the closer personal ties in such a structure. The objective is to enable a person to stay as long as possible in his/her familiar environment instead of moving into institutional (stationary) care and the fields covered comprise mainly home-help, home-nursing, and family-help. The helpers living in the vicinity of the clients get a small amount of monthly support paid by the provincial welfare office and are supervised by social workers who are also available for professional and organizational support to helpers and clients.

The Model of Social and Health Area Sectors in Tyrol

Tyrol is a province with 586,663 inhabitants, with the provincial capital of Innsbruck having a population of 117,000. Apart from the town of Innsbruck, the province is divided into eight administrative districts. In order to deliver social services, the Tyrolean administration developed an organizational model for the comprehensive cooperation between all actors in health and social welfare in a local community or on a sub-regional level. It is therefore, both a form of decentralization from the provincial/district level and a form of centralization between a number of small local communities.

Area sectors comprise a number of local communities; there are eight such sectors at the moment, serving a population of between 4,600 and 21,000 people (the largest sector at this time). Thirteen further sectors are in the preparatory stage. The aim of this form of organization is to replace large public support systems with smaller systems, which are more adapted to cope with differing individual needs. Furthermore, this system promotes private initiatives by encouraging a spirit of private entrepreneurship. The sectors make use of all services and organizations already existing and are supported by the provincial social welfare office (advice, information material, contribution towards staff and operational costs, etc.). The sectors employ trained professional staff and deliver different kinds of social services, such as family-help, home-nursing, neighbourhood help, help for the aged, visiting services, job creation, help for and supervision of self-help groups, etc.

Up to now the experiences show some very important advantages. The efficiency of the social welfare system has increased, because its structure became more apparent to the clients and because the comprehensive delivery of social services in a decentralized manner helped the administration to discover heretofore unrecognized needs. The cooperation of local communities within the social area sectors solved their financial problems by expanding the self-help groups. Last but not least, this system, too, decreases considerably the trend to push certain groups into institutional care.

Problems and Perspectives of a New Decentralized
Social Policy: The Case of Salzburg

The division of responsibilities between state, provinces and local communities stemming from the Austrian constitution also leads naturally to differing concepts of social policy on the provincial and local levels. However, differences arise not only from varying local institutional facilities for service provision but also with regard to demands. The pressures on the politicians and administrations exerted by the people interested in welfare services differ considerably from region to region. This is especially true for the committed advocacy needed for organizing the clients' interests.

This is one of the reasons for the choice of Salzburg for this case study. Need of social benefits as the only selection criterion for a case study would make Salzburg just about the worst possible subject. Salzburg has a much lower unemployment rate (2.1 per cent in 1985) than the whole of Austria, because of its very special economic structure: business is dominated by small and medium-sized enterprises and Salzburg is a centre of tourism based on the offer of 'high culture' available throughout the year (i. e. the different festivals) and almost completely independent of economic developments. A price level far higher than the national average (very clearly seen in housing, for instance) is compensated by higher than national average incomes and by lower than national average unemployment.

And yet, Salzburg is characterized by a very committed grass-roots level social policy. First initiatives for a semi-advocatory social policy came from Salzburg University, linked with important, though scarce, social initiatives. Public policy has reacted to this situation in two different ways: by a certain change in traditional policy-making, and by establishing new counselling institutions with the representatives of the traditional sector and the new initiatives.

Salzburg is therefore a very good example for a case study because the networking of the traditional sector and innovative social initiatives is a promising strategy for changes in the welfare mix.

An advisory body initiated by the province's governor and under his formal chairmanship was set up as early as 1978 under the title 'Salzburg Commission' and was used informally for questions considered to be decisive for further provincial development. Special sub-groups of that commission were particularly active in recent years in questions of social security and psycho-social care. A working group on 'new problems in connection with marginal groups' was established in 1981; after a first discussion about concepts, this group moved to work in model projects. We can therefore already see a direct support for innovative social projects.

In the town of Salzburg social conflicts became stronger from about 1982 on, mainly due to the increased pressure of demand in line with economic developments and the growth of citizens' initiatives: these became the third largest potical group within Salzburg's city council. The increasing conflicts in the social sector have led to consequences in the traditional public assistance system. The Federation of Social Projects has been given the right to represent individual clients of public assistance. Bearing in mind the understanding of public assistance as individual financial aid, this can be seen as a first step towards a change or collective help. The consequences are already evident in the amendment to the Salzburg Public Assistance Act (1986); it is now possible to use means of public assistance not only for individual help, but also for direct project support. However, project support suffers at the moment from a very limited allocation of funds (AS 500,000 was budgeted for this purpose in 1986).

Social partnership on the local and provincial levels has originally reacted in about the same manner as on the national level: slower, sometimes even not at all, but there have been some modifications in attitudes in the meantime. The provincial Chamber of Commerce and the provincial Chamber of Labour have increased their commitment to the establishment of a secondary labour market since 1985; the chamber of labour even indicated the possibility of direct financial support for employment initiatives. The provincial Trade Union Federation, however, is still clearly opposed to such initiatives.

This is the framework within which unconventional social projects in Salzburg have to work. Starting in 1979 as mere social projects with implications on employment policies, they have moved from 1982 onwards into unconventional training programmes with a focus on unemployed youth. The project has been incorporated in a Federation for Work for the Unemployed in 1982, limiting its activities not only to immediate objectives, but also trying to influence policy formulation in the traditional social sector.

The paradigmatic case in point is 'Treffpunkt' (Meeting Place), the oldest initiative in Salzburg. 'Treffpunkt' runs a social advisory centre and housing projects for formerly homeless people. The project mainly offers work on a low qualification level in order to contribute to the reintegration of clients. 'Treffpunkt's' advisory centre tries to place clients in the traditional labour market or official vocational training programmes, but also guarantees the opportunity to return to the project in case of failure. The annual average for 1985 shows that the project has been run by two full-time and one part-time staff members and by voluntary helpers. Altogether twelve full-time jobs and work by the hour for about ten people have been provided by the project. 'Treffpunkt' is financed by its own income and by public support. After an initial rather controversial discussion in the city council, the town has agreed to provide facilities for a symbolic rent; 50 per cent of the wage costs of the staff are covered in equal parts by the Federal Ministry for Social Administration and by the province. The costs for running the project (care, accounting, coordination) are covered completely by the ministry.

A working group specifically concerned with women originated from this initiative in 1984; the group considers gender-specific aspects to be especially disadvantageous in this field of social deprivation.

Most of the employment and social initiatives in Salzburg (five employment initiatives and six training initiatives, two being run be religious institutions) founded in 1982 the Federation for Work for the Unemployed as an umbrella organization. Those unconventional employment and training initiatives have only limited range in employment policy as far as quantity is concerned. However, their effects are underestimated when only considering their quantitative impact upon the traditional social sector. The effect of unconventional employment and social initiatives on the traditional sector could be shown by the way in which they influenced cooperation between the traditional actors of social policy. Individual projects have established advisory councils and have integrated the administrations offering support to initiatives into their advisory councils. That simplifies the sometimes very demanding individual negotiations with the different public institutions and has again affected the views of the traditional actors. However, the sector of unconventional employment projects seems particularly suitable as a model for traditional social policy with regard to the networking of missing jobs and social needs. These models should also enable new forms of work organization, i. e extensive self-administration. The networking between the traditional and the autonomous sector is sometimes criticized by members of the autonomous sector particularly the danger of becoming dependent. The projects' autonomy is limited by the dependency on public financing and by the supervision connected with this. Furthermore, necessary share of self-financing demands economic actions that run time and time again counter to the social and socio-political intentions of the initiatives.

Moreover, the problem of new inequalities is becoming acute. The domination of major projects, in particular that of 'Treffpunkt', is often discussed in the federation. The younger projects see themselves therefore at a disadvantage in competing for comparatively limited public funds. And this discussion has undoubtedly limited the persuasive powers of the federation.

Conclusions and Further Prospects

There still exists broad consensus between the social policy actors on the Austrian central level in the following matters:
Nobody questions welfare state support benefits seriously as far as quantity i concerned; there is also agreement on the future efficiency of the system.

This general agreement relies upon the assessment of future developments and that is based on an easing of the labour market situation and on demo graphic factors. The traditional instruments of social policy are assessed a quite sufficient, as long as minor reforms provide quantitative relief and/c qualitative required adjustment to services. The reform of the pension syste is seen as an example for quantitative relief, reducing total pension expenc tures with a simultaneous redistribution between the different pension-receivir groups. In the last year there have been some indicators for a deteriorating situation in specific issues of social policy due to economic development: the reform of the nationalized industries, where depoliticization is leading to the dismissal of about a quarter of the work force within the next three years, is an important step in this direction. Nevertheless, there is little Austrian support for offensive neo-conservative strategies in socio-political matters. However, individual elements of such strategies do find support. The state's contributions to the pension and health insurance schemes are, according to this point of view, not so much a measure of redistribution than an intimation of that 'deficit' which shows the limitations of the welfare state; social policy has to provide the reduction of this deficit. First ruptures in social partnership's consensus are visible in this respect, for some of the workers' representatives are in favour of redistribution effects.

In any case, there seems to be no disagreement over the comprehensive measures initiated by the Federal Ministry for Social Administration in order to combat youth and long-term unemployment and secure pensions.

The public official actors neglect to a large extent the problems of marginal social groups and newly emerging social and employment initiatives in this sector. Initiatives in this sector are started by either the labour market administration (Federal Ministry for Social Administration) or by traditional charity organizations. The social partners try to hinder both the development of innovative social projects and the ministry's initiatives in this field. The social partners' concurrent assessment of alternative projects (even though they use quite different arguments) is rather remarkable and has an important impact upon the policy vis-à-vis the innovative social projects:

- The employers argue against the potentially distorted competition due to the solid support for social and employment initiatives and self-administered enterprises;
- the workers' representatives argue against insufficient social protection which could give this sector a kind of forerunner function in the reduction of guaranteed social benefits and labour rights assured by collective bargaining agreements;
- individual trade unions use also a very traditionalist argument: entrepreneurial activities;
- and the alternative and self-administered sector belongs to this group – are not the trade unions' business.

After World War II the social partners did in fact comprise all social interest groups (capital, labour, agriculture); they had, therefore, a national claim and their extensive influence on economic and social policy decision-making was undisputed. The concurring interests of the groups represented by social partnership as well as the emergence of new groups outside the social partnership framework have now weakened social partnership's claim to represent society as a whole, so political action has shifted towards the political level. The groups outside the social partnership system are only very insufficiently taken into consideration by the system, but their political relevance seems to be increasing.

The Austrian constitution attributes an important role in social policy to provinces and local communities, and they react very differently to the new challenges. Also the interplay between the political traditions and newly arising social initiatives becomes most apparent on the regional and local level.

Public assistance, the traditional social policy task of provinces and local communities, is based on nine differing social assistance laws (one in each province). These social assistance laws have been drawn up in the mid 1970s, after the state waived the right to pass a general framework law for public assistance. Therefore, regulations differ somewhat in the individual provinces, which also means differing standard rates for financial support in the individual provinces. Provincial public assistance offers help to cover one's livelihood, help in case of special problems, and personal social services. The granting of public assistance is related to the client's opportunity to find a job. Verifying a person's willingness and capability to work becomes more and more problematic in times of a strained labour market. This leads to a 'shuttling' of public assistance clients between labour office and social welfare office (see also the diagram mentioned in the introduction). Furthermore, employment initiatives such as the 'Project 8000' could be misused and lead to forced labour: the client's refusal of a job can lead to the cut of public assistance.

Repeated attempts of economizing are being made in the present crisis situation, which concerns above all the ideas of the welfare state. These include, of course, also the discussion about the standard rate of public assistance. An increase in unemployment severely strains the public assistance's capacity for problem solving, both in regard to quantity and quality. Long-term unemployed people in financial difficulties are referred to the social welfare office and form a clientele for which social welfare offices were not originally intended (long-term unemployed, one-parent families and unemployed youth 'joining' the traditional clientele of the aged, homeless people and large poor families). It is likely that these budgets will soon be too small to cover demands. The preparedness to increase these social budgets seems, however, to decrease rather than increase. Personal social services (home-help, meals-on-wheels, home-nursing, etc.) are increasingly provided on a cost-sharing basis. A greater orientation towards the financial capacity of public assistance recipients will have to be made in the future.

The Austrian development of an 'autonomous' sector is rather inconsistent, although this sector pretends to be part of an answer in the problems mentioned above.

'Pure' enterprise in the legal form of self-managed enterprises seems to have a rather limited potential, but has not yet realized that potential fully. Self-managed enterprises account for about 1,000 jobs in Austria; the more pertinent projects have started in situations that have made specific support possible for labour market reasons (i. e. insolvent companies in problem regions). Neither employment initiatives nor social projects have yet realized their full potential. They do, however, show some efficiency in social service delivery and in labour market-oriented care for specific problem groups.

Some objections are that they support the stigmatization of marginal groups and create new segmentations within these groups. The trade unions in particular believe that this sector is being abused as a forerunner of more conservative concepts of social policy. Such an argument neglects, however, that the alternative sector has now acquired its own bargaining capacity and that this sector is very capable of making demands autonomously and in succeeding with these demands. A model which assigns to the alternative sector only the function of alliance in traditional class conflicts misses the societal realities of today: The new social and employment projects do contribute to the existing welfare system.

It cannot be ignored that social partnership in the past has led to astoundingly good and lasting services, notwithstanding the always pessimistic forecasts of social and economic scientists. And this causes the authors to be particularly careful with the following matters: the development of the economy and the labour market; the internal and the external capability for social partnership integration; the strength of existing support networks in case social partnership should be weakened.

All expert interviews with representatives from social partnership institutions have been optimistic with regard to future economic developments. However, these interviews have been made after the drop of oil prices (end of 1985/early 1986), but (with one exception) prior to the Chernobyl disaster, and at this time there was again optimism about a return to the post-war path of growth with the help of cheap energy. One can expect greater conflicts in the future due to ecological and economic problems, as well as to the increasing international conflicts. Therefore, some scepticism is legitimate regarding the optimistic assessment made by the social partners.

Social partnership's integrational capacity has been considerable in the past and there is no reason to be less optimistic about future developments for the traditional social partners. It is therefore highly unlikely that the present manifestations of crisis will lead to the dissolution of social partnership. It will undoubtedly be able to initiate adjustments to the social security system as long as the adjustments have the support of the groups represented in social partnership (e. g. the pension system). However, it must be emphasized that social partnership has always tended to represent a perspective for the whole of society and this is in danger of being lost because of the tendency to exclude marginal groups from social partnership care.

Social partnership seems to have problems in dealing with new movements. This is the experience of the ecology movement as well as that of the alternative employment and social projects (which the social partners consider to be qualitatively unimportant on the one hand, but, on the other hand, important enough to jeopardize social achievements). There is therefore one decisive question with regard to the future: How will social partnership represent the interests of the unemployed if the hopes for a new economic upswing do not come true? The authors are not fully convinced that social partnership will be able to introduce societal structural reforms.

They believe that it is highly unlikely that state, provinces, and local communities can cope with all the additional problems, if social partnership should break up. In view of the state's empty coffers, this would most probably lead to an attempted shift of problems from one level to another. The coordination between the many 'public hands' as well as the recipients of social policy measures would be left along the way as a result of such a breakup and its consequences.

Acknowledgements

In addition to her substantial contributions, major parts of the chapter were translated by Brigitte Rauscher.

This chapter includes the 'Case Study – Salzburg' carried out by the Institut für Alltagskultur, Salzburg. In particular the European Centre would like to thank Raimund Gutmann, Heinz Schoibl and Liane Pluntz of this institute for their contribution.

Furthermore the authors would like to thank Georg Ziniel, Chamber of Labour and Fritz Leitner, Office for Social Welfare, Vienna, who assisted this project in an advisory function.

Cash and Care
Different Concepts of Work and Employment and Their Impact on Innovations in the Field of Care

Adalbert Evers, Ilona Ostner, Helmut Wiesenthal

Theoretical Considerations and Framework for Research

Introduction: The Ambiguities of a Shift in the Welfare Mix

Everywhere the crisis of economic performance and employment is stimulating proposals that refer to the supposed virtues of either the market or the state as regulators of social welfare. While discussions, in the Federal Republic of Germany as well as in some other European countries, increasingly stress the importance of informal work for thorough innovations, it is becoming obvious that there is no going back to full employment in terms of the standards and framework conditions of the 1960s. No doubt, innovative answers to the welfare state crisis presuppose an extension of its policy agenda. More and probably better choices appear accessible if and only if

- Besides the 'traditional' regulating forces of the market and the state, the *'informal sector'* with its actual and potential capabilities is taken into account.
- The concept of labour both in analysis and politics becomes extended to the dimensions of the *quality* of (paid) work as well as to the different forms of *unpaid* work.

However, the reference to 'informal' features of economy and social life is ambiguous. Informal economy and unpaid work are mainly seen as a means to reinstall traditional arrangements of the welfare state. We object to the suggestion that the pattern of a new welfare mix ought to develop as a result of quantitative substitutions within the triangle of market, state, and households, simply by adding up traditional elements in another way, e. g. by having 'less state and more family'. Relating possible outcomes of social change to articulated demands, manifest activities and observable trends (such as the differentiation of lifestyles),

197

a new welfare mix comprises qualitative changes on all sides of the welfare triangle including the linkages of wage labour with unpaid work. Therefore one has to study a process of interaction and feedback between different actors and strategies rather than a mere shift of figures concerning time-tables of households or the share of state, market and household in the production of global welfare. A changing welfare mix should only be judged as positive if it activates new resources, enlarges options and creates more possibilities for people's activity and participation.

Thus, concerning the above-mentioned 'informal sector', questions and research should not be restricted to what households as units of production are capable of doing. There is good reason to focus on networks of informal and semi-formal social interaction between households, different forms of collective self-help and public institutions.

Relating to the extension of the concept of labour, we suggest a shift in the welfare mix not only by substituting informal (household) production with goods and services to be bought on the market. Of equal importance is its possible tendency to increase the impact of informal forms of work. The category of 'informal' work stems from sectoral economic analysis focusing exclusively on ('formal') wage labour and institutionalized exchange relations. Since, as is commonly assumed, a reinstallment of full employment is beyond the reach of mid-term policies, 'informal' work loses its character as a mere residual. Instead, it becomes a *distributional* issue and is seen as a possible subject of regulations to restructure opportunities for social integration and participation.

In short one might say that the ongoing shift in the welfare mix has an ambiguous meaning. Whether it is positive or detrimental to welfare depends on politics and decision-making. Therefore, the issue of 'work' is a good example.

A restricted access to wage labour, its widely-spread subordination to principles of flexibility as a means of economizing labour, and the discontinuities of ('formal') employment lead either to an enforced segregation of social groups or might give rise to a revalorization of 'informal' work as a regular feature of our life career. The second alternative could include a relative loss of importance of those social values, which refer to wage labour, its aspects of hierarchy, division of tasks, subordination, and exchange relations. For example, engagement in informal and socially valued work would no longer appear as a 'second best' opportunity, since it becomes generalized over social strata and supported by access to sufficient means of living and social security.

Another instructive example concerning the ambiguities of a shifting welfare mix is the issue of gender. Women especially mistrust every attempt to upgrade the role of the informal economy, mainly constituted by their work and activities in the households. With regards to women's limited access to wage incomes and their being occupied by the burdens of isolated housework and family care, women's movements often insist on measures to overcome this situation through enlarged participation in the formal economy and labour market. The 'incomplete women's integration in the labour market – including a significantly restricted access to wage-depending social security programmes – often leads to poverty that especially strikes single mothers and elderly women. Yet, one might argue that the focus on 'full' labour market participation according to the male employment pattern of past boom periods is probably misleading. It cannot avoid the trap of a double burden for women, since the expectation that culturally deep-rooted patterns of work division by gender in households could be switched off through administrative measures has failed. But the shrinking possibilities for a mid-term realization of an "equal partnership at the working place and at home" should not lead towards making a virtue out of the odds of the traditional gender divisions (for this debate, see also Erler 1985 and Durst/Ostner 1985; regarding the feminist debate on the question of care see Land/Rose 1985). To escape the danger of non-factual reasoning and to take seriously the erratic character of opportunity structures differing according to gender, we envisage further changes in the forms of and motivations for work as a 'job' and an 'informal' activity. *Both of these could be a point of departure for generalizing for both sexes the discontinuous work pattern of women.* This could occur in positive forms if networks of interaction develop which offer equal opportunities for participation in and allocation of personal services.

The Focus of the Study: Different Concepts of Work and Employment and Their Impact on Innovations in the Field of Care

As a field of research encompassing both these issues, the crisis of the welfare state and the future of work, the field of *care (for the elderly)* was chosen. Referring to empirical trends in this field, both on the level of structure and of action, we look to new concepts for the provision of care and their interlinkage with the broad issues of work. Social and political innovations in the field of care affect the different forms of care work (formal/informal, paid/unpaid) and vice versa: traditional notions of work affect the scope of options for innovations in the field of care.

Surely, care is not the most important topic on the agenda of social policy. However, we assume an extraordinary significance in this field regarding the growing strain in the traditional welfare mix and the respective forms of work:
• Given that social and socio-cultural tendencies will continue, demographic changes and unchanged priorities of the political system will result in a dramatic gap between supply and demand of care for the elderly.
Since there are relatively fast developments in the care sector, a good example of the more general topic of the research project would be the growing mismatches between inherited rules and regulations, the changing identities of actors and socio-economic settings.
The field of care is also an outstanding example of linkages between different

kinds of work: e. g. professional work, volunteering, informal cooperation, and self-service.

• Last, but not least, reform of care becomes the subject of a political conflict, not only on the state level but also as an issue on the local agenda.

It is not our aim to contribute to the debate of proposals for an overall reform of care services. Rather we assume that the field of care might serve as an example (i) of current changes of work and (ii) of the need to modernize our concepts of work which can be observed in other fields as well. We direct our attention to processes of reorganization and innovation at the intersection of 'formal' and 'informal' work. Here, within this *'intermediate'* sphere between private households and public institutions, different forms of self-organization arise (not always flourishing, but still spreading), which show similarities in respect to orientations, work attitudes and service aspirations. *An important component of such unconventional, often 'semi-formal' institutions are types of work and activity which – as we try to show – do not fit into the traditional dualistic model of work, which differentiates between a rather uniform type of regulated and paid work or informal and unpaid work.*

Dealing with these phenomena appears to be a challenge to traditional concepts of work in social policy, to which administrations, trade unions, and political parties still seem to cling. In order to make feasible innovations in care services as a central element of a changing welfare mix, it is necessary to take into consideration a greater variety of ways to activate, regulate and acknowledge 'work' as a central resource for the well-being of individuals and for social welfare. But before examining the case study, let us begin with a critique of the main concepts dealing with the problem of reactivating work as a resource for future care and welfare.

Prevailing Concepts and Recent Discourses

As Scharpf (1986) pointed out, in the Federal Republic of Germany a specific setting of items such as tax rate (ranked middle), the rate of state-provided services (low) compared with money transfers (middle), wage differences (middle), and women's labour market participation (low) indicates a widening gap between the need for and the supply of personal services. When political actors refer to the gap between supply and demand for care they usually argue in the context of one of three strategies assumed to be able to activate the resource 'work' and to make fuller use of it in order to match present challenges to the welfare state. Certainly, the term 'strategy' does not denote a consistent set of actions pursued by rational actors. Rather, it refers to processes of decision-making and different 'discourse universa'. Strategies, in the weaker sense, are conceived of as an inter-related stream of arguments sharing the same view of problems and remedies because there is a consensus of basic values. The following para graphs give a critical presentation of the three prevailing strategies of linking the issues of work and welfare, by privileging either the market, the state or the informal social and economic settings.

Privatization: The Market Strategy

Here, the common point of reference is the limits of taxation and bureaucratic efficiency. The actual share of social welfare expenditure in the Gross National Product (GNP) reached its peak level in 1975 (33.7 per cent) and is still seen as a major cause of insufficient conditions for private investment, though the Federal Republic of Germany does better than other Western countries. A second line of arguments focuses on the normative impact of state intervention on the individuals' willingness to take responsibility for themselves.

The debate of market-oriented reforms of welfare institutions is centred around the question of a proper framework for the economy ('Ordnungspolitik'). Options concerning the issue of social services aim at two targets:
• Enhancing the realm of efficient competitive market production.
• Enforcing the individuals' responsibilities and obligations subsidiary to their claims of universalistic rights.
Still, a trend of 'commodification' of social services does not yet fit the German case. With respect to the goal of making a more effective use of scarce resources, liberals and conservatives argue for the privatization of care services according to the same pattern of rationalization that underlies the removal of technical service functions from public hospitals to private firms (e. g. laundries, cleaning services). Since private production might stimulate competition, it is suggested to reduce costs below the level of public services. This might induce a decrease of wage-related contributions to social security funds, releasing the wage bill of firms, while the all-encompassing insurance system could be cut back to a system that provides only a maximum level of services and benefits for persons who are not well off. (Biedenkopf 1984) It is suggested that considerable demand would be 'priced out' of the market and left to self-help.

A critique of this strategy can be built on a variety of arguments. First of all, the market discourse on instrumentalizing self-help and other forms of informal work neglects the issues of employment and transfer income as prerequisites for the proper functioning of households and for individuals' propensity to engage in care and self-help. Insofar as the concept of commodifying personal services implies 'to make a job out of everything', it contributes to the erosion of the normative foundations of informal cooperation and gift relations. Furthermore, market strategies attempt to convert professional demands for more self-determination into the idea of free entrepreneurship. It is assumed that less costly private services would be provided as a result of deregulating measures, i. e. a deepening of the lines of segmentation in the labour market. Employment gains achieved in the United States indicate a causal relationship of lower wage and less social security leading to an increased supply of services. However, significant gains in efficiency do not only require lower wages and a rising share of part-time work. Such a strategy will, in the long run, inevitably damage standards of efficacy and quality since professional values are over-run by effects of dissatisfaction and alienation as a result of the pressure to economize on labour and rely on hierarchical task structures. Last, but not least, the commodification of personal services would contribute unfavourably to the 'emancipation' of women from traditional duties of care. The sphere of social, local and household economy and of non-utilitarian values would shrink, a process which would affect both men and women. The situation of women would worsen, with the majority only being able to choose between the dependent status of unpaid work at home and low paid precarious part-time employment.

Increasing Public Employment: The State-oriented Strategy

Both unions and professional associations deal with the issues of unemployment and shortages in welfare budgets as if they were merely the outcomes of discretionary political decisions which could easily be altered. Actual pitfalls of the welfare state are converted into simple questions of demand for labour which could be matched by extended public demand. Clinging to a concept of full employment in terms of life-long, full-time and well-secured labour, the defensive position of labour unions and social democrats has little impact on actual policies of deregulation in the law of labour relations and industrial action. Still today, unions do not appear capable of developing new visions of work allocation and of a fuller use of human resources, in terms of time, activity and skills, which consciously include the manifold forms of unpaid and informal activities. Moreover, when striving for public employment programmes, they seem to run into further difficulties: The recently adopted criteria for employment programmes such as social usefulness, ecological soundness, or unsatisfied social needs, tend to 'backfire' on the demands for the preservation of existing jobs. A focus on the social quality of work contradicts the plea for jobs.

Concerning the debate on concepts of care, unsatisfied needs are redefined as a lack of professional services and, consequently, are seen as a question of budget priorities, which is thought to be answered by increased taxation (see Bäck 1985). Unions tend to refuse proposals that do not fit to the 'standard employment pattern' (Normalarbeitsverhältnis). Until now, they refrained from the regulation of precarious and part-time labour (for a more detailed discussion, see Wiesenthal 1986). They opposed concepts of self-organized services as well as the critique of the quality of professional services. This neglect resembles the unions' organizational interests. Pointing at an ideal future with equal partnership at home and a 30-hour week for everyone, unions virtually ignore the dilemma women who have an overload of full-time employment and family duties, on the one hand, and a prolonged status quo of unequal partnership in household work, on the other. Denying intermediate forms of social participation above and beyond participation in a full-time job means waiting until men's values have changed so that women face no costs at all when subscribing to the model of 'equal rights' through assimilation.

There is little understanding that even striving for full employment requires, under present conditions, above all "flexible and experimental policies that are open to all sides and thereby encouraging learning processes" (Rothschild 1983: 31). State-addressed concepts which aim at further substitution of informal work by professional labour share the view of market-oriented concepts. These also neglect the normative foundation and important role of those activities and forms of social interaction which are not as directly guided by individual self-interests as are formalized paid work relationships. Since the state-oriented concept is in need of more money to be collected in the formal economy, without offering any opportunity for increased private investment, it appears less realistic than proposals for market-oriented reforms. Neither concept gives any consideration to investing in the economies of the 'informal sector', social self-help and informal care as a major arena, where human resources are either (over)used in an unplanned way and/or not met by adequate public policies.

Making Fuller Use of Informal Work: Different Approaches to Self-help

Proposals presuming a growing importance of self-help proceed from the assumption that significant increases in services provision can no longer be expected on the traditional path of welfare policies, i. e. by an extension of public employment. Thus, political approaches to self-help focus on informal work as a reserve fund of societal 'resources'. Under conditions of a highly differentiated industrial society with its political system being overburdened by competing demands and stagnating funds, self-help appears to be the only field offering an adaptive potential which is not yet exhausted.

Conservative concepts of self-help argue within the logic of *substitution*. Much of the work done by highly paid professionals (e. g. in hospitals, kindergardens, and nursing homes) is supposed to be shifted easily to the "working place of the family" (Blüm 1983: 61). Envisaging increasing needs for services already provided through public institutions, conservative policy planners opposed very early the vision of a high rate of women's labour market participation attained at the price of an enlarged share of public services. Instead, it would be less expensive for the state to give financial allowances to women occupied with care at home (Geißler 1975). In the context of such considerations it even seems to pay off in economic terms when new mothers become entitled to financial subsidies by refraining from formal employment. While measures of this kind aim at the reduction of the supply of female labour, they appear inefficient as soon as they become instrumentalized for a policy disclosing options already achieved, e. g. by neglecting women's problems in gaining access to the labour market. The conservative approach to self-help, which focuses exclusively on the family as the traditional locus of unpaid women's work, is bound to fail wherever the family itself is subject to rapid social change. Instead of opening up options and encouraging them to develop into self-conscious actors, conservative social policies of this kind seem mainly to be using money and entitlements in order to facilitate the fulfilment of old and new tasks and duties by women.

'Alternative' approaches to self-help are not yet part of clear-cut proposals for welfare state reform. Many of them refer to experiences of so-called 'alternative projects' which have arisen since the early 1970s and today appear subject to some kind of institutionalization. The lesson of the past fifteen years is obviously not that social initiatives will emerge when needed as a kind of functional welfare-state relief. The phenomenon of socially exclusive self-organization indicates rather that patterns of cooperative initiatives might emerge in other parts of society, too, where people are sufficiently encouraged. They will thereby become relevant actors instead of the mere objects of unquestioned duties. This question refers to "forms of association and lively traditions on the basis of which the often neglected potential for (self-)help could be activated and directed instead of getting drained up by tutelage and reglementations." (Offe and Heinze 1986; translated by the authors) The 'alternative' approaches are targeted to associational forms that are not yet widely established. But given the social and cultural changes also touching other societal sub-cultures and institutions like the family, an approach which underlines the strategic role of forms of association, community and social relationships might overcome the limits of its 'alternative' sub-cultural specificity. 'Associative' approaches possess three main characteristics:

• They refer to the concept of *optionality* and choice which contradicts the conservative appeal to duties and traditional norms.
• They envisage *collective* and interactive forms of work instead of isolation and compliance with restrictive roles. On the grounds of these two premises,
• The logic of supply is not only or predominantly substitution but *supplementation* of professional as well as lay services already provided, which attempt to change their respective characteristics and interactions in a climate of social innovation. The 'alternative associative' discourse has a developmental perspective since it refers to the 'double crisis of work': it takes into account the lack of opportunities of employment as well as of the change of attitudes to work – in the light of the critique of professionalization, alienation, industrial technology, and environmental deterioration. Related concepts for the development of collective self-help are assumed to fit to the crisis of the welfare state not only in terms of problems but also in terms of resources and motivations. Conceptualizing within this context requires dealing with interaction between existing institutions, reference to adequate motivations, and the issue of gender.

Data already available indicate that the vision of self-sustaining self-help groups lacks any substance. The demand for professional skills, acquaintance with legal regulations, and access to information on unsatisfied needs require some kind of inter-organizational cooperation. Consequently, from the perspective of professional organizations the development of efficient forms of collective self-help (CSH) presupposes some kind of investment, or more clearly: an additional input of wage labour even if no substitutional effect is intended. Whether the need for more personnel as a prerequisite for continuous and efficient service provision serves to legitimize the unions' quest for new jobs or whether it puts a stop to substituting unpaid work for wage labour, depends on the kind of services provided and the degree of autonomy of CSH groups resisting the tendency for substitution. There are also questions of adequate forms of acknowledgement and remuneration, both being a concomitant phenomenon of positive attitudes to engaging in CSH activities. Within the sub-cultural and, in some way, 'opinion-leading' centre, concepts of anti-etatist forms of isolated self-sufficiency lost support; now larger sectors of the 'scene' favour financial assistance by public funds. Current controversies concern conditions of access and the degree of autonomy of allocation.

Reference to Adequate Motivation

Due to its emergence on the margins of the alternative sub-culture, for a long time the discourse on CSH missed a link with the traditions of volunteering as well as with the structure of unsatisfied needs arising in 'ordinary' households. Far from being a road to a utopian society that might emerge out of a network of self-reliant alternative communities, concepts of CSH must tackle the question of how to link fragmented and discontinuous participation in CSH with the remainders of networks based on family, kinship, and neighbourhood relations. Answers can probably be found if the current trend towards flexible lifestyles and the inclination for discontinuous involvement can be grasped by organizational innovations.

The Issue of Gender

We envisage the possibility of an emerging pattern of women's participation that encompasses periods of wage labour (full-time and part-time) and family work which might both be accompanied by a time-consuming participation in CSH activities. Such an attempt obviously promises 'less' than a fulfilment of demands for equal distribution of work and incomes between the sexes. However, the possibility to opt freely for CSH activities meets the demands for social integration and access to the public of many women whose household work is marked by privatism and isolation. At the same time and by the same measures the probability of relieving excessive burdens of personal care duties may increase.

Since the debate on collective forms of freely chosen self-help did not start before this decade, it has not yet reached any convincing proposals for reform. But there is a latent consensus that answers are needed to the question of how to recognize appropriately unpaid work and how to secure it by measures of 'formalization' that allow for the application of "the same criteria of social justice that are claimed valid in the formal sector of the 'labour society'" (Offe 1983: 358; translated by the authors). A successful extension of self-help presupposes 'investments' which cannot simply be financed out of the savings that some promoters of reform wish to obtain by extending self-help. Even if the 'products' of self-help were substitutes, the effect of substitution could not occur simultaneously or within a mid-term time span. In consequence, the 'developmental' self-help strategy cannot work as a simple remedy for public budgets.

Polarization and Intermediation – Trends of the Welfare Mix in the Field of Care

During the process of modernization, private responsibility for care became a problematic feature in families, especially for women facing the duty of caring for elderly parents or for elderly persons having to care for themselves. Full employment, labour market participation of women, urbanization, and the increasing spatial mobility not only contributed to changes of households' time budgets but also to the normative horizon within which moral duties are weighed in the light of given opportunities. While there was a weakening of family care and of relations of mutual help in neighbourhoods, the opportunities for participation of the elderly in everyday life also vanished. As a consequence of this development,

• Family care lost its character as something 'normal'. While the involvement in relationships of care became, in some way, a matter of chance, family care in an increasing number of cases turned out to be a burdensome duty which some socially unfit persons had to perform.

• The same factors of modernization explain a constant decline of private care 'going public', i. e. (mostly) women's engagement in voluntary services. Since the religious foundations of motives, as well as traditional notions of citizenship duties, eroded, voluntary organizations face stagnation or even regression. Formerly linking lay and professional care, the development of charity organizations led to increased formalization and professionalization. They became semi-state organizations that provide a large part of public welfare (see Bauer 1985). With further individualization, clients now depend on hierarchical large-scale systems without any opportunity for participation in decision-making.

• These developments are accompanied by a shift of expectations concerning

206

assumed responsibilities. With the loss of adequate opportunities for family care, taking care of elderly people became a public issue. The history of the welfare state and industrial culture might therefore be written as a history of a simultaneous individualization/socialization of tasks and duties. Processes which free the individual from duties with respect to the family, community and collectivity reinforced as a consequence processes of a public institutionalization and professionalization of tasks and duties such as education, care, etc. This global historical trend cannot be reversed by simply substituting professional services through family care. While 90 per cent of all care needed is provided by families or within kinship and neighbourhood networks, the obvious polarization of care, performed either in public large-scale institutions or in private isolated households and through individual responsibility calls for an innovative refoundation of *intermediary* forms according to existing needs and motivations. 'Intermediary' means:

a) institutions bridging the wide gap between large-scale public and small-scale private institutions of care;

b) forms of interaction between the total anonymity of public institutions and the total intimacy and privacy of care in a family;

c) the strengthening of motivations for caring between professional interests and personal care giving new forms of visibility, acknowledgement and remuneration to solidaristic and community-oriented mutual aid and self-help activities.

Current innovations in the field of care such as forms of outdoor care, district services, home-help seeking to bring services nearer to people, might serve as a local point of analysis, and probably as elements of an intermediary structure of organizations in a future system of care.

With respect to the Federal Republic of Germany, the system of local *community care centres* (Sozialstationen) being built up in most of the cities during the 1970s appear as useful examples. Community care centres *(CCC)* are installed by public decision and mainly managed by voluntary organizations subsidized in part from local public funds; they organize and coordinate social and medical care for clients staying at home, in cases of both chronic and temporary sickness, through various forms of assistance in housekeeping, and by helping family members in caring. The elderly receive the largest share of care given through these centres, which operate on a district level (usually a district comprises about 40,000 inhabitants). To meet needs of a more social, communicative and animating nature is nearly impossible as long as institutions fail to develop an encouraging structure for collective self-help that might overcome the deficiency of the traditional volunteering system. Within the same field of tasks there exist some *autonomous intiatives* of professional care as well as of *collective self-help*. However, further development of such types of organizations between public state-help and informal self-help depends on changes which are difficult to realise. First, in political decision-making, strategies which tend to rely nearly exclusively on the market or the public professional services have not yet been recognized as insufficient. Second, the change of motivations to engage in voluntary service and CSH is still waiting for public acknowledgement and encouragement in terms of developmental strategies. Third, such initiatives and activities do not fit into the traditional concepts of work and employment.

Still, most politicians and administrators cling to a *rather traditional concept of work, which is deeply linked to the above-mentioned process of polarization* in the field of care activities. The more care work became a public task, the more the jobs to do there became professional jobs and part of the labour market. On the other hand, the more community networks weakened, the more family care became a private issue, a part of what Ivan Illich called "shadow work", to be performed either in the name of clear-cut female duties or out of compassion. While care as a duty seemed to have no link with work, money and social security, care as a professional job for individual clients seemed to have nothing to do with family networks, the spirit of solidarity or personal commitment.

Today intermediate attempts, organizations and groups, however, are based on a set of motives which seem to question the traditional strict separation of formal and informal work:

• In helping to extend our notion of work towards household (care) activities, they question that there is a clear-cut line separating marketed jobs and 'other activities'; private duties become a public issue.

• In expressing new forms of meeting demands, which are not strictly private they extend the question of regulating and organizing work as a social activity beyond the limits of paid work.

• In claiming public help, infrastructure and response they question a traditional arrangement, where care activities are either professional paid work or performed for moral reasons and as an obvious duty.

Consequently, the intermediate forms of care giving represent new types of organizing work as a resource, without a model, which knows only marketed jobs or private duties. The challenge of how to make fuller and better use of human resources questions thereby the equivalence of work and employment as well as the simple idea of recreating the very cheap and traditional models of duty, obligation and commitment.

Motivations Beyond Paid Work and Charity

The current differentiation of conditions of labour and lifestyles, the emerging diversity of working time and shifting involvement into different spheres of interest – these factors amount to the challenge of developing a modernized concept of incentives, intermediation and interaction between the different areas of care giving, the different sorts of care givers and their different motivations for engaging in care activities. Innovations targeted towards non-professional and, until today, mostly informal contributions, appear promising insofar as they refer to

• The interest of (older) persons outside employment who are not in need of a wage income.
• The probable emergence of a pattern of discontinuous work careers, in the course of which emphasis is shifting between wage labour and social activities.
• The prospect of further reductions of regular working time, probably combined with a postponed age of retirement.

Looking to such resources, potentials and groups means to take into account a wide diversity of motivational patterns of engagement. Especially with respect to women's needs and interests and to the problems of unequal opportunities of female employment in this area, the consequences of comprehensive strategies trying to activate these resources are hard to oversee. However, they offer many more opportunities for out-family participation than would be accessible under conditions of a highly economized (and for some reasons very improbable) extension of professional services. The more open the organization of recruitment and the allocation of non-professional care work would become when considering the diversity of motives to participate, the more it would attract persons irrespective of gender.

Considerations on changes in motivations for care within the present context remain tentative, since surveys on value orientations of persons engaged in care relationships are not available. Furthermore, the issue is strongly linked with general phenomena such as a change of social values and an increasing heterogeneity of orientations. They lead to an erosion of traditional norms and values of duty and charity. Also clients often appreciate being cared for by persons who are not part of the family. In the process of individualization, the distance underlying the interaction of professionals and clients is not always thought to be negative. Instead, intimacy and nearness of family members sometimes becomes undesirable. On the other hand, isolation, lack of social support networks and personal help in case of need seem to be among the most articulated problems of people when it comes to living conditions and critiques of today's social policies. As far as these factors indicate an emancipation from community ties and kinship relations, as well as the need for direct and personal social exchange and support between private obligations and anonymous public services, they tend to strengthen the demand for intermediary forms of care, giving access both to individuality, options and personal exchange – to a kind of involvement and obligation in care activities limited by the contemporary notion of individuality.

Today the set of motivations underlying a positive attitude towards care cannot be reduced to single values of pivotal importance. We assume, in the absence of adequate survey data, the presence of a wide variety of values, including traditional values of duty and obedience as well as egoistic and hedonistic patterns (see Ferrand-Bechmann 1986). Within a broad mainstream of value orientations, e. g. utilitarian calculations giving preference to public homes for the care of one's own parents, this in no way contradicts the preparedness to engage in care oneself if circumstances allow for limited involvement.

We suggest that at least four characteristics can be pointed out to indicate direc
tions for further examination. Their specific features might be traced out by com
parison with those motivational patterns which are predominant either in the
sphere of jobs or private duties in household and families.

• *Cooperation* with other persons taking care and *optionality* with regard to tasks
time, co-workers, and clients are appreciated. Part of this pattern is the quest fo
freedom of choice to start and to finish (or to interrupt) a period of engagemen
according to one's own plan of life.

• Unlike the altruistic brand of traditional motivations and in contrast to a patterr
of 'gift relations' of love and help as well as to patterns of reciprocal relations c
private or community-based mutual aid, there are diffuse but increasing expecta
tions of public *acknowledgement*, *reward* or even *remuneration*. In case benefit:
are expected, they are by no means valued as a kind of wage equivalent, but a:
a means for socially securing and backing one's own efforts. A monetary re
muneration itself serves as acknowledgement of the labourious aspects of worl
as well as of one's subordination to a task structure that inevitably requires com
promises and inconveniences.

• Similar to the quest for collective production instead of isolated private care i
the need for *autonomy* of work. Its articulation opposes hierarchical decisior
making in the realm of public services. However, the attitude towards autonom
does not claim dominance over clients. It concerns the definition of tasks, the or
ganization and division of work, and the distribution of remunerations. Accordin
to holistic concepts of needs, the quest for autonomy expresses the intention t
organize care with respect to personality, communication, and social integratior

• Taken together, the factors mentioned above amount to a certain degree c
flexibility, understood in a positive sense of adaptability, and in a negative sens
of indefiniteness; in view of the care relationships with clients, the need arises fc
an organized framework ensuring continuity and some kind of overall respons

TYPE OF WORK	LOCUS OF PRODUCTION		
	PUBLIC		PRIVATE
Wage Labour	Professionals in the Public Service	Care-taking Entrepreneurs	Privately Paid Professionals
		Collective Autonomous & Remunerated Caring	Mutual Help
Solidarity, Charity or Duty	Volunteers in Charity Organizations	Publicly Acknowledged Self-help	Women in Families

bility; in view of persons engaged in care activities, the problem of delimitation against precarious low-wage jobs arises.

Still, far from suggesting a well-founded concept of reform, we wish to make clear that any promising way of developing and making a fuller use of human resources by bridging the polarization of stagnating public care on the one hand, and overburdened family care, on the other, must acknowledge the patterns of present motivations sketched above. Especially as far as women are concerned, one has to reject traditional expectations of institutional actors with respect to volunteering that women "have to give up personal motives for career and self-development in favour of charity. This expectation and assumption is assumed to justify the limited degree of participation." (Backes 1985: 391 f.; translated by the authors) Recognizing the mixed motive-patterns for CSH one has to accept that the organization of intermediary forms of care is bound to a notion of work with strong ties to optionality and choice (instead of duties) as well as to feelings of social responsibility and to the expectation of rewards for non-contractual work. Therefore developmental strategies in the field of care will have to overcome a simple dualistic notion of work where motivation comes either through money or through a certain notion of duty and common sense. Creating incentives for caring calls for complex strategies with a whole range of 'mixed' emotions, needs and aspirations of those people they want to address. This simple 3 x 3 matrix might illustrate how we conceive the intermediary sphere located at the intersection of the two dimensions 'locus of production' and 'type of work'.

Aims and Questions of Research

Our *first* aim of research is therefore to look for *innovative manifestations of care activities*. Claiming that there are obvious limits to a further growth of market-allocated or state-provided social services, we will find that the traditional reality of institutions and work in the field of care, juxtaposing professional care institutions and lay contributions and/or combining traditional forms of professionalism and volunteering is already questioned. A closer look will be given to such efforts and experiences raising such issues as developing, backing up, improving and socially securing the opportunities of persons who care.

The *second* aim is to *analyze adaptations of ideology and practice* of the main social actors involved, especially *with respect to the traditional (dualistic) concept of work, limiting innovation in care activities*. As a consequence, we look for policies that give room for new types of work in the field of care in terms of new chances for an active and productive social participation, visible through the emergence of 'intermediary' organizations. We try to analyze political and organizational decisions recently made concerning the extension of ambulatory, home care and self-help, or linking innovative programmes for the creation of work, income, training and employment with the field of care. We will find that traditional concepts of work create severe limits in search for a fuller and better use of resources for care.

The case study refers to recent developments in two West German cities which are both marked by a relatively well-developed climate of social innovation and lively conflicts, also with respect to one or both of our central topics: care for the elderly and work/employment. Local social innovations concerning social services and social policy (in West Berlin) and local employment (in Hamburg) have been discussed also on a national level. Whereas social democrats relate to a Hamburgian model of an innovative local employment policy (related to the field of social services) the more progressive elements of the conservative christian democrats prefer to refer to social policy innovations in Berlin (which have their own specific reference to the issue of work/employment).

However, this is neither theoretical nor a departure from comprehensive empirical research. We are restricted to exploration and compilation, mainly accomplished through secondary analysis of studies and data already available. In addition, information and insights were collected through interviews with key persons in the social administration, in charity organizations and trade unions, as well as with representatives of organizations providing care or creating new initiatives for activity, work and employment linked to the field of social care services.

Two Explorative Case Studies

The cities we chose for the investigation of innovation, West Berlin and Hamburg, have prominent research status because, as semi-autonomous states ('Länder'), they have more opportunities for innovation than cities (such as Munich or Cologne) which are subject to the regulations of the federal government.

Both cities have some features in common that make it possible, to a limited degree, to compare their governments' political decisions. They have nearly the same number of inhabitants (Berlin: 1.85 million, Hamburg: 1.6 million). In both cases the average number of persons per household is very low (Berlin 1.8, Hamburg 2.1, FRG 2.4). In Berlin, more than half of all households consist of only one person (exactly 52.4 per cent, in Hamburg 40.6 per cent, FRG 31.3 per cent). The same applies to the portion of older people. Persons of 60 years and older make up 24.8 per cent of the total population in Berlin and 23.6 per cent in Hamburg (FRG 20 per cent). In both cities, governments strive for the modernization of their economic structure, compete for investors and are eager to maintain local conditions of investment, be it by increased expenditure for social services, or by proposals to raise local taxes instead of cutting budgets. They also initiated, from different angles of political orientation, innovative policies in the field of social services and especially care services. As far as 'work' is concerned, the accent in Berlin (governed by christian democrats) is on the endorsement of self-help initiatives, whereas in Hamburg (governed by social democrats), the concentration is on publicly financed employment programmes.

Looking to the interlinkages between a specific notion of the problems of work and employment on the one hand and the future of (care) services on the other, we dealt in both cities with ongoing initiatives and innovations concerning employment, innovative social projects and services through literature, documents, collected data and about twenty major interviews in each city. We took up the reality of a broad spectrum of activities and work, ranging from private and individual self-help to professional care, trying to collect and evaluate those areas in which new attempts towards local employment and encouraging other forms of work meet with questions of the future development of care services.

Focusing on the repercussions of the conservative and social democratic concepts of work on the systems of care, we did not study the political concepts of a whole range of other actors (the 'alternative' scene, the Green Party, etc.). By questioning the Hamburgian model concentrating on the 'work as employment' option, as well as the Berlin model with its 'strengthening self-help' option, we are referring to local government policy. Other social actors are quoted when they raise sharp criticism.

The Case of Hamburg: Innovations Within the Traditional Concept of Work as Employment

Hamburg politics are run by the social democrats, who occupy since 1982 a comfortable majority of seats in parliament. The city's government strives for economic modernization, at the same time securing a consensus with the trade unions as the guardians of traditional employment structures. But the coexistence of a certain liberal will for allowing experiments, along with some administrative repercussions of left social democratic thinking, more favourable to the fairly widespread scene of initiatives and projects, has brought about some remarkable social innovations in Hamburg, as well.

Elements of Innovation

To get an overview of the areas and elements of innovations concerning the crossroads of both work and employment and social services and care, we take a closer look at locally-backed employment programmes; the network of newly organized Community Care Centres (CCC); the so-called 'alternative sector', and the organization of self-help.

Employment Provision Through a 'Second Labour Market'

Hamburg's administration of social affairs won considerable attention with its concept of using funds from the Federal Institute of Labour (Bundesanstalt für Arbeit, BfA), and for measures aiming at increasing employment (Arbeitsbeschaffungsmaßnahmen, ABM). These measures were directed to cover innovative social tasks and to provide opportunities for social reintegration on a larger scale than that of other West German cities.

The BfA gives regularly 80 per cent of the labour costs to private or public institutions ready to offer an additional working place which does not replace existing ones. The funding of such a working place is limited in time (mostly one year); previously, one hoped that the employer would keep the ABM worker afterwards with a regular employment contract, something which has become increasingly difficult with rising unemployment. In 1985, the BfA spent about 1.6 billion DM and it was possible to create about 70,000 ABM working places in the Federal Republic of Germany as a whole.

The Hamburgian Experiment of a 'Second Labour Market' which used the BfA funding, began in 1983 with a total of 123 million DM including 40.5 million spent by the Senate of Hamburg. It was possible to employ about 3,500 persons per year (some employments limited for a year, others to be prolonged to two years); this meant four times as many people working and living on ABM than in past years; in 1985 the whole programme already covered a total sum of 177 million DM. Thus, every fourth unemployed person trying to get back to work received such a time-limited ABM job. A major goal of the programme is the integration of *young people* who are actually living on social welfare with no chance of getting a job or acquiring occupational skills. For this purpose the Hamburgian 'Work and Learn Corporation Ltd' (the most important of these projects) also received additional money from the local employment fund of the European Economic Community; there are between 500–700 people engaged in such forms of training and protected work for problem groups.

Bringing together all the individual ABM subsidies in one programme allowed *the allocation of work and employment to fields where new social and ecological tasks have become visible*: in the field of social services, energy (saving) programmes, slum clearing, etc. Nearly 37 per cent of the sponsored ABM jobs are situated in the field of improvement of the urban infrastructure; about 20 per cent are in the sector of administration and organization (mostly public), 37 per cent are situated in different sectors of services (local services, health, education, youth programmes). However, it has to be mentioned that ABM jobs are legally restricted to additional tasks not yet fulfilled. Furthermore, Senate and trade unions agreed not to end up with a programme unintentionally helping to substitute for regular jobs in the private or public area. This would be totally contrary to the basic idea of a programme which is – as far as the money from the BfA is concerned – not financed by taxes but by the national fund of the unemployment insurance.

For unemployed people, working in an ABM programme is equal to normal contracted work as far as social rights and security is concerned. After the period of ABM work people who do not find a regular job are entitled to unemployment benefits rather than having to resort to social welfare.

Reorganizing Social Services: Community Care Centres

Concurrently with the search for local policies to combat unemployment, Hamburg's social administration undertook a major reform initiative for domiciliary care: building up a network of *'Sozialstationen'* (Community Care Centres, CCC). This appears less remarkable because here, unlike its labour market-oriented initiatives, the Senate (as in Berlin) followed a trend which had developed in most of the bigger cities in the Federal Republic of Germany since the mid 1970s. There have been several private predecessors of the state-created CCCs; a programme for their development began in 1979. Before that time it was the churches which offered different forms of ambulant care, partly by professionals, and partly by volunteers; also the five different voluntary organizations of home care for the sick and the elderly and sometimes the district administration of the city of Hamburg offered certain services. The goals for developing a formal network of 40 CCCs covering all districts of Hamburg with each being responsible for an area of about 40,000 inhabitants, were set out in an initial document. It states that the further development of hospitals foresees lowering the number of patients and their stay in hospital, while family- and neighbourhood-based lay care still seems important, but is limited to expanded professional home care.

Every CCC has a basic staff of professionals, usually 20 people, most of them on a part-time basis (nurses, personnel for domiciliary care and housekeeping); two full-time workers are anticipated who are not paid because they do their civil service in the CCC. The establishment of 22 CCCs is planned for the end of 1986. Financial costs borne by the Senate are relatively low and are hoped to be offset by shrinking demands for hospital beds and homes for the elderly. The majority of refunding for the personnel costs is arranged through the reimbursement of the performances of the CCC, be it by the clients or their relatives, their insurance or the social welfare institution.

As an evaluation of the first three CCCs in 1980 showed, nearly 90 per cent of the cases the CCCs dealt with shortened hospital stays or avoided hospital and/or home for the elderly stays.

To the surprise of planners and administrators most of the CCCs installed expanded much faster than original plans for basic staff and hours of services had foreseen. Some of the CCCs also took over volunteers who had worked in the preceding institution, run by the church. But in contrast to the civil service staff regularly provided for in the organizational plans, no special funds or programmes are planned for developing further volunteering.

Collective Self-organization: The 'Alternative Sector'

A further element, significant for a 'changing reality of work' is the so-called *'alternative sector'*, even if it may be arbitrary to draw a sharp line between 'normality' and alternative 'deviance'. Social, economic and cultural activities or projects labelled as 'alternative' might be characterized by the relevance of social goals instead of mere profit orientation, by the striving for democratic and egalitarian ways of cooperating, which attempt to avoid too much specialization. Alternative projects prefer collective ownership and less anonymous forms of relationships with consumers and clients.

A local study using these topics as criteria for description concluded that in Hamburg there are about 4,000 – 5,000 people working in this 'alternative sector'. But only one-fourth of them receive a salary which is sufficient to live on. The alternative sector covers a broad field of economic, social and cultural activities (private services, women's projects, housing, special consumer goods, etc.); 30 per cent of the activities are production of goods; about 70 per cent of the projects comprise all types of services, but up to now, only a very small fraction has been care work.

We found three groups called 'Autonomous Care', or 'We care for you at home'. These groups concretized the 'alternative principles' mentioned above by

● Working with much more flexible time arrangements than the official institutions.

● Trying to underline the communicative side of 'home care' aiming towards more than just privatization of the former hospital care.

● Trying to be less specialized, thereby sparing the client from being addressed by different specialists.

They are refunded either by (i) the clients themselves, (ii) their social insurance or (iii) the local bureau for social welfare (depending on the kind of service and the income of the respective client). The initiatives, mostly founded by professionals who became disillusioned by the routines in the established institutions, are neither foreseen in the local plans for the development of public care services nor have a clear idea themselves about how to be integrated into any concept for a complex local care system. As long as they are acknowledged and refunded by the institutions of social security and welfare, they have the chance to develop their concept of care quite 'autonomously'.

Since 1984 representatives of the alternative project scene and the Netzwerk (Network) have dealt with representatives of the Senate and the Hamburg administration for installing a self-administered fund of about 10 million DM/year to subsidize projects. The chance to take a first step came in July 1985: since the social fund of the European Economic Community took over 50 per cent of the costs for the well developed and diversified 'Autonomous Youth Work and Education Centres' (part of the 'Work and Learn Corporation Ltd' already mentioned), the local Department of Work, Youth and Social Affairs (BAJS) spent 1 million DM to present a *'Programme for the Development of Local Employment Initiatives'* comprising

- The institutionalization of a fund for subsidizing projects which attempt to be self-sustained (while creating stable working places and becoming competitive on the market).
- A fund giving additional money for so-called 'social-economic projects' which are suspected to take much longer until they reach a state of self-sustaining growth (because they work in social fields such as services and education).
- A special fund for the field of housing.
- A full professional counselling service for projects.

Also here, the link to the field of care services is clear: such services are basically included under the label 'socio-economic projects'.

Projects that have been successful might apply for assistance at a special 'alternative' institution which is to be found in a dozen of the bigger cities in the FRG and in West Berlin: Netzwerk (Network).

Self-help Initiatives

While usually only a small share of 'informal' self-help activities becomes visible to the public, self-help groups in Hamburg became a focus of attention when – in the context of a research project – KISS (Kontakt- und Informationsstelle für Selbsthilfegruppen = Clearing house for self-help groups) came into existence. Since the beginning of 1984 the Department of Health in Hamburg contributes an annual subsidy of about 200,000 DM. With half of this money KISS finances rooms, technical infrastructure and three part-time professionals for the counselling of the local scene of self-help groups. The team of KISS estimates the number of self-help groups in Hamburg to be more than 900. Most of them are dealing with problems in the very wide field of health, whereby psycho-social problems and problems of social isolation, rated especially high in Hamburg, often correlate. It is remarkable that the wide field of self-help groups in Hamburg is not addressed by any official programme of public assistance offering rooms, infrastructure, casual counselling, etc. – except for the few rooms and people subsidized in the KISS Centre. Furthermore, the realm of self-help is relatively isolated from other institutions and fields, such as the state-administered health and care sector. Nearly all groups deal entirely with themselves and have only few organized outside contacts. This field is minimally politicized.

Analyzing the Programmes

Having acknowledged four fields of social innovation, where financial resources for employment and services provision as well as motivations for self-organization and self-help can easily be detected, we now turn to a critical assessment of the administrative policies described before. Is there a chance to combine the striving for social innovations in care provision with the goal of creating new and additional resources by stimulating special forms of work and employment? To what degree does a concept which limits work to employment and the perspective of a more effective use of human resources to the regaining of full-employment coincide with the need for a more comprehensive system of care? The following sections deal with the consequences of a certain idea of work for the possibilities of a renewed system of care.

The ABM Programme –
How to Create New Types of Work While Avoiding Repercussions on the Traditional System of Employment?

Measures of work provision in the 'Second Labour Market' were originally de signed as a way for leading unemployed persons into employment in the private economy. However, it is important to underline that the programme creating more than 3,500 employment opportunities (less than the so-called alternative sector, but all of them better paid and socially secured) is almost totally separ ated from the private labour market. 98 per cent of the 'work places' created by ABM are public work, be it in the administration, non-governmental voluntary or ganizations, or public enterprises owned by the state of Hamburg. Therefore, it is easy to see that the chances of transforming these ABM measures into regula employment are completely linked to the future of the general (local) public em ployment policy. There is little hope for stabilizing these experimental forms b using the ABM funds as an instrument for a policy of "social and ecological res toration", as one of the initiators of the programme called it.

Nevertheless, the rationale of the 'Second Labour Market' contradicts its poten tial applicability for the provision of services not yet offered by traditional institu tions. In an annex to a contract between the Senate and the trade union for th public employees (Öffentliche Dienste, Transport und Verkehr, ÖTV – trad union for public services, transport and traffic), concerning targets and condition for ABM employment the ÖTV insists on its demand for more and additional wor places in public administration, e. g. in the realm of social services, while the Sen ate, under the pressure of budget deficits, is going in the opposite direction. states "an undeniable necessity to reduce the costs of public employment b dealing with the employment offered and by eliminating also some traditional en ployment opportunities".

Thus, the contract foresees a group of measures which should guarantee that th 'second class' ABM labour should neither replace traditional public employme nor cover public duties already stated. These have not yet been realized due financial impasses. The consequence of such an arrangement which tries to sep arate 'normal' and 'ABM' work is that there are serious obstacles to a consciou and increased use of ABM in areas of clear-cut demands. In its annex to the co tract the trade union argues that ABM should be forbidden to get in touch wi areas where there are (i) established private activities already at work or (ii) gap

218

in public organizations due to fiscal constraints. The CCCs, already overloaded with demands of care, demonstrate well the pitfalls of such unemployment programmes. There is neither a programme to widen that part of the staff which is refunded by the Senate nor any programme for using ABM work within the CCCs. Since the additional work to be done here is not considered to be innovative, and since it is not seen to offer opportunities for unconventional youth integration, ABM measures cannot be applied legally. Facing such a large distance to areas of social needs, the "Second Labour Market" is, as a critical evaluation in 1984 rightly stated, "either creating poor pedagogical measures or projects where targets claimed for social and ecological reform remain a mere imagination".

The 'Alternative Sector' – Nothing But an Underdeveloped Labour Market?

Local Employment Initiatives' – this official label for a perception of what the alternative sector is or should develop into – is incompatible with the self-interpretation given by the organizers of this 'scene'. As underlined in our interviews, their main goal in establishing these projects is *not* simply to create employment, but to set up alternative, social, cultural and economic projects which might *as well* encompass unconventional answers to employment problems. One of their very basic features is that – within a framework of new cultural orientations – they try to look for new combinations of economic and social goals, paid work and social interaction, binding both together in a perspective for societal development. From that point of view the already quoted programme of the Senate for the development of Local Employment Initiatives, having as its main goal "to create stable work places and to reintegrate long-term unemployed back into the work process", is grasping only one dimension of the alternative projects it wants to address. Consequently, the so-called 'socio-economic projects' are merely seen in the Senate's programme as a special sub-division of the economic employment initiatives and therefore the only measure taken is to give them more time and credit to reach the employment goal, i. e. to create 'solid and stable work places'. Representatives of the project scene, who knew quite well that it would never be possible to finance themselves entirely many of the socio-economic projects, criticize rightly what they call an attempt to "economize social projects by forcing them to be entirely self-supporting in a medium-term perspective". When the Senate of Hamburg states that in the 'alternative sector' of 5,000 working people, only 20 per cent receive an income similar to that of the private economy, this statement is made in the perspective that the 'alternative sector' would merely be a less formal and still underdeveloped labour market. In fact, as we already showed, it is not, and the people working there do not consider it as such. Summing up, one can say that there is a basically different notion about the further development of new 'alternative' projects. Whereas the Senate from a merely economic point of view wants to reduce them to local employment initiatives, their initiators rate them as 'multifunctional', encompassing such different aspects as employment, cultural change and the creation of various forms of social participation in one and the same project.

Self-help Groups – Only an Extended Family Affair?

A similar practice of ignoring manifest motivations for work not contracted in the well-known forms of regular paid work can be seen when we look at the local clearing house for self-help groups in Hamburg, KISS. The fact that in Hamburg the self-help groups themselves receive no money (for infrastructure, current costs, etc.) seems simply to be because until now they have not claimed it. In fact, research work and polls have shown that 94 per cent of the members of self-help groups asked wanted the local community to give rooms and infrastructural help for such initiatives; moreover, 78 per cent wanted professional help for the phase of building up such a group. Such claims may nourish our hypothesis that these types of activity represent forms of work which are neither done for a wage equivalent of time and skills, nor executed without remunerations. In Hamburg, as in other places, no claim is voiced for remunerations and rewards of collective self-help work (even if it has social impact) just because people do not expect to be granted more than technical assistance. However, the less these self-help initiatives are acknowledged, the less they are or can be woven into a broader network of social policy. Self-help groups around KISS have until now only and first of all worked as extended 'private' initiatives with a very low level of contacts and conflicts with public institutions, be they represented by an office, a hospital, a home for the elderly or a CCC. As the annual report of KISS in 1984 states, there was only little interest for a regular meeting in a special contact group including representatives of the social security agencies, the administration, etc.

The Further Development of the CCCs – Creating Intermediate Activities or Economizing Public Care Services?

With the tendency to view the field of self-help as a world of its own, being as far apart from the world of professionalism as it is supposed to be from a world where performances are only given if financial remunerations are offered, it will not be surprising that the concept of the Hamburgian CCC network misses entirely a conscious integration and development of non-professional and non-paid contributions to care. While the predecessors of the CCC, run by the voluntary associations and churches still made systematic use of volunteers, the actual CCC only uses this heritage without further reflections on how to enlarge or develop it. Until now, all known concepts of the Senate do not even make reference to the fact that an earlier evaluation of the work done by the first three CCCs showed a remarkable difference between those CCCs which did not use informal contributions and the ones which made (given a specifically strong tradition) strong use of volunteers; here clients could be given back earlier to care providers by relatives, neighbours or volunteers and the burdens of the professional helpers to do everything were slightly relieved. Far from merely substituting their professional tasks, lay contributions played an important role whenever the social and communicative components of care won impact with respect to the specialized and more medical aspect of caring. This fact is of special importance since in all interviews with CCC leaders or professionals we learned that social care has expanded much faster than the demand for medical care. This might open up possibilities for lay engagement which had been until now denied in the name of skills and standards claimed for care as a specialized, mostly medical task. Since the building up of the CCC has not reduced intra-mural forms of care significantly but stimulated more demand for home care, the controversy over additional resources between the Senate subsidizing the upgrading of the CCC, and the local voluntary associations as the main holders of the CCC, has intensified. Yet, since additional resources from both sides, the Senate and the voluntary organizations, can only be imagined as additional public employed professionals, there are nearly no possibilities for broadening the offer of care. Also, the representatives of the health insurances, which provide a considerable refund for their members, complain that a mere restructuring leading from institutionalized (hospital/home for the elderly) professionalism to professionalized home care has not brought about the savings they had hoped to achieve.

In our interviews, CCC leaders and professionals did not deny that additional informal resources for caring (by self-help groups, volunteers, neighbours and others) and their activation by professionals, e. g. social workers, would be of considerable importance. Yet they emphasized that the existing concepts do not offer any legitimized and acknowledged space for the mobilization of such types of work. Being already overburdened with the given tasks and routines, the need for encouraging new types of non-professional and unpaid work is unheeded by the professionals.

Administrative Myopia: Assimilation and Exclusion

We have tried to show that the Hamburgian policies pretend that the unconventional combinations of income and activity through ABM are merely an immature form of widened public employment, and therefore either to be transformed into ordinary jobs or to be thoroughly separated from conventional public employment. They treat the multidimensional phenomena in the alternative sector only under the unidimensional aspect of creating local employment which is supposed to be totally self-sustaining; keep self-help initiatives and volunteering on a rather low level and well separated from professional care activities; conceive of the CCCs rather as decentralized public services than institutions linking different kinds of care work. In doing so, they are either targeted towards assimilation or exclusion. The principle of *assimilation* governs the local policies with respect to the attempt of turning new forms of remunerated work into an ordinary job, be it in the system of public employment or on the local private labour market. The principle of *exclusion* characterizes the local policies with respect to their attitude towards work and activities such as self-help and volunteering. They either try to separate them strictly from the spheres of contracted work or they neglect them totally as a possible resource for the creation of a renewed complex system of care.

Stating the limits of a concept, where work is still synonymous with employment and a fuller use of human resources equals full employment, one should note that the Hamburgian Senate has helped to support an innovative reality: ABM programmes open up new opportunities for combining income and social participation or for organizing socially useful activities through public programmes, even in times of financial constraint; the alternative sector badly needs every type of subsidy; the attempt to create a network of CCCs might also be seen from the aspect of guaranteeing the right to care under circumstances of a downgrading of the traditional system of highly institutionalized care.

We are attempting to demonstrate that the full scope of possibilities to be developed through such innovations is hindered as long as one clings to a traditional dualistic model of work which only knows regulated labour in markets and public employment systems or private informal activities. This leads to unintended dilemmas. Disregarding the empirical finding that only by the activation and integration of informal kinds of help and care, e. g. by relying on neighbourhood help, a CCC is able to offer more, better and comprehensive care, no side dares to discuss appropriate ways to further the development of informal networks, volunteering and self-help. CCCs are kept separate from cooperation with 'traditional' volunteers as well as from the new forms of collective self-help. Being already overburdened by the demand for often heavy domiciliary care, they lack resources to stimulate self-care and informal cooperation, e. g. by personnel responsible for the training of different kinds of volunteers. Facing a prevailing concept where formal and informal contributions are only seen from a substitutional and not from a complementary point of view, they fear becoming trapped by providing reasons for cost-cutting if they would point to the potentials of non-professional work and help. Bound into the latent conflict between unsatisfied demands for care and the union's ban on any unconventional kind of organized care work as a threat to employment, CCCs and voluntary organizations resort to significant increases of precarious part-time employment. More than 40 per cent of all care given by CCCs is supposed to be provided by female, low-paid workers with totally insecure jobs. Such a 'cheap' solution not only leads to a totally unequal splitting of the costs of social change under conditions of financial stress between the employed; it also disregards any possibility of activating *additional* and *complementary* resources. The conceptual exclusion of volunteering and self-help from a field of rising importance such as domiciliary care leads to a further segmentation in the labour market – paradoxically through public policies carried out in the name of protecting employment against every form of unpaid and 'self-exploitative' activity.

The Case of Berlin: Rediscovering Self-help

Berlin's specific geographical location and its political status intensified the socio-cultural change after the ruptures of 1968 which gave rise to the development of a broad and manifold 'alternative scene'. Since the social democrats lost power in 1981 to the conservative christian democrats (CDU), conflicts over many issues are highly politicized and polarized. This is so despite the fact that Berlin's conservatives are more flexible and innovative than other local CDU governments in the Federal Republic of Germany. Berlin's social policy, designed by the Senator for Health and Social Affairs, Ulf Fink, became well known for emphasizing the other side of work and care: the usually unpaid and less formalized activities labelled 'self-help'. But while the national Social Democratic Party has claimed the Hamburgian model as an important attempt to be generalized, the Berlin social policy is not that representative for christian democratic policies.

The main orientations of the so-called 'Berlin model' are:
- The development of qualitatively differentiated services and transfers instead of the traditional stereotype and 'covering-it-all' systems.
- An accent put on measures to combat modern threats to well-being: isolation, passivity, etc.
- A liberal reformulation of the traditional christian democratic concept of 'subsidiarity': the smaller units in social policy are promised the help of institutions and communities to stand on their own two feet.
- Thus, the focus is on stimulating social initiatives, a spirit of community obligation and care, hoping to re-establish social relationships and a new spirit of citizenship duties.

Elements of Innovation

While in Hamburg, the main field of innovation is centred around public employment measures, innovative social policies in Berlin centre on the contribution of social initiatives, projects and self-help groups to social care services. Therefore, we have to start with this field of action to grasp a different reality and its challenge to local social policy.

Collective Self-help and Social Projects

Berlin is, among all West German cities, the one with the most developed scene of 'alternative' projects, initiatives and groups. Their number is estimated to be

1,000 – 1,500. The considerable difference in the estimates already says something about the difficulties in obtaining clear criteria on what to judge as an alternative project. While the first estimate, which counts about 7,400 cooperators, including 600 paid workers, concentrates on projects offering services or producing goods, the second one also includes less formalized and non-professional self-help groups encompassing 10,000 – 15,000 participants. In 1983, self-help initiatives were addressed by a special fund for subsidizing and encouraging self-help activities brought about by the Senator for Health and Social Affairs. Explaining the targets and logic of the programme one explicitly referred to:
- A better fluctuation between work and leisure, family, and profession.
- The stimulation of non-governmental social initiatives.
- Volunteering and neighbourhood help not as a surrogate for but as a complement to the state's social policy.
- A new definition of work that is not limited to paid work.

The regulations of the self-help fund stipulate that every self-help initiative becomes entitled to subsidies (that cover part of infrastructural costs) if the project is (i) oriented to neighbourhoods or their respective city district; (ii) democratically self-administered; (iii) tolerant and open for participation and, thus, somehow serving as a model of social integration.

On the basis of these rather weak criteria, in 1983 4.1 million DM was spent, in 1984, 6.5 million and in 1985, 6.5 million. About 140 groups in 1983, 160 groups in 1984 and a few more in 1985 were financed.

Meanwhile part of the money can also be used for paying for work done in the projects. The subsidies are only for one year and every year a new decision is needed. Since 1986 part of the projects (the ones which are more formalized and have shown their utility) are granted permanent subsidies allowing for mid-term planning and security of existence.

Besides the self-help fund of the local government there are two other institutions providing access to finances and organizational advice. The Berlin bureau of Netzwerk, since its foundation in 1978, has given loans and grants of about 3.5 million DM to projects. However, today it has reached the limits of private fund raising. With financial help from the administration of social affairs, SEKIS (Selbsthilfe Kontakt und Informationsstelle = Centre of contacts and information on self-help) has been founded. It acts as a clearing house for self-help groups, offering them help, advice and rooms. SEKIS is managed by 7 (part-time) professionals and serves as a model for a broader infrastructure of clearing houses which, in the future, is supposed to cover all city districts. In contrast to KISS (in Hamburg), SEKIS engages in public debates on social policy issues, and especially on appropriate forms of assistance to and encouragement of self-help groups. It learned as well, by its own practice, that the assistance given to groups stimulates more activities and a demand for further assistance than it is able to respond to.

Reviving Volunteering

Another element of the Senator's concept to develop the more informal parts of care work is the *stimulation of volunteering*. By tradition, located with the church and the six voluntary organizations in Berlin, there are about 33,000 volunteers estimated to be working in the context of homes for the elderly, the hospitals, social work and aid. In 1985, the social administration officially issued some basic guidelines for "the political encouragement of volunteering". Volunteers are expected to assist in the CCCs, in hospitals, in homes for the elderly, in neighbourhood centres and similar institutions. Even when referring to features of free time, social motivations and semi-professional competence of volunteers, the administration explicitly denies any plan to substitute for professional work. In 1984, it started a public campaign in the local media called "Aktion Die Hilfsbereitschaft" (action 'ready for help'). About 1,000 people responded to the possibilities offered, although only less than one-third of them finally took over some function. In 1985, the campaign was renewed on the district level under the sponsorship of several associations ready to take over contributions of volunteers. 1,200 people responded, while there are controversial statements about the number of those who actually became involved later, ranging from 70 to more than 300. To encourage volunteers, the Senate provided

- An insurance against accidents.
- A special budget of 1.8 million DM for paying fees for volunteers, for further training, etc. to be spent by the districts.
- A central budget of 1 million DM for central campaigns, advertising, counselling, etc.
- 1.5 million DM for hiring a part-time social worker at every CCC whose task is the encouragement, counselling and care for building up an informal social network as a complementary part of the services offered by the CCC.

In addition, there is a special 10 million DM fund for the counselling and training of women who want to engage in social activities or return to formal employment. Out of the programme, minimum contributions to the pension fund are paid.

Restructuring of Care Services

In May 1982, the administration of social affairs started a programme establishing 15 CCCs, each being responsible for 35,000 to 40,000 inhabitants. Unlike in Hamburg, the whole network has been set into practice at once, although starting in most cases on a modest level of services provided. With one full-time professional per 5,000 inhabitants (on the average) the staff rate is slightly lower than in Hamburg. Even if precarious, non-secured work on an hourly basis does not occur as often as in the Hamburgian CCCs, most employees are part-time. According to different preconditions and district environments, some CCCs not only respond to the technical and medical duties of home care, but offer additional help by organizing volunteers, self-help groups, providing rooms for clients' meetings, e. g. a self-organized coffee shop or a communication centre. The subsidies for building up the Berlin network of CCCs have risen from 2.3 million DM in 1982 to 8.8 million DM in 1985. At the same time, a reduction of the number of beds in hospitals by about 1,000 helped the Senate to save about 10 million DM and, additionally, saved 90 million DM of expenditure for health insurances. While the average rate of hospital beds is still disproportionally high in West Berlin, the Senate plans further reductions and tries, as a compensation, to reach an agreement with the health insurances on an improved and specified reimbursement for those services of the CCCs which are more of a social and communicative, than of a clear-cut medical character.

Supporting Social Initiatives Through ABM

Since the whole design of Berlin's social policy innovations is basically linked with the idea of stimulating self-initiatives and volunteering, it is no wonder that questions concerning work as paid work and employment are usually left out. Not to enlarge public employment but to reduce it, wherever possible, is a silent precondition of the self-help-oriented strategies in Berlin. However, the Senator for Health and Social Affairs decided as late as the end of 1984 *to use 2,000 ABM working offers* out of the 10,000 reserved by the Federal Bureau of Labour for the City of Berlin, *for the sector of non-state voluntary organizations and self-help initiatives*. Due to a number of unsettled administrative aspects at that time, in 1984 only 400 out of the 2,000 possible ABM positions could be installed. As in Hamburg, the Senator for Health and Social Affairs in Berlin pays those 20 per cent of the ABM salaries not covered by the Federal Institution for Labour for these 2,000 places. Like in Hamburg, the Berlin ABM programme as a whole concentrates on public services. 95 per cent of all ABM work places in Berlin are located in the public sector.

In order to overcome the considerable difficulties of mediating between the labour administration, which is responsible for the allocation of the ABM fund and applicants for ABM measures in the area of projects, initiatives and self-help groups who are not accustomed to bureaucratic practice, an *ABM clearing centre* was established in early 1985. It is itself financed with ABM funds (as well as with some money from the self-help fund). In 1985 nearly 200 ABM work places were applied for by such groups and initiatives, a fairly negligible number in terms of employment policy, but which is seen by the groups as a considerable help for stabilizing the network of initiatives and social activities of which they are a part. Thus the ABM clearing house is working as a communicative bridge between the different cultures of bureaucratic institutions and social initiatives.

Most assessments of the impact of the innovations described above, especially those made by the left, usually concentrate on one special aspect: the attempt to make financial savings in the social service sector, judging the 'Berlin Model' to be "not much more than a simple cost cutting-strategy". Within our framework of references it is exactly the 'little bit more' which makes it so interesting to study the Berlin example. Its essence is the attempt to activate or at least use new and additional resources in the field of social and care services, such as those represented through the projects, initiatives, self-help and volunteering activities described above. If one conceives the Berlin model from this point of view, critiques and evaluations should be concentrated on the question of whether the concepts and instruments used for such a stimulation of new forms of work beyond jobs and professionalism are suited for such a target of social policy; this includes the question of whether they are really meeting the aspirations of those who engage in such projects and activities. With respect to these questions, our basic critique is concerned with the fact that the Berlin model, while forced to change in practice, in its theory and conception (unlike the Hamburgian) still upholds a dualistic concept of work, where it has to be either paid, secured and professionalized or given for altruistic reasons. Drawing a sharp line between paid work and volunteering, it is difficult to acknowledge a sphere between the formal and the informal, paid work and altruism. The activation of resources not only calls for public investments in terms of infrastructure, but also in terms of special acknowledgements and forms of remuneration for a kind of work and contributions to the broad issue of care, where solidaristic motives and the will to receive financial compensation for one's own efforts do not exclude each other. A dualistic conception of work is in Berlin, as in Hamburg, restraining reforms in social (care) services, which call for *intermediate* links, regulations and institutions not only *between* professional and lay contributions, institutional and home care, paid and informal work but also between public and private, marketed and non-marketed work and activities.

Subsidizing Projects: Difficult Adaptations to a Moving Target

Whereas the ideological background of Berlin's social policy innovations acknowledges actual tendencies of social differentiation and the flexibility of employment patterns, the approach to non-paid work, be it volunteering or collective self-help is rather traditional and insensitive to the self-image of people addressed. The Senator's view on alternative projects and their grass-roots forms of networking supposes, often counterfactually, altruism, solidarity, and a sense of citizenship as the dominating if not the sole motivation to be found there, but at the same time neglects that the 'multifunctional' setting and multidimensional approach which projects represent is as well marked by other motivations such as seeking employment, training, cultural innovation, and social interaction – issues not mentioned in the official programmes of the Senate. According to the historical development of the welfare state in the course of industrialization and an increasing inclusive labour market participation, the conservative view as well as the social democratic concept of reforms still cling to a strict duality of wage labour and professional work on the one hand and altruistic motivations for unrewarded help on the other. While social democrats claim to overcome what they mainly perceive as "self-exploitation" in the area of "compulsory altruism" (Land and Rose 1985) by transforming unpaid work into professional wage labour, their conservative counterparts tend easily to idealize informal care as a world of virtues which can often be revitalized by merely symbolic acknowledgement. In their view public initiatives might therefore be strictly limited in time and scope, to be mainly targeted to the preconditions of such initiatives and not to the questions of acknowledgement and remuneration of the work given there. Therefore, they assume that help for self-help initiatives should be temporarily restricted. The Senate's first official report in 1983 stated that "a steady subsidy does not meet with the intention of the funding programme. It only schedules time-limited kick-off phases".

Until today these basic principles are still being declared but they become less significant for the practice already developed. Today, revised self-help funding guidelines acknowledge a differentiation between projects to be seen as possibly self-sustaining in the future and others, where, as a declaration states, "a time-limited subsidy has not proved functional". As a consequence the fund for 'self-help' groups has been increased to 10 million DM while a quarter of the money is dedicated to *constant funding* (the groups receiving continued funding represent 40 per cent of all groups initially funded). This is also to be seen as an attempt at reconciliation with actual practices of project workers who already reallocate the subsidies they received from the social administration. From the beginning they use a part of the money for wage-like remunerations given to the most engaged activists of the group, the so-called "Stammkräfte" (permanent personnel). Principles of allocation range from a simple agreement on an hourly basis to the creation of socially secured work and its transformation into regular public employment, situated in the quite unusual context of an autonomous institution. A recent statement of the Senate of West Berlin on refunding wages within self-help groups is slightly more cautious, stating that "constant funding should not be a usual routine" and that the maximum amount of money in self-help groups devoted to paying for work done there should be limited to 40 per cent of the entire funding. Facing thereby a scope of projects ranging from the spheres of paid professionalism to the field of informal privacy, the question arises of why the entire activity is still assembled under the one and only label of 'self-help'. For the groups concerned it was surely an advantage that the self-help definition by U. Fink, the Senator for Health and Social Affairs, was always a rather unclear and thereby also a general one. This led to the fact that those initiatives received subsidy whose motivations were nearer to professionalization and the creation of income than to altruism or the spirit of community. Yet an analytical view ought to distinguish between self-help projects as loosely integrated groups of persons with a special need (or interest) who meet only for some hours a week to provide mutual help through (mostly) verbal interaction, on the one hand, and 'self-help' in a wider sense as an emblematic label for all kinds of innovative projects, activities and social experiments. The latter stay outside the traditional institutions as well as outside the private and semi-private area and, insofar as they represent social action, protests, efforts and self-defence, they cover all types of work, from unpaid social activities to relatively secure paid work. Therefore, as one of the representatives of the Berlin alternative scene rightly remarks, the differentiated reality of project work the Senate relates to under the 'self-help' label should be more correctly called a "scene of innovative projects and social experiments". Christian Wend, one of the founders of Netzwerk mentioned above, tries to differentiate between *(i) self-help groups* (private, very informal, mutual help for members), *(ii) self-help projects* (offering help to non-members; activity guided by political reasons, with solidaristic and citizenship motivations prior to professional values) and *(iii) new social service projects* (with a high level of professionalization, and priority given to income and stable jobs). The differentiation is similar to the one made in the *SEKIS* yearbook of 1985 which adds *self-help organizations* as representatives of and pressure groups for the wide range of associations in the intermediary sphere. Of even more importance for the design of policies is the fact, stated by Wend, that most of the projects receiving subsidies are 'mixed types' and not constantly maintaining one and the same structure of work. Rather, they develop and *move* within the range described above. "They are difficult to classify but even harder to administrate without ignoring the interest of at least a part of their operators", Wend adds.

As well as some groups may restrict themselves to mutual help without any reference to professional assistance or remunerations for activists, other projects, from their beginning, have "little to do with self-help and (are) difficult to distinguish from professional projects of the state or voluntary organizations" (Senator Ulf Fink). Since the administration's criteria of funding are based on a dualistic view of either professional paid work or self-help activity, they fail – even with a wide and vague notion of self-help – to meet a fluctuating reality between these poles. The SEKIS report of 1985 states that "organizations and initiatives are forced to label their work 'self-help' because otherwise there is no possibility to have access to the fund". Thus, there is still a conceptual lack of adequate patterns of funding an extremely differentiated field of different ways and degrees to formalize resources, namely work, including projects which intentionally combine unpaid lay work and professional activities usually done within employment-like relationships.

Intermediations in the Field of Care
Links Still Missing

When the Senate campaigned for an increased engagement in volunteering, it consequently addressed *individuals* who were supposed to be ready for voluntary services according to organizational definitions of problems and tasks. In so doing, a shift in motivation for voluntary action which possible arrangements should face has been ignored. Whereas in former times the spirit of charity and pure altruism prevailed, today the general emphasis is more on some kind of exchange where the ones who give voluntary work and care also receive emotional support in terms of social integration, but sometimes also something in terms of public acknowledgement and remuneration. Therefore, opening up new possibilities for volunteering calls for concentration on problems such as how to give the volunteers more autonomy and to organize in action groups, etc. As we were told by experts, it would be much better to give resources for restructuring 'the culture' of decentralized networks and institutions like some of the CCCs try to do, than to resort to simple advertisement through newspaper. Taking up actual motivations for volunteering presupposes a context of encouragement and acknowledgement that responds to the quest of potential volunteers for some minimum of autonomy, optionality and remuneration. Since voluntary services are provided not only in order to meet the needs of people cared for, but at the same time are seen, on the side of volunteers, as an opportunity to overcome social isolation and forced privacy and to gain some kind of recognition and access to the public sphere, there has to be a back-up structure: being connected to the social environment (neighbourhoods), offering differential opportunities for participation and rewards, and providing guidance and advice. Indeed, as already mentioned above, each CCC is joined by a part-time social worker as an animator for networks of help and volunteering. However, giving assistance for building up volunteering and organizing cooperation between the professional staff and semi-formal and informal networks in a district of 40,000 people calls for a greater capacity than that of one part-time employee. Appropriate links between the institutional system and present motivations to engage in unpaid work are still missing.

Another aspect of intermediations with respect to work is the transfer of definitions and standards of care from the new practices in the sphere of collective self-help over to the traditional routines in the sphere of professional services. While the former, in many cases, adopted professional standards of skill, continuity and responsibility, the latter became subject to rationalizing and economizing strategies, thus refusing to enhance its task structure and to meet the communicative and social needs of clients. Social projects face the entire burden of innovation. They cannot count on reforms in the public services in order to allow them to mediate and gain additional support instead of mere ignorance or even rejection. As in Hamburg, also in Berlin there is almost no official policy in sight with clear ideas about how to take up and evaluate the new social experiments as proponents for a changing culture in the *entire* area of services (especially in the area of hospitals, homes for the elderly, where only some cautious steps towards more individual rights for the clients are being made). Consequently, we face the danger of a forced dual reality of work. Thus, the administration's promise that the reform is not to replace professional services by 'self-help' activities, meant as an appeasement for all those who fear a mere decrease of welfare performances, might also be read as an appeasement for vested interests in the established field of health and care. Here, what the experimenting groups are doing is seen as a challenge for their established routines, privileges and power on finances and decisions. In such a context the funding programmes for self-help initiatives might get perverted into a mere deregulation of the area of social services. New "associations and initiatives, when forced to label themselves a self-help project, feel denied a regular access to the traditional system of public social services, within which they would be entitled to less precarious forms of funding." (SEKIS report 1985)

Decisive for Development, Neglected in Policies: The Employment Issue

As our description of the areas of alternative projects, the CCCs and the ABM programme, as already shown, the entrance into a promised land giving additional firm grounds for paid work and income has not been made here. Even in the near future the overall hours of professionals working in the expanding CCC networks will not exceed remarkably the working hours and places saved through a reform of the hospitals. And – as in Hamburg – the alternative scene offers a considerable amount of places where one can have a chance for social participation and sometimes also a certain amount of financial remuneration, but only in very few cases a paid job guaranteeing an income which is sufficient for living. If we take the multidimensional meaning of the alternative scene seriously, with its mixture of activities ranging from paid work to casual volunteering it is misleading to regard them simply as mere employment initiatives. Therefore, we are more than sceptical as far as slogans like "creating 10,000 and more working places inside the alternative sector" are concerned.

It seems *unrealistic* to us to view this new area only from the point of view of additional employment just as it is also unrealistic to leave the question of employment out of consideration, as Senator Ulf Fink does from a pure self-help/volunteering point of view, stating: "Social policy cannot solve the problem of unemployment. That is the task of economic policy." However, even if one is solely interested in social service innovations one cannot refuse to recognize that the work of most 'self-help' initiatives is mixed with or sometimes even governed by intentions of job creation. Nevertheless, legal regulations and administrative practice in dealing with employment measures like ABM fail to meet requisite conditions of continuity and growth of initiatives and social projects.

231

In defence of existing jobs, the trade union of the public services (the trade union for the public employees, transport and traffic – Öffentlicher Dienst, Transport und Verkehr) remarks that ABM measures usually function as a "special labour market of job rotation" and just "help to brush up the statistics of unemployment". Despite the aim of creating additional work places, local departments for infrastructure "would no longer be able to administer our parks and public gardens without the thousands of ABM people they employ; professional personnel for the care of the elderly, social workers, pedagogues, etc. are only employed through ABM funding". The ABM clearing house states in its official report 1985 that in these areas of public administration the practices are "at the margins of what can be seen as legal and not in the interest of the ABM workers in these precarious jobs".

But whereas the union comes to the final claim to abolish the ABM programme as a whole and publishes its demand in leaflets distributed in institutions like SEKIS, where we find just those people for whom ABM is the only available answer, the ABM clearing house in its report asks for more differentiated solutions. To make ABM measures accessible for initiatives and social projects on an enlarged scale might have more impact on further innovation and the creation of future new jobs in such areas than to use them as mere cost-saving measures in the existing public services.

A report of the ABM clearing house envisages three important effects of using provisional ABM employment as a resource for social projects:

● In projects there is the highest chance to transform time-limited ABM work into stable regular work places insofar as the economy of many projects is developing in contrast to the stagnation or shrinking of ordinary public employment.

● Within projects, there is no discrimination of ABM workers often found in the regular administration, because the social atmosphere here is more solidaristic and egalitarian.

● The effects of ABM work in terms of opportunities for qualification are usually much higher within projects than in most of the professionalized sectors.

In consequence, the report of the ABM clearing house argues that their work not just an 'alternative' addition to usual job creation (here, as they rightly state their legitimacy is very low), but that they are "giving a useful contribution to a integration of labour market and social policy". Moreover, one might state that every additional working place in a social project provided through public subsidies multiplies the opportunities for participation and integration of many more persons than those few being financed as ABM jobs. This view resembles the rare insights of politicians who begin to perceive that enhancing the range of voluntary services often stimulates the demand for more professionals as coordinators and advisers (such is an argument of Senator Fink). In a similar statement, the Berlin Senator for Youth and Education, Hanna-Renate Laurien, complains about short-term perspectives in social policy and the narrow sight of corporate interests in the well established social sector which blocks a positive interplay b tween the promotion of additional and new resources through volunteering and the need for new professionals and jobs. "If we want to engage volunteers in kindergardens and social work and in case we would ask for the employment of a few new professional trainers for this purpose, nearly every politically responsible person would actually reject such a project. One thinks in merely financial and not in broader economic terms. One only sees the initial and immediate costs, not the possible long-lasting and stable multiplier effects."

In fact, if we take together the fields of projects with and without ABM jobs, the area of the CCCs and the self-help groups around SEKIS, we face – under the heavy pressure of the crisis – a complex restructuring of demands and needs as well as of resources offered and supplied. Care needs become more visible by the establishment of institutions like the CCC; social networking seems to change the structure of demands and needs for caring and new social projects competing with traditional definitions of supply and demand in care and social services restructure or even enlarge resources offered. As far as these processes do not only concern regular jobs which become questioned (e. g. by lowering the offer of hospital beds) but also stimulate new forms of work and activities (e. g. in addition to a CCC), we face more than an expanding or shrinking of professional paid work and more than an expanding or shrinking in terms of public finances and economy. What is happening is a restructuring of the whole scope of resources for caring, a wider social process wherein a change of professional skills and the loss of old or/and the creation of new paid work places is only one aspect. Even if the 'Berlin model' gives a rather limited chance to initiatives, projects and experiments outside the established institutions of health, care and social service, it has shown the need for more than symbolic signs of active support to transform activated resources and innovative elements of the new experiments into acknowledged parts of the overall culture of health and services, which are now still dominated by what is called the 'social-industrial' complex.

Final Remarks and Conclusions

Our research dealt with traditional concepts of paid and unpaid work challenged and questioned by innovations in the field of care, as well as with new concepts of work and employment. Our central problem, shifting characteristics of and balances between the different forms of work and their organizational and motivational principles can best be studied in a field where by tradition professional and lay, paid and unpaid work, formalized and less formalized resources and contributions are closely linked. We have tried to examine the effects, limits and shortcomings of two different political concepts dealing with the topic of work and care in an innovative form; they are opposed because the one is mainly centred around work as employment whereas the other is centred around work as an unpaid social (self-help) activity; they are similar insofar as they both rely on a dualistic notion of work and a rather traditional concept concerning the guiding motivations for and regulations of its paid and unpaid elements.

In *Hamburg* we found a political concept still indebted to the heritage of the traditional welfare state and to concepts which refer to gaps of services solely within the framework of professionalization and full employment. We found tight limits for taking innovative steps within such a framework. This excludes the activation of possible resources and contributions beyond work as employment and professionalism. It provides the funding of new activities, initiatives and projects only under the aspect of assimilating them to public or private employment and working structures.

In *Berlin* we found a political concept trying to encourage a revival of the inherited and long neglected forms of activity, work and care outside the professionalized services; but as the modern reality of social projects and volunteer initiatives is different from the traditional culture of self-help and community spirit, it calls for new forms of public acknowledgement and funding, thereby also questioning every attempt at sharply separating the world of professional jobs and services on the one hand and an assumed world of self-help and altruism on the other. The potential impact of the activated new resources of work and care is moreover tightly linked with new investments to be made and to corresponding innovation in the professional sector.

In Berlin *and* Hamburg the traditional concept of work – be it as employment and paid work or self-help and volunteering – shows its limits even in innovative attempts, where the new forms of activity and work to be found in the intermediate area of socio-economic projects are addressed with a high and specific selectivity, *either trying to transform them into employment initiatives or to keep them restricted to the world of self-sustaining self-help activities.* (For further discussion see Evers 1986 and Trojan 1986) *However, their socio-cultural functions are neither compatible with full professionalism nor with a prolongation of the old virtues of gratuity, motherhood, mere altruism or charity.*

The two strategies in both cities, though sharing from opposite ends a traditional view of the problems of work, help with their endeavours to develop experimental forms of funding, a realm of activities neither to be identified with public professionalization nor with unpaid lay and private self-help activities. Projects partly based on subsidies, self-help groups and refunded socio-economic projects, as well as concepts of CCCs combining professional and volunteer work create a reality marked by new and differentiated forms of acknowledging (care) work and activities. Furthermore, they are incapable of *new relationships between individual or collective performances and income allocation.* We testify to the significance of new forms of remunerations created by state intervention; they differ from the prevailing concept of wage equivalence in formal employment relationship just as they differ from the norm of reciprocity with only symbolic public reward and acknowledgements of state-free private forms of mutual aid. (For further discussion, see Sichtermann 1985)

It is difficult to speculate about the future of new relationships between (i) work and gratification, (ii) activities and acknowledgement, and (iii) dormant resources and strategies for applying them. Perhaps we only testify to a deregulation on the labour market accompanied by a colonization of other informal resources whereby a part of self-help initiatives and projects turn into a kind of second-class labour. On the other hand, the whole development might be seen as a challenge and a chance to overcome some of the most remarkable deficits the welfare state is showing today:

● Tackling the silent and individualized exploitation (especially of women) of work and activities supposed to be given for free or being a compulsory cultural obligation, by using and developing these resources consciously as well as by acknowledging their social character as a basis for new regulations in securing and remunerating them.

● Tackling the trend of social disintegration into a mere sum of individualized clients and consumers by the introduction of acknowledgements of cooperative, communitarian and collective (co)producers of services and welfare.

● Thereby overcoming a concept of social rights only based on formalized work in the labour market. New links between performances and gratifications might contribute to the development of a 'post-industrial citizenship' with rights and duties based more on an enlarged notion of social participation than exclusively on participation in the labour market.

Bibliography

Bäcker, G., 1985, 'Sozialpolitik im Verteilungskonflikt — Anmerkungen zu den Finanzierungsproblemen der (auch alternativen) Sozialpolitik', WSI-Mitteilungen. No. 7. pp. 424–433.

Backes, G., 1985, 'Ehrenamtliche Dienste in der Sozialpolitik. Folgen für die Frauen', WSI-Mitteilungen. Nr. 7, pp. 424–433.

Bauer, R., 1985, 'Die Politik der Freien Träger': Aufgabenfelder, Handlungsorientierungen und Leistungspotentiale in Krüger, J., Pankoke, E. (eds.): Kommunale Sozialpolitik, München.

Biedenkopf, K., 1984, 'Die Zukunft des Sozialstaates', Gewerkschaftliche Monatshefte, No. 8. pp. 494–500.

Blüm, N., 1983, Die Arbeit geht weiter, München.

Durst, A., Ostner, I., 1985, 'Der private Haushalt — eine Ressource alternativer Sozialpolitik?' in Opielka. M. (ed.): Die ökosoziale Frage. Entwürfe zum Sozialstaat, Frankfurt, pp. 183–195.

Erler, G., 1985, Frauenzimmer. Für eine Politik des Unterschiedes, Berlin.

Evers, A., 1986, 'Zwischen Arbeitsamt und Ehrenamt. Unkonventionelle lokale Initiativen im Schnittpunkt von Arbeit und sozialen Diensten' in Blanke, B., Evers, A., Wollmann, H. (eds.), Die zweite Stadt. Neue Formen lokaler Arbeits- und Sozialpolitik, Opladen, pp. 15–50.

Geißler, H., 1975, Neue Soziale Frage. Zahlen, Daten, Fakten, Bundesfachausschuß für Sozialpolitik der CDU.

Ferrand-Bechmann, D., 1986, Moderniser le bénévolat, Université de Grenoble (manuscript).

Land, H., Rose, H., 1985, 'Compulsory Altruism for Some or an Altruistic Society for All?' in Bean, P., Ferris, J., Whynes, D. (eds.),Defence of Welfare, London - New York, pp. 74–96.

Offe, C., 1984, 'Perspektiven auf die Zukunft des Arbeitsmarktes. 'Orthodoxie', 'Realismus' und 'dritte Wege' in Offe, C. (ed.), 'Arbeitsgesellschaft'. Strukturprobleme und Zukunftsperspektiven, Frankfurt, p. 340–358.

Offe, C., Heinze, R. G., 1986, 'Am Arbeitsmarkt vorbei. Überlegungen zur Neubestimmung haushaltlicher Wohlfahrtsproduktion in ihrem Verhältnis zu Markt und Staat', Leviathan, No. 4, pp. 471–495.

Scharpf, F. W., 1983, 'Strukturen der post-industriellen Gesellschaft', Soziale Welt, No. 1, pp. 4–24.

Sichtermann, B., 1984, 'Gleicher Lohn – andere Arbeit. Überlegungen zu den Grenzen der alten Gleichberechtigungspolitik' in Baier, L., et al., Die Linke neu denken, Berlin, pp. 93–106.

Trojan, A. (ed.), 1986, Wissen ist Macht. Eigenständig durch Selbsthilfe in Gruppen, Frankfurt.

Wiesenthal, H., 1986, 'Zwischen Verkürzung und Flexibilität. Arbeitsumverteilung diesseits der schlechten Utopie der 20-Stunden-Woche', in Maier, E., Schmid, T. (eds.), Der goldene Topf, Berlin, pp. 116–131.

Constructing a New Welfare Mix in the United Kingdom: The Role of the Voluntary Sector

Stephen Humble and Alan Walker

Introduction

In this chapter we outline the main challenges to the British welfare state and the traditional relationship between different forms of welfare delivery. This general explanatory framework is followed by a detailed case study of the changing role of the voluntary sector in the provision of social services which we use to illustrate some of the factors underlying and the implications of the challenge to traditional mechanisms of social integration. What social and economic changes and policies have contributed to the current criticism of the welfare state? Why have privatization, informal support networks and voluntarism in particular been offered as the answers to some of the problems associated with the state welfare? How far are these two developments – the weakening of the post-war consensus on welfare and the emergence of alternative forms of welfare delivery – related? What norms and values underly this new policy? These are the main questions addressed in the first part of this chapter. In the second part we apply these general questions to the role of the voluntary sector.

Underlying the continuing critical re-examination of the apparatus of the welfare state and the assumptions underlying it is a weakening and, in some instances, breakdown in the political consensus on the welfare mix forged in the immediate post-war period. The chief opponents of public services argue that such services stifle individual initiative, divert scarce resources from private investment and inhibit freedom of choice. In the place of the role of the public sector in the mixed economy of welfare is proposed *both* privatization and individual and community provisions – that is, corporate care and community care.

In addition to this straightforward condemnation of the public sector from the New Right, there has been a longstanding critique of some aspects of welfare provision – especially the personal social services – from other sections of the political spectrum. These criticisms have mounted steadily in recent years. Similarly, interest in the role and potential of private services, volunteers and informal networks has not been confined to the New Right. But, as in other aspects of social policy, the motives behind this interest are functions of political ideology. This brings us to the fundamental assumption underlying this introductory commentary: recent and projected changes in the organization and distribution of welfare services are premeditated and planned. They result from conscious thought and action on the part of policy-makers rather than an evolutionary process – hence the title of this chapter. This structural approach to analyzing developments in the mixed economy of welfare emphasizes not only the fact that the particular balance between the constituents in the welfare mixture is constructed socially, but also that – in contrast to the implication of harmony in the term 'mix' – the different elements may be based on *conflicting* assumptions and practices. Thus there might be a structural incompatibility between the traditional mechanisms of social integration and the new social relations being promoted. Additional research is required to explore the precise relationship between existing institutions and practices and new ones, especiallly in the fields of social care and employment.

The Economic, Social and Ideological Challenges to the Welfare State

Recent challenges to the welfare state and the related growth in interest in the voluntary and informal sectors may be traced to two separate, though now conflated, sets of developments. On the one hand there is the fiscal crisis of the mid 1970s and the ideological and policy changes following it. On the other, there are various specific criticisms of state services which have evolved over the last 30 years.

The former often takes the form of fundamentalist critique of the welfare state aimed at replacing public with private welfare. More moderate policy-makers have been forced by a combination of financial stringency and increasing demands or resources to search for alternatives to state welfare. The latter is concerned primarily with the reform of public welfare services and, in particular, making them more responsive to the informal sector. Elements of both are apparent in current social policies.

The evolution of the liberal welfare state in Britain was based on post-war economic prosperity – the twin policies of economic growth and relatively full employment. Sustained growth and near full employment during the 1950s and 1960s delivered a welfare surplus which, although it did not create equality of condition (Le Grand 1982), did finance rising real levels of benefits and services with resulting reductions in economic insecurity and provided for the massive expansion in social expenditure over the post-war period. Thus, in the Unted Kingdom, the proportion of total public expenditure going to the welfare state nearly doubled between 1950 and 1984 and currently stands at 60 per cent of the total. This era of unparalleled growth in the welfare state was abruptly halted in the mid 1970s by the rise in world oil prices, a slow down in economic growth, a combination of rising unemployment and inflation and a growing resistance to taxation (for a fuller discussion of these factors see Walker 1982: 7–9). In the wake of economic change came political and ideological change – the rise of monetarism in response to the economic problems of the 1970s echoed the adoption of Keynesian policies in response to those of the 1930s. The election of the Conservative Government in 1979 (and its re-election in 1983) brought a thorough-going neo-monetarist strategy that, in important respects, marked a departure from the assumption underlying the post-war settlement.

Participation in the Labour Market and Wage Levels

At the heart of the social and economic strategy of the present Conservative Government is the labour market. The primary aim is to lift some of the constraints of a 'free' market and thereby, it is assumed, allow entrepreneurial activity to flourish. Four main elements to this individualistic neo-monetarist strategy might be distinguished.

First there is what amounts to the creation of unemployment: at best the unwillingness to adopt measures to create jobs and at worst the encouragement of de-industrialization, for example in steel manufacture, mining and shipbuilding. In contrast to the liberal-pluralist assumptions underlying the Beveridge/Keynes welfare state the present government argues that the causes of unemployment are *not* lack of demand, *not* lack of public sector investment and *not* technological change (Department of Employment 1985). It is due instead, the government argues, to the bulge in the population, the unwillingness and lack of initiative of the unemployed and, particularly, the interference of trade unions and the state itself in the labour market:

"The biggest single cause of our high unemployment is the failure of our jobs market, the weak link in our economy." (ibid.: 13)

Thus, on the one hand, the neo-monetarist strategy denies the structural significance of unemployment by assigning its cause to factors outside the economic system, or by attempting to minimize the numbers involved by repeated changes in the calculation of unemployment statistics. On the other hand, it explains the over supply' of labour by constraints on the free market for labour. The practical outcome is that policy is concentrated on the supply side of the labour market, there is no significant reflation and job creation and, conversely, the rate of unemployment is one of the highest in the Organization for European Cooperation and Development (OECD) at over 13 per cent and is the main reason for the substantial rise in poverty in Britain over the last five years.

Secondly, there is the increased commodification of labour. In the words of the recent White Paper on Employment (the first since 1944):

"To think of workers as part of a market is not to devalue them; it is to recognise that the realities of economic life are not waived just because the factors are people, not things. Skill and effort are traded between workers as sellers and employers as customers; and here as in all other markets, the customer cannot be expected to buy unless he is getting what he needs at a price he can afford. In the labour market the employer as customer is looking for the right people at the right price in order to carry on his business." (ibid.: 13)

When workers are viewed primarily as commodities their welfare depends on their selling price in the labour market. If some workers are paid less than others – for example, women, blacks, people with disabilities – it is because the skills and abilities they bring to the labour market are inferior. The commodification of labour is essential to the neo-monetarist strategy because it legitimates reductions in the *price* of labour.

Thirdly, there is the increasing casualization of labour. Recent policy measures – including the shift from a social insurance-based to an employer-based sick pay scheme and the removal of employment protection from those working for an employer for less than two years – may be seen as giving encouragement to employers not to hire permanent labour. Schemes such as the Youth Training Scheme (YTS) and the Young Workers Scheme have increased the casualization of young workers.

This policy has added impetus to a longer term trend in the labour market away from full-time towards part-time jobs and self-employment. For instance during the 1970s more than one million part-time jobs were created and it is estimated that a further million will be established by the end of the 1980s. There has also been a sharp increase in self-employment (600,000 jobs since 1979). Most of this increase has not taken the form of small businesses but casualization through the growth of sub-contracting – for example in cleaning and catering services, offering little or no job security and no social benefit rights.

The outcome of this policy is increasing economic insecurity for large sections of the working class in Britain, especially women. One of the main applications of casualization has been through the public sector. Virtually all women's normal work in health, education and the personal social services is organized on a part-time basis, as is most of the caring work in hospitals, residential establishments and houses for the elderly and mentally handicapped. As a result there is a significant growth in low pay among women and with it, the increasing feminization of poverty.

Fourthly, there is the pauperization of labour. This policy has two components. First there is the drive to lower wages, in order that unemployed people might 'price themselves back into jobs'. This has taken the form of a public sector wages policy aimed at minimizing wage increases, the repeal of the fair wages legislation requiring public sector contractors to pay the same rate for the same job in the public sector, the introduction of YTS with extremely low rates of pay (£ 27.30 per week) and proposals to remove Wages Council protection for work kers under the age of 21. Secondly, there are cuts in social security benefits – some £ 10,000 million has been taken from the social security budget since 1979. One of the main intentions of these cuts and the major review of social security undertaken between 1983 and 1985 has been to 'rationalize' the incomes of those in and out of work and promote work incentives. Thus the rationale for the proposed 'simplification' of benefits currently in the pipeline is that:

"Greater compatibility (between benefits to these in and out of work) is impossible while supplementary benefit itself offers such a wide range of potential extra help for claimants." (DHSS 1985: para 9.5).

The social consequences of these four aspects of the neo-monetarist labour market strategy are increasing unemployment, economic insecurity, low pay and family poverty. For example, the numbers of people dependent on supplementary benefit (the state minimum income for those not in work) have increased from £ 4.4 million in 1979 to £ 7.1 million in 1983. In 1983 one million children lived in poverty because of their parents' low wages and another one million because of unemployment. Official surveys of earnings show that inequalities have increased in recent years. Relative to medium earnings, top earnings have increased since 1980 and bottom earnings decreased.

Financial Stringency and the Public Burden

The second main plank in the government's social and economic strategy is its opposition to public expenditure and especially expenditure on the welfare state. Since the late 1970s attention has turned from the problem of how to divide up the extra annual increment for public expenditure to viewing this expenditure itself as one of the main *causes* of economic failure. The government is unequivocal: "Public expenditure is at the heart of Britain's present economic difficulties." (Treasury 1979: 1)

The result of these changes in ideology and policy towards the public sector is retrenchment in the growth of public expenditure on the social services (Webb and Wistow 1982). In fact public expenditure on the personal social services has *increased* over the last five years, largely through the efforts of some *local* authorities to maintain services in the face of central government structures, with the result that service provision is becoming more and more patchy. But expenditure has not increased sufficiently to keep pace with what is required just to maintain existing service levels in the face of demographic changes – particularly the growth in the numbers of very elderly people (Wicks 1982; Walker 1985).

Another aspect of financial stringency is the "cost-effectiveness imperative" which dominates the policy-making process (Davies 1981). Of course the close scrutiny of all forms of public expenditure, particularly in relation to an assessment of social priorities, is a desirable and long-overdue principle for policy-makers, but this is not always what is intended or what occurs in practice. At its crudest this cost-effectiveness imperative takes the form of a narrow concern with economic or cost-efficiency, which suggests that the lower the financial cost of a service the more efficient it is. (Taken to its logical conclusion this provides a crude financial rationale for privatization, which increases efficiency by shifting costs to the private sector or the greater use of zero or low-cost volunteers.)

Although budgetary restraint has been practised in most Western countries in recent years the differing impact of this policy on their social expenditure indicates that financial factors are not the primary cause of cuts in the welfare state. Social expenditure rose as a proportion of Gross National Product (GNP) between 1975 and 1981 in all countries of the European Economic Community (EEC) except West Germany, but despite the fact that one of the largest rises was that of the United Kingdom (20 per cent compared with 12 per cent for the Netherlands) it still had the second lowest proportion of expenditure in relation to GNP (Eurostat 1977). Moreover, in Sweden during this period social expenditure grew as a proportion of GNP by 32 per cent. That financial stringency has operated to some extent as a scapegoat for other motives is also suggested by the fact that expenditure on some programmes has *increased* while that on others has been cut back. For example in the United Kingdom some £ 10,000 million has been cut from the social security budget since 1979 while at the same time there has been an increase in defence expenditure of £ 9,500 million.

Underlying the Conservative Government's strategy towards the welfare state is the characteristic *laissez-faire* aversion to the public sector. Briefly, this encompasses the belief that public services stifle initiatives and responsibility. In the words of the former Secretary of State for Social Services, "our statutory services should be a safety net, not a blanket that smothers initiative and self-help" (House of Commons 1981: col. 136). Secondly, it is assumed that the private sector is necessarily more efficient than the public sector. Thirdly, the 'non-productive' public sector is held to be a costly burden on the 'productive' private sector (Walker 1984). For these reasons it is argued that the frontiers of the welfare state should be rolled back. In other words, less government means more corporate welfare enterprise and individual self-help.

The essential precondition for a thorough-going policy of privatization and self-help is the belief that the public sector is wasteful, inefficient and unproductive. This 'public burden' model of welfare characterizes expenditure on public social services as a burden on the economy (Titmuss 1968: 124–5). It has exerted a significant influence on both official and public attitudes to social expenditure over the whole of the post-war period, and is one of the main reasons why there were elements of privatism built into different parts of the Beveridge welfare state from the outset, and its influence may be detected in policies originating from left, right and centre of the political spectrum (Walker 1984a: 45–57).

The 'public burden' model of welfare is supported by the crude division between economic policy and social policy and the presumption of supremacy of the former over the latter. Narrowly defined 'economic' objectives such as profit maximi zation, economic growth and cost-efficiency are considered automatically to be legitimate, while 'social' objectives such as good health and community care must secure legitimacy in the policy system, and are believed to rest ultimately on economic policy for their achievement (Pinker 1974: 9). Thus the subordination of the equity concerns of social policy to the efficiency concerns which dominate economics and economic policy follows from and reinforces the assumption of the superiority of the market, and paves the way for the adoption of policies aimed at reducing the size of the welfare state when economic growth no longer provides a sufficient welfare surplus. In both capitalist and state societies social policy has been assigned a role as 'handmaiden' to the economy (Titmuss 1974: 31; Ferge 1979: 50).

Pressures for Increased Expenditure on the Social Services

At the same time as resource constraints have been imposed on the social services, three additional sources of pressure on resources have exacerbated their impact and deepened the dilemma facing policy-makers, including those seeking to maintain welfare expenditure at a time of low growth and reduced economic activity.

In the first place the massive rise in unemployment in recent years, common to all EEC countries but particularly severe in the United Kingdom, has increased not only social security budgets but also the pressure for expenditure on the health and personal services, while on the other side of the coin, it has reduced considerably revenues from taxation, social insurance, production and expenditure (Burghes and Lister 1981; Hakim 1982). It is estimated that the current Exchequer cost of unemployment – lost tax revenue and benefit expenditure – is some £ 20 billion per annum.

Secondly, in addition to the increasing demand created by unemployment, the need for social care in general and formal services in particular has been rising due to demographic and social factors. For example, between 1901 and 1981, the numbers of those aged 75 and over in England and Wales increased by 621 per cent, from 396,000 to 2,856,000, and the numbers will increase to an estimated 3,314,000 in the year 2001 (Walker 1985). It is among the older age groups that the greatest need and, therefore, the main demand for social services occurs. For example, those aged 75 and over are six times more likely than those in the 65 to 74 age group to receive a home help (OPCS 1982: 154). As the elderly population itself ages, with an increasing proportion reaching advanced old age, so the need for care increases. So, the proportion of those aged 85 and over who are unable to bath, shower or wash all over alone is seven times higher than it is for those aged 65 to 69 (OPCS 1981). This is not to say that the majority of elderly people require care or 'tending', they do not, nor is it to indulge in "demography of despair" by reinforcing false stereotypes of dependency in old age

(Walker 1980; 1985). It is simply to demonstrate that the scale of need is rising at precisely the same time as resources are diminishing. An indication of the future scale of need can be gained by estimating the impact of population changes: for instance, on present trends by the year 2001 the numbers of people over 65 who are unable to bath themselves will increase by 23 per cent (Henwood and Wicks 1984: 16).

The significance of these statistics and the population changes underlying them are heightened by two related developments. Not only are a large number of elderly people, and elderly women in particular, outliving their spouses for long periods but also there are a significant number of elderly people who have either never had children or who have none surviving (Abrams 1980). Also contributing to a possible widening informal "care gap" (Walker 1985) or shortfall are changes in the pool of potential family and other informal carers. The decline in fertility during the 1920s and 1930s, geographical mobility and recent increases in family breakup are likely to reduce the availability of family care. Although there was no evidence from the recent survey of the family care of elderly people in Sheffield that the size of the pool of potential family carers has a significant influence on the provision of such care; the crucial elements were the gender and proximity of carers (Qureshi and Walker 1987). On the other hand it is not possible to predict the future consequences of divorce and family reconstruction on the supply of family care and Parker's (1981: 21) question about who will look after dependent step-grandmothers and grandfathers of the next century remains an open one. Economic policies too might have unforeseen consequences on the supply of family and informal carers. It is sometimes suggested that the growth of unemployment might have a beneficial spin-off in freeing more men to take a greater share of caring tasks. On the face of it this is an appealing argument, entailing benefits for those cared for, female carers and unemployed men. But it contradicts all that research has revealed about the debilitating, isolating and psychologically damaging effects of unemployment (see, for example, Hakim 1982). What little evidence there is suggests that unemployed men are *less* likely than those in work either to provide care directly to elderly relatives or to support the caring activities of their wives (Qureshi and Walker 1987). Possible changes in the attitude of women to continuing gender divisions in the provision of care also raises a question mark over the future availability of informal carers – a point we take up again later.

Thirdly, the search for alternatives to public social services has been given added impetus by increases in the cost of formal care (Wright 1982; Tinker 1984; Knapp 1984). For example, the gross cost of old people's homes rose by two-fifths between 1970 and 1975 and net unit costs by three-fifths (Challis and Davies 1980: 2). Moreover when the financial costs of informal and quasi-informal care are compared with those of formal care the attractiveness to policy-makers of substituting the former for the latter are obvious. Among elderly people judged to be in the 'high dependency' category the cost of providing paid neighbourly helps and

244

home care assistants in 1981–82 were respectively 21 per cent and 23 per cent of the cost of a geriatric hospital bed and 71 per cent and 79 per cent of the cost of a place in a local authority old people's home (Tinker 1984: 112). Significant financial savings are possible when a high degree of care input is required and where paid carers are employed.

Criticisms of the Structure and Operation of the Social Services

The combination of budgetary constraint and increasing demand for formal care – in the absence of the welfare state's ally of former years, economic growth – is a major factor behind current official interest in the role of volunteers and informal support networks. When this is coupled with an ideological opposition to the welfare state, as in the case of the United Kingdom, the result is a policy aimed at cutting and privatizing parts of the social services and shifting some of the burden of care from the formal to the quasi-formal voluntary sector and the informal sector.

Outside of this ideological mould, quite a different critique of the welfare state has been developing over the last 30 years, based to the large extent on the direct experience of formal services and research into their impact. Although important elements of this critique are to be found in some anti-welfare state rhetoric, notably in the attack on rigid state bureaucracy, for the most part it is directed towards changing the structure, operation and assumptions of formal services, making them more responsive to individual, family and community needs rather than *replacing* them with private or informal alternatives.

Three main elements in the critique of the operation of formal social services may be distinguished, each of which points to the need for greater awareness of and responsiveness to informal support networks and the voluntary sector.

Community Care: The Death of an Ideal

First, there is a longstanding criticism of institutional forms of care. Disillusionment with the social services arose early in the life of the welfare state when the objective of the children's service to keep children, as far as possible, with their parents in their own homes was not translated into services for the elderly and handicapped. There followed a long history of independent research on the relationship between institutionalization and dependency. Numerous researchers have substantiated Townsend's finding in the late 1950s that a significant proportion of residents of old people's homes are physically and mentally capable of living independently in the community (Townsend 1962; and for a review of subsequent research see Townsend 1981). This body of research has also demonstrated that for a large number of elderly people admission to an old people's home rests on social factors such as the lack of alternative forms of care, rather than simply physical or mental disability (Townsend 1965). Related to this is the considerable reluctance of elderly people and their families to contemplate admission to residental care (Qureshi and Walker 1987). In recent years the analysis of the dependency creating aspects of residential care has been extended to a wider range of social policies (Walker 1980; 1982b).

The alternative to institutions was originally said to be 'community care', or care in a person's own home with necessary domiciliary support services (Walker 1982a: 14 – 15). The history of community care policy in the United Kingdom, however, is one of painfully slow progress towards timid goals. Official statements and policies quickly undermined even the limited goal of care in the community (Bayley 1973) and in recent years the term 'community care' has been enlarged to include some residential institutions and hospitals (DHSS 1977: 8). The failure to pursue the original intention of the policy is demonstrated by the continuing dominance of expenditure on residential care over community care in local authority budgets and the considerable and growing shortfall in community care services in relation to official targets. Expenditure cuts have contributed to the shortfall in services and, as the DHSS itself (1981: 67) has recognized, this has inhibited the development of community care as a replacement for residential care: "In the personal social services some elements of the package of care which might be provided as an alternative to long-term hospital care do seem to have been held back as a result of expenditure constraints. The growth in the number of home helps, for example, had not kept pace with the increasing number of elderly people."

The failure of community care is primarily a failure of political will but in addition, there are powerful vested interests supporting residential care: planners, politicians, builders and professional groups involved (for a full account see Walker 1982a; 1982b).

The Client is Allowed to Speak

This brings us to the second set of criticisms of public social services: their bureaucratic organization, complexity and lack of responsiveness to client need. Again there is a long series of research studies pointing to the divergence between the perceptions of need held by clients and the professionals working with them (see, for example, Mayer and Timms 1970; Sainsbury 1980). This problem of bureaucratic complexity was increased, and the professionalization of the social services encouraged, by the expansion of the social services and development of more rigid and hierarchical management structures following the report of the Seebohm Committee (1968). Rather than developing community-based services sensitive and responsive to local needs, the new social services depart

246

ments became more centralized both organizationally and professionally, and more remote from their users. Moreover the hierarchical structure of these departments meant that successful staff could quickly be moved out of the reach of clients into management roles and non-qualified staff left in their place (Goldberg and Connelly 1982: 93). The gap created between clients and professionals by increasing professionalization, job demarcation, administrative complexity and the ever greater demands placed on social service workers was reinforced by a retreat into techniques and bureaucratic procedures:

"Symbolically, nothing reveals more clearly the limits to traditional social policy thinking than the spreading use of such terms as "service delivery" and "delivery systems". Social services are seen as something owned by the professional hierarchy within the social sector, to be "delivered" to the clients according to some professional diagnosis of what and how much different clients need" (Eide 1981: 258). Reactions against professional definitions of need, articulated initially through the welfare rights movement, community development projects and community work (Sinfield 1969) encouraged developments in social work away from models of casework which concentrated on personal inadequacy or pathology. towards models of practice which recognized the influences of environment. including family and other sources of support (Pincus and Minaham 1973) and contributed to a growing demand for client participation in the social services (Council of Europe 1984).

Together with mounting pressure on resources these developments paved the way for proposals aimed at altering the relationship between the formal and informal sectors by making the statutory services more responsive to and supportive of informal care networks, more community-centred rather than client-centred (Hadley 1981). Further encouragement in this direction was given by the Wolfenden Committee (1978: 192):

'We place a high value on this (the informal) system of care both because of its intrinsic value and because its replacement by a more institutionalised form of caring would be intolerably costly."

Most recently the Barclay Committee (1982) added its weight to this trend towards the construction of a community-centred policy for the social services by proposing a greater community orientation for social work emphasizing the importance of informal support networks, including volunteers, in the provision of services. Integrally related to these sorts of proposals for community support work are those for the decentralization of social services into small local areas or patches' (Hadley and McGrath 1980; Bayley et al 1981).

The Carers' Perspective

The third strand of criticism against the social services also stems from people with direct *experience* of welfare provision: those caring for elderly, mentally han-

247

dicapped and physically disabled people. The vast bulk of care is not provided publicly by the state but privately by the family. The family is the major source of primary support. In turn, it must be emphasized, family care is a euphemism for care by female kin (Land 1978; Finch and Groves 1980; Walker 1981; 1985). Women carry out most of the help, assistance, support or tending that care comprises. A survey of carers by the Equal Opportunities Commission (1980: 9) found that there were three times as many women as men. A study of elderly people using short-term residential care found that 85 per cent had female carers (Allen 1983). To the extent that we have a caring society, therefore, it is the female half that is the active one.

The task of caring for disabled people is often arduous and exhausting (EOC 1980; 1982). It comprises physical work, such as lifting, washing, cooking, but there is also a great deal of mental effort involved in the management of care, for example in organizing the disabled person's meals and medication or in coping with a difficult relationship. Where a woman is at the same time caring for a husband and children and managing two households or regimes, the burdens are enormous (Nissel and Bonnerjea 1982). This is the unromantic, uncomfortable reality of a great deal of caring work: hard manual labour, dirty jobs, sleepless nights and mental stress.

As well as doing most of the unpaid labour women bear the main burden of guilt and worry that the other side of the caring coin, love or affection, usually entails (Graham 1983; Ungerson 1983).

It is in response to the enormous costs – financial, social, physical and mental – that caring can impose on families and the fact that it is overwhelmingly women who have to bear the brunt of them, that a critical analysis has developed of the role of the social services in relation to female carers. This points out that in practice community care policies have paid very little attention to the needs felt and expressed by carers. The state has done very little to actively *support* their caring efforts. Instead it has confined the community care services to crisis or casualty intervention, thereby putting a penalty on caring and rewarding the breakdown of a caring relationship (Moroney 1980: 2), while legitimating non-intervention through appeal to the ideological assumptions that it is 'natural' for the family to provide care and especially 'natural' for women to do so (Walker 1981a: 25 – 29). The assumption underlying the Beveridge Report (1942: 59) was that "During marriage most women will not be gainfully employed." This was reasonable enough at the time because that was what the 1931 census had shown. But today three-fifths of married women in the 16 – 59 age group are economically active. Remarkably this does not seem to have reduced their commitment to care. Indeed it is extraordinary what physical and mental costs many employed married women bear in order to care for relatives and keep them in the community (Nissel and Bonnerjea 1982; EOC 1980).

This critique of the state and the social services in particular has been augmented recently by calls, from carers themselves, for a greater recognition of their role social care and for more practical support (Oliver 1983). Out of the more fundamental feminist critique of sexist forms of care has come the demand for alternative approaches which do not exploit women (Wilson 1982; Finch and Groves 1983). The feminist critique of formal care policies remains the most potent force pushing for alternative approaches to care. It has articulated questions which will emerge in a different form in many families caring for disabled relatives in the future. Although opposition to sex-based inequalities is unlikely, under its own steam, to have a major impact on the provision of informal care in the short run, in the longer term when coupled with the changes in the role of women in the labour market and society in general there is bound to be a, long overdue, challenge to their normative designation as carers.

These are the main factors contributing to disillusionment with the organization and operation of the public social services, one set arguing for the replacement of formal services and the other pointing towards a reconstruction of the welfare state and a closer partnership between the formal and informal sectors. Both help to explain the recent interest in voluntary forms of care and informal support networks or, in Abrams' (1980: 12) terms why "nowadays neighbourhoodism is all the rage."

There are sound political, economic and social reasons why volunteers and informal support networks should be integrated more fully into the operation of the social services. The main issue concerns the basis on which this policy is implemented. There is a great temptation to view volunteers and informal support networks as a universal panacea for the problems – economic, organizational and operational – of the social services. There are worrying signs in the United Kingdom that current policies of privatization and greater use of informal carers are not based on a responsible assessment of needs and resources but a dual concern to reduce the financial cost and limit the scope of the social services. It does seem sometimes that in place of 'throwing money' at social problems the government is attempting to throw volunteers at them.

The Voluntary Sector in Britain

There are then a variety of political ideologies in Britain arguing for a variety of state and non-state solutions. There is also a variety of meanings put on non-statutory welfare. Part of what follows is given over to explaining what we mean by welfare activities that are non-statutory. We exclude from consideration the private or 'profit-making' welfare sector, which has grown rapidly in recent years but remains small-scale. This is also true, in a financial sense, of the voluntary sector. But the voluntary sector is widely regarded as a more serious contender for the delivery of welfare services and, therefore, it is important to subject recent developments in this sector to critical scrutiny.

It is difficult to give an encapsulated definition of non-statutory welfare activities, excluding the private sector. A more common term in English usage used to describe them is 'voluntary' activities, or the 'voluntary sector'. Yet there are many paid jobs in the British voluntary sector and voluntary activity is by no means wholly unpaid. One survey recently estimated a figure of 180,000 paid jobs in the voluntary sector, equivalent to the size of the present computer industry (Charity Statistics 1983). This apparent paradox –paid voluntary effort – is not unique to Britain. Other languages however are more precise than English about the meaning of volunteering, and it is well that people unfamiliar with English should be aware of the term 'voluntary'. A distinction can be made between volunteers (individuals giving their time unpaid) and voluntary organizations or charities (structured, non-profit, non-governmental organizations which may employ paid staff).

The rest of this chapter proceeds through a historical review of the British voluntary sector to an assessment of its extent so that we can gauge its capacity to respond to the new pressures being put upon it by policy-makers. We use the term 'voluntary sector' rather loosely to refer to the work of voluntary organizations and voluntary work undertaken through them by volunteers. This has already been distinguished from informal care, which is most often undertaken in families by women, and which cannot be considered as voluntary activity – in many instances it is involuntary – but which is 'non-statutory' activity and may be related to voluntary caring activity. Neighbourghood care is also treated as a special case in that it can and does entail voluntary activity between individuals, as well as activity organized through formally structured community and neighbourhood groups.

The Evolution of the British Voluntary Sector

The tradition of voluntary action is well established in British culture and voluntary effort has played an important role in Britain in the delivery of welfare service The importance of its role has nonetheless varied and it is interesting to compare the current emphasis being put in the United Kingdom on the voluntary provision of welfare services with the historical ups and downs of the voluntary sector as whole. Before the 1834 Poor Law Amendment Act, poor people and working people depended in large measure upon a paternal system of welfare provision one in which church, employer and aristocrat combined in one way or another dispense to the needy, though a sharp distinction was drawn between the so called 'genuinely' needy and those regarded as the simple fickle. During the course of the 19th century Britain witnessed the growth of voluntary organization caring for the sick and the underprivileged. There was for example the foundation of the Salvation Army, settlements in the large cities, and orphanages such Barnado's for children. It was towards the end of this century that analyses were presented (e. g. by Booth, Rowntree and Marx) showing a casual relationship b ween industrialization and the plight of workers, and in this period too, we saw he socialist foundations of the Labour Party being laid.

n the period between the two world wars many major welfare services were provided by voluntary organizations. Voluntary organizations were major providers of care for children and the handicapped. National insurance was partly voluntarly administered. There was a significant number of independent voluntary hospials.

At the same time marked inroads in the work of the voluntary sector began to be made by the state. The state began to lay down standard provision for medical nsurance, pensions, unemployment and the like. Criticisms grew about the partiality of voluntary-provided services. Advocates of state provision called for the establishment of comprehensive and standard service provision and recommended a supplementary role for the voluntary organizations. The real watershed was reached with the publication in 1942 of the Beveridge Report (Beveridge 942) which laid down the form of the welfare state in Britain as we know it today, consisting of national provision for health, education, social services, housing and employment.

The setting up of national standards and of a safety net for the underprivileged at rst deprived the voluntary sector of growth points and for a long period after the var ended in 1945 there were few initiatives taken by voluntary organizations. Following the Beveridge Report the pace of change was set by the state. According o a major contemporary review of British voluntary organizations, in the 1945– 960 period "the voluntary sector seems in some ways to have been marking me" (Wolfenden 1978). Table 1 provides an indication of the further. very significant expansion in the welfare services provided by the state.

is doubtful whether current public expenditure on the broad welfare services has o any marked degree been curtailed even in the past decade. The pattern of current expenditure appears to be more or less keeping pace with current inflation,

able 1
ublic Expenditure on Welfare Services 1961–76 (£m)

	1961		1971	1976
ducation	1,012		2,899	7,300
ealth	730		2,249	6,089
ersonal Social Services	66		310	1,169
ocial Security	1,628		4,308	11,237
ousing	555		1,310	5.084
otal	4,191		11,016	30,876
	(100)		(264)	737
of Gross National Product	17.3	22.5		28.2

urce: National Income and Expenditure 1976. table 9.4

although this has to be set against the fact that the demands on this expenditure are most probably outpacing these increases, demands mainly brought about by a significant increase in the number of unemployed people and an aging population.

The Character of the British Voluntary Sector

In spite of the remorseless expansion of the statutory sector, advocates of a strong welfare state – like Beveridge and, more recently, the Seebohm Report on the reorganization of social service (Seebohm 1968) – also supported the idea of a strong complementary basis of voluntary activity. Although the Beveridge Report envisaged a dominant role for the state in combating want. disease ignorance, squalor and idleness, by 1948 Beveridge himself granted an essentia role for voluntary action alongside statutory-based care (Beveridge 1948). Twenty years later, in a report on the restructuring of statutory social services. Seebohm accorded a place to local community influence in the planning of locally-based social services. The aspirations for non-statutory activity, however, were largely not realized. The Wolfenden Report on voluntary organizations concluded that fo some fifteen years following Beveridge, there was little or no expansion in the vol untary sector.

During the course of the 1960s and 70s the voluntary sector expanded on a con siderably more modest scale than the expansion of the statutory sector. There were a number of developments which strengthened the voluntary sector:

• The establishment of the Voluntary Services Unit in the Home Office as a coor dinating arm of central government for voluntary organizations.

• The specialization of the work of voluntary organizations to carry out functions not carried out by statutory bodies, e. g. in the care of children in children's homes.

• The commissioning by government of community development projects fo inner city areas.

• The growth of pressure groups in welfare services, such as *Shelter* in the hous ing field.

• The proliferation of local self-help groups, some with national headquarters, i an attempt to come to terms with a host of issues such as drug addiction, alcc holism and the needs of single-parent families.

Despite the impetus to voluntary and community activity in the 1970s the belie still held that statutory services in the main provided the right solution. The belie too was expressed that properly reorganized statutory services were the answe The reorganization of local government in 1974 and the hiving off of health se vices into separate health authorities reinforced the notion that the state bore th major responsibility for welfare services in the field of housing, health and the pe sonal and social services. Reorganization involved fewer. larger authorities tha hitherto and the introduction of "corporate planning" in which local authorities were meant to take a comprehensive view of their provision of services (Bains 1972). It was a period in which managerial reorganization was felt to hold the key to better public administration.

Almost as soon as the new statutory structures were in place, doubts began to be raised about their capabilities. Although experiments were introduced to decentralize local authority services, in particular in the form of area management (Hambleton 1978), the impression was left that, in general, citizens became more distanced from their elected local representatives and the machinery of local government as a whole. Furthermore, although plans for reorganization began to be made years before reorganization was implemented, the changes came about at the very time when Western economics including Britain's were becoming subject to intense inflationary pressures. Reorganization demanded more public spending just when it was felt that spending needed to be cut back. The time was therefore ripe for a new review of the provision of welfare services and opportunities began to be sought for innovative and inexpensive modes of service delivery.

During the period of the 1974–79 Labour Government, modest, piecemeal attempts were made to involve the voluntary sector in new ways of service provision: for example, the Department of the Enviroment set up inner city partnerships; and the Department of Health and Social Security promoted neighbourhood care schemes. Finance to the voluntary sector through the Voluntary Services Unit was maintained. But the government had other major problems on its hands, not least its precarious majority in parliament. With the advent of the 1979 Conservative administration and its decision to hold public expenditure back, new opportunities, and new dangers, were presented to the voluntary sector.

The publication at the end of 1978 of the Wolfenden Report set the trend. This was a major review of voluntary organizations carried out independently of government but with government's blessing. Some commentators believed that though Wolfenden opened the door, it did not go far enough. There followed a set of publications which made particular recommendations for more equitable balance of voluntary- and statutory-provided services, in particular three books by Hatch (1980), Gladstone (1979) and Hadley (Hadley and Hatch 1981).

These publications arrived at a turning point in statutory-voluntary relations and in British politics when it seemed possible to break with the orthodox two-party political system and create a viable third party. Here was a small cluster of academics and policy-makers in the voluntary sector, a number of them renouncing their allegiance to Labour politics and promoting new social democratic ideas. They were neither in favour of state monopoly of welfare nor wholesale privatization, but of a middle way with enhanced voluntary provision.

Hatch's book was an empirical work based on a study of three English towns which was completed as research support for the Wolfenden Committee. Gladstone wrote from the point of view of a staff member of the National Council for

Voluntary Organizations, the major national body in Britain for voluntary organizations. Both authors were in broad agreement as to the way forward. Both supported the idea of a greater role for the voluntary sector but for different reasons. Gladstone was critical of statutory social policy which he regarded as an expensive failure having little impact. Hatch blamed the statutory authorities for a "top-down" approach to the voluntary sector, making little use of its potential. He advocated an "integral" model in statutory-voluntary relations. Gladstone called for "gradualist welfare pluralism." Neither were too specific about what voluntary-statutory combination they would like to see although amongst other things Gladstone recommended an overhaul of the role and scope of government activity and of grant-giving to voluntary organizations.

Hadley and Hatch together reviewed the position of health and social services in Britain. They concluded that clients had been persuaded to adopt passive roles. Based on close study of social services, they argued for greater decentralization at the local level, greater involvement on the part of clients and new legal rights for every citizen to participate in the planning and implementation of welfare services.

The course set for voluntary-statutory relations for the 1980s and beyond was one for which monolithic welfare policy, regarded as tied to the Labour Party, was rejected in favour of a 'better' mix of the voluntary and the statutory. But the careful research and guarded phrases of the academics began to give way to new Conservative Government policy to hold back on public expenditure and expand 'seed corn' programmes in the voluntary sector in which it was hoped a little money would reap a rich harvest of activity. Social services were a particular target.

The following statement is a typical example of government intention. It comes from Patrick Jenkin, Health and Social Services Minister for the first two and a half years of the Conservative Government, who wrote:

"Unlike education of health where the state carried the overwhelming responsibility for the provision of services, the personal social services run by local authorities represent but a small part of the total care given to those in need in the community. Overwhelmingly, elderly and disabled people are looked after through their families, through informal networks of care, through self-help groups and through the voluntary movement . . . Family and neighbourhood care constitutes an essential part of our system. With encouragement these voluntary and informal sources of care can expand as needs grow. I see the statutory services as essentially providing a framework for the whole pattern of community care and giving that special, skilled help that is necessary when dealing with particular areas of need such as children in care and the severely disabled and the physically and mentally handicapped" (Jenkin 1981).

Measures of the United Kingdom Voluntary Sector

What is the extent of voluntary activity in the United Kingdom? What capacity does it have to meet extra demand? These questions are some of the questions needing to be posed if government decides to hold tight on public expenditure and look to non-statutory sources of provision.

We do not know for certain about the extent of the voluntary sector. We can be fairly sure that the 'formal' voluntary sector – broadly speaking, the work of voluntary organizations and volunteers – is rather small compared with the statutory sector. We also believe that informal care – relatives, usually women, caring for relatives – is extensive.

There has been some work done on quantifying the voluntary sector. and that work is referred to here. But the work done is far from sufficient to support policies which rely on a shift of emphasis from the statutory to the voluntary. More work on quantification is being undertaken. For example, government surveys planned for 1986–88 will tell us more about participation in volunteering and the extent and nature of informal care. But the work appears patchy and piecemeal compared with the significance of the change of emphasis from formal to voluntary and informal.

Moreover, the orientation of the existing and planned work is towards what voluntary and informal care *is* taking place, not what *might* take place. In making social policy, politicians are apt to pronounce on what *ought* to take place. This is true of the United Kingdom. Not much work is going on at mapping voluntary activity as it takes place at present. And still less is work being undertaken on the capacity of the non-statutory sector to cope with the fresh demand. The few indications from the data are that there is not much spare capacity. The indications are as follows:

Try as it might, central government is not succeeding in reducing public expenditure. As we have shown unemployment and the rapidly rising proportion of elderly in the population are making increasing claims on social security. The level of government expenditure on the voluntary sector is minuscule compared with expenditure on the statutory sector. Public expenditure on the voluntary sector is increasing. Central government is a minor spender on the voluntary sector compared with local government, but its share of spending is increasing.

Voluntary organizations are eagerly taking up offers of government finance. Very many short-term and part-time paid posts are being created. Some voluntary organizations are becoming large-scale employers in an expanding 'grey' area between unemployment and permanent employment. It may be that to some degree impermanent, low paid posts in the voluntary sector are replacing and displacing formerly permanent, higher paid posts in the welfare state.

The level of volunteering on a comprehensive scale is not high and cannot be significantly increased. Busy people, people in employment and people who are economically secure volunteer most. Neighbourhood activity is quite prevalent but may be mostly confined to 'one-off' helping activities. Important though these voluntary and neighbouring activities may be, they cannot be expected to sustain much extra demand.

Informal care is extensive and the primary source of care for most of those requiring it. It is unlikely that it could be made more extensive. On the contrary, as we have argued, the accent on equality for women is likely to lead to a push for less care carried out by women.

An idea of the relative size of the voluntary sector may be gained first by looking at the proportion of public funds devoted to the welfare state (table 2).

Health and social services combined form over 10 per cent of total public expenditure (with health getting by far the lion's share). Health and social services are themselves a minority spending programme in the total of welfare state expenditure. Expenditure on social security is well over that on health and social services, and there is also additional welfare expenditure to account for in housing, education and so on.

To take the National Health Service alone, it is very big business indeed. Since its inception it has grown threefold and its proportion of a growing national in-

Table 2
Public Expenditure in Cash Terms by Programme (£b)

	Estimated outturn 1984–85
Defence	17.2
Overseas aid and other overseas services	2.5
Agriculture, fisheries, food and forestry	2.1
Industry, energy, trade and employment	7.2
Arts and libraries	0.7
Transport	4.8
Housing	3.1
Other environmental services	3.8
Law, order and protective services	5.1
Education and science	13.7
Health and personal social services	15.8
Social security	37.9
Other public services	1.9
Common services	1.0
Scotland	7.1
Wales	2.6
Northern Ireland	4.1
Adjustments – special sales of assets	–2.0
Reserve – general allowance for shortfall	–0.5
Planning total	128.1

Source: The Government's Expenditure Plans 1985–86 to 1987–88 (HMSO. Cmnd 9428-1)

come has risen from 4 per cent to 5.6 per cent. It comprises more than 2,600 hospitals with 450,000 beds. It is made up of 6 million in-patients and 37 million out-patient attendances. It is a massive employer with 38,000 doctors and 415,000 nurses, 113,000 administrative staff and 211,000 ancillary workers. In addition there are 22,000 general practitioners in the primary care sector.

Government Aid

Government expenditure on the voluntary sector is minuscule compared with that on the statutory welfare services (Charity Statistics 1985). Central government grants to the voluntary sector totalized £ 182 million in 1984/85. Announcing this total early that year, the Prime Minister explained that this represented a 35 per cent increase in real terms since 1979/80. It also appears to mean that central, as opposed to local, government is increasing its share of finance to the voluntary sector (from about one-fifth of central and local government expenditure combined in 1978 according to Wolfenden estimates, to more than one-third in 1983/84).

Grants by quangos (quasi non-governmental organizations) increased considerably from 1982/83 to 1983/84. Even after substracting Housing Corporation grants, which are a special case, grants from quangos in 1983/84 were more than double those from central government. The grants from the Manpower Services Commission (MSC) more than doubled over the last two years, an indication of the massive scale of MSC operations in the voluntary sector and of the impact of employment issues upon voluntary work.

Although central government finance has been rapidly increasing, total cash payments from local authorities are still nearly twice those of central government, running at some £ 351 million in 1984/85. Nevertheless, central government is becoming a much more important benefactor to voluntary organizations than hitherto. It seems too that the combination of central government and quango grants now dwarfs local government grant giving (and company giving even more so). The abolition of the Greater London Council and the metropolitan counties is almost bound to reduce further the local government share.

The statistics of central government grants indicate that the Department of the Environment (DOE) has emerged as by far the biggest spender on voluntary organizations. DOE finance through the urban programme has become the most sizeable central government grant. However, of as much interest is the 42 per cent increase from 1982/83 to 1983/84 in Department of Health and Social Security (DHSS) grants. DHSS spending in that period overtook for the first time, and by a considerable margin, grants from the very department which houses the Voluntary Services Unit (VSU), the Home Office. The VSU is only empowered to finance 'generalist' voluntary organizations which cannot find finance from particular government departments. The relative decline in importance of the VSU grant is itself a sign that voluntary organizations are being financed more and more to undertake work which is oriented to departmental interests.

With these increases in overall government finance the voluntary sector has been enjoying a small bonanza. It is important to bear in mind how small government expenditure is on the voluntary sector, including expenditure by local government. Only a little over one per cent of total local government expenditure goes to the voluntary sector. This is hardly an indication that the state has been rolled back. Additionally, local government is finding it hard to give more to the voluntary sector as central government tightens its hold on local government expenditure.

What is required is more consistent data on local governement aid to the voluntary sector, in cash and in kind. This in turn calls for improved monitoring by central government. Assistance to the voluntary sector is, after all, largely discretionary and therefore vulnerable, and one can all too easily see how central government expenditure may simply be replacing diminishing local government expenditure.

Charitable Giving and Volunteering

In terms of public expenditure the voluntary sector is minute compared with the public sector welfare state. But the size of the voluntary sector obviously cannot be considered solely in terms of public expenditure. Considered in these terms one gains an appreciation of government policy on the voluntary sector. Government understands that the voluntary sector is essentially about voluntary giving and its policy is to provide 'seed-corn' finance, of a kind which it is hoped from the provision of a little money lots of voluntary effort will flow.

The size of the voluntary sector is indeed far larger than public expenditure indicates. For instance, one recent survey of charitable giving of money in the United Kingdom puts it at £ 7.3 billion annually, or 3.4 per cent of GNP (Charity Statistics 1984). This seems a high figure and no doubt a large proportion of finance does not go into domestic welfare services. But the data show that even with these caveats voluntary donations dwarf government finance to the voluntary sector.

Additionally there are in the United Kingdom considerable amounts of time spent by volunteers carrying out voluntary activities. Research undertaken for the Wolfenden Committee made particular manpower estimates (table 3).

The Wolfenden data were admittedly rough and ready but they broadly signify two things. First, there is the possibility that volunteer effort can outnumber certain state welfare services. Second, there is considerable variation in the popularity of volunteer tasks. Giving help on a personal basis and helping young people are, according to table 3, probably much more appealing than helping in the health and hospital field.

Table 3
Manpower Estimates of Volunteers and Paid Staff in Welfare Services

	Volunteers (full-time equivalents) (1976 estimates)	Staff (1975 estimates)
Personal social services	200,000	200,000
Health	25,000	850,000
Education	120,000 *)	2,000 **)

*) working with children and young people

**) full-time workers

Other data from 1980s surveys support the view that volunteering takes place out of all proportion to government expenditure on it. But they also show that volunteering is largely a minority activity mainly undertaken by middle class people. Estimates of the proportion of people involved vary, from 23 per cent of adults taking part in volunteering in the previous year (GHS 1983) to 44 per cent (Humble 1982). Of this second detailed survey of a sample of 2,000 adults (aged 18+) some of the main findings were as follows:
• Approximately 44 per cent of people had been involved in some form of voluntary action in the past year (25 per cent in the past month and 20 per cent in the past week).
• Men were almost as likely to participate in voluntary action as women.
• 'Caring' volunteering is mainly carried out by women. Men tend to do impersonal work such as helping on committees.
• More better-off people tended to be involved than not so well-off people.
• Volunteers in the past week each volunteered six hours on average of their time.
• Popular forms of volunteering were with schools, sports and hobbies clubs, churches and welfare voluntary organizations.
• Neighbourhood care was more extensive than volunteering (75 per cent of the sample had given some form of help to neighbours in the past year).
Could voluntary work be expanded? The question is not an easy one to answer. But the answer justified by the survey data to hand must be that voluntary work could not be significantly expanded. Broadly speaking the evidence contradicts the view, sometimes asserted or implied, that volunteering is an ideal way of filling spare time. The data do not support the hypothesis that voluntary workers would be drawn predominantly from those who would apparently have the most time to spare. On the contrary, groups that might be expected to have more time available, such as people without children, the unemployed, and perhaps the recently retired show lower than average participation rates in voluntary work. The data suggest that those who do voluntary work tend to have a relatively stable and secure lifestyle, so that some of the spare time they do have can be given to

voluntary work rather than to sorting out their own problems or adjusting to a new lifestyle such as that imposed by unemployment.

The number of unemployed in Britain is now considerable, some three or four million. Few studies have been conducted in the past few years on the extent to which unemployed people participate in voluntary work. One special study was a postal survey undertaken in 1982 of some 3,000 registered unemployed (and therefore seeking employment) in five localities. Non-response was high (nearly 50 per cent) so the statistics needed treating with caution. The overall conclusion was that "It seemed that the participation of unemployed people in voluntary work is similar to, though a bit lower than that found in the population generally" (Gay and Hatch 1983). Here, the authors compared their statistics with the Wolfenden survey, the closest comparable survey, finding that some 9 per cent of the unemployed sample reported voluntary work in the period of their unemployment.

The unemployed volunteer figures (only 130 participants) were analyzed by sex, age, social class, length of time out of work and locality: "Though time out of work apparently made little difference to participation in voluntary work, there were substantial differences between the five localities; women were more inclined to take part than men, and people in non-manual occupations than those in manual occupations; and those aged 25 or less were least likely to take part."

In terms of the kinds of people helped by volunteers "It seems that only a small number of the volunteers, and thus a tiny proportion of the total sample, were using voluntary work to occupy a substantial proportion of the time left free by lack of employment." It was found that about the same proportion (8 per cent) of the sample were taking education or training classes as were volunteering but that leisure pursuits such as gardening were being undertaken by up to six times as many of the people in the sample. Significantly, 28 per cent of the sample reported doing odd unpaid jobs for friends and neighbours, indicating that friendly and neighbourhood helping was at least three times as widespread as formal volunteering (a finding supported in the survey quoted earlier of the general population). It was also found that volunteering was not a replacement for other 'spare time' activities – the unemployed volunteers participated to a greater extent than non-volunteers in almost every kind of spare time activity.

Demands on the Voluntary Sector

We turn now to a summary of the current claims being made on the role of the British voluntary sector in the provision of welfare services. These claims come from a mixture of sources. They represent claims not centred exclusively on the functions traditionally provided in Britain by voluntary organizations but on the broad range of voluntary activity taking place, including volunteering through voluntary organizations as well as informal and neighbourhood care, and voluntary activity carried on through self-help groups. The list of claims below is necessar ily an incomplete one but it should be sufficient to illustrate the present shift in rolling back the state in favour of voluntary and community-based provision.

Claims from Within the Voluntary Sector

As a prime example the National Council for Voluntary Organizations – the national voice for voluntary organizations in the United Kingdom – calls for pluralist provision of welfare services (NCVO 1980). Voluntary activity, it maintains, does not simply involve volunteer-donated welfare services for the needy but also community-based activity, including influence on public policy able to be exercised by local communities. The demand for plurality of welfare provision does not represent a demand for dismantling the welfare state, rather a redirection of statutory attention away from professional delivery of care towards supporting care in the community.

Claims from Outside Reviews and Commissioned Research and Development

There has been a recent substantial accumulation of review and research evidence in favour of shifting the balance towards voluntary provision. It is difficult to disentangle this evidence from government influence since government has played a major part in prompting, stimulating and funding such reviews, research and development. A major example is the Barclay Report (Barclay 1982), which was a review at the behest of central government of the role and function of the professional social work service. Besides findings basically in favour of a professional social work service, Barclay supported the notion of a community-based service and distinguished between four types of community resources with which the statutory services might usefully interweave – informal carers, mutual aid (or self-help) groups, volunteers and formal voluntary organizations.

Locally-based Research and Development

Three examples are research and development projects located in Dinnington, Normanton and East Sussex. "At the heart of the experiment" (in the mining community of Dinnington) "lies the desire to create a working partnership between both formal services themselves and formal services and the community" (Tennant and Bayley 1984). The Dinnington project is not untypical of projects such as these which embody attempts to devolve social services delivery to the very local level, operating 'patch'-based systems in close conjunction with local voluntary and community groups. Some, like Dinnington and Normanton (Hadley and McGrath 1984), are collaborative efforts involving central and local government.

Others, like East Sussex (Hadley 1984), represent the efforts of local authorities in cooperation with sympathetic outside evaluators. These innovations in devolution may be counted as part of a larger contemporary movement in British local government towards 'going local'. This devolutionary shift however masks a variety of political motivations. The present attempt amongst a number of Labour-controlled urban local authorities to go local is heavily criticized by Conservative central government because it requires extensive public expenditure. Yet Dinnington, Normanton and East Sussex are Conservative-inspired experiments – the first two funded by the Department of Health and Social Security (DHSS), the third by the Conservative-controlled local authority of East Sussex – also on local area lines. The important difference is that the accent in the three social service experiments is on community care whereas the Labour-controlled councils are concerned with making local government services more accessible.

Claims from Central Government

The Dinnington and Normanton projects illustrate the limits of control by central government (in this case the DHSS), over local government. With these experimental projects, central government is hoping to indicate to social services departments across the country how they might work to support voluntary, informal neighbourhood-based and family-based activity. Central government is considerably constrained in Britain in what it can tell local government to do. True, it is taking steps to increase its control over local government expenditure. But in matters, say, of social service practice it is confined to showing the way by demonstration. Similarly, in the case of the voluntary sector, central government has instituted a set of programmes designed to convey the message that it wants greater emphasis upon voluntary-based activity. The following (taken from Stubbings 1983) is a list of examples of these programmes for 1980–84.
• *Good Neighbour Campaign.* Dept. of Health and Social Security, late 1970s: Development of good neighbour projects and activities.
• *Adult Literacy Campaign.* Dept. of Education and Science, mid 1970s: Utilization of volunteers to improve literacy.
• *Civil defence.* Home Office, 1980: Creation of emergency defence, volunteer-based forces.
• *Development of local voluntary action.* Home Office, 1980: Development of local intermediary agency functions in voluntary sector.
• *Voluntary Projects Programme.* Manpower Services Commission, 1981: Development of local voluntary action involving unemployed.
• *Opportunities for Volunteering.* Dept. of Health and Social Security, 1981: Development of local voluntary action involving unemployed in health and social services.
'Helping the Community to Care' is the most recent (1984) government pro-

gramme aimed at the voluntary sector, in this instance in order to improve care for elderly people, the mentally ill and mentally handicapped by providing assistance for volunteers, neighbours and others to care for them more effectively. Improvement to family-based care is also included in this programme.

Central government attempts to persuade public agencies to pay much greater attention to the voluntary sector. It also has increased the amount of research and intelligence on voluntary action. But overall central government policy on the voluntary sector is uncoordinated, unsystematic and *ad hoc*.

Where it is directed it tends to see voluntary action as instrumental to its own ends, rather than as a right to be enjoyed by individuals. In particular, as Westland argues cogently (Westland 1983), current government policy, including policy on voluntary action in the personal social services, lacks purpose and coherence. In the 1979–82 period ministerial statements in the social services field were exclusively directed at the need to involve the voluntary sector, not at support for the public sector. Yet the Department of Health has been unable to make significant inroads into local government expenditure on the personal social services. Westland calculates that in spite of government rhetoric in favour of the voluntary sector, its expenditure on special voluntary programmes in the social services amounts to only 0.88 per cent at most of the forecast social services expenditure.

In other words, while the rhetoric has shifted significantly in favour of non-statutory-based care, expenditure has not. Present central government policy in this area is to an extent a prisoner of demographic forces – for example, greater expenditure required through an aging population – and its other policies – for example, greater social security expenditure required through a larger number of unemployed. Taken in this light, government support for voluntary action is marginal. Public expenditure currently fails to keep pace with growing demand in the personal social services; and present government policy fails even in its own terms to shift the balance significantly away from statutory provision.

Unemployment and the Voluntary Sector in the United Kingdom

Some of the demand on the voluntary sector which has been illustrated so far has been stimulated by criticism of what are regarded as inherent weaknesses of state welfare, such as bureaucracy, inaccessibility and over-professionalization. New seeds also create demands on the voluntary sector, prominent among which is unemployment.

In relation to the significant problem of unemployment, the voluntary sector in Britain does not see itself limited to the provision of volunteer-based care to help cope with the negative side-effects of unemployment, nor simply to the provision of alternative voluntary activity whilst people are unemployed. Voluntary organizations are involved in both (Stubbings and Humble 1984). Agencies in the voluntary sector also believe they have a role alongside the statutory bodies and the private sector in helping provide

- Income maintenance strategies.
- Stimulation of specific employment opportunities.
- Restructuring of working time.
- Local economic development (NCVO 1983).

Local voluntary organizations have for some time been deeply involved in a variety of ways with unemployed people, whether providing financial advice for example, or providing voluntary work for them to do. Current government measures (e. g. the Voluntary Projects Programme, Opportunities for Volunteering) are specifically designed to promote the activities of the voluntary sector in the unemployment field. Thus far, finance provided through these measures has been eagerly taken up by voluntary bodies, which have historically been poorly funded. The twin dangers of these measures are first, that measures aimed at the unemployed provide finance in fact for bolstering the voluntary sector infrastructure; and second, that voluntary bodies become party to the creation of a subgrade system of employment which is poorly paid and operates on a temporary basis.

The chief direction in which the accumulating evidence on the proper relationship between the voluntary sector and the unemployment issue is pointing to is that involvement in voluntary action by unemployed people is not a substitute for paid work, and should not be regarded as such. But the potential of voluntary work in this field is "as a measure to the creation of small-scale employment, as a key ingredient in creating community businesses, as a means of redistributing skill and energy, as a way of helping to meet the social and intellectual skills of people who may be unemployed as a route to acquiring or sustaining new skills" (Stubbings 1984).

Conclusion

This chapter does not stake out a significant claim for a role for voluntary action in the changing climate of state welfare services. Rather, it has tried to place general policy on and activity in the British voluntary sector in relation to ideological shifts in policy, retrenchment in public welfare expenditure and various pressures on the formal services. The main points arising from the study are:

- A voluntary sector largely overshadowed by a burgeoning welfare state in the post-war period up to the 1960s.
- In the following period a growing number of local experiments to realize a more creative voluntary and public welfare mix.
- Demand for welfare services outstripping public expenditure on them.
- Public policy statements with an emphasis upon a greater role for the voluntary sector outmatching policy implementation.

• Greater demand being placed upon voluntary, informal, neighbourhood and kinship caring networks.

• Voluntary activity assisting at the margins in the problem of unemployment, but where the potential to assist is probably much greater.

We have attempted to explain these developments in the first half of this chapter. Government attempts to achieve welfare pluralism have been considerably more rhetorical than practical. Government has been adept in creating an atmosphere of philosophical support and has committed small funds for experimental voluntary-statutory schemes. But any shift of policy like that towards community care requires high expenditure in the first instance. Government has failed to show how the voluntary sector could significantly increase its funding to take on the extra burden.

Special employment measures like the Voluntary Projects Programme have distorted the concepts of paid work and voluntary work and increased the dependence of voluntary agencies on government. The danger is that voluntary agencies are tending to become agencies of implementation rather than of experimentation and innovation – an additional arm of the state rather than a source of alternative ideas, good practice and criticism of state-run services. It is essential, therefore, for policy-makers to recognize both the strengths and limitations of the voluntary sector (as well as those of the informal sector) if it is to make the most productive use of voluntary effort. The following points emphasize this need for caution about the potential of the voluntary sector.

First, the encouragement of direct action of the voluntary kind and increased public participation in the delivery of social services does not begin to tackle the problem of the unequal distribution of income and wealth. Voluntary organizations are not in a position to organize the equitable distribution of resources since each competes for its own discrete area of provision.

Second, more emphasis on the voluntary sector means less emphasis on the statutory safety net of support for the poor. Unless we are careful, it directs our way from the state's obligation to meet the needs of the poor and the deprived. This danger is particularly acute when the state attempts to *substitute* voluntary for statutory assistance as a means of reducing resources.

Third, we have had in Britain a modest programme for the voluntary sector – the urban programme – which has been found wanting in failing to increase public participation. It has had little to say about the new devices that might be open to us to allow people to feel more able to influence and organize social policy programmes.

Fourth, an accentuated voluntary sector requires more finance. The dangers of more money for voluntary organizations are obvious: it may increase their dependence on the statutory sector; it brings into question where their accountability lies; and it helps transform them into statutory organizations in the guise of voluntary ones.

Fifth, increased voluntary activity must rely upon the capacity of people in communities of neighbourhoods to care for each other. Yet this capacity may be over-emphasized. Work by Abrams (1979) on neighbourhood care schemes in Britain has questioned the assumption on which such schemes operate. His evidence is that neighbours often enter into neighbourly transactions for what they can get out of it, rather than from altruistic motives. Neighbourhood care 'networks' may thus be too fragile to cope with such schemes or to be able to deliver the right things in the right places.

Sixth, an expansion in the voluntary sector requires more volunteers. Where are they to come from? Commentators have pointed as a possible scenario to the increase in time given over to leisure and recreation as a result of massive technological change. Another scenario might be one of an increasing number of unemployed whose dissatisfactions are unlikely to lead them down the path of volunteering.

Seventh, the unions and unionized labour are unlikely to accept a growth in voluntary effort when it is likely to threaten jobs at a time of widespread unemployment.

Eighth, an increased emphasis on the voluntary sector may entail a growth in what might be called a voluntary sector superstructure, cutting across existing lines of accountability and responsibility between elected bodies, such as local authorities and their electorate. It is a superstructure whose accountability is confused. The danger is not so much that it will be more inflexible than present government, but that it will provide an excuse for elected representatives to place the blame elsewhere.

Finally, expansion of the voluntary sector costs money. Additional finance on its own does not yield the sort of results that are needed to fill the gap between increasing welfare need and the decreasing capacity of the public sector. Expanding the voluntary sector is not the answer. It is only part of the answer.

The Conservative Government in Britain has been attempting to engineer a new welfare mix by encouraging the non-statutory sectors. We have concentrated on informal and quasi-formal voluntary provision but assistance has also been given in the form of state subsidies, to the market sector. This policy stems primarily from anti-welfare state ideology, but is also draws strength from the more constructive criticism of the welfare state that has developed over the last 30 years. Research suggests that caution is required in accepting the new configuration of 'mix' of welfare provision as more effective than the old one. The hopes of politicians for a greater *substitution* of informal or voluntary activity for formal services are based largely on cost considerations. But if we are concerned with the effectiveness of services in the promotion of welfare we are more likely to focus on the relationship between the informal, voluntary and formal sectors and the need to interweave their respective strengths.

Contrary to the hopes of some politicians, informal and voluntary support cannot adequately replace the welfare state or counteract inadequate macro-social and economic policies. Nor can they substitute for public expenditure on the social services, they are dependent to some extent on such expenditure. Thus social welfare is not likely to be enhanced by cuts in social expenditure or an anti-welfare state ethic. Moreover it will not be helped and may be positively hindered by over-idealizing the potential role of informal and voluntary support with the presumption that they are superior to formal services. All three forms of welfare provision have strengths and weaknesses; all three may create dependency or foster independence and social integration. This danger of over-idealizing and therefore overburdening informal and voluntary effort can be prevented by the careful planning of social change in relation to *needs* rather than prescription for service provision. Research should play an important part in this planning, including comparative research. At the heart of the search for a more effective welfare mix must be an awareness of the strengths and limitations of all forms of welfare delivery.

Bibliography

Abrams, M., 1980, Beyond Three Score and Ten, Age Concern, Mitcham.

Abrams, P., 1978, 'Community Care: Some Research Problems and Priorities' in Barnes J. and Connelly N. (eds.) Social Care Research, Bedford Square Press, London.

Abrams, P., 1979, Neighbours, papers presented to the Volunteer Centre UK.

Abrams, P., 1980, 'Social Change, Social Networks and Neighbourhood Care', Social Work Service No. 22, pp. 12 – 23.

Allen, I., 1983, Short Stay Residential Care for the Elderly, PSI, London.

Bains Committee, 1972, The New Local Authorities, HMSO, London.

Barclay Committee, 1982, Social Workers: Their Roles and Tasks, Bedford Square Press, London.

Bayley, M., 1973, Mental Handicap and Community Care, Routledge and Kegan Paul, London.

Bayley, M., 1982, 'Helping Care to Happen in the Community' in Walker A. (ed.), 1982a, pp. 179 – 96.

Bayley, M., 1986, Address to the Volunteer Centre.

Beveridge Report, 1942, Social Insurance and Allied Services, Cmnd 6404, HMSO, London.

Beveridge, W., 1984, Voluntary Action, Allen & Unwin, London.

Bosanquet, N., 1983, After the New Right, Heinemann, London.

Burghes, L. and Lister, R., 1981, Unemployment: Who Pays the Price?, CPAG, London.

Challis, D. and Davies, B., 1980, 'A New Approach to Community Care for the Elderly', British Journal of Social Work, Vol. 10, 1, pp. 1 – 18.

Charity Statistics, 1983, 1984, 1985, London, Charities Aid Foundation.

Council for Europe, 1984, Proceedings of the Colloquy on Client Participation in the Operation and Management of Social Services, Steering Committee for Social Affairs, Strasbourg.

Davies, B., 1981, The Cost-effectiveness Imperative, The Social Services and Volunteers, The Volunteer Centre, Berkamsted.

Department of Employment, 1985, Employment: the Challenge to the Nation, HMSO, London.

DHSS, 1977, The Way Forward, HMSO, London.

DHSS, 1981, Growing Older, Cmnd 8173, HMSO, London.

DHSS, 1981, Report of a Study on Community Care, DHSS, London.

DHSS, 1985, Reform of Social Security, vol. 1, HMSO, London.

Ide, K., 1981, 'Breaking Out of the Traditional Social Policy Ghetto' in OECD, 1981, pp. 255 – 260.

EOC, 1980, Caring for the Elderly and Handicapped, EOC, Manchester.

Ferge, Z., 1979, A Society in the Making, Penguin, Harmondsworth.

Finch, J. and Groves, D., 1980, 'Community Care and the Family: A Case for Equal Opportunities?' Journal of Social Policy, vol. 9, Part 4, pp. 487 – 514.

Finch, J., 1984, 'Community Care: Developing Non-Sexist Alternatives', Critical Social Policy, Issue 9, pp. 6 – 18.

Gay, P. and Hatch, S., 1983, Voluntary Work and Unemployment, Manpower Service Commission, Research and Development Series No. 15.

Gladstone, F., 1979, Voluntary Action in a Changing World, Bedford Square Press, London.

Goldberg, E. M. and Conelly, N., 1982, The Effectiveness of Social Care for the Elderly, Heinemann, London.

Golding, P., 1983, 'Rethinking Commonsense About Social Policy' in Bull D. and Wilding P. (eds.) Thatcherism and the Poor, CPAG, London, pp. 7 – 13.

Graham, H., 1983, 'Caring: a Labour of Love' in Finch J. and Groves D. (eds.) pp. 13 – 30.

Hadley, R., 1981, 'Social Services Department and the Community' in Goldberg E. M. and Hatch S. (eds.) pp. 35 – 45.

Hadley, R. and McGrath M. (eds.), 1980, Going Local: Neighbourhood Social Services, NCVO Occasional Paper One, Bedford Square Press, London.

Hadley, R. et al., 1984, Decentralising Social Services: A Model for Change, Bedford Square Press, London.

Hakim, C., 1982, 'The Social Consequences of High Unemployment', Journal of Social Policy, vol. 11, Part 4, pp. 433 – 68.

Hambleton, R., 1978, Policy Planning and Local Government, Hutchinson, London.

Harris, C. C., 1983, The Family and Industrial Society, Allen and Unwin, London.

Hatch, S., 1980, Outside the State: Voluntary Organisations in three English Towns, Croom Helm London.

Henwood, M. and Wicks, M., 1984, The Forgotten Army, Family Policy Studies Centre, London.

House of Commons, 1981, Hansard, vol. 998, HMSO, London.

Jenkin, P., 1981, 'Economic Constraints & Social Policy', Social Policy and Administration, vol. 15 no. 3, p. 240.

Knapp, M., 1984, The Economics of Social Care, Macmillan, London.

Land, H., 1978, 'Who Cares for the Family?', Journal of Social Policy, vol. 7, Part 3, pp. 357 – 84.

Le Grand, J., 1982, The Strategy of Equality, Allen and Unwin, London.

Mayer, J. and Timms, N., 1970, The Client Speaks, Routledge and Kegan Paul, London.

Moroney, R. M., 1978, The Family and the State, Longmans, London.

Moroney, R. M., 1980, Families, Social Services and Social Policy, Department of Health and Human Services, Washington.

NCVO, 1983, Voluntary and Community Organisations and Long-term Unemployment, NCVO Consultative Paper, National Council for Voluntary Organisations, London.

Nissel, M. and Bonnerjea, L., 1982, Family Care of the Handicapped Elderly: Who Pays?, PSI, London.

OECD, 1981, The Welfare State in Crisis, OECD, Paris.

Oliver, J., 1983, 'The Caring Wife' in Finch J. and Groves D., pp. 72 – 78.

OPCS, 1981, General Household Survey 1980, HMSO, London.

OPCS, 1982, General Household Survey 1981, HMSO, London.

Parker, R., 1981, 'Tending and Social Policy' in Goldberg E. M. and Hatch S. (eds.), pp. 17 – 32.

Pincus, A. and Minahan, A., 1973, Social Work Practice: Model and Method, Aldine, New York.

Pinker, R. A., 1974, 'Social Policy and Social Justice', Journal of Social Policy, vol. 3, Part 1, pp. 1 19.

Qureshi, H. and Walker, A., 1987, The Caring Relationship, Macmillan, London.

Sainsbury, E., 1980, 'Client Need, Social Work Method and Agency Function: A Research Perspective', Social Work Service, No. 23, pp. 9 – 15.

Seebohm Committee, 1968, Report of the Committee on Local Authority and Allied Personal Social Services, Cmnd 3703, HMSO, London.

Sinfield, A., 1969, Which Way for Social Work?, Fabian Society, London.

Social Services Committee, 1980, The Government's White Papers on Public Expenditure: The Social Services, vol. II, HC 702, HMSO, London.

Stoller, E. P. and Earl, L. L., 1983, 'Help with Activities of Everyday Life. Sources of Support for the Noninstitutionalised Elderly', The Gerontologist, vol. 23, No. 1, pp. 64 – 70.

Stubbings, P., 1983, Central Governement Policy Towards Volunteers, MSC Thesis, Cranfield Institute of Technology.

Stubbings, P., 1984, Voluntary Work and Unemployment Study in the Countries of the European Communities: Summary, Commentary and Conclusions. Policy Studies Institute, London.

Stubbings, P. and Humble, S., 1984, Voluntary Work, Unemployment and the Labour Market in Britain, Voluntary Work and Unemployment Study in the Countries of the European Communities, EEC.

Tennant, A. and Bayley, M., 1984, 'Continuity of Social Work Ideas and Practice in the UK', in Nowotny, H., (ed.) Thought and Action in Social Policy, European Centre for Social Welfare Training and Research, Vienna.

Tinker, A., 1984, Staying at Home, HMSO, London.

Titmuss, R. M., 1968, Commitment to Welfare, Allen & Unwin, London.

Titmuss, R. M., 1974. Social Policy, Allen & Unwin, London.

Townsend, P., 1962, The Last Refuge, Routledge & Kegan Paul, London.

Townsend, P., 1965, 'The Effects of Family Structure on the Likelihood of Admission to an Institution in Old Age' in Shanas E. (ed.) Social Structure and the Family, Prentice Hall, N. J., pp. 163 – 187.

Townsend, P., 1981, 'Elderly People with Disabilities' in Walker A. and Townsend P. (eds.) Disability in Britain. Martin Robertson, Oxford, pp. 91 – 118.

Treasury, 1976, National Income and Expenditure, HMSO, London.

Treasury, 1979, The Government's Expenditure Plans 1979/80 to 1982/3, Cmnd 7439, HMSO, London.

Ungerson, C., 1983, 'Why Do Women Care?' in Finch J. and Groves D. (eds.) pp. 31 – 50.

Walker, A., 1981, 'Community Care and the Elderly in Great Britain: Theory and Practice', International Journal of Health Services, vol. 11, 4, pp. 541 – 57.

Walker, A., 1980, 'The Social Creation of Poverty and Dependency in Old Age', Journal of Social Policy, vol. 9, Part 1, pp. 49 – 75.

Walker, A. (ed.), 1982, Public Expenditure and Social Policy, Heinemann, London.

Walker, A. (ed.), 1982a, Community Care, Blackwell/Robertson, Oxford.

Walker, A., 1982b, 'Dependency and Old Age', Social Policy and Administration, vol. 16, 2, pp. 115 – 35.

Walker, A., 1984, 'The Political Economy of Privatisation' in J. Le Grand and R. Robinson (eds.), Privatisation and the Welfare State, Allen & Unwin, London, pp. 19 – 44.

Walker, A., 1984a, Social Planning, Blackwell/Robertson, Oxford.

Walker, A., 1985, The Care Gap, Local Government Information Unit, London.

Webb, A. and Wistow, G., 1982, 'The Personal Social Services' in Walker A. (ed.), pp. 137 – 164.

Wenger, C., 1984, The Supportive Networks, Allen & Unwin, London.

Westland, P., 1983, 'No Sense of Direction'. Community Care, 17 November.

Wicks, M., 1982, 'Community Care and Elderly People' in Walker A. (ed.). 1982a, Community Care, p. 97 – 117.

Wilson, E., 1982, 'Women, the 'Community' and the 'Family'' in Walker A. (ed.), 1982a, pp. 40 – 55.

Wolfenden Committee, 1978, The Future of Voluntary Organisations, Croom Helm, London.

Wright, K. G., 1982, 'The Economics of Community Care' in Walker, A. (ed.), 1982a, pp. 161 – 178.

269

Shifts in the Welfare Mix:
Significant Features in Countries with
Planned Economy

Similarities and Differences

Endre Sik and Ivan Svetlik

This preface is written to draw the reader's attention to some peculiarities of the European socialist countries. During the discussions in our research group we found that we used the same terms several times such as welfare state, social actors, economic crisis, market, voluntary sector, etc. but that they had quite different meanings. We think that this communication gap can be narrowed if one takes into consideration the differences in historical background, ideologies, economic and political structure that exist between socialist and non-socialist European countries.

Our task is first of all to point out *similarities* and also some *dissimilarities* among the socialist countries. In this way some light will also be shed on the differences between socialist and non-socialist countries.[1])

First we would like to familiarize the reader with the meaning of the central term of this introduction *the welfare system* and with the reasons why we chose it as opposed to the terms welfare mix or social policy. We then enumerate some fundamental historical facts and turn to the impacts of the ideology and economic structure of the European socialist countries on their welfare systems. Last but not least, we give some examples which show how these countries react to the present crisis.

The Welfare System

It is somewhat difficult for us to delineate adequately the subject of our introduction.

Although in socialist countries there has been a combination of planned and market economies, we can scarcely speak about a liberal state which assumes responsibility for the well-being of its citizens through a range of interventions in the market economy, e. g. full employment policies and social welfare services (Mishra 1984); i. e. we can hardly speak about *welfare state*. The socialist state is not a liberal one as it is known in some Western countries. However, its interventions in the economy and in other spheres of social life have been frequent. Had we accepted the notion 'welfare state', this would not have been a proper concept. The state is by no means the only social actor that assumes responsibility for the well-being of its citizens, be it directly or by means of welfare institutions. There are several social actors such as enterprises, volunteer organizations, families and informal groups which aim at incrementing their own or others' welfare without any state regulation.[2]) At first glance it seems that *social policy* would be a better term to circumscribe the subject of our contribution. If it refers "to the aims and objectives of social action concerning needs as well as to the structural patterns of arrangements through which needs are met" and if it "is not restricted to government action and arrangements" (Mishra 1981), it comes closer to the point. However, there are at least three reasons for our reservation regarding this term. First, in socialist countries, social policy has been conceived as a special aspect of economic policy (Ferge 1983; Šefer 1981). But it is doubtful that welfare for all citizens could be achieved only by means of economic regulation. The consequences of economic flows are to a great extent unpredictable and uncontrollable. Second, social policy relates semantically, more to the production of services than to welfare institutions, more to the dynamics than to the structural elements of welfare. Third, social policy has not been widely shared among Western scholars, which makes communication even more difficult.

We decided therefore to use the term *welfare system*. It is less ambiguous than 'welfare mix' and represents an open and universalistic concept. It includes private and social welfare sectors and welfare institutions; health care, child care, education, employment, social security and other welfare areas; service providers and service consumers, their values, norms and policies. It also includes various relations between these structural elements such as management, financing, service production and service delivery, and (de)centralization. The informal or semiformal welfare sector can be added without any difficulties. Moreover, this concept permits the examination of relations between the welfare system and its environment, e. g. economic and employment systems.

Social and Economic Development

According to A. Gerschenkron (1962), the most important outcome of the belated economic development of the European periphery during the 19th century up to World War II was the huge role of the *state* as the sole actor of economy which could collect financial means from the national economy in order to make at least the first steps towards economic development and to be powerful enough to bargain with the leading capitalists of the core economies.

This process also included bureaucratism, centralization, militarization and other forms as well as the deepening of social inequalities. This powerful state combined social policy with police force. As successfully as Bismarck used social policy as a weapon against the rising workers movements in Prussia, the emperor of the Austro-Hungarian Monarchy and Russia used the gendarmerie against the peasantry. Combining caritas with brute force, and personal rewarding systems with close mass control was typical in this world region.[3])

This state-centred system produced paternalism, ideologies of the omnipotentiality of the state, clientelism, nepotism, corruption, and servility on the one hand, and lack of civic consciousness and of decentralized (community level) administration on the other.

The afore-mentioned trends took place in peasant-type societies in all the East European countries. The isolated peasant communities preserved the 'ancient' forms of social policy, e. g. familism, interhousehold transfers, moral elements of economic behaviour besides (or instead of) market-oriented rationality. These post-peasant elements of behaviour survived in spite of the mass migration to towns and cities and working in industry. This was also encouraged by an overall religiousness.

The developments after World War II have led to the increasing power of the state and of the Communist Party in all the East European socialist countries which have made many efforts to modernize relatively backward societies. A part of the modernization process has also been the development of the state welfare system. After some successes during the first two decades, socialist countries have faced increasing economic and social problems since the beginning of the 1970s. This also holds true for Yugoslavia which has remained out of the Eastern block and which has made some attempts to find an alternative to socialism e. g. a highly decentralized administrative system and self-management.

The Ideological, Political and Economic Basis of the Present Welfare System in the European Socialist Countries

Social and welfare systems of socialist countries are built on the basis of a *Marxist ideology:* equal distribution of goods and services is desired in these systems, which can be achieved only after production and distribution of all resources are brought under state control. Once this is done, the market, family and private property cease to be the basic allocative institutions.

According to Mishra (1981), in socialist countries there exists a *structural model* of the welfare system which is characterized by: total state responsibility for meeting individual needs, the domination of the need-based ideology of distribution, comprehensive range of statutory services which cover the entire population, high level of benefits, high proportion of national income spent on state services, marginal use of means tests, clients treated as members of the collective, solidaristic orientation of services and a marginal role of non-statutory agencies in welfare. Social services are an expression of the basic values of society and are in this sense central to the social structure.

The ideal structural model described above is certainly not realized fully. *Quite*

275

the contrary. There have been several deviations from the model and several un-favourable consequences have appeared as a result of its application.

The state has not only been the dominant actor in the sphere of social policy but also in the sphere of economy. This has led to many interferences between the two areas. As a consequence, social policy is not conceived as a means for neu-tralizing the side effects of the economic system, which forces certain groups and individuals onto the margins of the labour market and the economic and social systems. As we stated earlier, social policy is conceived as an integral part of economic policy (Ferge 1983; Šefer 1981). There has been an assumption that social problems can be solved by means of economic growth and redistributive mechanisms of which social and economic systems in socialist countries consist. The most important is the employment system which should permit full employ-ment.

The ideology and practice of the state and especially of the Communist Party have been to limit individualism and to promote the collective forms of produc-tion and consumption. These collective forms have been introduced mainly *from above* without much respect for the traditional forms of collective life. Therefore, traditional forms of service rendering were destroyed or else they survived only in the 'civil society' i. e. in the informal sector. Instead of new collectivism which should appear in the formal service sector, forms of massive, typified and imper-sonal service rendering have evolved, often being rather ineffective and of poor quality.

One of the most widespread collective forms of service rendering can be found within the *enterprises* which have developed several services from highly valuable ones, such as housing facilities and educational programmes, and ranging to cer-tain everyday services like provision of clothes for work or hot meals. These ser-vices have evolved because of two distinctly different reasons. First, the state is interested in direct rendering of services to the employees by the enterprises in order to omit some responsibilities, to promote the idea of collectivism on a lower (quasi-community) level and to simplify the welfare system. Second, enterprises develop some services as a means of competition which exists on the labour market under conditions of full employment.

One should not neglect the special meaning that *work* has in the ideology as well as in the economic system. Work represents the cornerstone of Marxist ideology as well as of the institutional system of the socialist countries. In this context work is conceived as employment in the socialized sector and at the same time as a basis for participation in political and economic systems.[4] Employment, and not citizenship, is the key criterion by which one is entitled to welfare benefits and can participate in welfare programmes.

In practice the official working time in socialist countries is longer than in most Western countries, especially for women whose participation rate is high and who seldom work part-time.[5]

Besides long official working hours, *informal work activities* e. g. housework, ousebuilding, caring activities and other forms of self-production, as well as vari- us forms of informal paid work, have been rather extensive.[6] This can be ex- lained partially by the traditional forms of social life, *but mainly by lasting econ- mic deprivation of individuals and by the underdevelopment and rigidity of for- al welfare institutions which are unable to satisfy several needs of individuals.* ne can notice that some actors of the welfare system who play an important ole in West European countries are less important in the socialist welfare sys- ems. *These make up the private and the voluntary sectors.* Their role has been arginal because the state tends to exercise tight control over the welfare sys- m and to get rid of the competitive actors. The lack of an organized and wide- pread voluntary sector is caused also by the long total working time. However, e state is ready to tolerate or even temporarily encourage these system-aligned egments (informal, private and voluntary sectors) in order to ease the burden of conomic crisis and to strengthen the social peace.

he 'Present' Economic Crisis and Adaptation to It

or the European socialist countries, the worldwide crisis of the 1970s appeared rst of all in the form of sharply growing international debts. But this crisis was nly an unexpected extra burden on these economies which have faced structu- al 'mini-crises' since the end of the post-war 'renovation period' (Jánossy 1975). ow productivity, permanent shortage of goods, inefficient production and dis- ibution, underdeveloped infrastructure and service sector, growing technologi- al backwardness are the main elements (structural basis) of the lasting econ- mic problems of the European socialist countries.

uring the past 20 years different types of experiments have been made to hange or at least minimize the negative effects of these elements.

ust to mention a few of them: In Poland, Gomulka's reform, Gierek's experiment haracterized by 'quick modernization' based on Western credits and the Soli- arity mass movement. In Yugoslavia, economic reform in the mid 1960s fol- owed by institutional reform which brought about increasing decentralization, ew forms of direct democracy and ignoring market mechanisms in the mid 970s and another economic reform called the stabilization programme in the be- inning of the 1980s. In the German Democratic Republic, a permanent pursuit owards the perfection of the centrally-planned society based on 'intra-German' conomic ties. In Hungary, the 'invention' of the second economy, the New Econ- omic Mechanism in the mid 1960s. In spite of these differences, *in all European ocialist countries the worldwide crisis caused quite similar effects in the begin- ing of the 1980s:* declining real wages, falling standard of living and the tempor- ry (?) interruption of the very embryonic restructurization process.

he first reaction in all the European socialist countries to the rapid falling into ebts was the cut-back of state funds including social policy funds. In this respect

there are some basic similarities with other industrial economies e. g. Reagano
mics and Thatcherism. This cut-back together with the decreasing real wages an
rather poor social infrastructure caused great troubles for the population, espe
cially for those who are not in the labour force because, as mentioned earlier, th
overwhelming proportion of the social benefits in the socialist countries is base
on participation in the labour force.[7])

The reader will notice that the three contributions which follow deal with differei
segments of the welfare system in socialist countries: Hungary with labour ma
ket problems and their impacts on welfare and welfare policies, Poland with i
voluntary sector, its decline and professionalization and Yugoslavia with the re
sponses of its welfare institutions to economic and employment crises. He w
find out certainly that there exist many similarities as well as dissimilarities be
tween these three welfare systems. However, we would like to turn the reader
attention to one, most important problem, in our opinion, which all socialist cour
tries share. How to establish civil society which would be relatively independel
of the socialist state? The following chapters show that this problem has not bee
solved in a satisfactory way. Professionalization of the voluntary sector in Poland
the tension-ridden symbiosis between the first (socialized) and the second (ma
ket and household) economy in Hungary, and the dominant role of the stai
which prevent the real autonomy of self-managed communities of interests
Yugoslavia, can serve as good examples.

Notes

1) There exist also similarities between the two groups of countries e. g. the necessity of developir
several welfare programmes to counteract the negative social effects of industrialization, the bas
structure of educational systems, the role and the spreading of the state bureaucracy, etc. Ho
ever, we will not address ourselves to these issues in this work.

2) Even if one or more of these actors would be missing from the field of social action, a model wi
which a researcher could not explain the causes of these 'holes' would be incorrect.

3) Zsuzsa Ferge's description of the social policy of the 1930s in Hungary is a good example of th
nature of the mature form of this Bismarckian empire-like social policy: "the destitute and milita
working class, was subjected to strong police oppression but they obtained some concession
mainly in social insurance provisions. The coverage and the level of benefits remained low, ar
the concessions did not weaken the capitalistic relations. An unemployment insurance was nev
enacted. The first payments of old-age and disability pensions were postponed until 1939. Th
schemes covered less than one-third of the population and the whole rural proletariat was left ou
The urban and some of the rural poor, including the unemployed, the aged and the disabled, we
the target of state-organized, mainly privately financed charity, permeated by the spirit of the po
laws. The combination of forceful demagogy, police repression and some concessions su
ceeded both in assuring quiescence and in fragmenting the political potential of the oppresse
classes. The political logic of the dominant classes so marked the progressive movements ar
thinking of the time that the left became divided into many splits and schisms that weakened
and rendered it self-defeating." (Ferge 1984)

4) In Hungary the name of one of the highest govermental medals is the Hero of Socialist Work.

5) In 1984 the average weekly working time in Hungary was 42.7 hours, while in the OECD countri
in 1981 it was only 40.1 hours. (Timár 1986).

6) According to the level of living research carried out in Slovenia for instance, more than half of adults work over 12 hours a day (Level of living 1984). Ir. Hungary the informal economy took up 57 and 56 per cent of the economy's total work time. While time devoted to performing strictly defined houshold chores occupied a great but decreasing percentage (in 1960, 80 per cent, in 1980 only 67 per cent of work done with in the informal economy), there has been a 166 per cent increase in that part of the informal economy which includes small-scale craftmanship. paid and unpaid social work, and do-it-yourself work activities. (Sik 1986)
7) While in other socialist countries, no open unemployment exists, in Yugoslavia this problem has been rather severe. The unemployed, among them especially new entrants, who represent the majority, are in as bad a position as those who are not in the labour force.

Bibliography

Ferge, Zs., 1983, 'The Impact of the Present Economic Crisis of Hungarian Social Policy – from a Comparative European Perspective', Can There be a New Welfare State?, September. Baden.

Ferge Zs., 1984, 'Ideology and practice in a situation of Change and Uncertainty', Can there be a New Welfare State? Siófok, Hungary.

Gerschenkron A., 1962, Economic Backwardness in Historical Perspectives, Harvard Univ. Press.

Jánossy F., 1975, A gazdasági fejlödés trendvonaláról (Of the trend of economic development), Magvetö, Budapest.

Level of Living, 1984, Kvaliteta zivljenja v Sloveniji/Level of Living research projekt, Coordinator Veljko Rus, Institute of Sociology, Ljubljana.

Mishra, R., 1981, Society and Social Policy,MacMillan Press, London.

Mishra, R., 1984, The Welfare State in Crisis,Harvester Press.

Šefer, B., 1981, Socialna politika v socialisticni samoupravni druzbi (Social Policy in Socialist Self-management Society), Delavska enotnost, Ljubljana.

Sik E., 1986, 'Second Economy and Social Stratification'. Paper for the XIth World Congress of Sociology, New Delhi, India

Timár, J., Working time, Manuscript, Budapest.

New Trends in the Hungarian Welfare System
Towards 'Self-Welfarization'?

Endre Sik

The aim of this chapter is to describe the new trends of the welfare system[1]) in contemporary Hungary in a brief summary of the goals and rules of behaviour of the *actors* of the welfare system:[2]) the state, the enterprise, the private social service, the church, the voluntary association and the household.

Brief Notes on the Actors of the Hungarian Welfare System

The *state* is the dominant actor of the welfare system in contemporary Hungary. This is a result of both the imperial traditions of the Austro-Hungarian Monarchy and of the Soviet-type socialist model (which also has its imperial historical background).

This etatist development produced paternalism, ideologies of the omnipotentiality of the state, clientism, nepotism, corruption, etc.

As for the Soviet inheritance, I follow Ferge's (1984) description: ". . . (in a soviet-type state) . . . Any remaining problems were assumed to vanish rapidly and automatically, since all the actions and measures of our people's democracy, of its social and economic system *are* social policy".

Since everything 'was' social policy, and since poverty and other social problems were declared to have been abolished, no autonomous social policy was needed by the central power.

During the decade of the Cold War (the late 1940s and early 1950s) a centralized, hegemonistic state welfare oganization emerged.

From the mid 1960s until the 1970s, the Golden Era in Hungary prevailed: stabilition, economic reforms, international loans, a lifting of the Iron Curtain. Because of the favourable economic conditions there was no pressure to change the organization or behaviour of the state's welfare policy (described previously by Ferge) during these decades. There was a rapid growth of the state in social policy, with the number of creches, kindergardens, physicians and hospital beds multiplying during this period.

The *enterprise* has been an important actor of the welfare system since the early 1960s. (Previously it was only the final stage of the state's allocation chain with no autonomy.) The enterprise as an actor of the welfare system, due to the permanent scarcity of market labour, has always tried to use welfare funds as a means to obtain new entrants and to bind its core workers.[3]).

This is why the enterprise (as long as it could) has increased its welfare expenditures.[4]) Between 1960 and 1976 enterprises increased their welfare funds by 89 per cent. This was almost 10 per cent higher than the increase of the nominal wages in the same period. (Farkas 1982)

In 1976 the enterprise's share in financing the six most important welfare tasks was almost equal with that of the state's.

During the 1960s, due partly to the high proportion of commuters and partly to the very underdeveloped infrastructure, the enterprise was able to obtain new en

Table 1

The share of pecuniary state welfare expenditure by actor and task in 1976 (%)

	Enterprise	Local council	Central budget	Total
Welfare subsidies	34	29	37	100
Building and running nurseries and kindergardens	13	85	2	100
Organized holidays	56	2	42	100
Total*)	45	40	15	100

*) Including cultural and sport expenditures and the value of feeding at the work place.
Source: Farkas 1982.

Table 2

The percentage of pecuniary welfare expenditures by task in 15 enterprises (%)

	1968	1971
Meals at the work place	50	45
Building and running nurseries and kindergardens	12	14
Holiday	6	12
Housing	1	3
Others*)	31	26
Total*)	100	100

*) Cultural and sport expenditures. financial subsidies. stipendium for vocational aims.
Source: Szilágyi 1974.

trants (especially from the youth). It offered hot meals at the work place at a very low price, new working clothes every year free of charge, good conditions for changing clothes after work and having a shower.

During the 1970s these welfare benefits were handled as 'natural' conditions, thereby losing their value in obtaining entrants. This decade was the period of building holiday resorts, nurseries and kindergardens (especially in firms where the majority of the labour force were female, e. g. in light industry) and marked the beginning of housing welfare programmes.

It was during this period that the first attempts to create internal labour markets and to bind the core workers and low level managers were made. In the area of welfare activity, this has meant increasingly valuable benefits for the core, but only 'natural' welfare benefits for the peripheral workers.

Private social services should operate basically on market principles. There are only a few firms of this kind in Hungary despite the state's efforts in the 1980s to stimulate the creation of small, profit-oriented private enterprises by tax allowances. Previously this actor has been virtually missing from the list of the actors of the welfare system. These kinds of small and professional enterprises probably did not emerge because they have not seen any chance to gain profit from households with low and decreasing dispensable income.

Associations (both self-help and charity type) offering social services have also been rare in Hungary. During the 1970s there were some local councils who tried to organize groups to look after elderly people or to help the poor, as well as a few mental-hygienic self-help groups.

In addition, the traditional associations and communities within the *churches*[5]) have participated.

In a global perspective the role of the church and of the associations has always been negligible. This is mainly related to the state's aversion to them. It has never liked either its own 'deviancy' – when an agency or local branch of state organization invents anything new or tries to give non-profit extra-welfare service (see later) – or the entirely independent initiatives.

The final actor of the Hungarian welfare system to be mentioned is the *household*. The welfare activity has never ceased to be one of the main functions of the household. Ethnological descriptions prove that the household has always been the dominant actor of welfare in non-industrialized rural societies which composed Hungary until the early 1920s. One may even assume that despite the increasing welfare activity of the state and the enterprise – and perhaps until World War II, that of charitable associations – in the 20th century *the welfare activity of the households, though never recorded, and therefore invisible, has always played a decisive role.*[6]) The constant importance of households within the welfare system cannot be verified directly in the lack of comparable sociological data. However, it can indirectly be characterized by analysis of time budgets of households between 1960 and 1980. Through one and a half decades the proportion of time allotted to work at socialized economy has decreased. Time

Table 3
Proportion of working time spent in different economic segments (1967—1980) (%

	1967	1974	1980
Private sector			
households' self production	19	18	17
households' petty commodity production	20	23	25
Socialized sector	61	59	58
Total	100	100	100

Source: Tímár 1985.

devoted to chores was still maximal in 1980 and there was a sharp increase small scale production (of agricultural goods).

The time budgets of households with small farms reflect a similar process (Ag cultural. . .1982).[7]) Between 1972 and 1982 the "prosumptive" (Toffler) ar small-scale commodity productive working time increased from the daily averac of 4.5 hours to 4.9 hours. (And to this a constant 1.5 hours have to be adde which are spent for upkeeping, building and supplementary activities. On th other hand every household is engaged in reciprocal exchange of labour f 1,2 hours *daily*.) Working time of chores has remained constant in the pa 10 years (6.3 hours/day).

The Reaction of the Actors of the Hungarian Welfare System to the Economic Crisis in the 1980s

Let us begin the analysis with a short summary of the economic crisis at the tu of the 1970s–1980s. The main goal of economic policy since 1978 has been th reduction of hard currency debts accumulated during the early 1970s. For th aim, an active monetary and bank policy – among others new foreign loans, ar the increase of export to Western countries – has been necessary. That these e forts were not unsuccessful is proved by the positive Hungarian foreign trade ba ance in Dollars since 1980 and by the decrease of foreign debt.

However, the plan to perform the export of efficiently produced goods sold good prices on the world market has not been achieved. This was caused first k the deterioration of the terms of trade, and second, by the unfavourable struct ral conditions and obsolete means of production of the Hungarian economy.

Since the export had to be increased at any cost, investments and consumptic were reduced centrally, while exports were considerably subsidized, implyir that everything was exported which could be sold at any price.

The maintenance of the political status quo made it impossible to keep back co

284

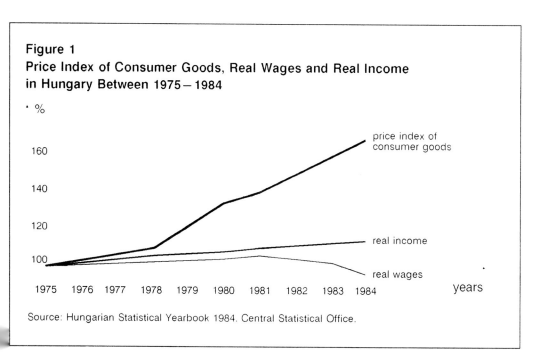

Figure 1
Price Index of Consumer Goods, Real Wages and Real Income in Hungary Between 1975–1984

Source: Hungarian Statistical Yearbook 1984. Central Statistical Office.

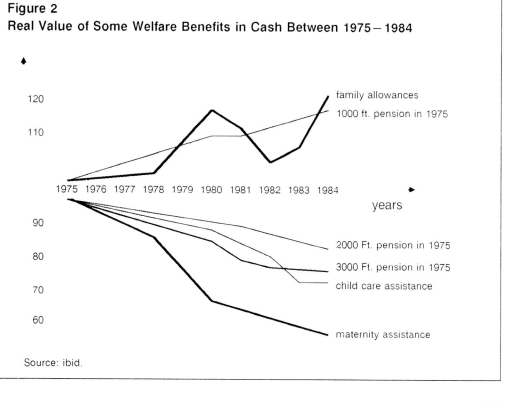

Figure 2
Real Value of Some Welfare Benefits in Cash Between 1975–1984

Source: ibid.

sumption by administrative methods (i. e. rationing) or by suddenly growing short. Therefore the state economic policy endeavoured to limit consumption by means of inflation or from the wage earners' point of view by decrease of real wages. In this way the state could reduce the budget's burdens of subsidizing the production of consumer goods and to decrease imports.

Figure 1 shows the official value of the consumer price index, real income and real wages from 1975.

The state as an actor of the welfare system acted in accordance with the aims of its economic policy. That is why most welfare benefits in cash did not preserve their real value, compared to the mid 1970s.

Figure 2 shows that, except for the lowest pensions and family allowances, all welfare benefits in cash decreased in real value. The investments and maintenance of welfare infrastructure (the hardware of the in-kind welfare service) were at best stagnating, more often declining in this period.[8]

Cancelling investments and decreasing the resources for upkeeping welfare service as well as declining real value of welfare benefits in cash naturally influences *the structure and functioning of the state's welfare organization.* One may observe renewed attempts at organizational refashioning and also conceptual changes, e. g. an altering relation to clients, the emergence of new 'economic' ideologies (i.e. selectivity increases to the detriment of universalism and there are many who wish to strengthen the discretional features of selectivity). At the same time 'welfare innovations' also appear on the 'edges' of the state's welfare organization, frequently in the form of 'deviant' behaviour of those working there. For example, in the middle of the general crisis in public health several groups, clubs dealing with children with Down's syndrome, ileostomics, or with chronic alcoholics have made their appearance.

Svetlik (1987) convincingly summarizes the habitual reactions of the socialist state on the economic crisis:[9]

"Welfare institutions have elaborated several responses which can be put together into three different strategies: the marketization of services, the rationalization of service production and the externalization of service production. In most cases, welfare institutions react to the crisis automatically, without any planned action and without an elaborated strategy. These reactions have significant impacts on enterprises, localities, volunteer organizations and also on informal welfare activities. Structural changes within the welfare system are in question."

As for the *marketization* and *rationalization of the state's welfare services* one can find almost all of Svetlik's Yugoslavian examples in Hungary, too.

The clients of the welfare organizations in Hungary are quite familiar with the situations when new and changed services appear tightly binding to or sometimes instead of traditional free of charge welfare services.

Another case is when enterprises and households are increasingly constrained to contribute to the resources serving the maintenance of hospitals, kindergardens, nurseries, etc. This mechanism works through a particular 'quasi-market'

286

type institution. This means that those households or enterprises who can afford it may jump the queue to institutions when – and it is very frequent – demand exceeds supply. Thus, for instance, enterprises may hand over their own welfare resources to the state's welfare, or they may offer their employees' 'voluntary' work for enlarging or upkeeping kindergardens. The households, in turn, may supply child care organizations with in-kind goods free of charge and 'voluntarily', e. g. pocket tissues, cleaning compound or used clothes.

Rationalization has also several forms and again all of them are very well – known to Hungarians. Firstly there are the efforts to reduce investments. Szalai (1986) gives very good examples of how the public health has been rationalized since the 1960s in Hungary. However, her excellent book is a strong argument against Svetlik's thesis that rationalization is a 'new' strategy and only a temporary reaction to the crisis. She stresses that the rationalization stategy is a constant attitude against the so-called 'non-productive' sectors, and its malevolance increases in accordance with the growth of investment costs (which is an imminent necessity of development).

She also describes the solutions which the central budget has always tried for easing its burdens by enlarging the already existing hardware almost without costs, developing without investment; e. g. by raising new buildings and using overburdened and underpayed physicians without modern equipment, such as the 'organized' growth of efficiency of hospital beds (beds in the corridors or five beds in rooms built for three).

Secondly, there is the rationalization by substitution of cheaper services for more expensive ones, e. g. outpatient care instead of hospitalization, cheaper medicines instead of more expensive ones.

A good example of rationalization is the changing balance between funds for regular and occasional welfare support. While the number of regular clients slightly decreased between 1970 and 1981, the number of cases giving occasional support increased rapidly.

Thirdly, rationalization is also rather frequent when there is a reduction in the timeframe or in the quality of the welfare programmes.

As for the *externalization* strategy, by and large I agree with Svetlik (1987) again: 'Essentially the externalization of service production means that certain professional activities aimed at carrying out certain welfare programmes are reduced or terminated within welfare institutions, while they appear for the same reasons in other spheres of the welfare system, for instance within enterprises, localities, volunteer organizations, informal groups and families . . . If human needs are satisfied by welfare institutions at a lower level, people try to mobilize other resources, either formal or informal. They exercise their pressure on the enterprise where they are employed, they seek other forms of social assistance, such as given by the volunteer organizations, or they start providing services on their own, either individually or in kin or neighbouring groups. This shift is easier if these types of service rendering represent an important part of cultural tradition, and if there is no rigid social control exercised by formal authorities and formal institutions."

However, while describing the real processes of externalization and also to promote the understanding of its possible social outcomes, it would be useful to make a distinction *among the variations in the attitude and structural position of the actors of the externalization process towards each other.*

Firstly, I think that there are crucial differences between the externalization process – in the course of which extra funds (to cover the surrendered expenses), professional knowledge and openly defined operational rules are allocated together with the new task – and the externalization process where only obligations and strict control 'come from above'.

Secondly, I think if there are mutual interests, open and constructive bargaining, similar sets of values and more or less balance in the power of actors the outcomes of the externalization process will be different as it would be in any other case.

Since the subject of my analysis is not the actor's inside mechanism, therefore, in *summing up the behaviour of the state as the dominant actor of the welfare system in Hungary in the 1980, I only point out that it takes upon itself less than before. Both the level of running in-kind welfare services and the real value of welfare benefits in cash show a declining tendency. So the state is becoming less capable of fulfilling the needs of households with decreasing real income.*

In a situation like this the mode of the externalization process can be characterized either as the *charging of or as the offering of a larger scope for non-state actors of the welfare system.* In the former case the externalization is a kind of *hidden exploitation,* in the latter it can be the *first step towards a more pluralistic welfare system.*

Now I enumerate the main features of the reactions of the non-state actors of the welfare system on the economic crisis and on the decreasing state welfare expenditure.

The *enterprises*, because of both the growing pressure of taxation and the continuous shortage of skilled labour *have been obliged to give welfare support while at the same time they are less and less able to do so.* Thus, their only aim is to preserve the former level. There is a growing inequality in the value and quality of the welfare services delivered to the employees both among enterprises and among core and peripheral workers within them. In addition to this growing and cumulative segmentation process from the households' point of view, it is also an extra burden that enterprises have rationalized their welfare services as well. While in 1978, the proportion of the value of charged service paid by the employees within the total welfare expenditures of the enterprises was 27.8 per cent, in 1982 it was 36 per cent. (Stuberné 1984)

Needless to say, the state has not given any financial aid to the enterprises. They are allowed – but by tacit understanding only – to surrender their funds to the state welfare organization and to use their own (and decreasing) welfare funds

288

freely. In brief, *less enterprises give less welfare services in a more unequal way and at higher and higher prices, while the state uses them as a means of marketing its own welfare services.*

As I mentioned before, at the beginning of the 1980s there were some efforts by the state to encourage the foundation of *private social services.* The most significant organization of this kind acts in form of a small cooperative: it is Lares,[10]) an organization established only because of negligence of the state welfare organizations. Here only the welfare demands (nursing, baby-sitting, cleaning, etc.) of solvent groups, can be met and it is not a solution for satisfying the urgent needs of poorer groups. The majority of the financial means for running this small cooperative comes from their matchmaker service and not from their welfare activity. As for the *church* and the *associations,* their welfare activity has also been growing during this decade.

For example, since 1981 there are eight newly founded care centres within the organization of the Catholic church, and their charitable activities cover some thousands of aged and poor people. (Szilágyi 1985)

There are also a growing number of specialized organizations of the churches, for example houses of charity and charity networks (i. e. supporting in the form of work, clothes and money). And there are also the less or hardly institutional initiatives of the churches, for example homes providing asylum for aged people, blind children, punks, neglected juniors, dope addicts, alcoholics. The welfare activity of small churches is also significant.

Some *associations* (both charity and self-help type) have also been formed in the past years. The Poor Supporting Fund (SZETA) organized auctions and collections (money and second-hand goods) to help the needy. The aims of the Cultural and Self-Help Association of Pensioners (consisting of 22 members) are to form self-help groups among pensioners, to build homes for themselves, "to fight against isolation and loneliness" and to form mutual helping networks for welfare services. (Horváth 1986)

In brief, the trend of the spreading of the private social services, of the church's welfare activity and of the associations indicates that perhaps (and to a limited extent and only if they have no political aim at all) the state allows a little bit more easily the functioning of these non-state welfare actors. However, *for the time being* – because of their poor financial means, of the almost unchanged suspicions by the state (very often by the local councils and the police) and of the lack of tradition to organize and use these institutions – *the scope of these welfare actors is very small, thus they cannot fill the widening gap, created by the withdrawal of the state (and partly of the enterprises) between the welfare supply of non-household actors and the constant or increasing welfare demand of the households.*

In a situation like this there are but two alternatives for the households: *to survive without having their welfare demands satisfied or to increase their own efforts by self-service, 'self-welfare' and self-production (of goods).*

According to opinion polls, people are very much aware of the fact that there is a growing gap between their needs and the state's welfare support. While in 1982, 55 per cent of a representative sample declared the economic situation of pensioners as serious and worsening, in 1984 this figure was 71 per cent. (Ferge 1984) Households would like to receive more welfare from the state. The proportion of those who want the state to increase its welfare activity was 45 per cent in 1982, but 59 per cent in 1984. (Ferge 1986)

According to its fundamental social function, the *household must at least try to satisfy the needs of its members.* It must be done, regardless of the dangers of the economic and social disadvantages of long working hours and of low productivity of self-production, self-service and 'self-welfare' in the long run. These characteristics can be summed up altogether as *self-exploitation.*

Unfortunately, I have only a few figures about the households welfare activity in contemporary Hungary. The only time-series data I have is on self-production of food. (table 4)

In cases of non-peasant type households, after the decline between 1960 and 1970, the amount of self-production rises again. In cases of peasants and peasant workers, there is a permanent decline, but still in 1982 the proportion of self-production is very high.

As for *self-service*, figure 3 shows that in every type of service, the use of domestic or reciprocal exchange of labour is more important than the service bought from the state or on the market.

The role of self-service[11] is the highest for building houses, repairing cars and washing. In the case of mending electrical appliances, due to the necessity of specialized skills and the state's monopoly on the allocation of spare parts, the households are unable to work for themselves.

The only direct figure concerning the *scope of welfare activity of the household*[12] is from 1980. In a representative questionnaire it was asked if there was any 'social help' received or given within a year. 62 per cent of the households reported themselves as active in this respect.

Table 4
The Proportion of Self-produced Food in Total Food Consumption by Locality and Strata (1960 – 1982) (%)

Household type	1960	1970	1980	1982
Urban workers	10	8	12	13
Rural workers	40	33	33	34
Non-manuals	14	12	13	14
Peasants	65	52	43	41
Peasant workers	56	45	39	36

Source: Háztartásstatisztika 1982.

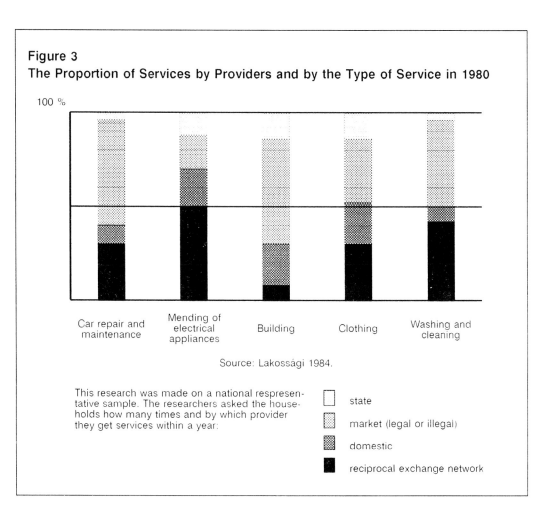

Figure 3
The Proportion of Services by Providers and by the Type of Service in 1980

100 %

| Car repair and maintenance | Mending of electrical appliances | Building | Clothing | Washing and cleaning |

Source: Lakossági 1984.

This research was made on a national respresentative sample. The researchers asked the households how many times and by which provider they get services within a year:

☐ state

▦ market (legal or illegal)

▨ domestic

■ reciprocal exchange network

Digression: Of Self-exploitation in House Building

It is not by chance that it is the case of house building where the households' reaction to the withdrawal of the state can be shown very clearly.

The right to housing has always been one of the declarations of socialism. However, during the 1950s – the period of forced industrialization and militaristic developmental policies in Hungary – both the building and maintenance of houses received low priority in the state budget. As a result, an enormous housing shortage developed by the 1960s, with the majority of the housing stock run down.

Then a long-term governmental housing programme was announced, aimed at eliminating quantitative housing shortages and improving the quality of houses as well. Still, while an annual 8.5 apartments had been built per thousand people in the 1970s, this figure dropped to 7.2 in 1981, 6.9 in 1982, 6.6 in 1984.

Table 5
Labour Resources for House Building by Types of Work Stages
in a Hungarian Village (%)

	Work done by						
	Domestic Work	Reciprocal exchange of labour	Household & reciprocal exchange of labour	Household and labour market	Labour market	Socialized labour	Total
Fence building	44	2	38	8	8	—	100
Foundation	14	10	44	24	7	1	100
Walling	18	5	35	20	19	3	100
Roofing	14	5	26	24	26	5	100
Electrical Fitting	8	15	23	7	39	8	100
Plumbing	13	9	33	14	16	15	100
Plastering	31	7	28	16	17	1	100
Concreting	32	10	33	14	10	1	100
Painting	52	3	28	5	10	2	100
Transportation	21	4	13	4	13	45	100

Source: Sik 1985.

The above decline in building activities was the total sum of a rapid decrease in state-run construction and an increase in that financed and performed by the households. In the 1970s households financed and built the majority (65 per cent) of new apartments. There has been a consistent increase in their share: it was 74 per cent in the years 1981-82, reaching 79 per cent in 1983 and amounting to 86 per cent in 1984.

The same tendency is found when focusing exclusively on labour performed in house building. Private building construction (including work actually done by the household members as well as work provided through reciprocal-altruistic networks and paid work obtained in the labour market) comprised 44 per cent of the total in the 1970s. The share of private construction reached 46 per cent by the years 1981-82, 49 per cent in 1983 and jumped to 59 per cent in 1984.

It has been demonstrated by historians as well as ethnologists that, except for the wealthiest urban dwellers, home building has always been done by the families and the households. The mixture of market and household labour with unchanged technology has dominated house building throughout the country, even with the appearance of large governmental housing programmes and estates (block houses). Table 5 presents the structure of labour resources in house building by the most important stages of the project in a contemporary Hungarian village. Apparently, the role of the first (socialized) economy is insignificant save transporation. It is the households that build the houses in the village, through labour exchange and, to a lesser degree, with a little help from the local 'second economy'. *Even in the cities, it is this organization of building that gradually fills the gap caused by the withdrawal of state redistribution from house building, consequently, the households' self-exploitation increases, the 'second economy' expands and the reciprocal network of households becomes stronger.*

Of the Future

I would sum up the structure and the likely trends of the welfare system in contemporary Hungary as follows: there are two dominant actors, the state and the household. *Their characteristics as actors of the welfare system* are very different: the state is a visible (sometimes loud-mouthed), bureaucratized, efficacy-oriented, monetarized, centrally-planned organization whose aim is to maintain the political status quo by satisfying (in a paternalistic manner) the basic needs of the average citizen.

The household is an invisible (sometimes consciously hiding) primary group which is often irrational (in a narrow economic sense) and is ready to 'overuse' its resources without plans or calculations just for the sake of the survival of its members. Its long-term stability, embededness into many-stranded networks, 'maternalistic' (woman-oriented) practice are the basis of its ability to react immediately in an emergency, and at the same time to bear long-term burdens.

If the trends I described in the previous sections continue, it could be the beginning of a self-welfare society, but quite different from Gershuny's self-service model (1983). This 'self-welfare'society would not be the outcome of the faster growth of productivity in the production of goods contrary to welfare production, or of technologidal development, but it can be a new 'peasantization' i. e. after the withdrawal of the state, the household would be charged with all the burdens. This kind of 'self-welfarization' could be advantageous for the central budget only in the short run. In the long run, the 'overuse' of the households' self-exploitative ability has many disadvantages, e. g. growing morbidity, the decline of labour productivity at the work place, tensions within the households and, as a result, the growth of several forms of deviance, the emergence of new kinds and the revival of old inequalities (e. g. in patron-client relations among generations, genders).

The outcomes of this trend would be completely different if:

● In the course of withdrawal of the state, the household receives financial resources and additional services to supplement its self-welfare activity.[13])

● The households are allowed (without suspicions and bureaucratic obstacles) to orm different types of associations (and not only the traditional interhousehold networks).

● The enterprises, the private social services and the churches are allowed and the first two also encouraged to enter the scene and give welfare services to the strata or groups they are connected with.

These conditions could ease the burdens of the households, could keep (or improve) direct and vivid connections between household and state on the local level, could help to flourish a more pluralistic division of labour among more than two actors.

But, even if all the afore-mentioned positive outcomes were possible, it would neither mean that the fundamental problems of the Hungarian economy can be solved by the welfare system nor that this system would operate without tensions, inequalities, wastes of human and material resources. But perhaps the idea of 'peaceful coexistence' between state and population could be improved in this way.[14]

Notes

The first version of this paper was written together with Ágnes Deák for the Second Project Meeting (Grenoble/France).

1) I use this term according to Ivan Svetlik's definition ". . .the term *welfare system* represents an open and universalistic concept. It includes private and social welfare sectors and welfare institutions: health care, child care, education, employment, social security and other welfare areas: service providers and service consumers, their values, norms and policies. It includes also various relations between these structural elements such as management, financing, service production and service delivery. An informal or semi-formal welfare sector can be added without any difficulties. Besides, this concept permits an examination of relations between the welfare system and its environment, e. g. economic and employment systems." E. Sik – I. Svetlik (1987)

2) Because of the scarcity of valid data the actors have been defined in a very broad way. The analysis could have been much more precise if I had been able to make a distinction between the state as a financial and as an administrative (policy-making) actor and between state-owned large firms (very often in a monopolistic position within an industrial branch) and small agricultural cooperatives.

   Last but not least, there are also differences among the actors from the territorial point of view. This is true both in a narrow economic sense (the state allocates larger funds in the capital than in small villages) and in a cultural-political sense; i. e. differences in the level of religiousness and of familism. On the one hand, are the spreading of traditional social interhousehold networks and the level of the state organization's bureaucratism; on the other, is the scope of action for the church and for voluntary associations.

3) In Hungary the trade unions have rather limited importance on the shop-floor or on the firm level (only the central staff of the unions has some influence on decision-making on the national level). The trade union within the enterprise is simply the allocator of the cash and in-kind welfare benefits and services.

4) The very rigid central limits of wage raising have also upgraded the welfare fund in the struggle on the labour market.

5) Both the Roman Catholic church and the Protestant church have played an important role in the welfare system up until 1949, when these were socialized or suppressed.

6) Another reason why households could always maintain their welfare activity is the network of social relations existing around the majority of the households. Through this network a mass of reciprocative and altruistic transactions and transfers have been flowing. This network has always been able to make considerable surplus efforts when required – naturally only for a shorter period and not always without negative side effects. (Sik/forthcoming)

7) Both in 1972 and in 1982 almost half of the population possessed small farms.
   Private farmers produce the majority of the value of the gross annual product in numerous labour-intensive products while, measured in natural terms, their share is overwhelming. (Approx. 14 per cent of agricultural land, 60 per cent of labour time and 33 per cent of the gross product value are exploited by small-scale family farming units.) (Gabor 1983)
8) The expenses allocated for upholding and increasing in-kind welfare services have been diminishing year by year in the 1980s. Welfare investments of state organs (in comparable prices) as to the previous year were 87.7 per cent in 1981, 85.2 per cent in 1982 and 77.4 per cent in 1983.(Hungarian. . .1984)
9) Except for the possibility of the emergence of the 'welfare innovations' within the state's organizational structure. Besides the 'deviances' in public health mentioned above there are other small-scale, often temporary forms (frequently in the disguise of an experiment and invented and managed by one or a few committed persons) of 'welfare innovations' in culture centres and local councils.
10) The example of this topic is from: Deák, Gere, Győri, Krémer (1986)
11) The reciprocal exchange of services can be seen as a special sub-type of self-exploitation in the course of which domestic work is shifted forward or postponed through interhousehold transactions. (Sik/forthcoming)
12) The spread of welfare transactions *within the kin* was proved by a nationwide representative cohort research (Sik 1984). According to this, two-thirds of the middle-aged generation have received help from their parents, half of them have given help through their life. Half of them have been in reciprocal relations with siblings, and most of them helped their children.
13) E. g. subsidies to nursing aged persons, handicapped children, 'social wage' to nurture wards, foster children; local (small-scale, non-bureaucratic, cheap, non-profit) state service to help home care, to give professional advice for 'self-welfare,'etc.
14) For the time being the labour intensive and therefore time-consuming informal economy serves this aim solely in Hungary. By this sub-economy the households earn money, get services which cannot be bought from the state because of the underdevelopment of the infrastructrue. In the past 10 years the state has tolerated, even encouraged this sub-economy, letting the people meet their needs by themselves. (Labour . . . 1985)

Bibliography

Agricultural Small Farms Time Budgets of 1972 and 1982 (1982), Central Statistical Office, Budapest.
Deák, Á., Gere, I., Győri, P., Krémer, B., 1986, 'The Shift of the Welfare Mix', Paper for the Third Project Meeting at Puchberg/Austria.
Farkas, 1982, 'The Current Division of Labour in Social Policy' in Of Education and Social Policy, Hungarian Academy of Siences, Budapest.
Ferge, Zs., 1984, 'Ideology and Practice in a Situation of Change and Uncertainty', Paper for the First Project Meeting, Siófok/Hungary.
Ferge, Zs., 1986, Fejezetek a magyar szegénypolitika történetéből, Magvető, Budapest.
Gábor, R. I., 1983, 'Second Economy in Hungary' in Labour Market and Second Economy in Hungary 1985.
Galasi, P., Sziráczky, Gy. (eds.), 1985, Labour Market and Second Economy in Hungary, Campus, N. Y. –Frankfurt.
Gershuny, J., 1983, Social Innovation and Division of Labour, Oxford University Press.
Háztartásstatisztika, 1982, KSH, Budapest.
Horváth, Á., 1986, Self-help Association in Hungary No. 22. 1983.
Hungarian Statistical Yearbook, 1984, Central Statistical Office, Budapest.
Lakossági szolgáltatások, 1984, Central Statistical Office, Budapest.
Sik, E., 1984, 'Interhousehold Transfers' in Cohort Analysis, Manuscript, Budapest.

Sik, E., 1985, 'Small is useful' or the Reciprocal Exchange of Labour in Galasi, P., Sziráczky, Gy. (eds.), 1985.

Sik, E., (forthcoming), Perpetuity of Reciprocal Exchange of Labour, Budapest Gondolat.

Sik, E., Svetlik, I., 1987, 'Similarities and Dissimilarities' (in this volume).

Stuberné, E., 1984, The Social Policy of Enterprises, Manuscript, Budapest.

Svetlik, I., 1987, Yugoslavia: Three Ways of Welfare System Restructuring (in this volume).

Szalai, J., 1986, The Diseases of the Public Health, Közg. és Jogi Kiadó, Budapest.

Szilágyi, I., 1985, 'A Római Katolikus Egyházi Szeretetszolgálat' in Szociálpolitikai Értesitö 3 – 4. sz.

Szilágyi, S., 1974, The Influence of Economic Regulation on Fringe Benefits, Research Institute of Trade Unions, Budapest.

Timár, J., 1985, 'Time and Working Time' in Közgazdasági Szemle No. 11.

Between State and Society: the Impact of Traditional and New Forms of Volunteering in Poland

Miroslaw Ksiezopolski and Irena Sienko

A Sketch of the Basic Characteristics of the Polish Social and Welfare Systems

It is not easy to delimit the social sphere in Poland. Some elements of social policy are comprised in almost every activity undertaken by the state and the costs of activities in the social field are not always calculated as social expenditures. The principal bodies responsible for the development of the social sphere are the state and its specialized organs, which carry out its social function. This means that they guarantee the realization of the citizens' social rights and promote social progress.

The social rights, as set forth in the Constitution of the Polish People's Republic, are as follows:
The right to work.
The right to health care and to help in case of disease or inability to work.
The right to education.
The right to mother and children care.
The right to rest.

The general directions in the development of the social sphere are determined by the Polish United Workers Party. The two other parties, the United Peasant Party and the Democratic Party, play only a supportive role and represent the interests of the social strata within which they operate (peasants and craftsmen). Other subjects of social policy in Poland are:

state enterprises and institutions – besides their statutory activities, all enterprises and institutions perform certain social functions for the benefit of their employees. They accumulate their own social Activities and Housing Funds. They also employ trained social workers. The dimension of the social activity vary depending on the size and character (productive or non-productive) of the firm. In recent years, the above-mentioned funds have not been sufficient for financing

297

social activities in the dimension the firms have provided up to now and it seems that they are trying to escape from performing some of their social functions.

Trade unions – in 1982 all trade unions in Poland were outlawed and from the beginning of 1983 a completely new union structure began to be organized. In the mid 1980s the unions represented little more than half of all employees in Poland. They provide assistance to workers and their families who have financial difficulties, severe disease or death of the main bread-winner in the family, birth of a child and broken home. The scope of such assistance is, however, less developed than it was before the 1980s. Many social activities, which were previously performed by the unions, have been transferred to the departments of social affairs, which have a more solid basis.

Social organizations – one of the features of the Polish social policy is quite a well-developed network of social organizations, which supplement the activities of the organs of the state. Some of them, representing old-age pensioners, disability pensioners, the disabled, veterans or other groups, conduct various mutual aid and social assistance activities. They assist their members by using funds derived from contributions and state subsidies. Many of these organizations have a similar scope of activities, coordinated by local administration, however, it is difficult to fulfil this task. Consequently it is possible to get different types of help from several institutions at the same time.

Cooperatives – they also perform certain social functions for their members and employees, most of them being similar to those performed by state enterprises. The role of disabled producers' cooperatives is especially important. They are one of the main subject responsible for rehabilitation of the disabled and for providing them with suitable employment. They also administer various forms of aid to the disabled, both in cash and in kind.

In Poland the social sphere can be divided into three main sectors: *general social services, the social security system* and *the different kinds of activities concerned with labour protection, conditions of employment and wages, subsidizing the prices of basic commodities*, etc. After the war, quite a well-developed system of social services and social benefits was established. In many respects this system is similar to that of the most advanced socialist and capitalist countries. Education is free of charge for every citizen and nearly 100 per cent of the population are entitled to free health care. There are only a few social benefits, however, which are granted upon citizenship, for example there are no flat-rate national pensions for all citizens, and family allowances are granted if at least one of the parents is employed. The majority of social benefits are related to earning, some of them, such as family allowance, partially paid parental leave and all social welfare benefits, are means-tested. The system of social benefits favours employees in the socialized sector of the economy and all so-called state employees. The social protection of self-employed (most craftsmen) and farmers has been greatly enlarged in recent years. Those, who are currently unemployed or who have not worked during a sufficiently long period time, must either rely on their families or on social welfare.

Two other characteristic features of the Polish social security system are: *lack of unemployment insurance and a weak protection of social benefits against inflation.* The indexation of pensions was introduced as late as 1986, but other social benefits are not indexed to inflation or to wages.

In Poland the social security system comprises social insurance, private insurance, social welfare, rehabilitation of the disabled and fellowship funds. In our report we will describe only the organization of the social welfare system.

The first law setting the course of welfare activities in Poland was the Welfare Act passed in 1923. This act imposed upon communes and relatives the duty of assisting the needy. This act is still in effect today, although it has since been almost completely amended by the Ministry of Health and Social Welfare.

Immediately after the war social welfare was determined by the needs of people who had been disabled and it had all the features of emergency aid. With the further stabilization of living conditions, it was generally believed that social welfare had become useless in the socio-economic system. In a socialist country, everyone has a right to work, so poverty should be automatically eliminated. This view hampered the development of social welfare in Poland during the years 1949-57. In the years following social welfare grew into a state-controlled system based on state obligations imposed by the constitution and devoted mainly to helping individuals who were unable to lead an independent life, especially the elderly.

At the present time the goal of social welfare is to promote social security for the population by supplying services and improving the income security of all deprived individuals and families. The principles which serve as a basis for the activities in this sphere are:

Responsibility of the state for providing a proper standard of living for all citizens and for the organization of care services.

A community-operated system of social welfare, the social services being based on participation of community agencies with stress laid on initiatives of social organizations.

The family as a basic institution responsible for providing the indispensable aid and care for dependent subjects (both moraly and legally imposed).

In practice social welfare is presently concerned with three categories of the population:

Those unable to work because of age, disability, chronic disease or other reasons who cannot provide for their needs by themselves (lack of right to social insurance benefits, no family responsible for their maintenance or care, inablility to work).

Those who despite their material status have no properly organized care.

Those who are able to work but are in exceptionally difficult situations.

The adult population of working age, however, remains principally outside the described system, as the services for this group are mainly work related and are delivered frequently by the private firm. This is the reason for several gaps in the social service system, such as in the case of young families in a temporary crisis caused by illness or accident. Except for financial help in special problem cases, young families are normally refused any personal service and therefore have to rely on other family members, friends or, in rare cases, the help of friendly neighbours.

The main body responsible for social welfare in Poland is the Ministry of Health and Social Welfare. At the province and county levels there are departments of health and social welfare with special divisions responsible for the problems of social welfare.

There is also a parallel system of social welfare agencies integrated into the health service. In 1959 the whole country was divided into social welfare regions, with a volunteer social worker being appointed to each region. Their tasks were to discover the needs of people living in the district and to organize ways and means of aiding them. The volunteer social workers come from various occupations, most of them being retired civil servants and professionals who live within the various areas of their activities. They are working without remuneration. In 1964 Social Welfare Centres were established at the district level. They were provided with trained social workers and consultants such as lawyers, psychologists, sociologists. At the beginning, the main task of these centres were coordination and supervision of the activities of volunteer social workers. They also helped them to solve more difficult problems and provided training. Gradually the plan of vocational social service development has been implemented. This plan assumes that one professional social worker will be working in a region with a population of about 2,500 in urban districts, or about 5,000 in rural districts. One such worker will cooperate with 6–10 volunteer social workers. The implementation of this programme is now in its final stage. In 1983 there were 9,500 professional social workers and about 44,000 volunteers. According to the programme, there should be about 14,000 professionals in 1990.

The tasks of professional social workers are the following: providing a systematic diagnosis of needs of the inhabitants in the district, applying for benefits or services for clients at the local administrative authority, cooperating with voluntary associations, collecting agency data and statistics, organizing training for volunteers. This listing clearly indicates that administrative tasks take precedence over the proper function of a social worker. In addition, the qualifications of the social workers are indeed poor. Most of them have been employed at their posts without necessary professional education and skilled social workers constitute only minority of the staff in the public social welfare sector. This results in the paradoxical situation that the majority of professional social workers are not professionals. It is estimated that in 1981 approximately 42 per cent of employed social workers had the necessary professional education, whereas in 1983 this fell to about 30 per cent. This unfavourable change resulted in a rapid growth of public social welfare manpower in 1982, when many unskilled persons were employed in social welfare centres all over the country. Due to these developments and to the predominance of money transfers, specific methods of social work have not yet found an appropriate use in social practice.

The situation described above demonstrates a very specific feature of the Polish system – poor qualification of the staff. To assess the level of professionalism in the social welfare sector, one has to consider a limited percentage of skilled persons among the employed social workers and the proportion of skilled social workers to volunteer social workers. The number of the latter is five times as high as the number of professional social workers with or without educational training. Thus, the Polish social assistance system may be described as being both, bureaucratic and not fully competent.

The social assistance programme in Poland is traditionally attached to the health system, which has proved to be very reasonable, as the majority of beneficiaries are the elderly or disabled. The cooperation between the district doctor, community nurse and the social worker also helps to fulfil the goals of the specific strategy of reaching people in need, described as active social assistance, which means finding needy people among the local population, the staff of social work centres are expected to be case finders and referral agents simultaneously with their basic task of delivering services. This approach requires the social worker to visit homes within the service district and involves interviewing people about their problems. This is contradictory to the approach applied in the majority of Western countries, which stresses the individual's responsibility in searching for help. This essential difference between both systems in organizing access to services results in a different type of social attitude towards organizing self-help or independent, voluntary structures in this field.

Another interesting feature of social welfare in Poland is the cooperation of trade unions and various social organizations in meeting the needs of people, especially in the organization of social services financed by state funds and by funds of the cooperating organizations, whose members are also involved in welfare work. The main social organization concerned with social welfare is the Polish Committee of Social Welfare. Its task is to supplement the state in the field of social services by initiating and organizing the actions undertaken by the citizens for giving the necessary aid and care to individuals and families, provided that they cannot cope with these difficulties themselves. This organization has at its disposal special financial means and its main activities are:

Organization of aid and care services for people unable to work and living alone, and for those whose relatives are unable to care for them.

Promotion and organization of services for facilitating the lives of aged and disabled people, their occupational and social activation.

Organization of neighbour assistance for those in need.

Guidance service.

Another important social organization in this sphere is the Polish Red Cross. It organizes and runs nursing services for bed-ridden patients in their homes and provides aid for disaster victims.

The basic task in organizing the lives of the elderly and disabled in Poland is maintaining them in their surroundings, which requires the development of different forms of social services. They are organized mainly by social organizations, but the costs are covered by the state. Home help is provided either by professionals or by neighbours or volunteers, mainly young people and pensioners. Fees are graded according to the beneficiaries' ability to pay. There also different kinds of outside help – washing, preparation of the meals, shopping etc. – and various forms of social activities, – cultural clubs, day care homes. For example, in 1981 about 20,000 nurses were employed by the Polish Red Cross, providing care for about 54,000 sick people and 6,000 people were helped by their neighbours. Home help was provided to more than 20,000 people, with more than 7,000 receiving paid help from their neighbours and about 8,000 being helped by volunteers.

Institutional care is reserved for individuals who, because of their age, disease, life and family situation or housing conditions, cannot be adapted to independent life in the place of their residence, despite application for other forms of help. The basic criteria for qualification are: the applicant's state of health, his/her financial situation, impossibility of the family to provide sufficient care for the applicant. Social services and places in social welfare homes are in great demand and it is not possible for state-organized social services and places in social welfare to provide this. For example, there are only 16 places in social welfare homes per 10,000 residents. In total there are about 66,000 places and according to estimates about 40,000 people waiting for a place. Then waiting time is between two to five years. Many of them must stay in normal hospitals taking up space assigned to intensive care.

To conclude remarks about the social sphere in Poland, it should be stressed that the Polish system is based on the activity ot the state which has taken on responsibilities for satisfying all major social needs. The role of other social actors is only supplementary. They do mainly what the state has commissioned them to do their own initiatives being limited. This has resulted in people being deprived c the responsibility for their welfare. On the other hand, people have gradually gotten accustomed to the fact that they have the right to obtain help from the socialist state. At the same time, despite a great quantitative and qualitative development of the social sphere in the last forty years, the state has failed to reach satisfactory level in meeting many major social needs. Difficult access or low quality of many services – not only social services, an inadequate network fc child care and old-age care facilities result in the family still being the main pro vider of services to its members. In many cases it also constitutes an importar or the sole source of support to its dependent subjects. This tendency is reir forced by the fact that the adult population of working age is excluded from th official assistance system, and also by the law which imposes on the family th duty of maintaining its poor or disabled members. Fulfilling this duty, howeve meets frequently with insurmountable difficulties.

Since the late 1970s Poland has been undergoing a deep economic, political and social crisis. In many respects the Polish situation differs substantially from that of other Eastern and Western countries which are participating in the research project. First, in spite of a significant decrease in the volume of production, there is no unemployment in Poland. To the contrary, there is a growing deficit in labour force. Rather than unemployment, Poland has to cope with the shortage of manpower, hence there is no need to special measures for creating substitute forms of jobs.

Secondly, the Polish economic crisis is not a crisis of overproduction, but one of scarcity – scarcity of food stuffs, manufactured goods, housing, social services, etc. This is the main reason why policy-makers are forced to confront all problems connected with the changing reality of work and with relations between free and working time from quite a different perspective than that of the Western countries. Polish people simply ought to produce more, to work more and harder in order to preserve the decreasing standard of living. The key problem is not if or how to reduce normative working time, but how to cope with a phenomenon which we call in Poland a pathology of work. This notion includes such negative sides of the Polish reality as: low motivation for work, excessive employment in some sectors of the economy, disappearance of work ethos, low labour performance, low quality of work, etc. Only by overcoming these phenomena can one improve the quality of life and reduce the real working time, be it paid work or household work. Better quality of work and not less work should be our passport to more disposable free time. Time for education and self-realization is now wasted trying to defend and maintain a material standard of living. Progress in the Polish circumstances means an achievement of a satisfactory level of labour performance in normal working time – so simple, but so far impossible.

Thirdly, the state in Poland is trying to release itself from full responsibility for satisfying all major social needs. Before the 1980s there was no debate in Poland about limitation of the social activity of the state. The responsibility of the state for securing social welfare and social security of the citizens was taken for granted and the existence of the social right filled policy-makers with pride. The economic crisis has changed this situation. The allegation that Poland has become an overprotective state has been given currency by some policy-makers, economists and journalists. The main argument against the present system is that it essentially hampers the process of escaping the crisis and introducing economic reform. They realize that the state has taken on too much responsibility for the welfare of the citizens. The state is not omnipotent and, especially in periods of crisis, it simply does not have enough resources to maintain the present system of benefits. Because of that it is necessary to limit the extent to which the state must protect its citizens.

The allegation that Poland has been an overprotective state is strongly denied by many Polish social politicians who are trying to prove that, in fact, the state in Poland is rather not protective enough. Independently of prevailing views, the economic crisis has not caused any substantial cuts in social expenditures, but in practice the measures provided have offered only minimal protection of social needs. The real value of most social benefits has been decreased, also extending to expenditures on the development of social services and social infrastructure. In fact one can observe a rapid depreciation of the social infrastructure.

Does this mean that the gaps in the social security system and poor social services are leading to the creation of a voluntary social activity in this field, which could replace or complement the statutory services and the services rendered by the family?

Voluntary Activity in the Sphere of Social Services and Social Welfare

In order to answer this last question and to find out what is the changing or new relevance concerning the role of the informal social networks, volunteering and self-help in the social welfare sector, we will cover three different fields of activity. Two of them comprise voluntary activities which are taking place in the framework of the officially recognized system of voluntary organizations and as part of the statutory social welfare services. As we mentioned, one of the features of the Polish socio-political system is a well-developed network of social organizations, which operate as an auxiliary to the public system. These organizations are intended to constitute an appropriate forum in which volunteer initiatives of the population could and should manifest themselves. Statutory social services, which from the very beginning were based on cooperation between professional and volunteer social workers, are another recognized forms of such activity. The possibilities for voluntary activity outside this officially established system are very slim. In order to be legal every new initiative in this sphere should be accepted by the state authorities, which in most cases means incorporating them into already existing forms of volunteer activity. Consequently the majority of voluntary actions which take place in Poland have a very formal character and are undertaken either by one of the above-mentioned social organizations or in close cooperation with state authorities.

There exists, however, a broader field of volunteering in Poland. In recent years one can observe an appreciable development of church-related activities in volunteering and backing informal networks for care and help. There are also more politically-based activities of a self-help character which rose around the delegalized trade union 'Solidarity'. The majority of these activities have an informal character, their scope is unknown and it is very difficult to get any concrete and comprehensive picture of what is really going on. The church activities are decentralized and information about them is furnished only reluctantly by respective parishes of church authorities. The activities which are connected with the former trade union 'Solidarity' are illegal and it is impossible to carry out ordinary field

304

research on this topic. In our research project, however, we intended to include both of these kinds of activities in order to get a picture of the whole spectrum of volunteering related to the main forces in Poland: the dominant political force – the Communist Party, the Catholic Church and the former trade union 'Solidarity'. Because of the already mentioned difficulties the length and precision of description of these fields of activity will be different, thus, we will concentrate on officially accepted forms of actions, the description of other kinds of activities being of a more qualitative character.

Social Activity of Voluntary Organizations in the Sphere of Social Services and Social Welfare

Three independent research projects on this topic have been carried out. The main goal of these projects was to find and assess the scope of voluntary activity of the members of these organizations, to analyse the activity of these organizations on behalf of certain categories of the needy, and to grasp the main feature of their functioning: the bureaucratic attitude towards the mobilization of voluntary social forces to manage the problems of people in need. We wanted to discover if social organizations are open to new problems and it they can serve as the potential forum for self-organization in the community.

The first research covered 20 major social organizations active in the field of social security and social services. The research was carried out during the years 1984-1985 and its principal findings have been compared to the results of similar research made in 1982. The analysis has been based on interviews with the staff of these organizations on the national level, questionnaires sent to social organizations and state administrative bodies on the local level and on the organizations' own reports.

The second research carried out in spring 1985, concentrated on the activity of six of the above-mentioned organizations. They were: The Polish Red Cross, the Polish Committee of Social Welfare, the Union of Old-age Pensioners and the Disabled, the Society of Friends of Children, The Polish Women's League and the Polish Anti-alcoholic Society. The research was based on 100 interviews with both paid und unpaid staff of these organizations on the national, provincial and local level and on reports written by the organizations themselves.

The third research consisted of working out monographies of the activities of local branches chosen from three social organizations: the Polish Committee of Social Welfare, the Society of the Friends of Children and the Polish Anti-alcoholic Society. These monographies were also based on interviews with the paid and volunteer staff and on available data concerning local activity of the respective institutions.

In the context of the above-mentioned research social activity means constructive and gratuitous or partially paid participation in an activity of social organizations or in collective action aimed at the common good and satisfaction of certain needs of other people, following a voluntarily accepted programme of statutory obligations or principles of collective action.

All the research findings presented a similar picture of the activities of the social organizations, so the main results of these projects will be presented jointly.

Organization and Programme

Social organizations in Poland participate in all major forms of activity in the social sphere (see table I). For some of these organizations, like the Society of the Friends of Children (TPD), the Polish Association of the Deaf (PZG), the Polish Association of the Blind (PZN), the Polish Committee of Social Welfare (PKPS), the Polish Red Cross (PCK), the Polish Union of Old-age Pensioners and the Disabled (PZERiI) and Monar, activity in the field of social security and social services has prevailed both in programmes and in practical work. The remaining organizations have concentrated on other issues, and activity in the social sphere has constituted only one of their several areas of interest. Generally speaking, social organizations assist public activity carrying out tasks commissioned to them by the state, or they simply relieve public authorities of certain forms of activities, especially in the most neglected areas.

In the first part of our report we described briefly the activities of the Red Cross, which in practice carry the main responsibility for providing home care services for old and handicapped people. Further examples illustrating the importance of voluntary organizations in the Polish social system can be given. For example, they make a diagnosis of people's needs, both in their social and individual aspects. In order to do this, social organizations run advisory bureaus (for example The Polish Organization of the Deaf: 15, the Polish Association of the Blind: 2, the Society for the Development of the Family: 20, the Polish Women's League: 473) consultative centres (Monar: 14, the Society for the Fight against Drug Habits: 6) care centres (The Polish Red Cross: 943), or make their own surveys. One can estimate that the diagnosis made by these organizations covers an average of 15 per cent of all people in need, but in some cases, like the blind and deaf, it covers up to 80 per cent of each respective group.

Social organizations also deal with supplementary social benefits and services. One can mention here:

- Supplementary food/for about 50,000 people yearly.
- Holiday camps/The Polish Anti-alcoholic Association and the Society of the Friends of Children for about 130,000 children yearly.
- Cash benefits/the Polish Committee of Social welfare for 70,000 people, the Polish Union of Old-Age Pensioners and the Disabled for 40,000, the Polish Association of the Deaf for 2,000 people yearly etc.

306

Table 1
Activity of Social Organizations in the Field of Social Security and Social Services

	Kind of Activity						
	a	b	c	d	e	f	g
1. LKP — Polish Women's League	●	●			●	●	
2. Monar	●	●	●				
3. PCK — Polish Red Cross		●	●	●		●	
4. PKPS — Polish Committee of Social Welfare	●		●	●	●		
5. PZERiL — Polish Union of Old-age Pensioners and the Disabled		●	●		●		
6. PZG — Polish Association of the Deaf		●	●	●	●		●
7. PZN — Polish Association of the Blind		●	●	●	●		●
8. PTWzK — Polish Society for the Fight against Invalidity				●	●		
9. SKP — Polish Anti-alcoholic Association	●			●	●		
10. TKKS — Society for the Propagation of Lay Culture	●						
11. TPD — Society of the Friends of Children	●	●	●	●	●	●	
12. TRR — Society for the Development of the Family	●	●					
13. TWP — Society for the Popularization of Culture and Science	●	●					
14. TZN — Society for the Fight against Drug Habits	●						
15. ZBOWiD — Federation of Combatants for Liberty and Democracy		●		●	●		
16. ZHP — Polish Boy Scouts' Union	●		●			●	
17. ZIW — Association of Disabled Soldiers Victims of War				●	●		
18. ZMW — Peasant Youth Union	●	●	●				
19. ZSMP — Polish Socialist Youth Union	●	●	●				
20. ZSP — Polish Students' Association		●	●		●		

a	Social prevention, resocialization	e	Social insurance
b	Health care	f	Out–family care
c	Rehabilitation	g	Special education
d	Social welfare		

● Funding of so-called housing savings books for orphans for about 2,000 children yearly.

Social organizations also perform important functions in the sphere of special education and home care. For example the Polish Association of the Blind and the Polish Association of the Deaf organize occupational education which comprises more than half of the blind or deaf youth. Out family care is performed mainly by the Society of the Friends of Children. It presently runs 44 nursery schools, 1,350 kindergardens, 883 day care centres, one holiday centre and one educational centre.

Our research has shown that the main function of social organizations was the representation of interests of their members of respective categories of people towards state administration. Besides being pressure groups, they have served as: organizers of social services, animators and programmers of volunteer activity, executors and transmitters of state decisions, advisory and consultative bodies.

In principle, the activities of almost all social organizations are financed from state funds. State subsidies amount from 15 up to almost 100 per cent of the total financial resources of the organizations surveyed. Contributions of members are very low in all organizations and the share of contributions in total expenditures of these organizations is usually small. Up to the 1980s voluntary contributions from enterprises were one of the main sources of financing social activity, but presently enterprises are very reluctant to grant funds for such purposes and this source of financing is diminishing. Members of voluntary organizations have also noticed that people's support for collections on behalf of their organizations is abating; more people seem to consider the state as the most proper source for financing this activity and the collections are sometimes considered as a form of begging.

Such a system of financing has caused social actors to be more dependent on state administration at the cost of the interest of their members and clients. In recent years some of these organizations undertook efforts to obtain certain organizational and financial independence, but these attempts have not achieved the desired results.

Another important instrument for controlling and directing social organizations is personnel policy – the Polish United Workers Party and state organs have an indirect, but decisive influence on the composition of statutory and administrative bodies governing these organizations. All representatives of social organizations were of the opinion that state and party organs influence the activity of their organizations, but a majority of them described that influence as average or small. Direct control in the form of official orders or recommendations is unheard-of; 80 per cent of the respondents stated that the main goals and the course for activity of their organizations were set by collective statutory bodies and not by outside forces. On the other hand, the research has shown that the members of the statutory bodies were at the same time either members of political and administrative authorities or accepted by such authorities. Furthermore, all key positions in the management of social organizations, on the central as well as on the local level, could not be filled without being accepted by the political and administrative authorities.

Due to the skilful use of the above-mentioned instruments (personnel policy and financing), political authorities have succeeded with the ground activity of social organizations on two principles:

Organizational unity – expressed in the creation of similar organizational struc tures in all social organizations, and *ideological unity* – expressed in acceptance and practical use of Marxist ideology.

These principles, when taken into consideration, have determined the political approval of the activity of each respective organization as well as their possibilities to obtain financial subsidies from the state. Furthermore, political and administrative authorities have been able to channel the articulation of interests of different categories of needy people as well as the managerial staff of the voluntary organizations.

The centralized organizational structure of social organizations makes such control much easier. It is a rule that programmes of activity are workerd out on the central or province level of the respective organization, with local branches making the plans and at the same time, having very limited influence on them. Such plans are often poorly fitted for local needs. Evaluation of the local branches' activity is based on the fulfilment of the plans and not on the degree to which local needs are satisfied.

During the years 1980-1983 all the major social organizations lost about 20 per cent of their members in spite of the creation of new organizations such as Monar, the Society for the Fight against Drug Habits and the Peasant Youth Union (see table 2). These figures are based on information from the respective institutions and include members, who do not pay contributions or have not been active for a long time; in practice the real figures are much lower. In the opinion of all respondents, we are facing a gradual but clear trend of diminishing volunteer activity of the population. The reasons for such a situation, according to the respondents, are as follows: concentration of people's activity on preserving one's standard of living, lack of tradition of work or activity for others, limited possibilities for spontaneous volunteer activity, deep disbelief in the possibilities of effective activity in the framework of existing social organizations and lack of free time.

All respondents underlinded the fact that activity of the social organizations has been based increasingly on paid staff, with the number of genuine volunteers decreasing. A majority of unpaid staff of social organizations are middle-aged or elderly people, many of them pensioners. These people are gradually vanishing and very few are coming to take their place. In the opinion of our respondents the problem of succession is becoming one of the most urgent. There is still quite a large group of experienced members of voluntary organizations, both paid and unpaid, who identify themselves with the respective organization and try to do something, hoping that their activity could be of use. Their successors are not as much engaged, many of them join social organizations through personal interest, while work for others is only of secondary importance.

Public opinion surveys made in recent years have confirmed the rising doubts of many Poles as to the sense of collective voluntary activity in the present institutional forms. This concerns primarily young people. Among reasons for their passivity they usually mentioned: lack of good climate for social activity, lack of need

Table 2
The Number of Members of Social Organizations in the Years 1980–1983

Name of organization	in thousands				
	1980	1981	1982	1983	1983*)
1. LKP — Polish Women's League	517.7	498.9	426.0	423.5	81.8
2. PCK — Polish Red Cross	—	0.2	0.4	0.5	—
3. Monar	5076.8	4840.5	4270.7	3960.5	78.0
4. PKPS — Polish Committee of Social Welfare	1970.3	1170.9	1597.7	1448.8	79.8
5. PZERiL — Polish Union of Old-age Pensioners and the Disabled	949.4	1075.1	1223.9	1332.5	140.1
6. PZG — Polish Association of the Deaf	18.6	20.3	20.3	21.5	115.6
7. PZN — Polish Association of the Blind	53.3	56.6	60.9	61.8	115.9
8. PTWzK — Polish Society for the Fight against Invalidity	7.4	8.6	8.6	9.7	131.1
9. SKP — Polish Anti-alcoholic Association	243.8	247.4	237.3	229.2	94.0
10. TKKS — Society for the Propagation of Lay Culture	370.0	280.8	234.8	151.6	41.5
11. TPD — Society of the Friends of Children	1100.7	1006.3	1007.2	981.8	91.5
12. TRR — Society for the Development of the Family	141.3	118.0	101.0	95.2	67.3
13. TWP — Society for the Popularization of Culture and Science	45.5	40.7	33.7	34.8	82.4
14. TZN — Society for the Fight against Drug Habits	—	0.1	0.2	0.4	—
15. ZBOWiD — Federation of Combatants for Liberty and Democracy	662.6	651.1	661.0	709.0	107.0
16. ZHP — Polish Boy Scouts' Union	3149.2	1890.7	1878.4	1910.8	60.7
17. ZIW — Association of Disabled Soldiers Victims of War	65.6	66.2	69.2	70.9	108.1
18. ZMW — Peasant Youth Union	—	126.1	248.3	314.6	—
19. ZSMP — Polish Socialist Youth Union	1993.0	1471.4	1471.4	1499.8	75.2
20. ZSP — Polish Students' Association	228.0	18.6	20.4	35.4	15.5
Total	16598.8	14190.5	13571.4	13292.3	80.1

*) 1980 = 100%

to be active, lack of clear ideas of what they could do, formal and showy character of the social activity and lack of free time.

Time budget research made in the 1970s showed that Polish families have been devoting more time to household work than their Western counterparts. In the 1980s the situation has changed more to our disadvantage. In 1976 an average time budget was as follows: physiological needs – 10.03 hours, paid work – 4.44, household work – 3.5 hours and free time – 4.06. In 1982 this sequence has changed: physiological needs – 9.41 hours, paid work – 5.03, household ork – 4.21 and free time – 3.38. Almost all time saved on physiological needs, aid work and free time has been devoted to household work. Various research ows that disposable free time is mainly used for passive rest. People concen- ate themselves on home matters and family life.

espondents in our research, asked about their reasons for undertaking volun- ry activity, have most often mentioned altruistic motives. In many cases, how- er, more instrumental reasons can be found: delegation from the employing in- tution, recommendation from a political party, greater possibility to receive ad- tional benefits or services. For many people activity in a social organization has en directly or indirectly connected with their occupational activity and volunteer ork has even been to some degree a performance of normal occupational ities.

e majority of paid staff are women due to low wages in all social organizations. en prevail among unpaid volunteer staff and most of them are well-educated ople, coming from the intelligentsia; members of other social groups such as ue-collar workers, craftsmen; and farmers undertake only exceptionally such an tivity.

other feature of Polish social organizations is the fact that the most active ople are usually members of several organizations often occupying respon- le positions. Such multi-organizational activity of top members constitutes one the reasons for the low efficiency of the organizations in question.

ew Initiatives

is somewhat critical picture of the activity of social organizations does not ean that they have no chances to activate volunteer activity. From among all tivities of social organizations covered by our research, we have chosen three amples of new voluntary action initiatives undertaken in recent years.

onar

onar (Youth movement on behalf of the drug habit counteraction) was estab- hed in 1981. Monar can serve as one of the most interesting examples of a new nuine volunteer initiative, undertaken outside the established system of social ganizations and public organs.

yone who reaches 16 years of age and who is not a drug addict can be a mem- er of Monar. Its programme proposes to make use of specific forms of treatment nich should change deviant behaviour into socially positive attitudes. In Monar's socialization centres drug addicts are undergoing not only medical treatment, ut are also being prepared for playing different roles in society or even for aying therapist to their drug addict colleagues. Monar works also with non drug-

311

addicted young people in order to make them conscious of all the dangers co nected with the drug habit and to prevent them from taking drugs. Instead drugs the Monar people offer personal contacts, help in difficult situations, frien liness and advice. Monar also tries to work with parents and teachers.

At present Monar has several hundred members organized in youth teams schools circles. The youth teams are supposed to create an alternative way of li in opposition to that of the drug addicts. This model is to be based on ideas help, self-help, self-improvement and self-development. Youth teams undertal various activities for the development and integration. In addition they render a for others, especially drug addicts.

For the time being youth teams are organized in several towns, the biggest grou of about 40 persons being in Warsaw. Monar intends to have such teams in eve large town under the common name 'House of Warmth'. Each house should b a centre for young people in danger of drug addiction, for those who feel lonel have personal or family troubles or difficulties in school. The main idea of Mon is to save young people on their own initiative, by organizing them into grou which will be able to stand in opposition to drug addiction.

Monar also runs 15 resocialization centres for drug addicts with about 400 plac and 15 consultative bureaus. The aim of the *consultative bureau* is to facilita contact with specialist health care agencies for young drug addicts. The ma forms of activity of these bureaus are as follows:
• Permanent turn of duty at a special telephone (hot line) of confidence.
• Preliminary talks, encouragement to undergo medical treatment.
• Guidance for families of drug addicts.

In the near future the majority of consultative bureaus will concentrate their a tivity on prevention, gradually transforming themselves into 'Houses Warmth'.

The treatment in a resocialization centre is based on cooperation between pr fessional staff and the inhabitants. They constitute a community which has pow of decision in every substantial matter, for example admission or expulsion of i habitants. A resocialization centre is a kind of school of life. Former drug addic learn here how to manage the problems of everyday life without drugs. The res cialization centres are largely self-sufficient. Their inhabitants study, work on ag cultural farms belonging to the centres and do all household work. Therapy based on mutual emotional help, a feeling of friendship and on common respo sibllity for effectiveness of treatment. Professional staff plays principally an a mative role, the working of each centre being based on the activity of the whc community. The effectiveness of resocialization in Monar's centres is very hig about one-third of all treated drug addicts are now free from addiction.

Recently Monar has been developing new forms of aid on behalf of people wl have had a resocialization treatment. In late spring 1985, a new agency, call Supermonar, was established. Its main tasks are: providing information abc jobs and accomodation possibilities, further education, financial aid. In the ne future a housing cooperative is planned, all members should contribute with their own work.

Every activity undertaken by Monar is based to a great extent on volunteer work. Even for those who get paid their work in various Monar agencies is a kind of volunteer work and usually they are as much engaged in the efforts to solve problems of drug addicts as other members of this organization.

Monar is still one of the most active and spontaneous voluntary organizations, altough it has not avoided losing its independence. At the end of 1982 all institutions run by Monar were incorporated into the public health care system. Public authorities thus took control over Monar's activity and have secured state influence on the shape and implementation of its programme.

In April 1986, while writing this report, the pupils from one of Warsaw's secondary shools, inspired by the activity of Monar, have declared their school to be a School of Pure Hearts. About 600 pupils have committed themselves to stop smoking and to take care of needy people. They are going to do voluntary work in hospitals, homes for the aged and orphanages. This should teach them how to enrich their lives by helping other people, by giving others something of their own. The declaration for the creation of a School of Pure Hearts has been sent to other schools and its authors hope that this initiative will spread all over Poland.

Self-help Groups of Parents

The Polish social services system is unable to meet the specific needs of children affected with various serious diseases such as mental retardation, children's paralysis of the brain, diabetes etc. Hence in practice the family invariably remains the basic support for such children. The economic crisis of the 1980s has deepened the difficulties of families. Parents have tried to organize themselves in order to help each other, to exchange experiences in the care and upbringing of handicapped children, to exert pressure on authorities. Efforts to officially register such self-help groups as independent voluntary organizations have failed. In order to carry on legal activity, members of self-help groups had to join one of the officially existing social organizations. They have chosen the Society of the Friends of Children. In consequence several national committees, affiliated with this society, have been created. There were: the national committee to help handicapped children, the committee of the friends of diabetic children and the committee to help mentally retarded children. They serve as a basis for exchanging information between particular self-help groups and represent them vis-à-vis the political and administrative authorities. At present there are several hundred different self-help groups acting in this field. They consist of about 10,000 parents of handicapped children and about 700 professionals, who are involved in the problems of such children due to their occupation or social interests.

In reality self-help groups are quite autonomous. Aid from the Society of the Friends of Children is rather symbolic as well as aid from the state authorities. Members of these groups have to organize and finance everything by themselves. They often complain not only of lack of help but also of difficulties they meet in contacts with their own society and state authorities, which are theoretically responsible for the satisfaction of needs of handicapped children. Despite all these difficulties, self-help groups have succeeded in overcoming many bureaucratic and economic obstacles in organizing proper care, education and rehabilitation of their children. For example they succeeded in equalizing the status of handicapped and normal children in different spheres of everyday life, in obtaining trained rehabilitation specialists, in initiating the production of special food, etc. Many self-help groups keep contact not only with each other, but also with similar groups in Western countries. Recently the parents of children affected with brain paralysis have begun preparing diagnosis of the needs of all such children in the country.

Initiatives of the Polish Boy Scouts

One can mention at least three initiatives of the Polish Boy Scouts in volunteering. The first one is called 'Unbeaten track'. This is the name for activities on behalf of children, adolescents and young adults handicapped either somatically or mentally. At present there are about 3,000 'Unbeaten track' squads, conducted by specially trained unpaid instructors. The main goal of these squads is to help young people, isolated from their colleagues by invalidity, to find their own place in society and to find joy of life. The 'Unbeaten track' squads also unite children from broken families and those coming from a criminal environment. The squads are usually organized in social welfare homes for handicapped children. They have year-round programmes of activities and in the summer they go to camps frequently organized with boy scout squads of normal children.

The operation 'Invisible hand' helps people without being noticed. Such action are undertaken from time to time by boy scouts from a particular squad or troop. They mainly help old and handicapped people in household work, shopping general cleaning, etc. It is especially popular during summer, when boy scout help farmers with harvesting and other work on the farm.

The boy scouts' winter rescue service was initiated in 1981 and is now being used by the whole union. Each squad finds needy people in its environment and help them in various everyday activities. It could take the following forms:
- Small repair brigades doing simple repair work, weather stripping etc.
- Shopping, help in household work, delivery of winter fuel, press or books, reading of books for the blind, etc.

The Future Role of Social Organizations in the Social Services System in the Opinions of Their Members

The clear majority of the population surveyed preferred to increase the role of public authorities rather than to extend the importance ot their own organizations. They declared that first of all state social services should be developed and modernized; one ought to improve their effectiveness by increasing financial means and augment investments in the sphere of public social services and by increasing employment of highly qualified professionals.

The remaining respondents wanted to modernize their own organizations, but in the same directions as above, i. e. more money and more paid professional staff. They demanded better possibilities to accumulate their own financial means by voluntary organizations and to loosen state control over their activities.

On the other hand, almost all respondents agreed that state and political parties' influence should be increased or more properly redirected. This means increasing interest in the activity of each organization, a participation in meetings of the statutory bodies of the voluntary organization, help in everyday activity, allocation of a proper office or telephone, etc.

Generally speaking, opinions expressed by our respondents confirmed a certain passivity of the social organizations, a slight feeling of responsibility shifted on to public authorities. The majority of respondents considered that the main activities undertaken by social organizations should be financed by the state and not by common means mobilized by these organizations. Despite these opinions, the representatives of voluntary organizations wanted to preserve the present system of many different social organizations. In order to be more effective, such organizations, however, should be more authentic; they should be created not by public authorities, but by local communities or by different groups of people with special needs.

The Role of Volunteers and Clients in the Provision of Social Welfare Services

In the second research area in the sphere of social services we have tried to gather opinions on desired future trends in the provision of social services and on the possibility and necessity of activating people to organize self-help and to participate in the management of services. In order to do this we conducted several interviews with representatives of the Ministry of Health and Social Welfare, experts (3), professional social workers (40), directors of province and district social welfare centres (5) and volunteer social workers (15). We have also used the results of research made by students of social work, graduated from our Institute of Social Policy. The questions were focused on three main problems:
* The role of the volunteer social worker in social welfare.

- The attitudes of clients of social welfare institutions.
- The desired development of the social services sector.

The Role of the Volunteer Social Worker in Social Welfare

The institution of volunteer social worker was set up in 1959. The concept of volunteer has a specific connotation in Poland, being a person who gives his/her free time to work without pay primarily in social services but in other areas as well. Volunteer social workers have an official status; they are appointed by the local government from among citizens of their respective areas, being at the same time active members of some voluntary organization. Up to the year 1974 they were almost the only social workers in the country and social welfare in Poland was chiefly based on their activity. This does not mean that they provided all services by themselves. Their tasks included ascertaining the needs of people in their district and organizing ways and means for aiding them. At the request of a volunteer social worker, the local administrative authority or respective voluntary organization granted benefits or provided necessary care services. These services were and still are mostly performed by paid staff employed by various social organizations. Voluntary unpaid activity in care services is not yet well developed. It usually takes the form of unregistered neighbourhood help, temporary actions undertaken in the framework of different social organizations or charitable activities of the church. In 1974, the programme for professionalizing the social welfare system was initated. In 1986, while writing this report, the implementation of this programme is in its final stage.

The remarks above are necessary for a better understanding of the opinions presented by our respondents.

All respondents agreed that the role of volunteer social workers is constantly diminishing and that this is especially visible in recent years. The reasons for this situation, according to the respondents, are as follows:

- Doubling of functions of professional social workers by volunteers. The tasks of the professional social worker include providing a systematic diagnosis of the needs of the inhabitants in the district applying for benefits and services for clients at the local administrative authority or the respective social organization, collecting agency data, etc. It comprises all those tasks which have previously been performed by volunteers. Almost all respondents were of the opinion that professionals perform these functions much better than volunteers due to lack of appropriate vocational training of the latter, lack of sufficient time, subjective estimation of needs or greater probability of not keeping confidentiality by volunteers. Thus there is a tendency to limit volunteer aid in all cases which professional social workers feel convinced they could manage by themselves. In recent years the number of professional social workers has rapidly increased from 1,200 in 197 up to 7,800 in 1984, which has strengthened such attitudes.

- The majority of volunteer social workers are elderly people, most of them being over 65 or even 70 years old, which significantly restricts their possibilities for activity. Owing to this and to their poor health, many volunteers ought to be qualified as clients rather than as providers of social welfare.
- Power of decision concerning social welfare benefits has been transferred from volunteers to professionals. Many people in need put their problems directly to the professionals, ignoring the intermediary link – the volunteer.
- The majority of professional social workers are young people, especially those recently employed, which makes cooperation with elderly volunteers difficult. Volunteers, who previously determined the scope of their work and had decisive influence on granting social welfare benefits, now have to submit themselves to the decisions of professionals, who often have limited social experience and poor occupational qualifications.
- A diminishing number of volunteer social workers – since the early 1970s their number dropped from about 65,000 to about 44,000 in 1983. This decline was due to death, aging or resignation from their posts, decreasing interest in volunteer activity in society and the weakening social status of volunteers. Young or middle-aged people show few signs of interest in undertaking such an activity. Newly recruited volunteers are not numerous and their commitment to volunteer activity is much weaker than that of their predecessors.

In the light of the above-mentioned facts one ought not to be suprised at the pessimistic views of the volunteers' responses. Many of them see no more place for themselves in the future development of social welfare. They feel unnecessarily underestimated and often unwanted. In many cases their role has been limited to the notification of needy people while they have been far less frequently asked to make social type inquiries. They have few possibilities of influencing the scope and forms of aid granted to clients. This last fact has especially caused bitterness among the volunteers. Their social status and esteem depended to a great extent on the right to grant or refuse access to state help. Now, in their own eyes and in the eyes of potential clients, intervention of volunteers has little or no significance. Possible gratitude is now directed to the professionals. Some volunteers pointed out a lack of mutual confidence between them and the paid staff. Inquiries made by volunteers are usually repeated by professionals. On the other hand, poor occupational qualifications of many paid social workers make it difficult for them to enjoy the volunteers' respect.

Those who would like to continue their activity as volunteer social worker pointed out the necessity of strengthening the role of volunteers; they want to do more or less the same as they did in the 1970s. They want primarily to be included in the decision-making process concerned with granting help to needy people.

In general all respondents agree that the future of the institution of the volunteer social worker in its present form is seriously in danger. One can distinguish two groups of opinions: Representatives of the first group emphasize that volunteer social workers are becoming steadily more unnecessary while the number of professional staff is increasing. When the coverage of professionals reaches the desired ratio (i. e. 2,500-3,500 inhabitants per social worker), they will be able to manage their work quite well without help from volunteers. Such help is of course desirable, but it should be limited to the notification of needy people, the rest could be done much better by professionals than by volunteers. A minority of social workers are still arguing in this way, but the number of people who share such opinions is growing.

The second group would like to preserve the institution of volunteer social worker, but are rather sceptical about this being accomplished without major changes in the present structure of social welfare and society's attitude towards volunteer activity. One can distinguish three major view points on the possible future role of volunteer social workers:

• The tasks of volunteers remain more or less the same as they were up to now. The main task of the volunteers should be aiding the professionals in finding needy people and making first contact with potential clients. In order to increase the volunteers'activity, professional social workers should try to improve cooperation with them by tightening contact with volunteers, enabling them to express their opinions about desired forms of help granted in concrete cases. Some respondents propose different forms of reward for volunteer work such as diplomas, awards or even cash benefits.

• The volunteer social workers should continue their present activity as before but they should concurrently become representatives of their local community They should represent the interests of the inhabitants not only towards professional social workers, but primarily towards all public authorities. Since mid 1985 the local government in Poland obtained more independence in the management of local affairs, thus volunteer social workers should, individually or in cooperation with professional social workers, prevent social welfare problems from being pushed out by more urgent economic problems within the sphere of the local authorities. Such views are shared, among others, by the Ministry of Health and Social Welfare.

• A further decline in the activity of volunteers is inevitable as long as they continue to double the tasks of professionals. The proper role of volunteers in the future should be cooperation with professionals in order to do *social work*. The volunteers have good informations about people in the district, about their needs and problems. The professionals have, or should have, the knowledge and skill needed to solve those problems. A volunteer social worker should integrate with the environment in order to help all people in need due to old age, disability, lack of care, social pathology, etc. As a member of the respective community he/she has more chances than a professional outsider to mobilize local forces, to organize self-help groups or to stimulate neighbourhood help.

At present social welfare in Poland is dominated by material needs. Professional social workers are occupied with administrative work, they simply distribute cash benefits among the most needy and try to secure a minimal standard of care s

318

vices for them. This tendency is reinforced by the fact that the official assistance system concentrates itself on the needs of elderly and disabled people. The domination of financial aid together with underdevelopment of personal social services and poor qualifications of the professional social workers make the fulfilment of the traditional goals of social work barely possible. Hence the proposition to activate volunteer social workers in that direction is a kind of wishful thinking and those who propose it know this perfectly well.

The Attitudes of Clients of Social Welfare Services

In light of the answers given by our respondents, the attitudes of clients of social welfare services could be described as both passive and active.

A passivity manifests itself in many different forms. The majority of the clients dispose themselves only to receiving help and not to doing or giving something of their own. Such attitudes are reinforced by the fact that the main form of social welfare are cash benefits granted to people unable to work due to old age or disability. Help for self-help constitutes only a marginal activity in the sphere of social welfare.

A certain number of potential clients never ask for help due to lack of information or low social status of social welfare beneficiaries. Most of them are ashamed of asking and receiving help from that source. This concerns mainly elderly. In recent years such attitudes have become less frequent, especially among the younger generation and among those who need care services. Another form of passivity is a refusal to give consent, when social welfare authorities want to start legal proceedings against members of families of needy people obliged to help them. In this way needy people are practically resigned from their right to be helped because according to existing rules formal applications for financial help from such persons should be dismissed by social welfare authorities.

Some clients take everything they get with gratitude. They are satisfied with every kind of help independent of its amount or form. They never actively try to get more.

Another kind of behaviour was most accurately labelled by one of our respondents as acquired helplessness. The clients very quickly learn that social welfare operates according to a strict scheme; benefits and services are almost entirely granted in situations defined in advance. Social workers have very limited possibilities to go beyond these schemes. Hence only those needs are articulated which have a practical chance of being met by social welfare authorities, satisfaction of other needs or wishes being beyond the power of the social worker. The possibility to choose a form of aid is also elusive in most cases. The underdevelopment of almost all social welfare services means that the only form of help at the disposal of the social worker are cash benefits, which must compensate for lack of care, poor housing conditions, etc.

Active attitudes manifest themselves first of all in demands for help. They vary from simple notification of one's needs to the open questioning of the amount of aid granted by the social worker. The active search for help is a phenomenon of recent years, the economic crisis having forced many people into this situation. At the same time the state has allocated more money for social welfare benefits and the right to such benefits has gradually been taken for granted. Attitudes of self-restraint or shame gave way to claims, manifested not only by the most underprivileged groups, but also by others since the economic crisis has diminished the standard of living of the majority of the population.

One respondent described the attitudes of clients as generally uncertain. The facultative character of social welfare benefits and their inadequate supply mean that the clients do not know what could happen in the future; what they get now is theirs.

The majority of our respondents, when questioned about the possibility or necessity of activating clients of social welfare in order to secure their participation in the decision-making process, were rather sceptical. One can distinguish three main groups of opinions:

• It is hard to imagine the introduction of a participation model. In the present economic situation and the present structure of social welfare, such participation would be undesirable and unnecessary. Social welfare authorities have a very limited field of manoeuvre and, apart from material aid, they do not have too much to offer. Thus even justifiable needs of people cannot always be satisfied. Therefore, a right to co-decision for clients would mean more claims and more disarray.

• The clients could participate in a provision of services, but only in an indirect way. Such participation is, after all, already exercised in practice. The clients apply for help to satisfy concrete needs; these needs are taken into account when the plan of further development of social welfare services is being prepared. In that way the clients have indirect influence on the shape of social welfare services. There is no need, however, to involve them in the decision-making process which determines the forms and amount of aid in concrete, individual cases. This should be decided according to objective criteria and regulations stipulated by law. The clients are incompetent in their own cases because they do not have enough knowledge about applied criteria, complicated regulations, the extent of unmet needs in their district or the resources, which are at the disposal of a concrete social welfare unit. Their opinions could of course be taken into account but final decisions should be taken independently by professional social workers.

• An active participation of clients is both needed and desirable. It could take different forms. For example the clients could cooperate with social workers in concrete case; a recognition of needs and determination of forms of aid should be made by all the interested parties. In most cases the clients have better knowledge of their needs and necessary forms of help than anybody else. The task the social worker ought to be the proper use of this knowledge in order to in prove the effectiveness of social welfare service and to free the potential possibilities for self-help activity which people have. Such participation common in many countries is exercised in Poland on a very small scale.

Furthermore, all recipients of social welfare benefits should be given full information about existing possibilities of granting help to them. They could elect their own representatives. Social workers should organize meetings with such representatives, devoted to acquainting the clients with all social problems in a district and with the possibilities of the social welfare authorities dealing with these problems. This knowledge could promote better understanding of all difficulties in the work of social workers by the clients. It could serve as a solid foundation for further cooperation; difficult decisions on how to divide scarce and inadequate resources could be made jointly. In this way a rejection of a request by one group of potential clients on behalf of another group, having more urgent needs, could have social acceptance and understanding. It could also stimulate those, who have a relatively better situation than other clients of social welfare, to do something on their own instead of holding out hands for more benefits.

All respondents who are in favour of clients' participation emphasize the fact that it could be possible only in certain cases depending on the intellectual level of the respective group and on the specific features of different needs. This is, among others, the view of the ministry. They also stress that an evolution towards greater participation has slim chances without major changes in the working or the whole social welfare system. The concentration on financial aid does not create proper conditions for the greater involvment of the clients. Their cooperation will not really be needed before social workers will be able to concentrate on the realization of the traditional goals of social work.

Future Development of Social Welfare Services

All respondents have presented more or less similar views on the desired development of social welfare services in Poland. All of them put first *further professionalization* of social welfare. It is, on the one hand, an absolute and forced necessity because no other subject is able to fulfil goals of social welfare in a proper and complex way. People's volunteer activity is diminishing as well as the family's to perform care functions. On the other hand, it is also desirable because highly qualified professionals (and there is no doubt that they should be highly qualified) are the most competent subjects to cope with the difficult tasks of the social welfare sector. In order to achieve the above-mentioned goal, it is not enough to employ more staff. It is necessary to raise the occupational status and social prestige of professional social local administrative bodies and different social organizations, the right to grant social welfare benefits should be exercised entirely by social workers. All other subjects active in this sphere should be more or less directly subordinated to the decisions of professional social workers.

Some of the respondents have proposed to convert the present centres of social welfare into centres of social work, which would integrate all state and volunteer institutions in a given area delivering social welfare services or granting benefits. Such concentration of all resources could lead to a better satisfaction of people's needs and better coordination of activity undertaken in this field.

In order to increase the prestige of social workers it is also indispensable to put their wages at least on the average level in the country. At present their wages belong to the lowest. It makes it very difficult to have a proper personnel policy and to prevent the best and qualified social workers from searching for another, better paid and less troublesome job.

All respondents agreed that professionalization should be accompanied by a significant, qualitative and quantitative development of the state social services. The state is the main body responsible for satisfying all major social needs and it cannot free itself from performing care activity. Social welfare services must gain a more prominent place in the activity of state organs instead of being treated as marginal and unimportant.

Quite surprisingly many respondents put in the second or even parallel place the necessity to increase the family's responsibility for satisfying the needs of its members. In Poland, contrary to some other countries, the family is by law obliged to provide the indispensable aid and care to its dependent subjects.

In recent years, however, fulfilling this duty meets frequently with great difficulties and a growing number of families fail to do so. This concerns care and maintenance provided by children for their old or disabled parents. Social workers have to dismiss application for financial aid coming from such families and in consequence many people are left without help. In order to avoid such a situation, social workers try to find ways to solve this dilemma. Some of them demand that the state should take responsibility for the maintenance of individuals when the family does not want to do so. The majority of our respondents, however, are of the opinion that such families should be forced to fulfil their obligation, if they are in a position to do so. To force does not necessarily mean resorting to legal methods, but it is more important to create proper conditions making it easier for families to fulfil their care functions.

Social welfare services and benefits should be concentrated more on help for families that on help for individuals, as they are at the present time.

Other possible trends in the future development of social welfare services were ignored by the respondents. The prevailing view, shared also by the ministry, was that professionalization and further development of statutory social welfare services does not mean an elimination of volunteer activity. The state alone is unable to satisfy all people's needs. In the present situation, however, one cannot rely on volunteer activity or on the activity of social organizations. Hence professionalization is the only possible choice for assuring that people are not left without help.

Catholic Church-related Activities in Volunteering and Backing Informal Networks for Care and Help

In the years 1945-1950 Catholic Church activity in the sphere of social welfare was mainly concentrated around the church's charity organization Caritas. In 1950, Caritas was for all intents and purposes nationalized, it changed its name to Catholic Union 'Caritas', and from that time up to now it has been a social organization of Catholics under supervision of the state. The church has never reconciled itself to that fact and is demanding that Caritas be returned to its auspices. In spite of the state character of this organization, many priests, monks and nuns are still participating in the activities of various care institutions run by Caritas. At present Caritas is one of the most important social organization active in the sphere of care services. In 1984 it had: 56 homes for mentally retarded children and 16 homes for mentally retarded adults, 35 homes for the chronically ill, 18 homes for patients with central nervous system diseases, 12 institutions which provide medical treatment and education for handicapped children, 46 special educational institutions for children with moderate and slight retardation, 2 pre-schools and 7 homes for orphans. Many of these institutions are among the best in the country, some of them providing unique services or treatment. About 2,300 nuns and monks are employed in the Caritas network.

In spite of significant limitations of legal possibilities to carry on charitable activity, the church has continued to be involved in these activities now carried on within the scope of so-called charity priesthood. The character of this activity, however, has been substantially changed and its scale has been greatly diminished. It is very difficult to discover a comprehensive picture of present church activity in the sphere of social welfare. In most cases such activities are of a very informal character, and are usually undertaken only occasionally. It is rare to find aid in a well-organized form. Most volunteer activity is initiated and organized by the respective parishes and such actions are not revealed in any official statistics. Church authorities are quite reluctant to provide informations about their charitable activities, hence reviews by the Catholic press and interviews reveal only a partial idea of church-related activities in the sphere of social initiatives in volunteering undertaken or backed by the Catholic Church.

• In 1982 the Primatial Committee of Brotherhood Aid was created. It later changed its name to the Charitable and Social Primatial Committee. The main task of this committee is to give evangelical help to all people, in particular to those who are ill and disabled, old and lonely, ailing and oppressed, and to those deprived of work. All aid should be provided on a voluntary basis by clergymen in cooperation with laymen. The committee carries on activities in different sections. There is a section of aid to old and bed-ridden persons, delivering food and clothes, distributing hot meals and organizing common celebrations of the church holidays.

A family section, called Pro Familia, concentrates its activity on preserving lives of unborn children. This section takes care of pregnant women who are in diffi-culties in order to prevent them from resorting to abortion. It has organized a spe-cial telephone service which provides moral and legal advice to all pregnant women. Such women can also receive modest in-kind aid. In the last two years this section has helped about 500 women.

The committee also provides aid to the political prisoners. Up to the present, all activities carried on in the framework of this committee have been on a relatively small scale.

Each October the church organizes a 'Charity week' on a nation-wide scale, which is devoted to a particular group of people in need. By organizing charity weeks, the church is trying to encourage people to undertake voluntary activity and to be more responsive to urgent human needs in their environment. In pas-toral letters issued on this occasion, practical advice is given on how to organize and promote voluntary activity and on what each person can do in order to help other people. At the same time the church emphasizes that it is the responsibility of the family to provide care for its dependants.

Care activities for elderly and ill people are mainly undertaken within the frame-work of the charity priesthood. These care activities are organized on a parish level. In order to provide care on a regular basis some parishes employ parish nurses. She could be a nun or a lay woman, specially trained to do care work. Parish nurses organize all care activity in the respective communities and provide more specialized forms of care. Other simple care functions are performed by vol-unteers, organized into parish teams, who locate people in need.

The church authorities are opposed to the institutionalization of too many charity activities. They stress that a parish, which does not include volunteers in such ac-tivities, could not perform its care functions satisfactorily. Besides providing care, some parishes try to satisfy psychical needs of dependent people by keeping per-sonal contacts and by organizing their free time.

Charity activity is carried on by a majority of parishes. In some of them, especially in the countryside, such activity is still of an occasional character. The parishes in towns usually provide more systematic services. For example in the Warsaw Archidiocese 48 from a total of 385 parishes provide specialized nursing care.

Another form of activity in the social sphere is the use of foreign aid. In recent years, Poland has received a significant amount of foreign aid in the form of food-stuffs, medicaments, hygienic articles, etc. Most of this aid went to the Catholic Church, which had to organize its delivery. The charity commission of the Polish Episcopate has been appointed to coordinate the distribution of foreign aid on the national level. Most parishes have constituted special charity teams who are in charge of direct distribution of aid. These teams consist of volunteers enjoying community confidence and having a certain knowledge of the unsatisfied needs in their environment. The main tasks of charity teams are as follows:

• Card indexing of all needy people in a parish and of all beneficiaries.
• Sorting out of received goods.

● Organization of delivery of aid to beneficiaries.
● Being on duty in parishes, giving information and registering applications for aid.

Parish charity teams have accomplished a great deal, especially during 1982 – 1983, when foreign aid had assumed considerable proportions. In the past two years, both aid from abroad and the activity of this type has been rapidly decreasing.

Recently the church authorities in an effort to prevent people from terminating their own self-help activity and from relying entirely on foreign aid have organized a campaign to promote charity initiatives based on the communities' own resources. Money and in-kind aid have been collected and then divided among the most needy. Another interesting form of activity carried out under the formal or informal auspices of the church are movements. Some could be mentioned here:

● *Family of families* and *Faith and light* – both these movements constitute communities consisting of disabled persons, their families and their friends. In the Warsaw Archidiocese there are presently about 2,500 families and 300 persons participating in the activities of these two movements.

● *Civilization of love* – a movement which is to some extent related to the medical circle. One of its main goals is to fight against alcoholism.

● *Maitri* – a youth movement patterning itself on the activity of Mother Teresa in Calcutta. It is active in some towns, providing aid to the most needy.

● *The Adam Chmielowsky Society for Help* – this society was finally registered at the end of 1981, after a long struggle. Its goal is to restore human dignity to the homeless, to take care of them and to help in their resocialization. The specific needs of the homeless are not really within the sphere of public social welfare authorities. The society is almost entirely financed by private grants. At present there are six regional branches running several shelters for homeless men and three houses of friendship. These are the only institutions of this kind in the country. The first shelter for the homeless, opened in Wroclaw at the end of 1981, bears the name of Brother Albert, which is the monastic name of Adam Chmielowsky. In spite of difficult housing conditions, the shelter provides homeless men with night lodging, food and care. It also helps them to deal with their personal matters and to find a job. The shelter is run for the most part by volunteers, who are supported by the work of monks, and is managed by a Catholic priest.

The houses of friendship are situated in Warsaw and its surroundings. One of them is assigned to women. These houses are working on the family principle and are self-sufficient. Their maintenance is based on volunteer work, individual grants and fees from those who are in a position to pay. The houses of friendship are intended to receive a notion of common utility work and to promote a need to serve others unselfishly.

In the spring of 1986 the society opened another new home for mothers who are pregnant or in post-childbirth. This home is situated in an old presbytery near the town of Kielce.

At present all the above-mentioned institutions have only a few dozen places at their disposal. In the future the Adam Chmielowsky Society intends to run four kinds of shelters: shelters for provisional stay, old people's houses, hospices and houses for alcoholics.

It is worth mentioning one other new initiative, which is very loosely connected with the activity of this society. A short time ago two individuals created a 'Farm'. This is an agricultural farm which provides homeless people, especially drug addicts, with accomodation, food and work. It is run on a community basis and its main goal is mutual resocialization. Apart from the above-mentioned activities, efforts are presently being made to let the church open several hospices in which old and chronically ill people could spend the rest of their lives in a dignified way. The first of these hospices will soon be opened in Cracow.

Self-help Activities Connected with the Former Trade Union Solidarity

In recent years one of the most important reasons for undertaking a self-help type of activity has been political factors. One of the outcomes ot the introduction of martial law in Poland at the end of 1981 was the suspension and subsequent delegalization of all hitherto existing trade unions. All activity constituting a continuation of Solidarity activity is illegal, independent of its forms.

This also refers to actions of a self-help nature. Such activity is, nevertheless, carried on. It is mainly concentrated on helping those people who, because of their political activity, have been imprisoned, arrested or interned, or who have difficulties in finding a job. In some firms contributions are still being collected from among former members of Solidarity. A part of this money is distributed among families of the above-mentioned people, covering maintenance of such families, costs of lawyers or costs of possible fines. In many cases fellow workers of those imprisoned are taking care or their families helping them in everyday activities such as looking after children, household work, small repair work, etc. The Catholic Church is also very much engaged in providing different forms of aid to political prisoners and their families. These activities were quite well-developed during martial law in Poland. At present the number of people imprisoned because of political reasons is much lower, hence the need for such help is decreasing.

In some firms money collected from contributions of former members of Solidarity is assigned to ordinary trade union benefits, paid in case of childbirth, death of a family member, economic difficulties, etc.

Activities of a self-help character remain, however, in the background of the former trade union Solidarity. It also seems that these activities are diminishing, although one cannot be sure about that. The real scope of self-help activities ha never been known due to their illegal and, in most cases, very informal charac ter. The contributions are collected and distributed secretly, and mutual help i provided on a basis of close personal contacts.

Conclusions

In this chapter we have tried to present recent trends in the development of volunteer and self-help activities in the social welfare sector in Poland. We have learned that, although there would be room for such activities, our society does not show a great tendency in this direction, and in general voluntary activity is decreasing. It manifests itself in the decline in membership in many voluntary organizations and the growing number of voluntary social workers, in the increasing utilization of paid professionals in voluntary organizations and the growing number of people who are not interested in volunteer activity. Many members of volunteer organizations are passive, in most cases the activity of local branches being based on only a few people, the rest limiting themselves to irregular payment of contributions. This situation requires some explanation, taking into account the general socio-economic background of the process in question. Two types of reasons seem to underline the lack of interest in volunteer activity: barriers of a socio-economic nature and barriers of a socio-political nature. To the first ones belong several fundamental features of the socio-economic scene:

• A decreasing standard of living forced many people to undertake additional work to compensate for this trend.
• Insufficient salaries for taking care of the family forced women to become the second money earner, thereby excluding them from possible voluntary activities.
• The overall underdevelopment of the service sector and the time consuming process for obtaining most commodities and the market should also be taken into account. This refers equally to men and women, thus forcing disposable free time to be increasingly consumed in running the household.
• Also the free time accumulated by the large number of people who recently took advantage of the temporary possibility for earlier retirement (about 540,000 people) or of the partially paid parental leave (about 800,000 mothers of small children) was almost totally consumed by the households, which have to provide more and more services for their members.

Socio-political barriers include more complicated phenomena. First, the new society, although socialist, did not develop the necessary tradition of work or activity for others in the sphere of social welfare services. Social activity which has been promoted and favoured by state authorities has been concentrated on common utility initiatives such as: building of a new school, health care centre or cultural centre, building of a good road or water supply services in the countryside. Such initiatives are quite similar to the self-imposed contributions in Yugoslavia. They were and still are widespread in Poland, many institutions of the social infrastructure having been built by volunteers.

On the other hand, there is no tradition of self-help in smaller circles, except for family, good friends or familiar neighbours. People tend to be circumspect about their problems to strangers and withdraw themselves from a broader social activity in favour of family life. This is perfectly demonstrated by the escape of people from their work places in case of earlier retirement.

Another important factor is that every initiated voluntary activity in the form of a group or an organization has to be registered with the state and, thus must adopt a more or less bureaucratic structure, which is a real obstacle to spontaneous action in small groups. In addition, many people do not believe their action would be effective because of complex bureaucratic procedure. Therefore, many of them address their demands and complaints directly to the state or party organs or to the mass media. These channels usually proved to be more effective than looking for help at lower levels. Perhaps these facts have even been responsible for suppressing the need for local voluntary organizations. The existence of several separate channels for obtaining services (school, enterprise) where an individual can apply for help may have the same impact on voluntary actions.

Moreover, in recent years new social initiatives lay themselves open to suspicion that they are covering activities detrimental to the state. The state authorities favour initiatives undertaken by already existing voluntary organizations, and thus the creation of new organizations usually meets with many difficulties. This is to a certain degree justifiable in the present socio-political situation in Poland, as a volunteer activity in the social sphere could, in many cases, be of a more political than humanitarian nature. An informal blockade of possibilities of voluntary action outside the officially established system of social organizations, connected with a rather close subjection of these organizations to political parties and state authorities, has caused diminishing interest in undertaking voluntary actions. It is hard to force voluntary activity, when there is little room for autonomy and spontaneity, consequently, the existing forms of voluntary activity are more a result of state policy than an effect of authentic and spontaneous local initiatives.

Special attention should be paid to a very specific feature of the Polish social scene – the fact that the state is commonly believed to be the only subject responsible for meeting people's needs. Generally it is expected that the state would guarantee welfare services, which is a remainder of the centrally planned economy. It is also worth adding, to complete this picture, that the welfare services' delivery system is principally organized to serve passive clients and not to involve them in the management tasks or the decision-making process.

To predict future trends, the most probable development in the sphere of social welfare services will primarily be the professionalization of the delivery system and its further bureaucratization, as more detailed regulations are still required by the staff aiming at easier case treatment. At least the opinions presented by respondents in our researches clearly pointed in that direction. One has to stress, however, that our respondents could not divorce themselves from seeing all problems in the context of the present difficult socio-economic situation. For all people engaged in social activity, regardless of their status, the most important problem was the low status of social welfare in the state policy and in consequence the very low status of all social workers, professionals as well as volunteers. The desire to increase the role of paid professionals is an expression of the wish to increase the status of social welfare activity both in society and in the eyes of politicians. At this time, social workers, who are active in public social services as well as in voluntary organizations, are often powerless and rescue activity clearly prevails over genuine social work. It would be possible for a large group of qualified social workers to exert strong pressure on local and central authorities in order to promote better understanding of their clients' problems. On the other hand, in the situation of scarcity and underdevelopment of statutory welfare services, it is quite understandable that social workers want to concentrate the power of decision concerning welfare benefits and services in one place. It is difficult to rely on volunteers or volunteer organizations when many signs indicate the decline in volunteer activity in society. Professional social workers alone cannot reverse this trend. Unfortunately, it is also true that most of them do not even try to counteract diminishing volunteer activity. This is due to lack of sufficient skill, disbelief in the success of such efforts, or simply ignorance of the role volunteers should and could play in the provision of social welfare in Poland.

Meanwhile, our research has also shown that, in spite of these difficulties, new initiatives in volunteering and self-help activity are emerging and developing both in the framework of existing social organizations as well as outside them. Monar, self-help groups of parents of disabled children, unbeaten-track squads, the school of pure hearts, parish charity teams and different church-backed movements or organizations could serve as the most prominent examples of new genuine social initiatives undertaken in the sphere of social welfare. They speak volumes for the existence of a quite appreciable potential for voluntary activity in Poland.

In the beginning of the 1980s, many different social initiatives have been manifested, as a matter of fact, in all spheres of people's activities: in the work place, education, science and culture, health care, protection of environment, housing and social welfare. These initiatives have demonstrated that people want and can take over from the state responsibility for their own welfare and security. In the following years, however, people's activity in these areas has diminished and again it has become more controlled and less spontaneous. In the present complicated economic and socio-political situation, it is very difficult to carry on an active social policy, directed towards awakening the feeling of affiliation to a community, to support solidarity, to awaken volunteer work motivations. Such a policy also implies a risk of uncontrollable changes, a risk which, in the present situation, politicians would rather overestimate that underestimate. In consequence many people, having no other choice, want and demand to be helped by the state, to improve or even enlarge state welfare services. The opinions presented our respondents, demanding further professionalization of social services, correspond with people's expectations.

On the other hand, it is a well-known fact that the state alone is unable to meet people's needs on a satisfactory level. Hence all activities contributing to a better satisfaction of these needs are of great worth because without them many people would be left without any help. In such a situation, it is indispensable to utilize fully all potential for volunteer work available in the Polish society. This requires an introduction of greater freedom of voluntary actions in the sphere of social welfare and suppression of all bureaucratic obstacles to undertaking new initiatives.

A rush for spontaneous development of self-help or mutual aid groups similar to that ones active in many West European countries is hardly to be predicted, but an appreciable increase in volunteer activity is possible despite the above-mentioned circumstances. It is the task of the policy-makers to transform existing potential for volunteering into practical activities.

This chapter has been written in cooperation with G. Firlit, J. Hrynkiewicz, E. Les, M. Tobiasz.

Yugoslavia:
Three Ways of Welfare System Restructuring

Ivan Svetlik

This chapter deals with important recent changes within the national welfare system. The first part is a description of the development of the Yugoslav welfare system and its basic characteristics, based on the analysis of laws which have regulated the welfare system on the one hand, and on the literature (Bilandžic 1980), on the other.

The second part is the central one, presenting the analyses of some key changes within the welfare system as well as between the welfare system and its environment. We analyze the official statistical data and several reports about the situation in the welfare sector, especially about its outputs and the resources needed. We had several interviews with the experts who work for various welfare institutions and with officials who are in charge of welfare in the state administration. On this basis we identified the main trends that have appeared in Yugoslavia during the crisis which started in 1980 and which is still rather severe. We presented the results obtained in the first phase to experts and officials asking them to comment on the results and especially to evaluate the strategies that seem to be likely in the near future. To get the answer about future changes in the welfare system we also analyzed several plans which had been passed at the beginning of 1986 at the community and republic levels, as well as specialized plans for child care, health care, education, social security, employment and other welfare areas.

In the final part we present our interpretation of the results and give some conclusions by which we would like to point at some implications and possible developments of the welfare system.

Basic Characteristics of the Yugoslav Welfare System

The Yugoslav welfare system consists of two main structural elements, one formal and the other informal. We will focus on the formal welfare system which has been increasingly replacing the informal one, but has had many deficiencies. The formal welfare system comprises three sectors: welfare institutions which are ser-vice-producing organizations in the social sector as well as the administrative structure that regulates them, welfare activities exercised within enterprises, and, at the local level, volunteer organizations. No formal private welfare sector exists in Yugoslavia. The structure of informal welfare activities is less clear. Some illus-trations which indicate its size and domain will be presented, however.

Development of the Formal Welfare System in Yugoslavia

After World War II, a social system of the Soviet type was introduced in Yugosla-via. It was a strong and centralized state guided by the Communist Party. On one hand certain needs of the population were recognized and certain rights were given to the people. On the other, the state founded special centralized agencies led by its administration, which were responsible for the production of services needed for the satisfaction of the recognized needs. The state school system, health care system, pension system and social security system were founded. The majority of the population was equally entitled to numerous benefits, equally throughout the country.

At the beginning of the 1950s a radical deviation from the Soviet type of society began. It was characterized by two developmental streams that represented a cornerstone for the introduction of changes in the social system. There were decentralization and de-etatization on one hand, and self-management on the other.

In the 1950s the state's tight control over the welfare system slackened. Special institutions were founded at the federal and republic levels that were not meant to be under the direct supervision of the state administration. There were institu-tions that took charge of pension, health and disability insurance, employment and unemployment insurance, health care and educational systems. Those in-stitutions had to carry out decisions made by the assemblies that existed for each respective area mentioned. The assemblies were composed of representatives elected upon a territorial principle. However, the state control over financial re-sources and budgeting, as well as over rules upon which the welfare system was regulated, remained rather high.

In 1963 a new step was taken towards de-etatization. According to the Constitu-tion of 1963, the federal assembly and republic assemblies were composed of several chambers based on a functional principle, including the chamber of so-cial security and health care. It was supposed that such institutional arrange-ments would permit the respective welfare representatives (schools, universities, theatres, health care centres, hospitals, etc.) to exercise influence on relevant laws and plans, on budgets, and on benefits to which the population was entitled. In addition, it was supposed to diminish the influence of the federal and republic administrations.

In the late 1960s, the decentralization of the welfare system began. Republics and provinces received some autonomy concerning welfare jurisdiction and budgeting. Only a general framework, including basic rights of people, was determined on the federal level by means of laws, resolutions and other regulations. Republics and provinces agreed upon the size ot their welfare budgets, but within the limits of the agreement, they distributed the resources for their welfare programmes and welfare organizations fairly autonomously. They had to provide the population with the guaranteed programme, but they could extend it if they had enough resources. In some respects they could organize their welfare systems in a specific way. Eight increasingly different welfare systems started to grow in the country.

During the 1970s, the decentralization of the welfare system in Yugoslavia increased further. Many responsibilities previously given to the republics and provinces were pushed down to the level of the commune. Decentralization, however, is not a guarantee for de-etatization. Quite the contrary.Instead of having one centralized state bureaucracy which would control the welfare system, tens and even hundreds of them were developed at the communal level. The bureaucratic apparatus experienced a rapid growth. This constatation influenced another radical change in the welfare system which had been introduced by the latest Constitution in 1974.

The Structure and Functioning of the Present Formal Welfare System

According to the Constitution of 1974, the welfare system should be almost completly separated from the state. Instead of state bureaucracies which mediate between *service providers* and *service consumers* and which can control both of them, the service providers and service consumers should confront their interests directly. The institutional form which enables confrontation of and bargaining between the two 'parties' consists of the so-called self-managing communities of interest.

Self-managing communities of interest (SCIs) are located at the level of communes, towns or regions and the level of republics. There is one SCI at each level for the following sectors of the welfare system: education, culture, recreation and sport, employment, health care, child care, social security and social assistance, and research. Some other SCIs can be founded in other fields, such as housing construction, power production and transport, if service providers, service consumers or public authorities consider them desirable.

Self-managing communities of interest deal in these ways with problems that are important for a specific level. At the communal level, for instance, SCIs for education deal primarily with primary schools, at the regional level with secondary schools and at the republic level with universities. SCIs for health care deal at the communal level with health care centres, at the regional level with regional hospitals and at the republic level with clinics and the health insurance system. In fact they deal with the planning, financing and management of the welfare pro grammes for which they are responsible.

The structure of an SCI is simple. There is an assembly for each SCI which is composed of two chambers. The service providers' chamber consists of the dele gates who are elected from among the workers of service organizations which render a particular type of service, e. g. schools and hospitals.

The service consumers' chamber is composed of delegates elected from among the workers of non-service-providing enterprises and from among the inhabitants of localities of a respective commune in which the SCI operates. Special boards are appointed, usually by the members of the assembly, to deal with more com plicated problems, to make proposals for the assembly and to decide upon less important questions.

The third structural element of an SCI is its professional staff composed of vari ous experts and coordinators. It takes charge of data banks, makes analyses about the quantity and quality of services, as well as about the cost of service production, surveys the inflow and outflow of money, checks the relevance of standards, arranges sessions of the assembly, sends invitations, writes notes etc. It can also suggest discussions for the assembly. One staff can perform these tasks for one or more sectors of the welfare system.

There are three main sources of money needed to finance welfare programmes and welfare organizations. First, there are contributions of the enterprises. The percentage of gross personal income determined by the SCI assemblies is allo cated for each welfare sector. This money is paid directly to the account of a com munal SCI. Representatives of communal, regional and republic SCIs negotiate and decide upon the sum to be allocated to regional and republic programmes and organizations.

The second method by which welfare organizations obtain resources is the sale of services. Certain services are marketable. For some of them, like special edu cational courses, utilization of certain recreation facilities or some special medi cal treatments, full price must be paid. On the other hand, services such as child care, medical prescriptions and other medical treatments or cultural performan ces must be covered partially by individuals or other consumers, e. g. enter prises.

The third source of money which can be used exclusively for investments in new welfare facilities, e. g. schools, day care centres, health centres, cultural centres etc., are the so-called self-imposed contributions. For one or more neighbouring communes a programme of new investments is made, and a percentage of the personal income of individuals to be contributed during a certain period is pro posed. People vote for or against a self-imposed contribution.

The assembly of a SCI holds several sessions per year. At their sessions dele gates discuss and make decisions on issues such as the quality and quantity of services, new investments, the price of services that are paid partially, etc. Ses vice providers should propose programmes for services to be rendered as well as indicate the costs. Service consumers are supposed to demand additional services or reject some of them, demand improvements in the quality of services and bargain about the costs. It is expected that finally both parties agree upon the programme and that the assembly approves it. The programme should serve as a basis for the rendering of services and for paying contributions to service-providing organizations.

In fact, the above described procedure is modified by several external regulations, some of which must be mentioned. First there are some rights and benefits guaranteed by federal or republic laws either to the total population or only to some specific groups. This is a guaranteed programme which includes items such as free primary education to all young people, health insurance or paid parental leave, which must be fulfilled by all SCIs first. If the SCIs have resources that enable the extension of a guaranteed programme or the financing of an additional programme, they can participate. If SCIs in some communes do not have enough resources to carry out a guaranteed programme, they are given subsidies from a special solidarity fund to which all communes of a republic contribute.

Second, the federal government proposes and the federal assembly accepts resolutions for the yearly economic policy. Each resolution determines also the share of Gross National Product (GNP) that can be allocated to the welfare system. It means that the resources of SCIs cannot be increased over the determined margins even if the enterprises would like to do that. Otherwise the SCIs would come under strong political and administrative pressure or, if they insist on programmes which are too extensive, they would remain partially unfulfilled or unpaid. Certain SCIs can spend more resources only at the expense of the others. This implies an uneasy bargaining among SCIs.

The third problem is the lack of autonomy given to the welfare system. Institutionally, the welfare system is decentralized and separated from the state to a high degree, but in practice its autonomy is limited especially by the decisions of the federal administration concerning economic policy. There is also a state administration equipped with professional staff at the levels of commune and republic that takes charge of a welfare system. It must control the behaviour of service organizations to be in conformity with laws and other state regulations. Therefore it quite often interferes with the work of assemblies and the professional staff of SCIs.

The fourth problem is therefore the entropy of the welfare system itself. Frequent changes in the institutional arrangement lead to overlapping of the old and new structures, e. g. SCIs and state administration. As a consequence, the administration of SCIs is expanding. These changes also demand of all participants an adjustment to the new patterns of behaviour and therefore a decrease in their work effectiveness.

We should also mention another important segment of the formal welfare system which has been developed rather independently within the enterprises. Several welfare items are provided for workers, such as nearly full employment, security, housing facilities, child care, holiday, recreation and health care facilities, education and training funds, scholarships, hot meals, subsidized cultural performances and firms' cultural groups. Recently responsibility has been given to work organizations to finance training, employment and medical care for their workers who suffer from work accidents and professional diseases. Yet most of these services are not produced by enterprises, which for the most part purchase and distribute them among the employees.

The third segment of the formal welfare system, located on its margin, are local networks for self-help and mutual aid, and volunteer organizations. They are recognized as part of the welfare system, but their activities are based mainly on their own initiatives, financing and work. In fact they are semi-formal.

At the level of the locality, i. e. a village or a small quarter of a town, a commission for health and social care can be found. Its members are usually volunteers who are trained for home attendance of the sick or elderly.

Among the volunteer organizations whose aim is mutual help of their members or help for non-members, the following can be mentioned: Friends of Young People Association, Pensioners Associations, Organizations of the Disabled and Red Cross Organization. They act mainly at the local level.

The Role of the Informal Welfare Sector

The informal welfare sector shrank as the formal one expanded. Although formally unrecognized and separated from the formal welfare system, it represents a supplement to the latter. Usually it enters the areas which are not covered by welfare programmes of the formal institutions.

It is difficult to estimate precisely the size of the informal welfare sector and to find out what its internal structure is. There are some empirical results which show that it must not be neglected.

In 1981 it was estimated that the output of the informal economy amounted to about 16.6-33.1 per cent of the Yugsolav GNP (Kukar 1984), part of which were certainly services.

In other research conducted in 1978, it was found that informal paid work of Yugoslav workers equalled 38,000 work places, while the respective figure for informal unpaid work was 72,000 work places (Prpič 1978).

In the Level of Living research (Level of Living 1984) performed on a representative sample of the Slovene adult population, we obtained some results which show how widespread this informal work is. Of those people who possess their own houses or apartments, 49.6 per cent built them themselves. This is 23.6 per cent of the adult population. Compared to the statistical survey from 1973 the number of adults who built their houses or apartments has increased by 3.

per cent. The same survey shows that 42 per cent of adults in Yugoslavia live in the houses and apartments which they built on their own. While building, 71.7 per cent adults in Slovenia were assisted by their parents, relatives or friends. In most cases, a reciprocal exchange of labour is involved. It is shown also that 41.7 per cent of respondents solved their housing problems exclusively with the help of their relatives, as compared to 23 per cent of respondents who solved their housing problems exclusively with the mobilization of formal resources, i. e., they rented an apartment of their enterprise or commune.

Household work occupies 64.5 per cent of the adult population at least one hour a day. This group comprises 95 per cent women and 32.7 per cent men. These respondents spend on the average 25.7 hours per week for household work. Women spend thus 29.3 hours and men 14.8 hours per week. About 40 per cent of adults have children who are younger than 15 years. These parents devote on the average 23.3 hours per week to their children.

Among the adult population there are 16.3 per cent employees who do part-time farming. They cultivate land and breed different animals on an average of 24 hours a week. Moreover, nearly 70 per cent of adults are occupied in gardening. They grow vegetables and fruits and some also breed rabbits and chickens. In 1984, 18.8 per cent of the adult respondents in Slovenia answered that they had to stay in bed due to some illness in the previous year, while 10.4 per cent had to be hospitalized for the same reason. The relative importance of informal 'hospitalization' is obvious (Level of Living 1984).

Recent Trends in the Development of the Yugoslav Welfare System

This is the central part of the report in which one or more new and significant issues from the country's agenda should be presented. However, we decided not to deal with only a few cases or with changes in just one area, but to present recent global trends that we identified while analyzing the welfare system and welfare programmes. The reason for such a choice is quite simple. The changes within the welfare system as well as in its environment are so turbulent that it is practically impossible to estimate the right meaning for a particular case, especially with reference to its impact for the future. Therefore we took into consideration a broad scope of information obtained from statistical publications, official reports, interviews and research works[1]) in an effort to compose a mosaic which would best correspond to reality.

We conducted our research at two levels, the republic and communal level. Due to time and cost limits we were able to analyze the situation in only two republics: in Serbia without the autonomous regions of Kosovo and Vojvodina, that reached the average level of development in the country, and in Slovenia as the most developed republic. The attitudes of different social actors about the strategies followed by the welfare system were analyzed only in Slovenia. As to the commune level, we analyzed in detail only the situation in Maribor, a town with six communes. However, we included in this report also the information describing the situation in other communes and republics as well as in the entire country.

In this part of the chapter we describe the dynamics of the welfare system and its interaction with the environment, especially economic and work environments. We deliberately limit ourselves to descriptive analysis. The only theoretical inputs are a model according to which the generating of the crisis of the welfare system could be explained, and a synthesis of various responses to the crisis offered by the welfare system; these are combined in three main developmental strategies. Our discussion concerning wider social impacts of the described developmental trends is given in the final part of the chapter where we employ some theoretical speculation.

Our main hypotheses dealing with the relation between the welfare system and its environment, especially with the economic and work areas, are presented in chart 1.

First, we presume that the economic crisis has accelerated the internal crisis of the welfare system which can be described in terms of a unidimensional development of formal welfare institutions at the expense of the informal ones (Pulliainen and Pietilä 1983), and in terms of a productivity gap rising between the service and the industrial sector (Nilsson and Wadeskog 1985).

Second, this acceleration takes place in two ways: directly, through the intervention of the state administration that would like to reallocate the national product in favour of industry; and indirectly by the employment crisis. The employment crisis influences the decrements of financial resources for the welfare sector because of the falling individual demand for services, and because of the falling contributions of enterprises for the welfare sector; these contributions are determined as a percentage of gross wages per worker. On the other hand, the employment crisis increases several social problems, e. g. unemployment, which are expected to be solved by the formal welfare institutions.

Third, the crisis of the formal welfare system has important negative impacts on the employment situation, for there has been a tendency to slow down employment growth in the service sector.

Fourth, several reactions appear within the welfare system as a response to the crisis. They can be described in terms of strategies which we call marketization, rationalization and externalization strategy and which in fact mean an attempt to achieve a new balance between structural elements of a welfare system, especially between formal welfare institutions, industrial enterprises and the semi-formal and informal sector.

Let us present the case step by step.

Chart 1
The Relationship Between
Employment and the Welfare Crisis

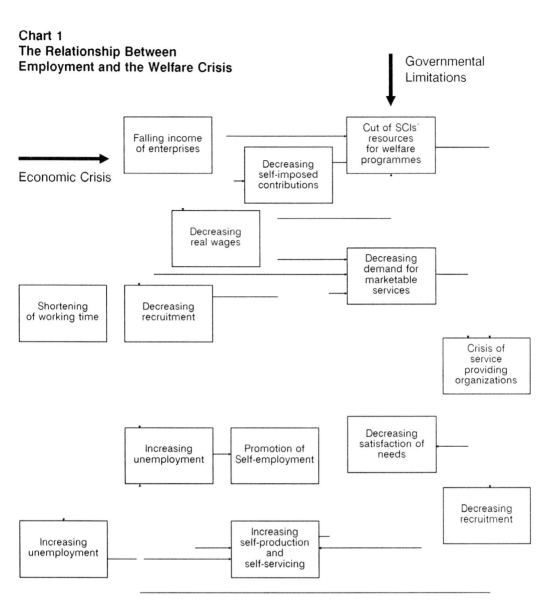

Governmental
Limitations

Economic Crisis

Falling income
of enterprises

Decreasing
self-imposed
contributions

Cut of SCIs'
resources
for welfare
programmes

Decreasing
real wages

Decreasing
demand for
marketable
services

Shortening
of working time

Decreasing
recruitment

Crisis of
service
providing
organizations

Increasing
unemployment

Promotion of
Self-employment

Decreasing
satisfaction of
needs

Decreasing
recruitment

Increasing
unemployment

Increasing
self-production
and
self-servicing

Economic Situation at the Beginning of the 1980s[2])

By the end of the 1970s, the Yugoslav economy had fallen into a deep crisis
which was followed by a general social crisis (Savremeno jugoslovensko društvo
1982). In the period 1965 – 1980 the annual growth rate had been nearly 6 per
cent, while during the period 1980 – 1984 it fell to only 0.6 per cent. The growth
rate of the GNP per capita fell as far as – 1.1 per cent.
The balance of payments and foreign debts became the most important prob-

Table 1

Indicators of the Employment Crisis in Yugoslavia, Slovenia and Serbia (%)

	Yugoslavia	Slovenia	Serbia
Labour force participation rate in 1984	27.7	43.2	27.5
Average annual employment growth			
— in the 1970s	4.8	4.0	4.2
— in the period 1980 – 1984	2.3	1.0	2.1
Workers in welfare services in 1984	16.7	15.3	18.0
Average annual employment growth in the welfare sector 1980 – 1984	2.2	1.9	2.1
Rate of unemployment in 1984	13.3	1.8	14.4
Deficiency demand unemployment of the total open unemployment 1976 – 1983	74.1	50.1	56.5*)
Women among the unemployed in 1984	55.9	54.3	61.3
Young people (below 25) among the unemployed in 1983	59.4	55.2**)	53.6
Qualified workers among the unemployed in 1984	55.5	46.3	55.2
Self–employed out of the active population			
— in 1971	43.0	24.0	54.0
— in 1981	29.5	15.2	41.7
Average annual growth of non–agrarian and non–professional self–employment 1979 – 1983	2.6	7.8	0.2 4.0***)
Average annual employment growth in private sector 190 – 1983	3.7	6.0	0.2 3.3***)

*) period 1980 – 1984
**) below the age of 26
***) period 1980 – 1985. non–agrarian self–employment

Source: Yugoslav Statistical Yearbooks (Statisticki godisnjak Jugoslavije).

lems. More than 5 billion dollars must be paid to foreign banks each year, in spite of the rescheduling schemes. The balance of payments has improved, so that in 1983 imports were less than exports by 81.6 per cent, compared to the period 1974 – 1980 when the respective percentage was between 50 and 60. But this improvement is mainly due to decreasing imports.

Inflation went up to over 70 per cent in 1985; real wages that were increasing by 5.4 per cent to 7.2 per cent in the 1960s and by 0.9 per cent to 1.5 per cent in the 1970s, have been falling ever since 1979 by nearly 6 per cent annually. In 1984 they reached the level that we had had in 1966 and were still falling.

The economic crisis has an important impact on the welfare sector. The bulk of money for the welfare programmes comes from the enterprises. It is determined as a percentage of gross wages. Since the economic growth has slowed down, employment growth has decreased and since real wages have fallen radically, there has also been a cut in resources for welfare programmes. The percentage of GNP for welfare has fallen from 19.21 in 1979 to 15.1 in 1984. The delegates of SCIs would have probably voted for a higher percentage of gross wages to be allocated for welfare programmes, had they not been blocked by the decisions of federal and republic governments that reallocated national resources in favour of economy and foreign creditors.

The fall of real wages has two important consequences for the welfare sector. First, real value of self-imposed contributions that are used for investments in welfare facilities has decreased. A public opinion survey in Slovenia (1982) indicates also that the percentage of people, who would vote for new self-imposed contributions, has decreased. Second, there has been a shift in the consumption pattern. From 1979 to 1982 the share of marketable services in total consumption of the individuals fell from 17.4 per cent to 16.6 per cent, while the share of natural non-market consumption increased from 7.9 to 8.7 per cent. This means that the demand for marketable services has been reduced.

Employment Crisis and Labour Market Policies

While the economic situation is similar throughout the country, this is not the case in the area of employment. When analyzing welfare programmes, we must also take regional differences into account. These differences will become obvious in the following pages where we shall analyze the employment situation and welfare programmes in more detail.

The employment crisis in Yugoslavia has been influenced by the economic crisis. As shown in table 1, Yugoslavia is still a developing country in regard to the labour force participation rate. Nearly the same situation can be found in Serbia, while Slovenia reached the level of developed countries with its labour force participation rate of 43.2 per cent in 1984. We must bear in mind, however, that self-employed persons are not included in this figure.

During the 1970s, the average annual employment growth in Yugoslavia, Slovenia und Serbia was over 4 per cent. In the period 1980–1984, employment growth in Yugoslavia fell to 2.3 per cent, in Slovenia to 1 per cent and in Serbia to 2.1 per cent. Employment growth has not diminished as drastically as the growth of GNP. Therefore it has influenced the deepening of the economic crisis. In the period 1980 – 1984 productivity was falling by 0.5 per cent annually.

The employment situation in the welfare sector has not been better than the general situation. In 1984, 16.7 per cent of people were employed in welfare services in Yugoslavia, while the respective figures for Slovenia and Serbia were 15.3 per cent and 18 per cent. It is interesting to note, that the percentage of workers in welfare services remained constant in the period 1955 – 1975 and that it has been increasing only after that period. Average annual employment growth in the welfare sector in the period 1980 – 1984 was 2.2 per cent in Yugoslavia, 1.8 per cent in Slovenia and 2.1 per cent in Serbia.

The most serious employment problem in Yugoslavia has been unemployment. Up to 1975, the rate of unemployment was below 10 per cent. But in 1984 the number of job seekers was well over one million and the rate of unemployment was 13.3 per cent. In the same year the rate of unemployment in Slovenia was 1.8 per cent and in Serbia 14.4 per cent.

During the period 1976 – 1983, an average of 74.1 per cent of open unemployment in Yugoslavia was deficiency demand unemployment of which the major part could be defined as growth gap unemployment (Addison and Siebert 1979: 412). While the gap between labour demand and labour supply was shrinking up to 1979, it widened again since that time. In Slovenia, an average of 5.1 per cent of open unemployment in the period 1975 – 1983 was deficiency demand unemployment, and it was of a cyclical nature. In Serbia, an average of 56.5 per cent of open unemployment in the period 1980 – 1984 was deficiency demand unemployment. The gap between labour supply and labour demand shrank substantially, but we can suppose that structural unemployment increased.

Young people are the largest group of the unemployed. In 1983 59.4 per cent of young people below the age of 25 were among the unemployed in Yugoslavia, 55.2 per cent below the age of 26 in Slovenia and 53.6 per cent below the age of 25 in Serbia. In Yugoslavia, more than three-quarters of job seekers are younger than 30. Women, too, are over-represented among the unemployed. In 1984 55.9 per cent of women were among the unemployed in Yugoslavia, 54.3 per cent in Slovenia and 61.5 per cent in Serbia. The rising qualification level of the unemployed is the problem demanding special attention. In 1984 there were 55.5 per cent qualified workers among the unemployed in Yugoslavia, 46.3 per cent in Slovenia and 55.2 per cent in Serbia (table 1).

Apart from unemployment, Yugoslavia is facing a severe problem of sub-employment. Mencinger estimated that in 1982, Yugoslav economy could have produced the same output with 4,959,000 workers as it had with 6,159,000 workers. This makes a difference of 1.2 million workers. The private sector, particularly private farmers, were not included (Mencinger 1983). A similar situation could also be anticipated in Slovenia and Serbia.

A large part of sub-employment could be explained by working time utilization. Yugoslav workers utilized effectively only 33.2 hours of the 42-hour working week

Table 2
**Share of GNP for the Welfare Sector in Yugoslavia, Slovenia and Serbia
in the Early 1980s**

	Yugoslavia		Slovenia		Serbia	
	1979	1984	1979	1984	1979	1984
Education	4.65	2.92	4.31	3.05	4.93	2.76
Health Care	5.05	4.36	5.22	3.88	5.47	4.25
Pension and disablement insurance	6.72	6.02	6.64	6.06	6.92	6.08
Child care	1.16	0.86	1.67	1.16	0.98	0.77
Employment	0.22	0.14	0.12	0.09	0.22	0.12
Social Security	0.36	0.27	0.46	0.34	0.32	0.21
Others	1.04	0.73	1.20	0.96	1.02	0.61
Welfare	19.21	15.10	19.62	15.54	19.86	14.80

Source: Planning Institute of Slovenia (Zavod za druzbeno planiranje SR Slovenije).

in 1981. A shorter real working time could be found only in Norway and Sweden (Kukar 1984).

In spite of the poor utilization of working time, some measures have been adopted in this field to improve the employment situation. Enterprises with a poor working environment in which jobs are performed with great physical strain can shorten their working time. In Serbia several hundreds of such firms can already be found, e. g. mines, steel mills and foundries. As a consequence, there could be less utilization of equipment. Therefore, some measures have been taken, such as special loans for firms which would like to introduce additional working shifts. In Slovenia there are several enterprises that have shortened the working week from 42 to 40 hours for experimental reasons. However, a general shortening of work time might be expected.

The consequences of working time reduction have not been evaluated so far. One could expect at least four: the reduction of sub-employment, the worsening of equipment utilization, the introduction of additional work shifts accompanied by employment growth, and the increasing work activity of individuals in the informal sector.

Other measures connected to the working time have also been: the limitation of overtime, the limitation of the possibility of keeping a second job, and the possibility of early retirement and of job sharing. Except for job sharing, these measures have been successful to some extent. In Serbia, for instance, during the period 1983–1984, 2,000 workers retired early. A possibility of partial retirement is given, but data about the number of 'part-time' pensioners have not been available so far.

As a consequence of employment problems and of changing work time, we could expect the expansion of part-time, casual and temporary employment. Unfortunately we do not have enough data to illustrate these changes, except for temporary employment and part-time employment in Slovenia. In 1980 there were only 25.5 per cent who became unemployed due to the termination of their temporary job. In 1983 this figure rose to 42.6 per cent. Young people are the largest group of those who get temporary jobs. According to the Level of Living research (1984), only 2.5 per cent of employees in Slovenia had a working week shorter than 42 hours.

In the Yugoslav employment system, self-employment has been given priority. According to the 1981 census, there were 70 per cent employed and 30 per cent self-employed members of the active population in the country. In Slovenia only 15.2 per cent were self-employed but in Serbia the rate was 41.7 per cent. The respective figures for Yugoslavia, Slovenia and Serbia in the year 1971 were 43 per cent, 24 per cent and 54 per cent. Self-employment in general is thus declining, largely due to de-agrarization which will probably continue in the future.

When considering non-agrarian and non-professional self-employment, quite different trends can be observed. In the period 1979–1983 it was increasing by 2.6 per cent annually in Yugoslavia and by 7.8 per cent in Slovenia. In Serbia, the non-agrarian and non-professional self-employment growth was only 0.2 per cent in the same period, but it has improved so that non-agrarian self-employment growth in the period 1980–1985 reached the level of 4 per cent. In the period 1980–1983 the annual employment growth in the private sector was 3.7 per cent in Yugoslavia, 6 per cent in Slovenia and 0.2 per cent in Serbia. In Serbia, employment growth in the private sector improved substantially and reached the level of 3.3 per cent in the period 1980–1985.

The figures presented above indicate that non-agrarian self-employment shows more vitality in the period of crisis than does employment in the social sector. Even more, the case of Slovenia particulary supports the hypothesis that self-employment represents a real opportunity for the reduction of unemployment. Self-employment trends in Serbia have been encouraging as well after 1983.

These trends represent a positive feedback for the labour market policy which elaborates measures for the promotion of self-employment. The following measures are already in use: the import of equipment was facilitated for the self-employed; the administrative procedures needed to start one's own business were made more flexible; information centres for self-employed producers are being founded at republic chambers of commerce; in Serbia, there is a project for 1,000 new self employed production units, of which 500 were already founded in different communes; in the agricultural sector, the acreage of land that one can own in the mountain area was increased; for self-employed farmers, pension and disability insurance was developed; agricultural cooperatives of the traditional as well as of the modern type have been supported; associations of handicapped persons started to create their own production units. Quite naturally, some cooperatives have spontaneously appeared as a form of collective self-employment in Serbia and a few experimental cooperatives have been founded in Slovenia by the Youth Organization.

Labour market policy not only deals with working time and self-employment. It concerns especially the position of youth, women and qualified workers on the labour market. In Serbia, for instance, each enterprise is obliged either to offer one post per 40 employees for apprentices[3]), or to pay a contribution to the apprenticeship scheme. About 20,000 places for apprentices are provided annually, although 35,000 would be needed. In Slovenia, a similar scheme exists. About 7,000 places are provided annually for the apprentices, this being insufficient as well. When the apprenticeship period is terminated, several young people lose their jobs and they are registered as unemployed.

The scholarship scheme is another programme which aims at the improvement of the position of young people on the labour market. It has become a universal programme in Slovenia. Everyone whose family income per capita is below a certain minimum can get a scholarship to cover his/her living costs while studying. Some scholarships, given directly by firms, are favoured by labour market policy because firms bear the responsibility of giving an opportunity for apprenticeship and employment to scholarship holders. Those who cannot get a firm's scholarship can apply for a communal one. There were about 52,000 scholarship holders in Slovenia in 1984. Apart from scholarships, students in Serbia can get a special loan for their studies. But these resources are rather scarce. Only 5,000 scholarships and 20,000 loans were given in the school year 1983/84.

In Serbia, enterprises are obliged to offer two-thirds of new placements to qualified job seekers and to women. As a consequence, the average employment growth for women was 3.8 per cent compared to 1.2 per cent employment growth for men in the period 1980–1985. A programme to stimulate the migration of qualified workers to less developed areas has been introduced without reasonable success.

Labour market training is also an important area of the labour market policy. In Slovenia it has not been as extensive as in Serbia. In the period 1980–1984, 3,000 unemployed workers took part in several training and retraining courses in Serbia. Enterprises can also apply for financial aid to cover training costs of their workers. In some cases the administrative workers have been retrained and re-employed in production units.

Throughout the country great efforts have been made to increase the number of students for manufacturing occupations, both at the secondary level and at the universities. The share of these students increased from 55 per cent in 1979–80 to 68 per cent in 1984-85 in Serbia, while in Slovenia their share rose from one-third to two-thirds in the same period. It is hoped that such labour supply will better suit the existing labour demand.

Because of rising unemployment, an ever higher share of the population is covered by the employment security programme. However, only a small percentage of the unemployed are given unemployment benefits and other financial as-

345

sistance. New entrants and re-entrants are not entitled to it. The duration of th
unemployment benefit depends on the length of one's former employment.
amount depends on one's previous wage and on the minumum cost of livir
criteria. Those who receive unemployment benefits have pension and disabl
ment insurance covered as well. When the unemployment benefit is terminate
workers who have no resources to live on can apply for supplementary financ
assistance. In Serbia, unemployment benefit was given to 61,000 and su
plementary financial assistance to 7,500 unemployed workers in 1984. In Slov
nia, about 10 per cent (1,500) of the unemployed are covered by this programm
Apart from the items above, there have been some other important measures
ming at the improvement of the labour market situation: the banks finance inve
ments with regard to employment effects, firms are not obliged to pay some cc
tributions or taxes for a certain period for newly employed qualified workers,
Kosovo and in Bosnia resources for the creation of new jobs are mobilized on t
basis of public loans, in some communes and regions people vote for self-i
posed contributions with the intention of supporting investments in new wc
places.[4])
To sum up: the economic crisis has also caused the crisis of employment,
which unemployment is the most important and long-lasting problem. As a cc
sequence, temporary employments have increased in number. Labour marl
policy has reacted in several ways to improve the employment situation. The
has been a tendency to reduce working time, self-employment has been pi
moted and several measures have been applied to improve the situation of you
people and women and the labour market. Social security of the unemployed
rather low.
The employment crisis substantially cut the flow of money into the welfare sect
but on the other hand it caused several problems which should be solved by t
welfare programmes – including those developed by the labour market poli
The contradiction is evident.
Self-employment has been promoted in the industrial sector quite successfu
Supposedly self-employment would have risen even faster had it been allowec
the welfare sector. It could have also represented an opportunity for the develc
ment of the formal welfare sector itself in terms of cost reduction, diversificati
of service supply and individualization of services. However, there have be
strong ideological blocks against changes in this direction.

The Responses of the Welfare System to Its Crisis

We have already seen that the economic and employment crises also influer
the crisis of welfare institutions. Speaking in terms of self-managed communit
of interest, service consumers now have a decreasing amount of resources wh
can be allocated for these services. Moreover, this allocation is not complet

346

free from state decisions. On the other hand, service consumers need more and better services rather than less services of a lower quality. Therefore they are looking for a non-reduced supply of services at a lower price. Since this strategy is undermined by the reactions of service providers, service consumers withdraw from the joint action and act on an increasingly individual basis. This means that some enterprises buy additional services for their workers on a free market and individuals who have enough money to afford it also react in the same way. Nevertheless, the aggregated demand for services is declining.

Service providers are thus given less money for the programmes that they are expected to carry out. This became quite evident after 1979, as shown in table 2. Neither can they expect that the demand for services by individuals and enterprises would offset these losses.

Apart from external reasons, the crisis of welfare institutions is caused internally as well. There has been a widening productivity gap between social services and industry which causes social services to become complex and rigid, which renders services impersonal and heightens organizational entropy. In spite of increasing professionalization, costs and organizational complexity, the needs of the population are not met in a satisfactory way (Huber 1983).

Welfare institutions have found themselves in a difficult situation. Their financial resources were cut and the demand for marketable services decreased, but they have not been able to make their personnel redundant and their obligations to carry out welfare programmes have remained unchanged.

They have therefore elaborated several responses which can be formulated into three different strategies[5]: the marketization of services, the rationalization of service production and the externalization of service production. In most cases, welfare institutions react to the crisis automatically, without any planned action and without an elaborated stategy. These reactions have significant impacts on enterprises, localities, volunteer organizations and also on informal welfare activities. Structural changes within the welfare system are in question.

Marketization of Services

In order to acquire additional financial resources, welfare institutions will increase the production of services which can be rendered for at least a full or partial price. This does not happen by introducing new programmes but rather in four different ways.

First, welfare institutions try to qualify some services as additional, i. e. services which are not supposed to be rendered as part of guaranteed programmes which in principle must be free of charge. Additional services can be charged. Therefore schools turn to parents to either cover the costs for excursions of their children and for outdoor school: otherwise they would have to discontinue these activities. They expect the children to bring along things like nappies, books and notebooks from their homes.

Second, welfare institutions tend to increase the number of those clients who contribute more for the services rendered and to decrease the number of clients who contribute less. The percentage of inmates in elderly centres in Slovenia who bear the costs of treatment themselves, was 38 in 1983 and increasing. Some high schools would prefer to enrol more adult students and less regular ones, because the former must pay educational fees themselves or else the enterprises where they are employed pay for them.

Participation for some health care services can serve as an example of the third possibility. Services such as medical examinations, prescriptions, hospital treatments and dental care must be paid partially by some patients. The role of these contributions is supposed to be merely educational. It is intended to make people aware of the cost of health care. However, 2 to 3 per cent of the total costs of health care programmes in Slovenia are covered in this way, and the possibility that this may influence the number of patients, which is falling, cannot be neglected. In the period 1979 – 1983, the number of patients in Slovenia in general and special outpatient care fell by 4 per cent and the average hospitalization period decreased from 13.9 to 12.7 days.

The fourth way in which marketization takes place is the production of services for enterprises. Some large enterprises invest in their own health care, child care and educational facilities in which welfare institutions render services for the workers for a full or partial price, depending on the type of service and on the investments of a particular firm. Even more services for the employees are rendered on the basis of contracts between enterprises and welfare institutions, using the facilities of the latter. The distribution of services among the employees is determined by self-management bodies or by trade unions.

Marketization of services is not extensive, however. With the exception of the fourth possibility mentioned above, it does not represent a real possibility for the improvement of the situation of welfare institutions. Moreover, it is in contradiction with the idea of welfare itself, according to which those who do not have enough resources should be protected, and everyone must be guaranteed equal opportunities for a decent living. A general and extensive marketization of services would soon deepen the crisis of welfare institutions, because individuals would not be ready and able to cover the rapidly increasing costs of services. good example for this statement is child care. Many parents cannot afford child care in a day care centre although the costs are subsidized. Therefore they search for alternatives such as private baby-sitting, shift work of mother and father and the help of relatives, friends and neighbours. At the same time, the facilities of day care centres are ever more poorly utilized.

Rationalization of Service Production

Rationalization strategy too is composed of several responses. The first one is the attempt to utilize more effectively the available resources: financial means, equipment and labour. A good example of this response is the reduction of investments in educational facilities in Slovenia by more than 50 per cent from 1981 to 1983, while in the same period several schools had to organize the pedagogical process (teaching) in two shifts. In Serbia, 85 per cent of hospital bed facilities are utilized and improvements are planned.

The bulk of costs in welfare institutions are the labour costs. In 1980 the costs of labour in educational institutions in Yugoslavia represented 64.2 per cent of the total costs. In 1983 these costs in Slovenia rose to 80 per cent.

Although, relatively speaking, these costs increased, they were reduced in real terms. Real wages of teachers, physicians and others fell by 32 per cent from 1979 to 1984. Their wages were reduced more than the wages of industrial workers. In 1980, the average wage in primary school was 17 per cent higher than the average wage in industry. In 1983 it was higher by only 7 per cent. The reduction of wages in welfare institutions has a negative impact on recruitment and promotion of personnel. One of the few colleges in Slovenia which did not get enough applicants in 1985 was the Pedagogical Academy.

This response has long-term negative consequences. It erodes welfare institutions; gradually only the less qualified personnel are left; work morale is falling and long-term plans for development are lacking. During the crisis period there has been an increasing number of slowdowns and strikes in health care and educational institutions.

The productivity growth is one way of better utilizing labour. Welfare institutions try to increase productivity mainly by changing the standards of service production because they have no money to invest in more advanced equipment and in knowledge of their personnel. Up to 1980, for instance, one group in day care centres included 20 to 24 three to six-year old children. In 1981 this number rose to 30. The maximum number of pupils in one secondary school class also increased in the 1980s from 32 to 36. University lecturers are required to teach 7 hours per week while their teaching obligation before the crisis was only 5 hours a week.

Productivity growth is no guarantee that the services maintain their quality. On the contrary, one can expect the fall of service quality. In some cases even more favourable standards do not influence the quality of services positively. In health care, for instance, the number of physicians who worked in outpatient services increased from 4.7 per 10,000 people in 1971 to 7.2 in 1982. In the same period, the number of diseases registered in outpatient services increased from 1,790 to 2,161 per 10,000 people.

The third response that can be qualified as rationalization is a substitution of cheaper services for more expensive ones. This response has been widely used.

In the employment area, the programmes for labour market training and for rehabilitation of the disabled have been reduced while the employment security programme and placement services have been given more resources. In the total
budget of employment services in Slovenia, the share of resources for labour
market training fell from 8 per cent in 1981 to 6 per cent in 1983 and the share of
programmes for the handicapped fell from 9 per cent to 8 per cent in the same
period. The share of resources for employment security programmes rose from
28 per cent to 33 per cent in 1983.

In the health care area, hospitalization and special outpatient care have been reduced and general outpatient care extended. Physicians also prescribe cheaper
medicines. The share of the health care budget for medicines fell from 11.4 per
cent in 1979 to 10.1 per cent in 1983. Workers who suffer from work accidents
and professional diseases have been more frequently offered part-time employment and re-employment cash compensations instead of occupational rehabilitation.

The substitution response can be successful in the short run, for it reduces the
costs. Its long-range effects, however, could not be equally positive. In most
cases the reduction of service quality is in question.

Fourth, there has been a shift from universal to more selective programmes. The
limited resources have been allocated in favour of the most affected groups. Here
are some examples. The criterion according to which one is entitled to child allowances has become more severe so that only the lowest-class parents are entitled
to it. In health care, preventive examinations have been reduced so as to save
money for medical treatment of sick persons.

The value of real pensions has fallen, on one hand, but on the other there is an
increasing number of pensioners who receive pension allowances because their
regular pensions are not sufficient to live on. In 1980 the average pension in
Slovenia amounted to 73.5 per cent of the average wage, but in 1984 it decreased
to 71.3 per cent. In 1984, 53 per cent of pensioners in Serbia and 22 per cent in
Slovenia were receiving a minimal pension. In 1979 there were only 11.5 per cent
of pensioners in Slovenia and 5.9 per cent in Serbia who received pension allowances, while in 1984 these figures rose to 14 per cent and 16 per cent respectively.

The reduction of universal programmes has caused an increasing burden of welfare to be carried by the individuals themselves. However, the increasing selectivity in favour of the lowest strata and of other marginal groups reduces social inequalities.

The most widely used response has probably been a reduction of programmes.
In particular, additional programmes have been reduced, since the services
which they provide are not guaranteed by law. The reduction of a particular programme is seldom total and direct but takes other, more subtle forms.

The first possibility is the reduction of enrolment. This can be achieved by the introduction of new criteria according to which a smaller number of people are en-

titled to services, or by the introduction of quota restrictions, e. g. a limited number of students in a particular educational programme. As an example of the first possibility, we can mention the new criterion of unemployment. The unemployed have been divided into two groups: truly unemployed who have no other resources to live on besides employment, and other unemployed, who have additional resources, such as a piece of land.

Because there are many criteria related to the individual or family income, the margin up to which one is entitled to free or partially paid services can be easily pushed down and the number of entitled individuals falls. For instance, the number of parents entitled to child allowances in Slovenia was reduced in 1983 to one-third of that from 1971. In 1983 only 6.4 per cent of employees were receiving child allowances which covered only 13.6 per cent of minimal living expenses for a child. The age criterion can be used in a similar way as the income. In Slovenia, for example, one must be 5 years older than in Serbia to be entitled to old-age pension.

By using quota restrictions, the number of first-degree university students in Serbia was reduced by 43 per cent in the period 1980 – 1984. Enrolment in secondary schools in Slovenia declined on this basis as well.

The second possibility is to reduce the network of welfare programmes and facilities. Consequently a student has to commute a long distance if he/she wants to attend a specific educational programme as compared to the previous situation in which he/she had the same programme nearby. This has happened with some secondary school programmes and could serve as explanation for the falling enrolment in secondary education institutions.

The third possibility is to reduce the amount of services rendered to a non-reduced number of individuals. We can enumerate the following examples of this sort: the shortening of programmes of labour market training and the real value of child allowances and pensions.

The reduction can be even more subtle, especially as far as the quality of services is concerned. This results from interference of several factors. The reduction of resources causes welfare organizations to pay greater attention to the services which are marketable than to other services, although the former are less essential. Since welfare institutions try to improve the utilization of available resources, they do not change their equipment, they increase the work loads of their personnel and they search for cheaper services to substitute for the more expensive ones. The involvement of personnel is reduced because of decreasing money incentives, increasing work loads and out-of-date technologies. The individual service consumer can thus expect a decreasing number of free services which are rendered with increasingly outdated technologies, decreasing personal involvement of service providers and which are less individualized and reduced in quantity.

Externalization of Service Production

Essentially the externalization of service production means that certain professional activities aimed at carrying out certain welfare programmes are reduced or terminated within institutions, while, for the same reasons, they appear in other spheres of the welfare system; for instance, within enterprises, localities, volunteer organizations, informal groups and families. In some cases they are exercised by professionals, although usually it is laymen who carry them out. This transfer of service production relates primarily to those phases of service rendering which are labour intensive and for which highly specialized knowledge and complex technological equipment are not needed. It relates to the care of the infirm and not to surgery. Because production of welfare services is to a high degree labour intensive, while general education of the population is improving and specialized knowledge is available to a large number of people, real chances exist for externalization strategy to play an important role in the development of the welfare system.

If humans needs are satisfied by welfare institutions at a lower level, people try to mobilize other resources, either formal or informal. They exercise their pressure on the enterprise where they are employed and they seek other forms of social assistance, e. g. that given by volunteer organizations, or else they start providing services on their own, either individually or in kin or neighbouring groups. This shift is easier if these types of service rendering represent an important part of cultural tradition, and if there is no rigid social control exercised by formal authorities and formal institutions.

It is important to bear in mind that the transfer of service production from welfare institutions does not mean that there have been no other widespread welfare activities in other segments of the welfare system. They existed long before the welfare sector evolved. However, externalization could stimulate their revival. Let us examine the main directions of the externalization strategy.

The first is the transfer of the production of services to the enterprises. In the crisis period the enterprises have been given many responsibilities for the welfare of their workers in addition to those which they bore before. They are expected to give scholarships, especially to the students of relevant educational programmes whom they expect to employ after they graduate. In Slovenia, about two-thirds of all scholarships in the period 1981 – 1984 were given by enterprises. Enterprises are expected also to provide training facilities for their scholarship holders and they are responsible for the retraining and re-employment of their redundant workers. Only in the case of a poor economic situation can they apply for additional resources from the employment programme. In the period 1981 – 1984, 70 per cent of redundant workers in Slovenia were re-employed within their enterprise and another 18 per cent by other enterprises. The retraining of workers is carried out by the enterprises themselves, by employment offices or by schools for regular education, but nearly always at the expense of the enterprise where redun dancy appears, or by the enterprise which intends to employ the retrained workers. In addition, the enterprises are expected to carry out the apprenticeship scheme.

A transfer of responsibilities for sick leave compensations from health care programmes to the enterprises has also been effected. Workers have a right to sick leave compensations as well if they attend a sick member of their family. Similarly, there has been a transfer of responsibilities from the pension and disablement insurance programme to the enterprises for disablement as a consequence of work accidents, professional diseases and travel to work.

This system of externalization is combined with a marketization strategy. Only in some cases the enterprises develop their own service producing units. Usually they merely cover the costs of services rendered to their employees, by paying directly to the welfare institution in question. Their responsibility is mainly financial.

The second method for the externalization of service production is its transfer to the localities. While in the enterprises, services are provided for the most part formally and by professionals, in localities the informal and semi-formal rendering of services by laymen prevails. Here we give some examples of some, which were initiated by welfare institutions.

A type of the externalization of service production has appeared in the health and child care areas in Slovenia. Within health care, home care is expected to be given an important role. Instead of being hospitalized, some patients can stay in bed at home where they are attended by their relatives or neighbours and also by medical personnel from health care centres. The data show that this type of service is increasing gradually.

Another type of externalization can be found in the case of foster families, who take care of a few homeless or retarded children for a longer period. The families are paid for the service and may also take advice, but the individuals who render the service are not employed. In Slovenia there were 2,263 children in foster families in 1980 and 2,419 in 1983. This is a great number compared to the 2,748 handicapped children who were enrolled in training programmes in 1983, or to the 7,253 people who were in various social institutions in the same year.

For the third example, the initiatives of community centres for social work can be taken. In Maribor, professionals of the centre for social work initiate, advise and organize various social activities in town localities. They deal mainly with senior people, retarded children and those who return from prisons and similar institutions.

Senior people are advised on how to use their time for various activities, such as artisan work and crafts or for recreation, and how to organize help for the infirm or ailing people in the neighbourhood. The centre for social work initiates alternative activities for old-age centres, such as day care for the elderly, home delivery of hot meals and washing for the elderly. Volunteers are also trained to be able to help the retarded children and ex-delinquents.

In Maribor, as in other communes, a professional service exists which advises parents who have problems with the education of their children. About 10 to 15 per cent of the children have various psychological or social difficulties when they start attending school. In order to help them, professionals invite about 40 students each year who are being trained during a four-week period; when the training is finished, they begin to work with groups of school children. Two volunteers work together with one group comprising 5 to 8 school children and use game playing as the main activity. This programme has been deemed successful and it is interesting to note, that there are more applicants for this kind of volunteer work than can be trained.

The fourth example are the Commissions for Health and Social Care which carry out various activities at a local level. In Maribor, for instance such a commission was founded in 1980 for each locality, i. e. a village or a small quarter of the town. Members of each commission are usually volunteers who are trained for home attendance and are chiefly older women, a representative of the locality, the local Red Cross organization, the local youth organization, a social worker and a nurse who are responsible for that locality.

Members of the commission try to find people in the locality who need their help. These are mainly elderly persons, young families and children of lower-class families. The following services for the elderly are organized:
• Regular help coming from the members of the commission, young members of the Red Cross or neighbours who bring hot meals and fuel to the elderly, or do shopping for them.
• Temporary volunteer help of the neighbours or young members of the Red Cross consisting of preparing meals and attending the elderly, cleaning and heating their apartment, shopping and bringing mail.
• Regular paid help of the neighbours consisting of the same items as temporary volunteer help. This service is paid for by the elderly themselves.

In addition, members of the commission organize various entertainments, social activities and recreation for the elderly. A commission provides lower-class children with subsidized holidays at the seaside and with clothing. Young families are helped to find an apartment or employment.

The third direction of the externalization of service production is the transfer of services to the volunteer organizations, such as the Friends of Young People Association, the Pensioners Associations, the Organizations of the Disabled and the Red Cross Organization.

The Friends of Young People Association is an organization of parents, various professionals and young people whose aim is to enrich the free time of school children, especially during summer and winter holidays. Members work in groups. They organize various competitions, trips and holidays and they also provide facilities like playgrounds for children. They train parents and youngsters to carry out the activities of the association and organize various courses for parents. They also initiate volunteer work among school children, such as collecting thrown out newspapers.

Pensioners Associations are organized in localities or communes as well. Their aim is to enrich and ease the life of retired persons. Therefore they organize various activities such as: sports, recreation and competitions, cultural activities, craftsmen and artisan circles, trips and holidays. They also help pensioners to solve their housing or legal problems and organize the mutual aid of pensioners. In 1983, 325 Associations of Pensioners could be found in Slovenia which organized 461 sport circles, 71 choirs and over 3,000 trips. In some communes or localities they organize consultations and medical examinations, visit the inmates at their homes and purchase fuel for the members. Most Associations of Pensioners have their own clubs where they meet, plan and carry out various activities. A number of specialized organizations of the handicapped also exist, such as: Association of the Blind, Association of the Deaf, Association of the Paraplegic and Association for Recreation and Sporting Activities of the Disabled. There were over 55,000 members of such associations in Yugoslavia in 1980. They organize members to help each other, mobilize relatives and friends of the handicapped to help them and try to ascertain some privileges for the handicapped in society.

The Red Cross Organization probably has the most developed and widespread network. Its activity is twofold: health care and social security.

Concerning health care, there are several educational activities such as courses on general health education, first aid courses and courses for training the volunteers for attending sick people at their homes. Active members of the Red Cross organize some activities to improve the hygiene of living environments. In the period 1980–1984, 2,780 courses were organized in Slovenia alone. About 113,000 people took part in these courses. The number of courses as well as the number of participants is increasing throughout the country. In Croatia, the Red Cross organized 15 services employing 159 people who attend sick people at their homes. There is also a widespread activity connected with blood donation. In Yugoslavia, the number of blood donors increased from 2.09 per cent to 2.56 per cent of the total population in the period 1980–1983. Out of the total population in 1983 in Slovenia, there were 5.65 per cent blood donors.

Social security activities include: collecting of clothing, shoes and linen, collecting of secondary raw materials, neighbourly help to senior and disabled people and child care. They also train volunteers. According to a datum, about 30,000 senior and disabled people receive continuous help offered by Red Cross volunteers comprised mainly of youth.

In Maribor there are 3,500 active adult members of the Red Cross. The number of young members in primary and secondary schools varies. They help the elderly, the disabled, families with many children and sick people. They bring them meals, clean accesses to their houses, purchase and bring fuel, do shopping and bring mail and newspapers.

In 48 of the 80 localities there is an office of the Red Cross where people who fall into some kind of trouble can find an activist who is ready to talk to them, give them financial aid or clothing, advise them on how to draw long-term financial assistance and check their blood pressure. Members of the Red Cross also visit about 3,500 individuals a year who need their help.

Active members of the Red Cross collect about 18 tons of clothing, shoes and linen a year. Due to the activity of the Red Cross, there are about 6 per cent blood donors among the active population in Maribor. Red Cross activists also organize courses on medical first aid, the attendance of the sick at home, general courses on health care, protecting from work injuries and environmental protection. The Red Cross subsidizes hot meals and holidays for lower-class school children. It also maintains a holiday resort for children where about 2,500 children spend their holidays each year.

Externalization can be oriented towards the entirely informal sector as well. There are several manufacturing and service activities such as house building, land cultivation, household activities, child care and health care, which have already been mentioned in the first section of this chapter. No doubt this is an important sector of a welfare system, however we can only judge its development indirectly.

Using an economic model we find that informal economy in Yugoslavia is increasing. In 1961 it represented between 0 and 8.8 per cent of GNP, while in 1981 its share was between 16.6 and 33.1 per cent of GNP (Kukar 1984).

Another indicator that shows the expansion of the informal sector, especially in the field of services, is the consumption pattern of the population. Table 3 shows that the share of non-market or natural consumption has increased since 1979, while before that year it was rapidly decreasing. Consumption of marketable goods has stagnated, while it was increasing before 1979; and consumption of marketable services has fallen, while it was increasing up to 1979.

Because the consumption of marketable goods stagnated and the consumption of marketable services declined, we could expect that the natural consumption of goods and services increased.

The externalization of service production has been initiated by welfare institutions, but it has also been supported by the state administration. The state has also

Table 3

The Structure of Individual Consumption of the Yugoslav Population (%) in the period 1953–1982

Type of consumption	1953	1963	1973	1979	1982
Natural, non–market	33.5	18.9	10.7	7.9	8.7
Marketable goods	57.5	66.5	72.8	73.9	73.8
Marketable services	10.2	13.9	15.6	17.4	16.6

Source: Yugoslav Statistical Yearbook (Statisticki godisnjak Jugoslavije) 1984.

made an effort to improve the welfare in some other sectors. In fact, the state has cut the resources for welfare on one hand, but on the other, it has passed the following measures to influence more equal distribution of work and services:
• Several measures for the promotion of employment and the reduction of unemployment that were already mentioned.
• Parental leave was prolonged in several republics to one year and the right to parental leave was given to farmers who cooperate with the public sector.
• In 1984, pension insurance was extended to the total population of adults who are employed, self-employed, entitled to unemployment benefits and to elite sportsmen.
• Social work centres were founded in most communes in Slovenia and in 80 per cent of the communes in Serbia.

Strategies in the Eyes of Social Actors

The responses of the welfare system described above were summed up by three strategies: marketization, rationalization and externalization. Then the fourth was added, i. e. the extension of the existing programmes and the introduction of new programmes. Furthermore, we summarized separately the principal changes in the employment sector. We sent this summary to various social actors of the Maribor commune and the republic of Slovenia, asking them to make comments on the presented strategies and to estimate the role or these strategies in the future.

In Maribor the managers of the staff services of SCIs for health care, education, child care and social security gave their answers in the form of short reports. The president of the local government committee for social services reported in the same way. Two discussions, were also held, one with the experts of the local employment agency and the other with the representatives of the local political organizations, i. e. the Communist Party, Socialist Alliance and Trade Unions.

The answers given by the community social actors do not differ in basic features, with the exception of those given by the representatives of political organizations. They try to find various apologies for the strategies they are supporting. Obviously they feel responsible for the consequences of some strategies which have not always been favourable.

All social actors in Maribor estimate the rationalization strategy as the most extensively used and the most important. They have made a significant distinction between the rationalization that implies restrictions and reductions of welfare programmes and that which implies structural changes in the welfare system, e. g. more prevention and less remedying, more rehabilitation and employment and less disablement pensions, more retraining programmes and less unemployment benefits, more homeless children in foster families and less in institutions. It is expected that these structural changes will reduce the costs of service production with no risk to the quality of services. In the opinion of the social actors, structural changes have been modest while reductions have been severe.

Representatives of political organizations agree that rationalization has proved to be the most extensive and important strategy. However, they accentuate its positive sides. They claim that some programmes were made cheaper, that some norms according to which the delivery of services was regulated were too loosely defined, that the worsening of service delivery is only temporary, and that the implementation of some programmes has been in most cases slowed down and not reduced.

Social actors in Maribor put the marketization strategy in the second place. It has developed in two directions. First, individuals pay ever higher shares for the services delivered. Second, welfare institutions deliver an increasing amount of services to collective consumers such as enterprises on a market basis. This manner of service delivery is called the direct exchange of labour.

Representatives of political organizations estimate that the second method of marketization is socially and politically acceptable and desirable. According to their opinion, it has not been used extensively enough. They do not admit that the first method of marketization has been widely used. In addition, they point at the third method of marketization, i. e. the exportation of services which, according to their opinion, should be socially controlled.

Of the three strategies, the externalization of service production is estimated as the least important. It has been used mainly in the field of assistance to senior people. Political organizations support it verbally. However, they are primarily concerned with the problem of regulation and control of those welfare activities which are not carried out within welfare institutions, and not with the problem of initiating such activities. According to political organizations, control should be exercised by centres for social work. The exaggerated concern with control could be the main block against promotion of the externalization strategy.

In the 1980s, the primary concern of the employment agency has been the reduction of unemployment. Several retraining programmes for the unemployed, especially for the handicapped, were organized. Labour supply was regulated by means of scholarship apprenticeship schemes. Two-thirds of new placements should be carried out through the apprenticeship scheme. The experts of the employment office claim that new forms of employment are needed; however, there are several legal and ideological obstacles.

For the social actors in Maribor, the future is a prolongation of the past. It means that they will seek further rationalizations in the welfare sector, particularly those connected to structural changes within welfare institutions, that they will allow some forms of marketization, and that they will accept some forms of controlled externalization.

This is in accordance with social plans in which the share of GNP for welfare programmes is not expected to increase. Some welfare sub-sectors, e. g. education will receive more means at the expense of the others. This is intended to eliminate the damage that education suffered in the early 1980s and to improve slightly the quality of programmes, e. g. to lower the number of pupils in one class. Therefore, various forms of rationalization will be needed as well. The substitution of cheaper services for the more expensive ones is planned especially in health care. Investments in new welfare facilities will be based exclusively on resources obtained by self-imposed contributions.

The marketization of services has also been foreseen in the social plans. All the additional (not guaranteed) programmes will depend on direct financial contributions of collective service consumers, e. g. enterprises. The improvements of the quality of some programmes, e. g. child care, will be based on additional payments of parents.

In connection with the security programme, community externalization is mentioned in the social plans of Maribor. It is expected that enterprises, localities and volunteer organizations will make endeavours for the increment of social security for employees, the elderly, lower-class people, handicapped people and similar groups. The centre for social work is supposed to initiate and coordinate the activities of welfare institutions on one hand, and semi-informal and informal welfare activities on the other.

At the level of the republic of Slovenia we obtained the answers to our questionnaire from two governmental committees, two SCIs, Communist Party representatives and an association of the disabled.

According to the answers obtained, rationalization especially takes the following forms: limitation of investments in welfare facilities and in new technical equipments, worsening of norms by which the delivery of services is regulated, which in turn causes decrements in the quality of services, the substitution of cheaper and selective programmes for more expensive and universal ones. Most social actors agree that there has been a combination of reductions of programmes and of structural changes within welfare institutions. Yet a representative of the Communist Party, whom we interviewed, claims that there have been no reductions. Except for the Communist Party representative, who estimates that the marketization of service production has been modest, all social actors share the opinion that it has expanded rapidly. The Communist Party representative considers the externalization strategy desirable, but shares the attitude of all other social actors that it has not been widely used in any form.

All social actors confirm the extension of the following welfare programmes: prolongation of parental leave, new rights for disabled persons, foundation of new centres for social work and purchasing of new technical equipment, e. g. computers needed for the modernization of the welfare system.

In the employment area three programmes have been put forward: scholarship and apprenticeship schemes, and a selective reduction of working time.

Concerning future trends, there is hope, shared by all social actors, that the share of GNP for welfare programmes will increase; this would enable the quality of the welfare programes to be improved, as well as the increment of wages in welfare institutions. Rationalization measures will be necessary however. Social actors point at various possibilities for cost reduction. The advantage will be given to selective instead of universal programmes oriented towards the most vulnerable groups, and the norms that regulate service delivery will not be improved.

The marketization of service production is seen as desirable by all social actors. They claim that the direct financial contributions of individual and collective consumers for the services should increase. There are possibilities for the exportation of services, especially in the health care area. Yet social actors are aware of some obstacles which may prevent the utilization of the marketization strategy. Above all: the standard of living will experience no fast rise, the economic situation in most enterprises will not be substantially improved in the near future, and welfare institutions will not be able to purchase the most modern technological equipment essential for competition on the international market.

All social actors support certain forms of the externalization of service production, especially into localities where semi-informal welfare activities should be exercised by volunteer organizations. They mention staying in bed at home and assistance for the elderly. Centres for social work should initiate this strategy. The Communist Party representative strongly supports the externalization strategy, although she expresses fear that it would demand structural changes which would not be easily accepted by SCIs.

In the employment sector it is expected that scholarship and apprenticeship schemes will continue. An extension of retraining and re-employment programmes is also expected. It is clear that the working week will be reduced from 42 to 40 hours. Concerning the possibilities for the new forms of employment, e. g. collective self-employment, part-time employment and work at home, all social actors are rather sceptical, most of all a representative of the Communist Party. Self-employment in the welfare sector cannot be expected.

In a similar way to the situation in Maribor, the three analyzed strategies are ranked as follows at the republic level: rationalization, marketization and externalization. This order stands for both past and future development.

The analysis of the republic plans throws a different light on these strategies. Here the externalization of service production is very much accentuated, especially in the field of social security, but in education and health care as well. Externalization is not conceived as a complete withdrawal of welfare institutions from certain welfare areas. But it means certainly that welfare institutions will make their services more flexible and more adjusted to the needs of consumers. Welfare institutions will tend less towards including clients, and more towards rendering services in localities and at homes. This opening of welfare institutions introduces possibility for the individual and group volunteers, as well as for the clients themselves, to participate actively in the production of services. It also stimulates some forms of self-servicing.

The rationalization strategy can also be found in the welfare plans. Some structural changes are foreseen which should contribute to the reduction of costs with out reducing the quality of services. The health care area can serve as a good illustration; it plans to extend and develop general and special outpatient care, reduce hospitalization, extend preventive dental care and reduce the number of visits to the dentist. Some rationalizations are also planned in the education area. Marketization is not favoured in the republic plans, which is understandable as direct exchange of labour takes place at the lower levels. It is interesting also that in some areas, such as child care, a fast extension of programmes, increasing enrolment in programmes and new investments are planned, which may seem a bit unrealistic.

Contrary to the general statements of social actors, the employment plan contains new forms of employment, such as self-employment in cooperatives, part-time employment, job sharing and work at home. It is also planned to stimulate employment in small enterprises and to reduce working time in order to save more time for education and training of the employees.

Conclusions

The Three Strategies: To Whom do They Belong?

An important question that remains to be answered is: If economic crisis is the main reason for the crisis of the welfare system, why have three strategies appeared as a response to it? What is the relationship between the three stategies and the principal social actors?

We would like to remind the reader of the basic characteristics of the present welfare system in Yugoslavia, including its management. On one hand, self-managed communities of interest evolved as an institution, which should enable direct bargaining for the production and distribution of services to service consumers and service providers. On the other hand, the state retained some key functions, e. g. control over the bulk of resources to be allocated for welfare programmes. With SCIs and the state is also the third actor, the individual whose needs often remain unsatisfied, in spite of the services guaranteed by the state and the services provided by SCIs in the form of additional programmes. The individuals exert pressure on the representatives who make decisions within SCIs and state bodies; however, the most direct and many times the most successful way to receive additional services is self-servicing, individually or in groups of friends, relatives or neighbours.

The state represented by the government (at the communal, republic and federal level), government committees and political organizations, formally has a limited influence on the welfare system. Nevertheless, this coalition is the only strong political power in society which always tends to make concerted actions. Therefore can interfere with the welfare system rather arbitrarily, irrespective of the autonomy formally given to SCIs. This is neatly illustrated by the decreasing share of GNP allocated to the welfare system by the state, which has been in contradiction with the demands of SCIs.

The state policy has been to organize as much production of services as possible within welfare institutions. This pattern of service production simplifies the state control over the production and distribution of services, i. e. over welfare institutions and service consumers. The state welfare system has become a means of social and political control of citizens.

The state favours universal welfare programmes. This seems to be particularly important in socialist countries where an alliance between the state and the political oligarchy exists on one hand, and large groups of loosely organized workers on the other (Denitch 1976). By means of universal welfare programmes workers are rendered several services free of charge or at a partial price; this is a necessary condition for them to support the power elite. This way political power is legitimized.

Universal welfare programmes are congruent with the egalitarian value system of the Yugoslav population (Županov 1970). They represent a means for the fulfilment of the principle called "distributive egalitarianism" (Županov 1983). Every citizen participates on an equal footing in the distribution of guaranteed services such as free education or free medical care for certain diseases. Therefore the majority of people support the state's endeavours to develop and preserve universal programmes.

The most natural reaction of the state to the crisis of welfare institutions has doubtlessly been the rationalization strategy. This strategy implies only marginal changes in the structure of the welfare system. An attempt has been made to preserve all universal programmes and to carry them out even under condition of reduced resources. It is safer for the state, in order to improve the utilization of capital, labour and knowledge to exert pressure on a relatively small group of professionals who work for welfare institutions, than to run the risk of losing support among large masses of workers because of the enforced reduction or termination of some universal programmes.

The pressure of state administration on the welfare institutions was gaining in intensity until teachers, physicians and other professionals started to react openly. Since the crisis of the welfare system is continuing the state must make some concessions to the marketization and externalization strategies. These two strategies imply a certain decline from universal welfare programmes. There also a risk of increasing social and regional differences. This is why representatives of the state and political organizations advocate marketization and externalization rather cautiously. They are in favour of that type of marketization where enterprises and not individuals themselves pay for the services rendered because it is easier to control enterprises than individuals. They accept controlled externalization and want centres for social work to exercise initiation, coordination and control.

The longer and the deeper the economic crisis and the crisis of welfare institutions become, the greater are the chances for the marketization and externalization strategies. In this situation, SCIs have the opportunity to build a structure of direct agreements for the production of services for certain enterprises and localities; there is also an opportunity to develop local networks for self-production of services. This would prevent the state from treating the marketization and externalization strategies as only two temporary measures, which would be terminated at the moment of economic recovery. According to chart 1, one would expect economic growth to influence the welfare system as in just the opposite way as economic stagnation. Therefore the state tries to preserve the existing structure of the welfare system as intact as possible, limits the space of action of SCIs as much as possible, advocates the rationalization strategy and allows marketization and externalization as an emergency.

Self-managed communities of interest are given the responsibility and resources to carry out universal programmes, guaranteed to the citizens by the state. Yet, these programmes would have been implemented with no less efficiency even had the SCIs not existed. The rationale of the SCIs lies in the possibility of direct bargaining between service providers and service consumers, the result of which are services adjusted to the needs of people of a certain enterprise, village, town or region. The additional programmes financed directly by collective service consumers are in question. Therefore SCIs favour the marketization strategy. It represents a chance for their economic emancipation which would decrease the dependence of welfare institutions and collective consumers on the state.

Self-managed communities of interest in which service providers are the dominant party, favour the institutionalization of service production. They tend to render services on a professional basis and to control their clients. Since they receive a decreasing amount of financial resources for the accomplishment of universal programmes, they tend to diversify their supply of services and to adjust it to the needs of clients. They also develop their technology of service rendering. They are increasingly ready to render services in enterprises, localities and at homes. This is a step in the direction of externalization which, according to their belief, should be controlled by welfare institutions.

The third strategy does not have its 'natural social actor'. It has been an emergency strategy for the state as well as for the SCIs; a practice used by those individuals and groups whose needs remain unsatisfied in spite of universal and additional programmes and in spite of the firms' welfare activities. These individuals and groups are not given enough services due to the discriminative norms, or because their needs are developed beyond the point where they can be met by the existing welfare programmes. They may not have enough resources to buy additional services on the market or else, the services they need may not be available on the market or they are of inadequate quality. Some of them find in self-servicing and volunteer activities a mode of self-fulfilment and utilization of non-working time (see Pahl 1984: 324–325).

363

The more insufficient the rationalization and marketization strategies, the greater is the need to initiate welfare activities outside welfare institutions and to support various practices of self-servicing, mutual aid, self-help and volunteer work. The initiation and support represent the core of the externalization strategy and a method for mobilizing the unutilized informal resources.

It seems that the differences between the various social actors concerning the three strategies are greater than their answers reveal. We can see, that the answers of political organizations deviate from the answers of other social actors. However, all them put the rationalization strategy in the first place, marketization in the second and externalization in the third. We can explain this situation by the existing power structure. Political organizations, together with the state, are the only strong power. Therefore they also define the space of social action for other social actors, such as SCIs. The range of the three strategies in fact reflects the power structure. If the economic crisis continues, there will be more room left for the marketization and externalization strategies; the result will also be a shift in the power structure. Self-managed communities of interest, as well as semi-informal and informal groups will act more autonomously. There are only two alternatives: fast economic growth or political and economic regression of the state.

The Impact of the Three Strategies on Welfare

The three analyzed strategies represent the outcome of the crisis into which Yugoslavia's economy and its welfare system has sunk. Do these strategies represent a positive or a negative deviation from our course of development? Do they jeopardize the achieved level of welfare or do they promise its improvement? The answers are more ambiguous than they are clear.

Speaking of rationalization, we have made a distinction between reductions or one hand and structural changes within welfare institutions on the other. It is clea that reductions of the enrolment of people in a cerain programme, reductions o the quantity of services as well as of their quality, influence also the reduction o welfare. The meaning of structural changes, e. g. the substitution of one pro gramme for another or changing norms that regulate production of services, i less known. A criterion for the real positive rationalization would be the produc tion of a non-reduced amount and quality of services by substantially reduced ir puts, e. g. labour and capital. This is a productivity criterion. The improvement in this direction are severely limited because the production of services is pe sonal by definition (Bell 1973). This means that the production of services is no only labour intensive but also human and knowledge intensive. It means also tha the introduction of new highly productive technologies is very limited, because would demand a transformation of services into goods and would decrease th welfare. These are after all the main reasons for the widening of a productivity ga and therefore rationalizations in most cases lead to reductions.

The consequences of the marketization strategy are even more ambiguous. Economically weak individuals and groups who occupy marginal positions in society, could be pushed into an increasingly worse position, instead of being protected by welfare programmes. Marketization could accelerate social inequalities and social differentiation. On the other hand, marketization makes individuals and groups more responsible for their own welfare. They do not wait passively to be given a certain social assistance, but they search for adequate solutions, either individually or collectively. Their autonomy may increase and their dependence on welfare institutions decrease.

And what about externalization? It implies not only the externalization of the production of some services or of some phases of this production process, but also the externalization of the costs of welfare institutions. It implies also the mobilization of informal and semi-formal resources for the production of services. This is a chance for welfare institutions to get rid of labour intensive phases of production, to lower the costs of labour, to retain the most demanding phases of the production of services, which are based on highly specialized professional knowledge and on complex and expensive technological equipment, and to become primarily research and development, consultancy, educational and training centres. It is a chance for service consumers, too, to be involved directly in the production of services which they need, to adjust the quality of services to their personal demands and to enrich their personal and social life in the domain of non-working time (see also Gershuny 1983). However, some services will remain labour, human and knowledge intensive at the same time and will not be externalized. The externalization of services often demands that laymen perform the activities otherwise performed by professionals, which can jeopardize the quality of services. It is not easy to organize the production of services in the informal or semi-formal sector on a permanent basis. The involvement of individuals and groups can vary. Externalization implies also a variety af arrangements and services and as a consequence, it increases the differentiation among individuals and groups.

Is it possible to employ simultaneously more strategies and to acquire a viable combination which would represent an efficient answer to the crisis of the welfare system, and which would increase the welfare? Our idea could be summarized in the following statements.

Two opposite extremes should be avoided: the liberal one, according to which individuals themselves are primarily responsible for their welfare and should therefore buy services they need on the market; and the totalitarian one, according to which the welfare of individuals is a responsibility of society, i. e. the state, which should provide all services needed by means of universal and guaranteed programmes.

Services should be delivered at three levels, according to the needs they meet. The services that meet the essential needs of people, e. g. average education, basic health care and minimal old-age pension, should be guaranteed to all citizens on an equal basis by means of universal and guaranteed programmes. Such guarantees should be given also to the weakest and marginal social groups, e. g. the disabled.

Certain groups, e. g. employees of an enterprise, residents of a large building or inhabitants of a village or a town quarter, would like to have some services rendered equally beyond the point determined by the guaranteed programmes. They have the possibility to make an agreement with certain welfare institutions that would render services needed on a market basis. Contributions to welfare institutions can be in money or partially in money and partially in work (see Gershuny 1983). Individuals can contribute equal sums, equal shares of their income or according to some other criterion. They also have a possibility of organizing the production of some services, e. g. child care, study circles, attendance of the elderly, and cleaning and decoration of their street, on the basis of complete self-production or they can pay someone to coordinate these self-producing activities.

There are always individuals who would like to have more services rendered than they can expect from the guaranteed and collectively arranged programmes. For such people, services should be available on the market, at market prices. However, if they would like to obtain certain services of special quality, self-servicing would be the only way.

Instead of mechanic equality that could be achieved through universal and guaranteed programmes, we follow the idea of organic equality which acknowledges that basic needs should be met on an equal basis, regardless of the differences between the individuals, and that beyond this point individuals and groups should be enabled to meet their different needs to different degrees and in different ways. Individuals and groups should take an active part in the production of services they need. This will be possible only if welfare institutions carry out welfare programmes more openly, if they come to their clients and not the other way around, and if service consumers organize their networks for self-production of services. The idea we advocate is thus a universalistic or institutional model of special policy (Titmuss 1974), combined with marketization and externalization strategies.

It seems that under these conditions the relationship between work and welfare must change substantially. The employment crisis influences the welfare area in two ways. First, there has been a decreasing inflow of financial resources into the welfare system. Second, unemployment has risen and there has been an increasing number of irregularities on the labour market, e. g. temporary employments. Thus the number of problems in the employment area to be solved with the help of the welfare system is increasing, while the ability of the welfare system to cope with these problems is falling. Because of this vicious circle, employment should not remain the only or the main criterion for a person to be entitled to services provided by the guaranteed programmes. Otherwise an increasing number of people will not be entitled. We can agree with the idea of citizenship criteria (Donati 1985).

One of the reactions of the welfare system to its crisis has been the externalization of service production. This could lead to various innovations in the sphere of work. It could be expected, specifically, that certain informal activities, aiming at increasing individual or group welfare, would be shaped in a new way and would enjoy social recognition. A new welfare mix in itself brings about new forms of work as well.

Notes

This chapter was written in cooperation with Ida Hojnik, Zinka Kolaric and Maja Vojnovic.

1) We consulted primarily: Yugoslav and Slovene Statistical Yearbooks (Stasticki godišnjak Jugoslavije, Statisticki letopis Slovenije); reports and plans of the Planning Institute of the Republics Serbia and Slovenia (Zavod za druzbeno planiranje SR Slovenija, Zavod za društveno planiranje SR Srbije); reports and plans of Self-managed Communities of Interest for education, health care, pension and disablement insurance, child care, employment and social security in Serbia, Slovenia and in the town of Maribor; reports of government committees dealing with various welfare areas in Serbia, Slovenia and Maribor; reports of volunteer organizations: Friends of Young People Association, Pensioners Associations, Organizations of the Disabled and Red Cross Organization at the federal level, in Serbia and Slovenia and in Maribor; other reports and research works that we refer to in the chapter.
2) Figures presented in this section are taken out or computed on the basis of Yugoslav Statistical Yearbooks (Statisticki godišnjak Jugoslavije).
3) The status of an apprentice is given to every graduate from a secondary school or university who is starting his work career anew. The apprenticeship lasts up to 12 months.
4) The information about labour market policies is taken mainly from the reports of republic employment agencies of Slovenia and Serbia.
5) The responses and strategies are described on the basis of reports from various welfare institutions of Slovenia and Serbia.

Bibliography

Addison, T. J., Siebert, W. S., 1979, The Market for Labour: an Analytical Treatment, Goodyear Publishing, Santa Monica.

Bell, D., 1973, The Coming of Post-Industrial Society, Basic Books.

Bilandzic, D., 1980, Zgodovina Socialisticne federativne republike Jugoslavije (The History of SFR Yugoslavia), Partizanska knjiga, Ljubljana.

Denitch, B., 1976, The Legitimation of Revolution, the Yugoslav Case, Yale University Press.

Donati, P., Colozzi, I., 1985, 'Institutional Reorganizations and New Shifts in the Welfare Mix in Italy after the 70s', in The Shift in the Welfare Mix, May, Grenoble.

Ferge, Sz., 1983, 'The Impact of the Present Economic Crisis on Hungarian Social Policy – From a Comparative European Perspective' in Can There Be a New Welfare State?, September, Baden.

Gershuny, J., 1983, Social Innovation and the Division of Labour, Oxford University Press.

Huber, J., 1983, 'Public Help and Self-help' in Can There Be a New Welfare State?, Baden.

Kukar, S., 1984, Obseg sive ekonomije in tendence v njenem razvoju v Jugoslaviji (The Scope of Grey Economy and the Tendencies of its Development in Yugoslavia), Institute of Economic Research, Ljubljana.

Level of Living, 1984, Kvaliteta zivljenja v Sloveniji (Level of Living Research Project), coordinator Veljo Rus, Institute of Sociology, Ljubljana.

Mencinger, J., 1983, 'Registrirana brezposelnost in zaposleni brez dela' (Recorded Unemployment and the Employed without Work in Gospodarska gibanja, No. 128, Ljubljana.

Mishra, R., 1981, Society and Social Policy, MacMillan Press, London.

Mishra, R., 1984, The Welfare State in Crisis, Harvester Press.

Nilsson, I., Wadeskog, A., 1985, 'The Fourth Sector' in The Shift in the Welfare Mix – A Challenge under Conditions of a Changing Reality of Work, January, Puchberg, Austria.

Pahl, R., 1984, Divisions of Labour, Basil Blackwell, Oxford.

Prpic, K., 1978, 'Neregistrirana radna aktivnost stanovništva SFRJ i SRH' (Unrecorded Work Activity of the Population of Yugoslavia and Croatia) in Naše teme, No. 10, Zagreb.

Public Opinion Research, 1982, Slovensko javno mnenje, 1982 (Public Opinion Research Project), coordinator Niko Toš, Research Institute at the Faculty of Sociology, Political Science and Journalism, Ljubljana.

Pulliainen, K., Pietilä, H., 1983, 'Revival of Non-Monetary Economy Makes Economic Growth Unnecessary' in IFDA Dossier, No. 35, June.

Savremeno jugoslovensko društvo. Sociološko istrazivanje uzroka krize i mogucnosti izlaska, 1982 (Contemporary Yugoslav Society, Sociological Research on the Causes of the Crisis and on the Possiblilities of Way Out) in Jugoslovensko udruzenje za sociologiju (Yugoslav Sociological Association), May, Ljubljana.

Šefer, B., 1981, Socialna politika v socialisticni samoupravni druzbi. Social Policy in Socialist Self-management Society), Delavska enotnost, Ljubljana.

Titmuss, R., 1974, Social Policy – An Introduction. George Allen and Unwin, London.

Županov, J., 1970, 'Egalitarizam i industrijalizam' (Egalitarism and Industrialism) in Sociologija, No. 1, Belgrade.

Županov, J., 1983, 'Znanje, društveni sistem i klasni interes' (Knowledge, Social System and Class Interest), Naše teme in No. 7 – 8, Zagreb.

Shifts in the Welfare Mix:
A Summary
of Trends and Prospects

The Evolving Welfare State Mixes

S. M. Miller

Changes, expectations about changes, and belated recognition of new conditions are reshaping welfare states in Europe as well as in the United States. Profound changes and issues are emerging. We take up first eight important changes in welfare state contexts in Western Europe and then the four models which are evolving.

Changes in Context

First is the widespread feeling that a growing and glowing economic future is unlikely. The enormous economic growth of post-World War II Europe and the near-full employment that accompanied it are not deemed possible in many countries. Indeed, European unemployment rates have been at levels once regarded as intolerable.

Europe seems to have learned to live with high unemployment rates. In the 1960s British social scientists told their American counterparts that if the United Kingdom had United States unemployment rates of 5 or 6 per cent, a revolution would occur. Today, of course, all of Western Europe outside of Scandinavia and Austria have scandalously high unemployment rates. Their political tenability suggests that expectations about the future have collapsed rapidly and deeply and/or unemployment can coexist with 'good times' for many others. Or, that employment benefits and informal economy participation make unemployment less burdensome today – the conclusion of neo-classical economists. Whatever the reason, continuing high unemployment is a shock. Fear of competition from Japan, the United States and the newly-industrializing countries of the Third World is lowering economic hopes. One set of consequences is high unemployment, which increases welfare state outlays, and financial stringency which reduces governmental funds for welfare. Another consequence is a drive to lower taxes, wages and fringe benefits in order to increase a nation's international competitiveness. A continually expanding welfare state – the condition of post-war European capitalism – is no longer anticipated. The political talk is much more of contraction of social programmes than of their expansion.

Second, unemployment has led to a re-evaluation of the sources of employment. For some time the unexamined belief has been that large and modern industries and firms furnished the bulk of jobs. Increasingly, it is clear that medium-sized and small firms provided the majority of employment opportunities. In some nations these smaller enterprises have been the growth centres, constituting a major absorber of the increased labour supply. Indeed, in Britain, this recognition has led to the enshrinement of the small businessman, 'the entrepreneur', as a major hope for economic recovery and employment expansion.

Great importance has been assigned to the 'discovery' that an 'informal economy' resides alongside the 'mainstream' economy of easily identified large and medium-sized firms. 'Informal economy' is an exceedingly elastic term with many synonyms and connotations: 'irregular economy', 'black economy', 'grey economy', 'off-the-books economy', 'penny capitalism', 'dual economy', 'illegal economy'. Sometimes it refers to illegal evasion of taxes by large and small enterprises engaged in legitimate business activities; sometimes, it refers to the income and evaded taxes of illegal enterprises. Often, it refers to under-reported wage income and 'home work', the domestic putting-out system of yore. Legal operations also have this label as in the case of smaller enterprises, the household economy – particularly the unpaid household labour of women – or self-help cooperatives, voluntary activities, or exchanges of labour (reciprocity) and goods (barter) without the exchange of money.

It is not clear whether informal activities have grown or are newly discovered. That part of the informal economy that refers to tax evasion has certainly grown as have purely illegal activities. But the other parts of what are sometimes lumped under the 'informal economy' rubric may not have grown; they are only receiving attention after neglect.

As presently used, 'informal economy' carries too much freight to do much analytical good except to point out that official measures of national and individual production, income and wealth, are grossly inadequate, at times misleading. If one could legislate usage, the term might be restricted to legal activities like small businesses, household labour, home work, voluntarism and the like, even if some tax evasion occurs. Basically illegal activities would have another term, like 'illegal economy'.[1])

One result of the renewed interest in the informal economy is to stress the level and possibilities of employment in its legal side, and the desirability of some of the flexible arrangements (reciprocity, cooperative behaviour) and processes (self-help, mutual aid) involved in it. In some nations the informal economy is complacently regarded as improving the well-being of many who are officially designated as unemployed or poor; therefore, these economic and social problems are deemed to be less severe than they appear.

For many who think in terms of a new welfare state with greater choices, autonomy and cooperativeness, the (legal) informal economy is an important avenue of experimentation and modeling for flexibility, self-help, and solidarity. For some

372

with this viewpoint, it is the arena in which a new type of economy and society can be constructed on a smaller scale with less bureaucracy and more self-determination.

In a period of intense internationalization of trade and spread of new, expensive technologies, how much and what kind of employment can be provided by smaller enterprises may be limited. On the other hand, at least half of the great expansion of United States employment in the 1970s and 1980s is attributed to small enterprises largely in service fields; the negative side of this expansion is that much of it is low-paid with low fringe benefits, non-career ladder jobs. While frequently providing the flexibility of part-time employments, they do not offer much income support.[2])

Third, irregular employment patterns are becoming more frequent, especially for households. Instead of the expansion of full-time jobs with security of employment and rising real wages and fringe benefits which would be accompanied by a labour force attached to a particular firm, unemployment, reduced hours of work, or part-time jobs are a frequent experience of many workers. Good jobs have become less good as labour market regulations are curtailed or softened by government. Low-wage jobs have grown; real wages are frequently threatened; and protection against lay-off – a great gain of the European post-war era – is eroding as the Western European labour force is being made more 'flexible' and 'adaptable'. This process is occurring rapidly and will have important negative effects on unions, wages and the welfare state. Slow or no real wage improvement impinges on the welfare state because revenues fail to keep up with growing needs.

The great hopes for European employment, according to their respective enthusiasts, seem to rest in high-technology or informal sector activities. The United States also experienced great hopes that high-tech would expand and offer an enormous number of jobs. While certainly jobs have grown in this sector – which has many definitions, yielding very different estimates of its employment effects – it has made only a minor contribution to the great job spurt in the United States. How much high-tech growth can offer in terms of European employment is uncertain as competition grows. Similarly, estimates of employment in the informal economy sectors are very uncertain. Even if prospects for expansion are great, these jobs do not offer high security or income.

The European employment discussions are dominated by hard-nosed neo-classical economists espousing high unemployment, lower wages, and reduced fringe benefits and welfare state programmes. Opposing viewpoints are scarce and fail to present an attractive, realistic-appearing alternative.

Fourth, this jagged pattern of employment, low wages, and job shifts is particularly common among particular groups who have become an increasingly significant part of the European (and American) labour force: women, youth, and immigrants. Their employment problems have mounted. Much of new social policy is oriented to dealing in some way with the fears arising from widespread and prolonged youth unemployment. To a lesser extent, the problems of female-headed families and immigrants have also received attention.

Fifth, the welfare state is becoming economized in two senses: one effort is to reduce welfare state expenditures, seeking economies by not maintaining cash benefits in real terms and contracting the level of services or demanding some payment for services (medical care is the main area for such efforts). The other sense is to enforce economic criteria and conceptualizations in decisions about the organization and benefit level of benefits and services. Of special concern are the level and duration of unemployment benefits as providing a disincentive to accept employment at lower than previously attained wages. In the United States, Aid to Families with Dependent Children (AFDC) is sometimes seen as offering higher income than minimum pay jobs, thereby discouraging female heads of households from moving off welfare rolls to these jobs. 'It pays not to work' is the assertion.

Sixth, social programmes are increasingly used to deal with unemployment (or, at least, to reduce official unemployment rates). One way is to reduce competition for employment by drawing older workers out of the labour market by providing early retirement and disability benefits through the social security system.[3]) Also widespread are efforts to promote youth employment by setting up temporary work programmes administered usually by non-governmental organizations. In Italy, transfer payments *(cassa integrazione)* are used to supplement the income of workers whose weekly hours of employment have been reduced. In France, the estimate is that 40 per cent of unemployed youth are in such programmes; the British counterpart, though smaller, is still substantial. Or, in Britain, unemployed workers who start an enterprise may continue to receive their unemployment benefits for a year.

The notion of 'autonomous social policy', independent of and offsetting to some extent market outcomes, is overturned. The possibilities of using social programmes as part of a transformational agenda are much reduced. Instead, social policy is becoming a micro-employment policy as transfers are used to promote employment, not to maintain income for those who have suffered in the labour market. This tendency to use social policy as a micro-employment policy has some positive effects but it is part of the increasing push to make all things subservient to economic pressures. That tendency would not seem to aid efforts to deepen and expand welfare state benefits and challenge the supremacy of the narrow economic calculus. One issue is how effective these micro-employment policies will be; their possibilities seem oversold. Another question is whether they will become a substitute for economic policies which deal with more basic, structural realignments; a third is what will happen to the transfer benefits of those who are not in the labour market or who fail to attain employment through the micro-employment programmes.

Seventh, feminist critiques of the welfare state have made clear the extent to which the welfare state provides services to women and through them to their

374

children and the continuing importance of women's (unpaid) activities in the overall welfare functions of society. The welfare state performs, then, only an important slice of societal welfare activities which still mainly occur within the family. Welfare state programmes in many nations, as Martin Rein has been emphasizing, also provide many of the better (professional, semi-professional) jobs that women hold.

The welfare state is thus largely about women. But that understanding has not shaped the discourse about the welfare state. One important implication of that statement is that shifts in welfare state activities – whether an increase, decrease, or change – have to be viewed particularly in terms of their impact upon women. For example, decreasing the role of formal governmental welfare agencies is likely to mean increasing the burdens on women, while diminishing the number of good jobs available to them. Another implication is that reshaping welfare state services and benefits so that they are more useful to women, especially those with children and without a mate, is a major need. A major difficulty here is that welfare state benefits are tied in many countries to labour market status. Women are less in the labour market than men (although rapidly increasing) and receive lower wages which affect benefit levels. The result is that women tend to get inferior benefits, especially when there is not a male bread-winner in the household. The growth of female-headed families and the pressure towards increasing means-testing of programmes are likely to result in more women using welfare state programmes but receiving meager benefits from them.

The rethinking of the welfare state in terms of women has not proceeded effectively in Europe or the United States. Trade unions as well as governments and political parties have been slow to adjust to the changing labour force and welfare state. Changing labour markets and demography disturb and challenge welfare states.

Eighth, the post-World War II political consensus around the achieving and achievability of full employment and the continuing expansion of the welfare state no longer exists in many nations. In some, the size, scope, performance and financing of the welfare state are important political questions. Welfare state policies have shifted from relatively easy acceptance of expansion to criticism, reform or change, retrenchment and privatization.

The welfare state is not simply 'evolving' as the population ages. It is assigned new roles, undermined by economic difficulties, and made into a political issue. Partisan political considerations will affect it to a greater extent than in the 1960s. In short, the welfare state is politicized in new and deeper ways, particularly in the use of political groups opposing its size, cost and performance. This situation pushes the discourse about the welfare state from an analytical-policy framework to a political-economic one.

Surprisingly, the welfare state appeared more politically durable and attractive in the mid 1980s than seemed to be the case at the beginning of the decade when many pundits described or foresaw 'the crisis of the welfare state': economic constriction and escalating costs (especially in medical programmes) would threaten the economics and politics of welfare state funding. The 'economic crisis' in Western Europe and the criticism of the welfare state in many countries, e.g. Italy, seemed to make reductions politically inexpensive. That expectation was wrong. The welfare state has many critics but that has not meant that people do not recognize its value. Apparently, the near-universality of programmes and the variety of household needs met by the welfare state have maintained or garnered support of social programmes. Also, continuing high levels of unemployment have not prevented national economics from experiencing some positive growth. The post-1973 'economic crisis' may not be over but it is not as severe as feared (at least for households with employed members). Many national economies are in a 'recovery' stage. But a deep recession could reduce welfare state support.[4])

The durability of the welfare state has been an agreeable surprise. If 'the crisis' worsens, there may be stronger pressure to reduce social welfare expenditures and wages. But the support for the welfare state may resurge in those circumstances. The diversity of response to pressures for change has also been surprising. Obviously, it is misleading to speak of the European welfare state; there are many European welfare states; there is no stage process of advancing to the 'Swedish model', but rather a diversity of models and paths. Particularly striking has been the range of responses to current pressures for change. Across-the-board cutting has not prevailed; new programmes have been added with characteristics which differentiate nations even where they have a common purpose like alleviating youth unemployment.

Finally, questions about goals (as well as effects) are also reshaping the way that the welfare state is thought about. Those who espouse some form of privatization usually advocate greater choice for citizen-consumers of social programmes as a prime need; others decry the bureaucratic and alienating character of public programmes and call for the promotion of social integration as the major objective. Still others want to promote independent, autonomous initiative and see self-help and self-direction playing the central role. Democratic control of services by its users compels the devotion of others. We categorize these competing goals and models as: defend-and-change; participation and economic transformation; social integration; and privatization. The next section discusses them.

Models of Change

Defend-and-Change

Because of attacks on the welfare state, many once-critical supporters have become uncritical defenders of it. But few want to maintain or restore the welfare state exactly as it was. Unfortunately, a careful elucidation of what is to be defended or changed has not emerged.

This uncertainty is not surprising since critical supporters fear that negative comments will be misused to attack the fundamentals of the welfare state. But that worry is not the only reason for slow movement along the defend-and-change channel.

A major reason for this hesitation is that the sources of resistance to change are diverse and deep. The staff of the welfare state agencies are frequently reluctant to change, fearing reductions in employment, shifts in routines, and diminution of professional control. Recipients or clients worry about reductions in benefit eligibility and levels and in provision of services. Finance ministries are sometimes fearful of changes that do not directly reduce costs; often, a change in a programme has the opposite effect. Indeed, to win better coordination and acceptance of changes frequently requires increasing expenditures.

The basic issue of course is what is to be changed and what is to be defended? The questions are about: cost and effectiveness; organization and performance; allocation and finance. Cost and effectiveness are troublesome issues. Should some programmes be reduced or eliminated because they have limited effectiveness or yield little benefit in relation to their costs? Or can they be changed to improve their effectiveness and benefit/cost ratio? Underlying these issues is the difficulty in defining, estimating and measuring effectiveness. Furthermore, should the impact of changes and the possibilities of measuring or reducing long-run political support be factored into the economics of cost-effectiveness calculations?

The operations of the welfare state are criticized as bureaucratic, alienating, disempowering, inflexible and providing low quality services. The frequent call is for more participation by clients and less unnecessary professionalism, less red tape and control, more local control by service recipients rather than administrators, providing incentives for higher quality services or to induce recipients to find employment.

Allocational decisions involve such issues as providing cash payments which can be spent as the recipient desires or (non-cash, in-kind) services which limit choices; or relative expenditures on medical care or education, or on programmes for the young or for the elderly.[5] Finance concerns the source of revenues for the welfare state – through pinpointed taxes or general revenues; through national or local taxation; through user charges or free services. The type of financing affects political support for programmes.

A political base has to be built to make the important changes involved in these three sets of questions and challenges. Can welfare state staff and beneficiaries be brought together early to forge joint programmes of change? Can the broader public be better informed about the need to both defend and change? So far the answer seems to be 'no' to both questions.

Obviously, it has been easier to defend than to advocate defend-and-change. But changes (e.g. tightening of eligibility criteria) unwelcome to the defenders of the welfare state are taking place even where the defenders seem to have been successful. Can the defenders take the initiative for pursuing positive directions of changes rather than responding to the pressure of the critics? This is likely only if they believe that the best defence of the welfare state requires changing it to meet old problems and new desires (especially for empowerment).

Participation and Economic Transformation

Stimulated by the left movements of the 1960s, some critics of the welfare state call for much greater participation of clients-recipients-beneficiaries in the welfare state. They call for local neighbourhood control and empowerment themes, more emphasis on self-help in usually professionalized medical, social work, and economic development activities. Supported in part by some conservative critics of the welfare state, this is a value-oriented, perhaps populist agenda.

Another starting point has been the analysis which argues from the assumption that full employment will not occur again in late capitalist nations (a perspective notably found in the Federal Republic of Germany). Even reductions in the normal work week or early retirements, it is asserted, will not overcome grave unemployment problems. Since national (macro) economic policies will be only limitedly effective, the scope for local (micro) activities should be enlarged.

The participatory adherents have to accept that not all welfare state functions, e.g. pension programmes, can be turned over to localities. And that funding for programmes, especially in lower-income areas, requires taxation on a broader basis. Who pays the piper will always influence the conduct of programmes.

Despite its democratic focus, localism has problem. It can create inequalities as some communities do much better than others. Those with high resources of physical and human capital are likely to gain more than those with low levels of these resources. Non-local government will have to play an equalizing role as well as assuring that localities do not discriminate against particular groups (e.g. minorities).

Nor is localism an effective answer to all ills, as some localists imply. Localism can mean xenophobia, parochialism, autocracy, manipulation, segregation, and narrowness. How localism is done is important – which again means that some controls need to be lodged outside the locality and that ways of building democracy and intolerance enforced.

Localism is likely to be used by retrenchers as a way of reducing welfare state expenditures. Rather than providing funds to promote participation and empowerment, conservative populism aims to reduce public spending on general welfare 'Individuals can do it' becomes a substitute for 'Government funds are needed for an effective welfare programme'.

The desirability of self-help and allied activities is high but not unalloyed. The fear is that increasing reliance on self-help, family, voluntarism, and community rather than national or city governmental agencies means more work for women. I practice, decreasing the governmental role in welfare functions is likely to in crease the already heavy burdens borne by women. For studies point to little increase in male involvement in the basic welfare functions of the family, even in the two-earner family.[6])

These doubts about the participation and empowerment approach are not arguments against them as goals. The issue is how they are carried through. Indeed, those who want to defend the welfare state need to adopt many of the objectives of the empowerment adherents.

The transformationalists go further than those advocating participation and empowerment.[7]) They are determinist in approach and regard the capitalist economic system as requiring a drastic change if decent jobs are to evolve and all are to have an adequate standard of living.

Many new jobs are low-wage and boring (as in expanding service employment in the United States). Nor are old jobs desirable in terms of work satisfaction. People should not be forced by income pressures to take such jobs. The need is for a broad political coalition that will seek a transformational agenda that will reduce the nexus between employment and income. This rupture can be accomplished by a vast expansion of the cash transfer system of the welfare state and more self-help and voluntary activities. Paid work will absorb less of the hours of people's lives and be less important in attaining the households' standard of living (which in any case will be redefined in more qualitative terms). Current difficulties are not regarded as a phase of the economic cycle but as a dramatic change in late capitalism to a condition thought of as 'post-industrial'. Unemployment, lousy jobs, and low wages will be rife unless the transfer system is greatly expanded. This transfer expansion would push up the wage levels of jobs for individuals who would now have the option to receive public transfers rather than take low-wage jobs. The number of poor jobs will decline as they are unable to meet the rising expectations about wage levels: workers will have an alternative – public transfers – to low wages. This is desirable because workers should not be subsidizing employers by working for sub-standard wages. The link between employment and income will be broken. A transformation in the nature of society is envisaged: work will be less significant for people in terms of time, standard of living, and self-image; the creativity of leisure or non-paid time would become more significant for self-actualization.

These are indeed bold objectives, involving more transformational aims than other approaches to reforming and reorienting the welfare state and welfare functions. What questions does the transformational agenda face?

s the future of paid work so bleak? In 1945 if someone had prognosticated that the next twenty-five years in Western Europe would see full employment and rapidly expanding and deeply significant welfare states, great restrictions on employers' rights to fire or lay off workers, enormous gains in the real income of working classes, an opening of higher education to those of lower-income families, reductions in the normal work week – that economist or social analyst would have been characterized as delusional.[8])

True, this is a glossy picture of what occurred in the post-war period but it should lead to hesitation about predictions in general and in particular to those insisting on late capitalism's inability to adapt to changing conditions. Certainly, the United States have experienced great job growth and not all in low-wage jobs.

Without political pressure, capitalist nations will try to have high levels of unemployment as ways of making wage rates and work conditions more flexible. It is dangerous, in my opinion, to accept high unemployment levels as inevitable and not fight to reduce them. The result will be higher unemployment rates than would have occurred in the absence of struggle against them. Even if the transformationalists are right about the low possibility of 'real full employment', the economic-political-social-psychological differences between a 9 per cent and 5 per cent unemployment rate are exceedingly important: at 9 per cent, unions are weaker; wage rates, working hours and incomes are down; conservative economic policies are likely to be ascendant in today's intense international competitiveness; low tax revenues lead to pressures to contract the welfare state, the already bad situation of many youths would worsen. If 'real full employment' is unlikely, we do not want to make high-level unemployment economically and politically feasible. If Barbara Wooton is right in her conclusion that full employment did more for working classes than did the welfare state, the future looks bleak unless full employment or something akin to it can be reachieved.

A strong and more expensive welfare state in the absence of an expanding economy is hard for me to picture, both economically and politically. If unemployment rates were high, as transformationalists expect, then funding for livable welfare state benefits would be threatened. If national income is not increasing rapidly, then tax rates would have to increase in order to cover increased cash transfers of the welfare state. Perhaps the great productivity and value-added production believed to be associated with the post-industrial state would advance national income but then the political obstacle would be garnering part of the rising incomes of some so that the state could support adequately others who are not working. It is difficult to imagine today the source of the solidaristic feelings that would promote such a political development.

New forms of stratification would likely emerge between those whose employment yields much of their command over resources and those whose resource command comes primarily from governmental transfer programmes. The former are likely to do better as lines of cleavage between the two grow, especially if general economic conditions are bad, as the transformationalists expect.

The transformational agenda envisions a profound change in the way individuals are viewed and valued, a change that is appealing to me but difficult to see coming about through the device of expanding transfer benefits. I value decommodification, taking many goods and services out of the market, autonomy, reduction of work hours, solidarity, making command over resources less tied to work, and increasing equality. But can the cash nexus be enduringly cut by expanded transfers? While embracing the transformational goals, I do not see the political, economic or socio-psychological basis for those goals.

380

Can the goals be achieved partially through reforms of the welfare state that do not veer towards the dramatic change envisaged by the transformationalists? The localists/autonomy/self-help groups seem to believe so as do some of the defend-and-changers.

The transformationalists may be right in their doubts about what can be achieved by these reformers; on the other hand, I fear that the transformationalists' apparent acceptance of high unemployment rates as given would make these rates more likely, an outcome that would undercut the welfare state as spending exceeded what is politically feasible as revenues.

I do not offer as a put-down the observation that it is important to have a far-reaching critique of current society and the welfare state but that there are dangers in seeming to acquiesce in the move towards living with high unemployment rates. Three observations about the transformationalists' approach intrigue me. One is the assumption that under conditions of high unemployment and international competition great redistributive gains can be won, that the economic difficulties facing nations produce a propitious time for profound transformations. This might be feasible if part of the economy is doing so well that it can lose substantial income to lagging parts and maintain its effectiveness. Is it likely that prosperous sectors of the economy would generate sufficient income to make a substantial difference? Is the assumption that international trade need not be very important and that the domestic economy could be self-generating and expanding? This position would certainly need defending.[9] The present moment of 'crisis' appears a very unfavourable time for making positive and sweeping social changes. Activities are becoming increasingly economized, rather than less as is emphasized in the transformationalist outlook.

A second question is why the transformationalists have emerged and are strongest in the Federal Republic of Germany. For this country has by far the largest percentage of its labour force in traditional industrial production of any advanced industrial nation. Whatever 'post-industrial' means,[10] it certainly is not pointing to traditional industrial activity. Why then the Federal Republic of Germany for the 1980s resurrection of the transformational agenda?[11] The contrast between West Germany's industrial present and putative post-industrial future leads to my final observation that there is a danger of self-deception if we are not careful in delineating between our desires for the future and our analyses and predictions of what is likely to occur. Self-deception is a parent of political failure.

The Social Integration Approach

This approach has important similarities with the localistic model but differs in its emphasis on social integration as the important principle for restructuring the welfare state. The present welfare state is seen as contributing to the sense of social isolation, excessive individualism, atomism and anomie which is said to prevail in many societies. The objective is to change the system of social welfare so that it becomes part of the solution to the overall problem of social fragmentation rather than an important contributor to it.

Changes in the welfare state are deemed necessary at the policy level as well as at the organizational level. In policy, the need is to strengthen family activities and encourage the stability of families, thereby avoiding female-headed households, by providing policy incentives to stay together. Some adherents might advocate policies which reduce the pressure for women to work by improving family and children's allowances. Community-help and mutual aid activities are to be encouraged.

At the organizational level, the intention is to move from government-centred social programmes to non-governmental, non-profit agencies which would carry out social policies that are framed and financed by legislation. These non-profit agencies would be locally based and would be free of what are regarded as the bureaucratic and alienating effects of governmental organizations. They would strive to promote a sense of closeness and sharing. Fewer professionals and civil servants would be employed as volunteers and neighbours become more important in providing services and assistance. Religious organizations might be the agencies providing services.[12])

In many countries, welfare state programmes are not exclusively or even mainly provided by governmental agencies. What Martin Rein calls "the public-private mix" is very extensive and significant. The social integrationists, then, are calling for a much more dramatic shift to an already prominent non-governmental sector. On the other hand, the social integrationists while calling for strong support for voluntarism do not advocate the grass-roots, informal, uncentralized form that is advocated by those seeking participation and localism. The social integrationists seek an institutionalized voluntary sector based on a national organization or organizations. The participation-minded desire a non-institutionalized, locality-controlled development.

The social integration approach faces some important issues. Some see it as having a traditional orientation which would be coercive and burdensome to women. They fear that women will be pushed back towards more traditional, less liberating roles and will be forced to spend more time in welfare activities. Voluntarism, in this view, usually means more work and responsibilities for women.

The organizations that would administer the social integrationist programmes are unlikely to be democratically run: neither beneficiaries, staff nor volunteers would have an important role in decisions. As private non-profit agencies, the voluntary organizations would not accord rights to those they serve as governmentally-administered programmes do. Creaming and inequality would likely grow. Some of the difficulties might be checked by strong monitoring and accountability administered by governmental agencies. How effective this policing activity could be – especially where the private agency is politically strong – is uncertain.

The personalism which is an appealing quality of the social integrationist ap proach has problems. In some circumstances anonymity, impersonality and bureaucracy have advantages in preserving privacy and dignity. People needing aid may not want friends and neighbours to know their plight. Where one cannot reciprocate and 'mutual aid' is one-sided, a sense of becoming a beneficiary of 'charity' may emerge and be harmful.

Whatever difficulties the social integrationist approach faces, it is raising a crucial question about the objectives of the welfare state. Like Richard Titmuss, who was the premier writer on the welfare state, its ambition is that the welfare state functions to encourage a feeling of national cohesion, integration, community and mutuality, a concern for 'the other', 'the stranger'. The social integrationists, unlike Titmuss, see the only possibility for the moral vision to occur if the welfare state becomes less governmentally-centred. Titmuss' concern for equality led him, by contrast, to stress the importance of governmental administration.[13]

Privatization

Privatization is heralded as an alternative to governmental programmes. Like 'informal sector', privatization is a broad, ambiguous term.

The general theme is to move to market relationships. Rather than governmentally-provided services, individuals would purchase current government social services in 'the market' where private firms would compete in attracting customers. Poorer individuals and households would be enabled to choose among private services by governmental cash grants or vouchers that would be earmarked for purchase of specific services (as in the case of educational vouchers or food stamps). Better-off individuals would be able to choose and pay for these services because their social security and like taxes would be reduced. In another form of privatization, government would purchase services from private firms rather than providing them itself as it once did. E.g., public laundry services in the United Kingdom would no longer be performed by the public hospital staff but purchased from private firms that would compete for the business.

The competition of private market firms in the social welfare field, it is asserted, would reduce costs and promote efficiency; it would also assure better treatment of the users of the service because they would be customers, not clients, who could move their business elsewhere. The social control element in governmental-controlled and provided services would be eliminated.

The proponents of privatization seek efficiency, less governmental expenditures, and increased choice through market competition. They differ among themselves in the weights attached to these different goals. They are united in regarding the governmentally-based welfare state as inefficient because of its monopoly state and what they see as inevitable bureaucratic structuring. Current difficult economic times, in this view, call for reduced public expenditures to lower taxes and for lower social benefits so that they do not support wage levels and disincentives to hard work, conditions that are harmful to a nation's competitive position in the world economy.

On the negative side, would consumer-clients have adequate knowledge to make choices? Would they be well enough organized to exert political pressure to improve or change services? The sorry condition in the United States of private nursing homes, paid for out of public funds under Medicare and Medicaid programmes, does not offer high hopes for the cash nexus leading to a high degree of care and concern. The elimination or reduction of state provisioning is likely to lead to greater inequalities as those with more private funds can purchase services not available to those with meager governmental vouchers or cash benefits. The business organizations providing social services are likely to cream. The aim of reducing governmental social welfare expenditures is likely to harm the scope and quality of services available to lower-income individuals. Greater 'choice' does not necessarily result in more equality, adequacy, and concern.

What Mix?

The myth of the government welfare state dies hard. Despite Titmuss' emphasis on the importance of fiscal and occupational benefits, despite the variety of household, self-help, and mutual aid activities, despite the importance of non-governmental organizations in providing social welfare aid with or without governmental funding and despite the sale of medical care, the belief still seems to persist that governmental activity encompasses the welfare functions. True, new ideas about organization and structures are loose on both sides of the Atlantic, but the basic theorizing still seems focused on the state in welfare activities.

What we see in the four approaches are adaptations or recommended adaptations to changing economic circumstances and lifestyles. Not only does the welfare state have many critics; they want to move it in very different ways. Some of these objectives might be reconciled with each other but other pairs (e.g. private markets and social integration) are not easily brought together.

One result is that 'experimentation' and 'innovation' are becoming fashionable terms in social welfare in Europe as they have long been in the United States. A number of countries permit, perhaps encourage, small-scale experimenting with different ways of conducting social programmes. Even in the large, well-established Swedish welfare state, flexibility and adaptability are evident. A group can take over the operation of social programmes in small geographic areas or take responsibility for local economic development. In (Social Democratic) Bremen and (Christian Democratic) West Berlin, the city-state governments provide funds for local groups to initiate new activities. In many nations small-scale projects are permitted which deviate markedly from the national model.

As is frequent with social innovation, the issue is whether the experiment is a forerunner of broad policy changes or becomes encapsulated, restricted to a narrow slice of the policy arena and gradually declining in significance as it placates critics of mainstream policies. Judging from the American experience, experiments run the danger of encapsulation and fragmentation: they are not planting a flag and exercising sovereignty over a sector of social policy; they need to spread and root if they are to occupy a policy territory. If not, the main sectors of social policy may continue with little change while those who seek transformational change will busy themselves with approach roads while the highways of social programmes continue largely as before. The United States landscape is littered with experiments that became approach roads to nowhere.

Looked at more positively, experimentation can indicate the recognition of the need to change. In that sense, experimentation can lead to new mixes which are significant. Whether the desire for change can outmatch the pressures for contracting welfare state expenditures is the main issue. The experiments may be flowers that singly break through the concrete of fiscal conservatism but they may not produce a garden.

Organizational structure is not seen as a given in the four approaches. The general orientation is to reduce the organizational role of the formal governmental structures or, at least, decentralize to smaller governmental units as repositories of authority and service provision. Despite the differences in the four approaches, some common threads seem to emerge: more participation, local control, flexibility, mutual aid and voluntarism. Significant differences appear in the locus of authority and organization sought by the four approaches.

The main issue lies however not in differences about organizational loci but in the values that are regarded as central. In the defend-and-change model, equality and lessened stratification accompany adequacy as dominant goals with decentralization and participation becoming more important than before. The transformationalists prize autonomy and self-development. The social integrationists focus on the links among individuals while those seeking privatization are most concerned about reducing costs and increasing choices through greater reliance on private markets.

These are quite different sets of agenda. They seem difficult to reconcile despite some overlap. Obviously, political strength will determine which road will be followed.

Surprisingly, none of the goals or models is primarily oriented to the specific interests of the new groups which require special attention today: immigrants, youth, female-headed households. Since these groups are now the most likely to receive any new, flexible funds, they would seem to be the sectors in which change might be easiest to structure. In practice, however, a major way that the differences in outlook is being played out is in the definition of what is the central group to help today: the traditional family, the female-headed family, unemployed youth, the unemployed, immigrants, the marginalized, traditional proletarians, the elderly, or cultural and counter-cultural opt-outs. A choice of new policies is a decision about which group is most important to aid today, a decision which can be made on a variety of grounds. The choice is made in the context of strong pressures to reduce welfare state spending.

For an American it is heartening to learn about the variety of new ideas and approaches that are debated in Europe. For in the United States, the policy arena lacks imagination. The discussion veers largely between disturbing contraction and uncritical defence of the welfare state as it was – although some progressive approaches are beginning to surface. The Western European nations which pioneered the diverse welfare states may again point the ways in which it should be changed. Clearly, welfare states are being changed; the issue is in what ways. Today's welfare states are vastly different from what existed in 1945; the next twenty years will be significant changes. That is what is debated in Western Europe and largely ignored or mystified in the United States.

Notes

1) More categories may be needed.
2) Why Europe has not experienced the enormous expansion in paid employment that has been occurring in the United States is not clear. One difference is that the United States has had sizeable population growth in contrast to the European situation. Whether that difference is sufficient to explain the disparity in new jobs is dubious. The United States has not experienced the 'jobless growth' that a report of the Organization for Economic Cooperation and Development (OECD) predicted in the late 1970s while Western Europe has. True, the job growth of the United States has not been particularly in high quality jobs, though there is some controversy about that, but it is clearly different from recent European history.
3) The Netherlands is spending great sums on such programmes.
4) The inroads into welfare state aid for female-headed families in the United Kingdom have been drastic and disheartening even though Prime Minister Thatcher has been unable to reduce the percentage of Gross National Product [GNP] devoted to social programmes. While some important programmes have been reduced or terminated, the costs of unemployment benefits have risen because of the continuing exceedingly high level of unemployment in the United Kingdom. Apparent stability in terms of spending masks harshness in policy.
5) The latter generational issue is likely to swell into an important political Rubicon in the United States. In Europe, the belief is that both young and old should be helped and that they should not be put into competition for governmental benefits.
6) Nor does less work time automatically result in more voluntaristic communal involvement.
7) Barbara Ehrenreich, Frances Piven, and Fred Block have Americanized the transformationalist position but they seem so far to call only for raising benefits rather than modifying the way programmes are conducted.
8) Or, to move to the Far East, if that economist had predicted that Japan would become a high-quality, high-value added producer and that new nations like Taiwan, South Korea or Singapore would become 'newly-industrializing countries' and effectively compete with the high-capitalist nations in the production and sale of mass production and high-technology goods, he would have seemed a prophet not deserving of honour anywhere.
9) In "Beyond the Wasteland", Samuel Bowles, David Gordon and Thomas Weiskopf espouse this position for the United States.
10) I have questioned its many meanings in "Notes on Neocapitalism", Theory and Society, 1975.
11) Robert Theobald in his book of the affluent 1960s on abundance in the United States heralded

the great productivity of automation, the massive unemployment that would ensue, and the desirability of increasing transfers and making work less central.

12) In Ireland, they do provide many social and educational services; in Italy, some important intellectuals pursue the objective of widening the role of religious agencies by providing them with government funds to provide social services that governmental agencies had provided.

13) See my introduction to Brian Abel-Smith and Kay Titmuss, eds., The Philosophy of Welfare: Selected Writings of Richard Titmuss, Allen & Unwin, 1986.

Main Findings and Common Orientations in the National Reports

Adalbert Evers and Helmut Wintersberger

The main points of reference from where we will discuss the presentations in this reader[1]) (mostly shortened versions of larger studies) are identical or at least closely linked with main questions in the research agenda presented before. Problems and open questions touched upon here might also be seen as a point of reference for future research. Some work done within the European Centre for Social Welfare Training and Research owes a lot to the approach built up by this research.[2])

'Unpaid Work' and the 'Third Sector' — From Residual Categories Towards the Discovery of a Differentiated Social Field

Since the main characteristic of the research framework is to move from a bipolar state/market discussion forward to a concept which integrates household and the social sphere as a realm of actors as well as of productive activities, the respective definitions of 'unpaid' work are of crucial importance. In the course of the discussions there have been several attempts to come to terms with such analytical tools as the 'third sector', or the 'informal economy'. Miller rightly states in his contribution that these are "exceedingly elastic terms with many synonyms and connotations", and at first sight, there has been no big success in classifying these issues. The labels still vary between the papers or the same label is being used for slightly different things. Nevertheless, all contributions make clear that the sphere of unpaid activities and the informal sector exclude 'black labour'. In all the papers the latter is seen as a less regulated and formalized part of the (market) economy.

Yet, if one gives a second look, there might be an important step forward to be detected with respect to the debates on the 'informal', 'third' and/or 'fourth' sectors. It is related to the attempts to describe in *positive* terms the 'informal' kinds of action and interaction studied, (a) the different motivations guiding them, (b) their change within the course of modernization processes, and finally (c) their intermingling with other spheres of work and activity.

As far as *motivations* are concerned, one might start with the simple question why there is work at all, since it is not paid in these areas. The simplest answer might not be entirely wrong but yet not satisfying: one has to do it unpaid because there is no paid work in sight. Even if there is a lot of truth in this answer, especially with regard to the women's situation, it covers only a limited aspect of the problem. There are complex cultural and historical reasons why family- and householdwork have not been totally either commodified or socialized, and only in the extreme liberalistic or rationalistic doctrines can one stick to an approach which reduces social activities to individual options and strategies of private individuals, trying to accumulate as many gains and to avoid as many losses as possible. If we conceive social relationships in a more complex sense, we detect that paid work is just one – relatively new and still limited – social relationship wherein work is given and exchanged. Within most of the papers one finds reference to a series of different motivations for 'unpaid work', characterizing the informal economy, namely:

• Altruistic values and gratuitiousness, establishing kinds of *'gift relationships'*: these motivations are of special importance for the fields most research contributions presented here are dealing with: the field of social services, especially care services and the 'economy of care'. The paper from the UK but also from the FRG yet underline, how much such motives are mingled with aspects of hidden pressure, constraints, and burdens – namely as far as women are concerned who do the main bulk of such care work.

• Reference is made also to all types of *non-monetarized reciprocal relationships,* visible – as the Hungarian contribution shows – in all kinds of mutual help, be it housebuilding, repair work and similar tasks in neighbourhood networking; the contribution of the UK points out, that the often one-sided care relations might be difficult to establish where reciprocity is prevailing.

• Finally, there are other motives, constituted through public discourses and social action beyond tradition and informality; they are represented by the traditional values of 'charity', 'benevolence', but also by *'solidarity',* constituting collective action as a specific form of mobilizing hitherto hidden resources of activity and work in self-organization; there are no clear boundaries between motivations reproduced through cultural heritage, and those which are constituted through protest and political action; the Italian (T)[3] paper states with respect to the forms of women's solidarity studied, that this unionized action seemed "to depend more on a sense of ,togetherness' than on the militancy of the political or trade union affiliations of its members."

Trying to analyze the dangers of political attempts to instrumentalize these 'cheap' types of work, especially the FRG paper says something about the *'modernization'* and changing natures of the main principles guiding such work relationships. It states that in line with the process of individualization, the impact and meaning of such motivations like commitment, solidarity, etc. have changed. New principles and orientations like creativity and self-expression are winning a growing impact as motives for volunteering, self-help and similar types of activities.

Furthermore, the FRG paper is raising the question of the consequences of the secular increase of paid work relationships and the consecutive *intermingling* between the private and the public sphere, e. g. by a monetarization of household economies and by a rising influence of social rights and entitlements to 'private' life in general and especially for care work in informal, semi-formal and community initiatives. The FRG paper states that as a consequence, (women's) household work loses the character of a mere hidden duty and increasingly calls for public acknowledgement. Likewise, social innovations and initiatives, e. g. in the field of care, realize that they are producing a 'public good' which might entitle them to public remuneration.

Consequently, instead of being able to separate in a clear-cut manner the informal sector from other 'sectors', increasing interconnections between private and public, state and socially productive action become visible. Volunteering may well mix with money, while 'work' organized through public institutions must not always mean employment. The French contribution, while referring to such an unconventional type of raising and funding work and jobs (the 'TUC'), rightly states that the TUC participants' "monthly stipend is not a wage, but neither is it a welfare or unemployment insurance payment, because they provide goods or services in return for it". This is just one striking example for the complex character of motivations and relationships wherein new forms of work and activity are brought about, situated between the 'sectors' where either 'money' or 'solidarity' rule as motives for work and action.

Summing up, it can be stated that within our common research, a new field of challenges for further theoretical and empirical work has taken shape. It deals with the different motivations constituting private and collective action and work outside labour, and the way these motivations mix and change in their respective impact in the course of modernization processes. Insofar, as the latter have multiplied the public-private relationships in the welfare triangle, one has to study the 'grey zones' between paid work, remuneration through public institutions and their connection to the hitherto 'private' informal activities. It might well be that 'work' and 'money income', so clearly connected in an 'employment society', tend to be connected with each other in more diverse and often looser forms instead of being simply disconnected as it is often claimed.

Shifts in the Welfare Mix: Socio-economic Trends with Different Meanings for Social Policy and Welfare

The research contributions have developed quite similar typologies concerning the political strategies which accompany or introduce shifts in the welfare mix. The papers of Miller, the FRG, Italy (B), Hungary and Yugoslavia deal explicitl with such strategies.

Marketization/privatization strategies changing the welfare mix, or – as the Yu goslavian and Hungarian contributors put it – the 'welfare system', are explicitl discussed with similar accents in these papers.

With respect to the role of the state one can find a diversity of strategies and way to describe them in the papers. While a defence or even strengthening of the in herited trend towards a kind of 'welfare-etatism' is only discussed in the contribu tion by Miller and the FRG paper, the Italian and Yugoslavian contributions con centrate on shifts, where the state's role is defined by selectivity, rationalizatio and externalization, be it with respect to financial benefits or services.

- Selectivity takes for instance place where the basis for an entitlement or th criteria for a respective group is redefined in a stricter sense.
- Rationalization is defined mostly as the attempt to cover the tasks in the fiel of social services with less manpower, changing teacher-pupil ratios, work organ ization in hospitals, etc.
- Externalization stands for attempts towards conscious substitution of centra state welfare performance be it through households and associations, private-fo profit types of institutions, or (local) institutions at the margins of the state.

It might be interesting whether one can generalize the thesis of the Italian (E paper, judging those central state welfare strategies as "jammed up" and theore tically as well as practically impossible, which limit themselves to an either/c concerning the question of 'more market' or 'more state'. In addition the FR paper tries to show that both marketization and etatism are 'exits' that are politi cally everless viable. Within the multiplicity of arguments given in favour of th thesis (see especially the papers of Miller, the FRG, Italy (B) and Sweden), th observations made in the Yugoslavian paper concerning the limits of a rational zation strategy in the realms of social services might deserve special attention. states that there is a contradiction between further rationalization in the name c increased productivity and the quality of the services, or, as one might put it, th services' task. It seems that in general all services which have special commun cative and emotional aspects and cannot therefore be simply commodified or re duced in time (like care or education) cannot be placed in the usual model of in creasing productivity by decreasing the input of (labour) time. There seem to b tight limits to such a strategy following the concept of productivity in industri production. This holds especially true with respect to care services. Creating better, yet in broader terms more effective, and less costly type of care seems t depend on social innovations in the relationships between professionals and no professionals, formal and informal co-producers – a problem impossible to grasp within a concept restricted to market/state alternatives.

Such a statement leads us directly to a second potential generalization, which is at the heart of the whole research and can be found in the Italian (B) paper, arguing "that currently the fundamental knotty problem of social policy is the interweaving between private initiative/self-management and public regulation/support". With respect to this, nearly all strategies discussed in the papers, be they market- or state-oriented, are similar to the degree that they ignore this challenge or leave it aside, trusting that society or those directly concerned will somehow be willing and able to cope with the by-effects of either marketing, rationalizing, using stronger selectivity, or externalizing welfare tasks. One might also put this statement the other way round: new types of policy, whatever their orientation concerning balances between state and (market) economy, might make a difference insofar as they consciously include individuals, households and the social sphere as actors and co-producers of welfare. This difference is visible through an increasing impact of the problem, how to relate to, communicate and exchange with these actors and co-producers. The research reports give remarkable insights into the follow-up effect of strategies, which hide their link to households and the social sphere as a strategic variable. By using people's informal creativity and the social sphere just as a 'strategic reserve', they produce *ruptures* in the mutual relations of the welfare triangle. Households and social organizations are left alone in coping with the consequences of less income, social security or services. Especially in the contributions from the countries with planned economies, like Hungary, Poland and Yugoslavia, an increasing impact of the informal and household economy becomes visible through *a regressive type of 'informalization of welfare',* by increasing black work, barter, unplanned self-production and consumer-work with mostly poor means, instruments and little space for decision-making, in order to compensate the losses of welfare contributions in terms of social rights and financial incomes. Such a type of "self-welfarization", as the Hungarian contribution labels it (described as well in the Polish and Yugoslavian contribution), is the more difficult to overcome, the more (a) the role of households and social organizations as potential co-producers of welfare is not a public issue, and the more (b) there are no countervailing powers or strategies defending the social sphere from such forms of increasing hidden exploitation or articulation of unfulfilled needs.

In contrast to this type of shift, it is interesting to look at the positive references the Yugoslavian report makes with respect to 'externalization' strategies, depending on the degree that they involve more productive divisions of labour and a better sharing of responsibilities between the formal and the informal sphere or, for instance, between professional social services and informal care. 'More productive' means here that a service is more viable and cheaper not by reducing the offer from the formal side, but through a new use of resources on both sides. This might happen by changing the professional contribution from a 'full service' orientation towards an educational and consultancy-oriented type of service and by conceiving the lay contributions not as a mere consumption but as a type of consciously integrated co-production to be stimulated and enabled. The Swedish paper gives a number of examples for such a new type of service or care economy, where the question of productivity has to be formulated as a question of cross cutting the borderlines between the formal and the informal.

Beyond such a "cooperative exit", as the Italian (B) paper calls it, social innovations aiming at a new division of tasks, at different exchanges and a changed use of resources between a plurality of public and private, organized and informal actors, can also take another more 'protest'-oriented exit. In the latter case, also referred to in the Italian contributions, the papers from Sweden, FRG, the UK and Austria, it is the social sphere itself which develops types of self-help or self-management, which on the one hand escape the limits of the defensive privatism which often shows in barter or single household economies and on the other hand establishes itself as an alternative to public services, due to their lacking or non-fitting quality.

Since shifts in the welfare mix and the way they are conducted are shaped by power relations, the challenge of changing the relationships towards the social sphere and the individuals as actors for and producers of welfare, without at the same time dismantling welfare rights largely depends on the role played by *collective* actors, movements and institutions. Therefore, the Hungarian paper rightly insists on the fact, that shifts in the welfare mix (as described by Rose through the proportional role of household, state and (market) economy in the production of "welfare goods") can take completely different socio-political meanings. This depends on the fact whether such shifts are including changes in the command over political and financial resources. More social self-management requires an upgrading of the role of (traditional and new) associations as collective actors in welfare. Identifying in a differentiated way such factors, decisive for the kind of link between shifts in the welfare mix on the one hand, and the level and quality of social welfare and well-being on the other, might introduce more clearness in a debate, where often still an arbitrary notion prevails judging marketization, informalization, or more state as either fruitful or detrimental to people's welfare, disregarding the social context and political strategy they are placed in.

Social Innovations: Unconventional Ways of Linking Different Elements in the Welfare Mix

Looking towards actors and action, significant for a shift in the welfare mix, the majority of the national reports has concentrated on what might be called social experiments. Such unconventional initiatives become visible through experiments in volunteering in Italy, the TUC programme in France, the Austrian economic and social projects, the Yugoslavian experience with what the paper calls externalization strategies, the debate in the FRG about projects and self-help in the field of care for the elderly, the Swedish "fourth sector initiatives", the Polish experience with new forms of volunteering and solidarity, or the UK experiences with different types of community care. Mostly there is a mix of marginal, often time-limited state-programmes 'from above' and of social initiatives coming 'from below'; sometimes the former, sometimes the latter aspect is standing in the foreground. The claim that these areas of experimenting, small by size, cannot be "neglected as just a minor phenomenon in the outskirts of the welfare society" (the Swedish paper, a view common to all participants) is best understood if one considers the relatively high degree of immobility characterizing central state action in social policy (with few exceptions, it is to say, like in the British case). When speaking of a "very subtle, qualitatively new phenomenon (. . .) sometimes private, sometimes public, sometimes informal, but most of the time a little bit out of everything", the Swedish paper puts it as simple as drastic. With the notion of "fourth sector initiatives" it tries to show that such movements and their organizational and institutional features both mix up and rearrange in different ways the three sectors of (market) economy elements, state regulation and activities around households and in the social sphere. With respect to the well-regulated system of social reproduction, its norms, rights and benefits, such innovations start often as a puzzling kind of 'deviation'. As it is written in the Hungarian contribution, "welfare innovations also appear at the 'edges' of states' welfare organizations, frequently in the form of ‚deviant' behaviour of those working there".

Most of the research reports concerned with social innovation observed their potential role for a change in social welfare on two levels:

• On the level of their *immediate effects,* as far as they are e. g. organizing voluntary work, help to integrate jobless young people or to care for frail elderly.

• Another level of discussion is concerned with their *indirect effects,* seeing them as a challenge for the legitimacy, the routines and divisions of resources in their surrounding: as an attempt to combat a certain practice of 'social help', the privacy of household-related activities or the medicalization of health.

Both dimensions are closely linked and dependent on each other. Miller states: "As it is frequent with social innovation, the issue is whether the experiment is a forerunner of broad policy changes or becomes encapsulated, restricted to a narrow slice of the policy arena and gradually declining in significance as it placates critics of mainstream policies". Therefore, with respect to innovations in volunteering, including changes in the voluntary sector, the UK paper states that "expanding the voluntary sector is not the answer. It is only part of the answer". Since no research paper claims that innovative practices are already visible on a mass level and competing on equal footing with traditional practices, mostly hidden challenges through such innovations are discussed. Usually their organizational features are marked by the "existence of a large inclination to multivalence" as the Italian (B) paper puts it. Trying to describe the essence of their contributions, it can be said that they, themselves, placed somewhere in between the poles of attraction as represented by 'market', 'state' and 'household', represent the attempt to link what is generally separated or opposed in the welfare triangle, and to change the traditional character of links. This might be described on five levels.

• Some of them establish *new links between the social and the private:* organizing self-help groups, social projects, employment and training initiatives, gathering together for changing local development makes it evermore difficult to reduce the social sphere to a mere sum of individuals or households; at the margins of privacy, such innovations change the household economy into more complex types of 'short distance economies'; these aspects of informal or semi-formal associations and communities are stressed in the Swedish, the UK, the FRG, the Italian (B) and the Yugoslavian paper.

• Most of them are establishing *more and renewed links between the formal and the informal:* the Swedish fourth sector initiatives describe lifestyles and not only work or services; the question of changing care for the elderly in the UK is formulated in terms of a better integration of what lay carers, neighbourhood networks and decentralized public institutions might do; and for the Italian (B) report it is the most central question, whether it is possible to establish types of cooperation in social services, where the professionals enable the former clients, while they, acknowledged as co-producers, might help to redefine the professionals' role. The links between the formal and the informal do, however, not only appear in the dimension of the social services offered, but also with respect to the problem of work and job creation: strengthening a voluntary sector and answering new needs, first by unpaid volunteering competing for resources, then by acknowledgement, remuneration and professionalization might open up an additional perspective on the whole problem of job creation.

• A special aspect is the frequently occurring *link between state- and socially-initiated innovations,* put in the Swedish paper as initiatives "from above" or "from below". Since both elements mix, like the French contribution shows with respect to the local TUC scheme, or the FRG paper with respect to the Berlin and Hamburgian scene of self-help and employment initiatives, the outcome of a running innovation is mostly not to be determined beforehand; instead of being a clearly 'good' or 'bad' thing, it represents at once both sides of social reality.

• Another feature is *the mix between social and economic rationales:* the social projects in Austria are financed by the labour market administration in order to become after a certain time self-sustaining economic organizations – but meanwhile their field of action is social help and social services; the Swedish social initiatives, while concentrating on questions of local social development, make new economic solutions more viable; finally the programmes, bringing people to work, like the TUC scheme, combine social purposes of different kinds (integration of young people, establishment of new goods and services) with economic goals of employment and cost saving.

• This is mirrored on the level of *links between economic and social policies* both changing profiles and practices. The Austrian report informs us that the labour market administration sponsors many projects which are in fact reform initiatives in the field of health, social help, etc., hoping, that social policy will take up these initiatives and, by integrating them, turn these "special working contracts" into ordinary employment; while the Hamburgian case referred to in the FRG report shows similar developments, the Berlin example stressed there, is demonstrating that an innovative social policy, sponsoring a variety of self-help initiatives has at a certain point to arrange with job creation programmes and the labour market administration. It seems that just creating labour is everless viable, while at the same time the appraisal of volunteering and self-help turns into mere rhetorics if it cannot show the implications for peoples' problems with jobs and income.

With respect to both, work and social services, the Italian (B) paper formulates as a goal that social innovations "should move freely for social non-profit-making purposes with the aim of creating new flexible work opportunities and new services that are not administered directly by public administrators." How much this might mix up all kinds of traditional representations of work, welfare, service and related policies, has been described most clearly in the French contribution with respect to the TUC schemes: "The TUC programme is a highly original creation; it defies easy classification. It is not a classical economic policy to create an over-all upturn in employment by encouraging investment or consumption, nor is it a selective programme offering aid to specific sectors. The TUCs do, however, create jobs; the young people are doing something and no longer part of the unemployment statistics. The programme is not a traditional welfare policy either; the young participants must work for the 1200 F they receive. Neither is it part of a traditional unemployment insurance programme. The measures are not simply new means of making it easier for young people to enter a given occupation, by increasing their training or making it cheaper for employers to hire them, because their activities take place in a production space that is different to regular employment. The TUC programme is a hybrid; its economic and social objectives are intermingled and any attempt at labelling is impossible."

Summing up, it can be said that the social innovations observed and analyzed in the research contributions have an *intermediary* character in a broad sense of the word. It is unclear how many may survive, how many are stabilized and how many either assimilated to the normality of state institutions or survive as an 'alternative' exit. One might further debate (a) options and limits for an expansion of such intermediary bodies and programmes, and (b) the consequences for a different logic of public policies and new types of their (co)operation.

Work and Job Creation in the Field of Social Services

Beyond the description of the main elements of a deregulation process on the labour market (in the Eastern countries: rising problems of irregular 'overoccupation' in the enterprises; in the Western countries: stagnation of job supply, questioning of solidaristic wage policies, segmentation, growth of less secured precarious work contracts), the research papers look to the threat of unemployment and job creation in a prospective way. The experiences of the limited traditional forms of enlarging the labour market form the background for the discussion of possibilities of job creation in the 'third sector' and the more informal societal areas. Besides strategies of industrial and technological modernization, where new jobs are a welcomed by-product (not discussed in our research), there is scepticism concerning three types of conventional job creation which rely directly on the (labour) market element of the welfare triangle:

(a) The politics of a state-administered crowding out mainly by strategies of a paid earlier retirement are, as the French paper underlines, very costly; the crisis of the pension systems in a lot of West European countries are accentuated by such strategies using the pension insurances as a tool and the elderly as an "intermediate good" (Swedish paper) in such type of labour policies.

(b) Special programmes which try to enlarge the employment capacities of the enterprises by subsidizing additional jobs and education facilities, produce, as the French and the Italian (T) paper rightly remark, often a mere "take-over-effect" or even a counterproductive result "of subsidizing the employers for job places which already exist, but which now risk to become less stable". (Italy T)

(c) The third possibility (an integrated part of the Scandinavian model) just to enlarge public sector occupation, especially in the realm of social services, is actually nowhere to be found anymore – a still often desired concept but practically a fiction. It is important to remind that this fact, like a lot of others in social policy, cannot be discussed on a mere economic and financial level (as the Scandinavian model shows, more or new public service employment did not necessarily prevent growth); it is to a wide part a problem of legitimating future rising tax rates under conditions of only small progress in wages, and the growing public opinion that in an enlarged cost-efficiency quota such measures do not really pay off and should not be supported and implemented.

With this background of mostly high unemployment problems and decreasing possibilities for counteraction in the formal sector, the interplay and dynamics between the informal and formal areas of the welfare triangle receive more attention. As the reports, especially of the FRG, Austria and Italy (B) show, there is still a perception prevailing, which claims, that the processes of an intensified structuring and formalizing of non-paid third sector activities, self-help, volunteering and other activities alike, have no or just a negative impact on the possibilities of additional job creation. One can, however, argue that this might be the consequence of a specific political option for cost-cutting, like in the case of the UK, but partly to be prevented by clear-cut regulations, stating what is up to volunteering and what to professional services. Beyond such defence arguments, the Swedish, Italian (B) and the FRG paper try to push an offensive attitude by conceiving a further 'articulation' and formalization of needs and activities outside the formal markets of labour, goods and services as a possible way to prepare the grounds for new social demands, action, activities, and – in this wider framework of 'work' – also for new jobs.

- The FRG report shows, with respect to the Berlin situation, that a growing formalization of informal help and care structures and a sponsoring of the self-help projects by the federal state leads to a mixed structure of work and activities: the projects subsidized represent a mix of paid work and volunteering; more than 40 per cent of the money in the 'help to self-help' programmes are spent on the creation of jobs, settled in these new networks, groups and organizations.
- The Swedish paper shows, how "activities aimed at alleviating social problems create human capital and social networks, thereby increasing the local aggregate production function. Secondly, this leads to businesses and jobs in trades that ordinary development agencies, banks or authorities never even consider."
- The Italian (B) paper states, that "a positive use of volunteers within the framework of services does not determine a zero outcome, but a positive addition, in the sense that normally this does not substract public positions but creates new work opportunities in finding new sectors for intervention and response methods."

It could be added that this unexpected view on the job creation problem has its historical predecessors: the history of the voluntary agencies in many welfare states has been such a process of creation of needs and demands, of facilities and jobs as a part of a broad articulation and formalization of the informal. Until now this new kind of (mostly public) employment is marginal in quantitative terms. But it is – in opposition to the classical forms of additional public employment – nevertheless *real*. Maybe it comes into reality because it can claim public support for two reasons mentioned in the FRG and the Swedish paper.

(a) The new fields of activity wherein the new jobs are created have through their process won a considerable local public support – the work done here is perceived as useful.

(b) Investing in the formalization of social networks might be most effective both from the point of additional service inputs and from the point of socially integrative effects; "tax payers get more service out of every swedish crown they pay" for the implementing of "more informal elements in the production of social services", the Swedish paper states. The FRG paper underlines the multiplicator effect with respect to social integration, if jobs and professionals become sponsored, which form the core of projects and networks offering additional chances for volunteering and social participation.

From State Welfare to Welfare Pluralism? In Search for a Changing Welfare Paradigm

In his contribution, Miller makes a striking attempt to differentiate between four strategies for the future of the welfare state, which he labels as "defend and change", "transformational", "integrationist" and "marketization". With respect to his classification one might say that the majority of the research contributions come within the framework of the second and third option, characterized by the search for a new role of employment and work, and/or the search for new bridges and services towards social integration. The research reports indicate six orientations largely shared when it comes to the history and the potential future of welfare arrangements and the desirability of new 'mixes'.

(1) With respect to the given welfare state arrangement, two characteristics are repeatedly noted. The first is the clear-cut *labour centring* of welfare rights and regulations to be stated commonly for countries with market and planned economies. This is no wonder, insofar the process of the "Great Transformation" meant in both cases to establish employment as the most widespread social relationship, and a welfare system, where male 'full-time' work became the desired overall norm. What is expressed in the Italian (B) paper holds also true with some minor corrections for the other countries included in this research project: "Welfare state structures and features are strongly based on what we can call the 'industrial citizenship'. In other words, social expenditures privilege regular workers, prefer money aids and use social services only as marginal services. The latter are increasingly identified as pathological needs of the population rather than physiological ones. In any case, services in kind and other services cannot compete with money benefits by importance and are granted to the weakest and marginal people". One conclusion might be directly drawn: the social consequences of changes in the employment systems are only partly counteracted by the social security systems; in addition, they are intensified by them because social rights and claims are built on the traditional normality of employment patterns. The second main feature is the tight and sometimes nearly exclusive link between state and welfare. As the Hungarian and Polish contributions underline, their "system is based on the activity of the state which has taken on responsibilities for satisfying all major needs. The role of other social actors is only supplementary" (Polish paper). While there is still an enormous difference between the degree of etatism in welfare policies of Eastern and Western countries, one cannot deny that at least in ideology in the latter there have been attempts throughout the 1960s and 1970s to see the state as the nearly exclusive actor for a perfect welfare planning. In manifold ways the notion of the welfare mix is spoiling these links between a certain conception of (male full) employment and (state) welfare, which in the Western countries has been labelled as the "Keynesian welfare state", or became visible in Eastern countries through a high degree of etatism denying any autonomy both to the economic and the social sphere.

(2) A different view on welfare emerges as soon as one begins to think in terms of (what also the Hungarian paper calls) a "welfare pluralism", to be constituted through the exchange between an independent formal economy, state institutions and individual as well as collective action in the social and household sphere. Each of the three elements is viewed as being useful but also as imper

fect: the (market) economy, which stimulates competition, gives freedom in terms of destroying links and opening up choices, yet creates all kinds of inequalities; the state, which is able to counteract the latter, to enhance equality and to accentuate common interests beyond particularism and individualism, might yet limit freedom of choice and space for self-organization; the social sphere can create all kinds of lively solidarity but also dependence on communities and local egoisms. The utopia of welfare is in fact everless characterized by the aim of abolishing markets or independent economies like the socialist utopia wanted to; vice versa it seems evermore unrealistic to minimalize state intervention by maximizing the impact of market rules as it has been envisaged in liberalistic utopias. And the social-democratic compromise between state and market seems to be seriously threatened with respect to the role of the social sphere: by citizens who want to become acknowledged as participants, not only in political terms but also in terms of being co-producers of goods, services and benefits. Introducing the 'third sector' might change the whole debate. In this context it is no wonder that the Yugoslavian contribution, after discussing strategies of rationalization, marketization and externalization, opts for "a possibility to employ simultaneously more strategies and to acquire a viable combination". The report underlines that this "implies also the mobilization of informal and semi-formal resources for the production of services. This is a chance for welfare institutions to get rid of labour intensive phases of production, to lower the costs of labour, to retain most demanding phases of the production of services which are based on highly specialized professional knowledge and on complex and expensive technological equipment, and to become primarily research and development, consultancy, educational and training centres. It is a chance for service consumers, too, to be involved directly in the production of services which they need, to adjust the quality of services to their personal demands and to enrich their personal and social life in the domain of non-working time." The quotation shows quite clearly the basic idea of the concept of welfare pluralism: the attempt of strenghening the virtues and reducing the odds of all three elements of the welfare mix, resp. the welfare system, by underlining the state's responsibility for equality, the citizen's ability to guarantee quality and responsiveness to individual needs and the market's ability to give space for choices on the basis of a guaranteed minimum.

(3) A second axis for a changed welfare paradigm, introduced with the notion of the welfare mix, might be *the strengthening and upbuilding of new relationships between the formal and the informal, state and market institutions on the one hand and the social sphere on the other*. It is built on a view, where the latter is seen beyond mere political terms as a productive sphere with its own individual, private but also collective and social actors and organizations. Once the productive aspect of household economies, 'short distance economies', social networking, etc. has been acknowledged, this might have consequences for a renewed culture of both, service and work, partly outlined in the papers.

• In *services* this means first of all, as the UK contribution underlines, to overcome a global view, where only ecnonomic activities are seen as socially productive, while all kinds of social services are seen as a mere load; by perceiving people as co-producers of welfare, a new basic paradigm for a changing culture of services is taking shape, linked more with investments than with benefits, with co-producers than clients, with the formal services' role as complementary 'helpers for self-help' than covering all professionals, with increased productivity more as the outcome of a new use and share of resources between formal and informal elements of service production than of a rationalization of the inherited service institutions.

• With respect to *work and employment* this means first of all to perceive people's duties in employment as part of their broader work and activities; the dissolution of the former male-oriented normality of an uninterrupted full-time working career might be not only seen as irreversible but also as desirable; as the FRG paper argues, 'full' employment is a notion not to be rejected or restored, but an issue to be redefined: as the challenge to open up the option of taking part in the labour market for as much people as possible and in more varied ways. It should be the aim of a future welfare system not to discriminate and marginalize but to protect and stimulate those types of divisions between different kinds of work, income and priorities over the life cycles, women try to patch-work, or young people are experiencing in work programmes. This is the message of the Swedish, the FRG, the French and the Yugoslavian paper, when it comes to the future of work.

(4) At least in part of the papers there is a *different perspective on people's future lifestyles and use of time, especially time to care* (see the Swedish, the FRG, the French, the Italian (T) and the Yugoslavian contributions). Their common hidden agenda with respect to this field might be constituted by the fact that the 'economy of care' does not allow to reduce time in a way comparable to other productive activities. 'Time to care' therefore might become both a scarce resource and an often most desirable element of welfare, playing an increasingly central role in future life plans and divisions of time and work of people. While (even if actually most unevenly distributed) a decreasing part of time is used up by other productive activities, be they formal or informal, it will largely depend on how people perceive their relations to others, whether we turn into a narcissist type of individualism, or towards a conception of welfare and well-being, largely constituted by the image of a 'caring society'. Since nearly all papers, except the French, the Hungarian and the Italian (T) ones, concentrate on the area of care (services) and its impact on future working, living and welfare arrangements, this might indeed give the impression of a largely decentralized society, where localism is prevailing as it is taken up in Miller's "transformational" and "integrationist" strategies. While a future economy and culture of caring might point towards such a direction, it should yet not be overseen that in most of the other areas of production and activity we might face adverse trends. All in all, one might say that the discussion of how to place and secure 'time to care' in a future welfare society has only just begun.

(5) Since today structural changes create more deregulation, accelerate traditional and create new inequalities, it is not surprising that *changes in those basic values on which welfare traditionally has been built* can be observed. Going through the papers one can find assumptions about at least three shifts in the value system (a) there is an obviously growing importance of freedom in terms of choices (beyond freedom as a right to participate, or freedom from poverty); (b) solidaristic values are more referred to in terms of micro-solidarities between groups on the local level than in the former terms of class and mass organizations; (c) while there is more acceptance for diversity, equality is weakening, turning more into reflections on basic levels to be secured than on overall levels of equity to be constructed.

(6) In this context the papers frequently deal with the question of a *recontruction of basic welfare rights.* Given the inherited tight links between labour and social rights as represented by the 'industrial citizenship', the question arises, how to remodel basic transfer systems, in case new patchworks of paid and unpaid activities, training, working, caring and leisure time constitute new patterns of work. As far as we can see, no contribution really opts for what Miller describes as an essential of the "transformationalist" strategies: the breaking of the link between employment and income. Instead of that, there are some ideas about a looser link between the two and better provisions in case of an imminent drop-out. Some contributions stress that the former systems of social help with their discriminating measures should be changed into a basic safety network in order to ensure "a possible rise as well as a protected fall" (the Italian (B) paper). In this respect the Yugoslavian, French and FRG papers argue similarly. While nearly no paper discusses the consequences of changing patterns of participation in employment (with respect to social security and income) in more details, the FRG paper tries at least to outline a perspective, where income and work performances might be linked in other ways: "The actually still prevailing answer concerning the problems of a changing role of paid work for the organization of income security of the individual is the basic income strategy . . . it is somehow accepting that paid work should be secured by a basic income; but, as we argue, all the new performances represented by private-social activities in groups, initiatives, etc. would thereby receive no specific acknowledgement and remain invisible if there would be no clear link between fundings and performances; therefore (beyond the question that no one should fall under a minimum level) we argue for the establishment of larger and richer relationships between work/performances and incomes/refunding, helping to give those activities which are not paid work more visibility, rights and stimulation."

Closing this section, one might say that the concentration of the research on work and social services has led to patterns of a future welfare paradigm, where one misses ideas both for the future of income policy and social security. How far can society go in loosening the link between one's role in the labour market and one's resources for social participation? How far might it be possible to upgrade, secure and remunerate hitherto unpaid activities and performances to a degree, that private and social activities in these fields pay off, not only in moral and psychological, but also in material terms? To what degree might it be possible to build up a new basic safety network which helps to protect and to reintegrate? These are the unanswered questions in the attempts to link our research work with perspectives on a new welfare paradigm.

Welfare and Democracy

With respect to a future paradigm of welfare some challenges for political democracy have already become visible. What might hopefully be labelled as a crossover from welfare state or state welfare to a welfare society or welfare pluralism, should be based on new relationships and mutual sharing of responsibilities between the formal institutions of state and (market) economy on the one hand and society and its individuals on the other, on a relationship, wherein the latter become increasingly acknowledged as actors, producers and decision-makers to be protected, but even more enabled. This orientation has been outlined in most of the papers with respect to (1) the role of the social sphere, (2) the role of the state and (3) the type of relationships which might arise between them.

(1) A changing role of the social, envisaged in the papers, which the Polish contribution calls a "delimitation" of the social sphere, has always been the utopia of discourses on political democracy, especially under the label of a 'civil society'. What the contribution of the research work in this reader accentuates, is the fact, that forms of association and 'public', constitutive of a civil society, should not only be thought in terms of social and political organizing, in terms of cultural creativity, of pressure and bargaining, but as well in terms of material production, the animation of household, short distance or more formalized social economies. As the Italian (B) paper states, they take today both, the form of a more informal "social-private action . . . defined as a sphere with management independence in both labour and services" (like informal or semi-formal self-help and neighbourhood-oriented networks) and the shape of "a collective mobilization in forms of self-management" which might be linked with types of voluntary organizations or other formalized bodies like associations, cooperatives, etc. Throughout the papers, their role for an upbuilding or strengthening of political democracy is underlined with respect to three aspects:

• Their possibility to *create and reproduce values* like solidarity, togetherness, altruism, which is vanishing, in case the direct vis-à-vis of individual privacy and state public action is dominating.

• Their possibilities to *influence or reconquer fields of action,* which might otherwise be subjected to a pure economic logic; hence the expression 'social economy' and the emphasis on a new mix of social and economic reasoning in new organizational forms of social service production.

404

• Their role as *"countervailing powers"*, as the Swedish paper puts it; they might play this role with respect to the conflicts between local and central interests, specific and global viewpoints, and, as one might add here, as an instrument to express the right to diversity versus uniformity.

Beyond influence on state power by protest and open political conflict, and contrary to a concept, which concentrates on 'taking over' the power of the state, this might be an option towards the strengthening of societal forces gaining political influence and power by ways of self-management. No wonder that especially the contributions of Poland, Hungary and Yugoslavia underline this kind of potential link between discussions on social innovations in welfare, independent organizations in the field of social policy, and the search for the development of a more 'civil' society.

(2) This perspective includes a different look at the *role of the state.* On the one hand, it might be a plea for a minor role with respect to the traditional concepts of 'full services', 'global' social protection and monopolistic solutions accompanied by an attitude, which is concerned "primarily with the problem of regulation and control of those welfare activities which are not carried out within welfare institutions, and not with the problem of initiating such activities" as the Yugoslavian paper puts it. On the other hand this leads already to those points, where state institutions should assume new responsibilities: to enable individuals to take their own initiative, as well as to stimulate collective initiatives. This might link with the increasing strive for autonomy and freedom in terms of 'having options'; the state should see to it that this does not remain the privilege of a few, but becomes reality for more people. Such a vision of the state's role as an 'enabler' and guarantor for people, communities and associations to become more autonomous actors is easy to be outlined. It points, however, to a complicated problem not evoked in the research: the more the possibilities for individual and social action are co-produced by political rules, guarantees and interventions, the more the concept of an 'independent' civil society vis-à-vis the state seems to fade. Autonomy can be everless defined as a room of 'state-free' action but as the outcome of a specific regulation of the interactions between the economic, the state-political and the societal.

(3) This leads us directly to the question of *relationships between state and society.* With respect to new initiatives and social innovations characterized by their multivalence and the fact that they are not foreseen in the traditionally established interplay of political institutions and social organizations, at least three types of 'exits' were perceived in the research contributions (see especially the Italian (B) contribution):

• An exit towards *'protest' and 'community'*, the attempt to obtain autonomy irrespective of or beyond the realms governed by state rules; obviously this is the more difficult, the more such collective action is formalized and expressed on a level beyond the realms of privacy. As the Austrian contribution puts it, "there is first of all the question whether unconventional initiatives lose their autonomy by networking with the traditional sector. And it is also said that the autonomous sector contributes to the cementation of stigmatization if the projects are not integrated into the traditional sector."

• Therefore *'assimilation'* can be seen as the other side of marginalization, a danger which increases with the unwillingness of the established institutions to change. As the UK report remarks, "the danger is that voluntary agencies are tending to become agencies of implementation rather than of experimentation and innovation – an additional arm of the state rather than a source of alternative ideas, good practice and criticism of state-run services"; in case that there is hardly any room left for protest and every self-organization is under heavy pressure for assimilation, 'authentic' volunteering nearly disappears as the Polish paper shows; the social is threatened by an increasing mutual nourishing of etatism and privatization.

• No wonder that most contributions look for possible *'collaborative exits'*, based on a certain state-guaranteed room for autonomy for the respective initiative, association or experiment. Regarding such examples as the TUC in the French contribution, the FRG programmes for stimulating work and self-help, the Italian volunteer organizations, it seems to be a question of the ability to develop modes of negotiating and contracting, whether such a collaborative exit comes into being.

Within such a perspective once again the whole research project has not answered but revealed some basic questions and problems. One of them is stated at the end of the FRG contribution: "Until now projects, initiatives and voluntary organizations have neither clear instruments and routines, nor rights and access to negotiate their performances or at least to participate in processes, where a society or a local community has to state, how much this or that performance in the field of care should be worth; therefore, the slippage from traditional work relations into new forms of work and activity is combined with a dramatic loss of rights and bargaining power." Also Miller's contribution underlines that it might be too harmonious a perspective, where state-guaranteed benefits or basic incomes, not related to performances but to a new 'social right', fill the gap which might arise alongside a changing labour market relation and a relative loss of trade-union guaranteed bargaining power. Unconventional forms of combining work, use of time and income arise often around the social service sector. Therefore the already visible conflicts concerning the 'terms of trade' of public guarantees for such projects and the people working there might well be not a very special detail or just a question of cheaper service provision. Instead they might be the first signs of new types of social conflicts concerning future ways to negotiate and regulate the links between claims on and rights to work, income and use of time.

Social Innovation and the Costs of Change

When discussing modernization not as it is expressed in terms of technological and economic investments, but as it is in terms of values, ways of arranging working and living as well as organizational rules, all papers give a similar picture when it comes to the present balance between traditionalism and change. Except the UK, which has undergone consciously-initiated drastic social changes, in nearly all other countries there seems to exist what the Italian (B) paper has called a "jammed up" situation and a high degree of immobility on the central levels of decision-making and in the core areas of societies' institutions and organized interests. At the same time, the papers feature micro-types of social innovations as a complementary side of this phenomenon. It is remarkable that state action, interventions and programmes of big social organizations linked to such micro-innovations are mostly labelled as 'time limited', 'provisional' and an exception from general rules to be still safeguarded. In such a situation it is a most crucial question, to perceive correctly the complicated links between 'normal' patterns and dissidence, tradition and innovation, which become visible here.

All the papers show that the observed micro-innovations have a double face. While the power is with the main traditional elements and holders of wealth, power and welfare, the social experiments 'accumulate' both: elements of restructuring and strengthening, but also the burdens and disadvantages of socio-political change. As the French paper puts it, the social experiments (like TUCs) are the less costly ones because they are suited to take over a lot of costs of socio-political change, which the majority of the society tries to avoid. "The TUC programme is an important innovation (and thus unclassifiable according to any prior system of categorization), but it is a localized innovation. If the young people involved in the TUC programme seem to be agreeable to the division of time, work and income, this does not prevent public opinion and the large majority of wage-earners, as well as most occupational associations, employers and labour unions, from refusing to envisage such an arrangement. Essentially, the institutions continue to live in the hidden hope of a return to the 'good old days', to the methods of social regulation that were in effect when there was full employment, growth and a strong welfare state." It is instructive to look to the OECD report on local employment initiatives, quoted in the Swedish paper, which is doing exactly the same: pragmatically accepting change, insofar as it helps to administer the marginal strata of society, yet ignoring the costs to be borne by societal centres: No wonder that local employment initiatives are suggested in that report (I) to have "low requirements for capital and energy", (II) to "accomplish a great deal with little support" and (III) to "create supply and demand with minimal substitution effects on existing markets". In this context the French paper is rightly insisting on the "abnormal" aspects of a situation marked by the coexistence of drastic but small changes in micro-relationships at some societal points and a still relatively high degree of immobility but also security and welfare in the societal centres, which try to 'externalize' the costs of change from some more static and powerful groups to those groups which are both: suitable and vulnerable enough for such a way of installing *and* avoiding social change. Therefore, it is no wonder to see especially (sometimes highly qualified) young people "saddled with the main burden of the costs of changes in our industrial society" (French paper). In the Italian (B) paper an opposite view is quoted as an option of political minorities, trying to grasp that volunteering and other new developments in the areas beyond state and market point to "the start of a general social change around the hubs of self-management and solidarism. This can affect the process of accumulation which increasingly tends to confine investments of resources to technological rearrangement, financial speculations, and safe sectors while being close to any investment aiming at the formation of larger job opportunities". This observation finally leads towards two phenomena which receive increasing interest in the actual public debates on welfare.

(1) There are many discussions about *perverse effects of welfare regulations* under conditions of rapid changes. Some say they produce actually new inequalities and injustices. This might for example be the case with welfare regulations, which have been built around the traditional image of the continuously and full employed worker, which disregard the spreading of other types of work contracts or treat them as a rare exception. Such regulations, rights and securities, which do not anymore refer to today's different social reality turn into mechanisms, which safeguard inequality and privileges even if formerly constructed as a means towards equality.

(2) It is a commonplace that welfare regulations are products of struggle and compromises. It is, however, far less a commonplace to deduce from that fact a *shared responsibility* for the present and future. If e. g. the big organizations of labour are denouncing trends towards a 'two-thirds society', excluding one-third from the rules and standards of the majority, the question remains which changes they are willing to make and which price to pay, in order to find a more integrative type of regulation.

Reflecting the need for changes in such a way, means to step out of a conservative type of 'labourism', where new needs, life models and individualisms are only seen with defensive distrust, whatever form they take:

• As 'a mere luxury' in case they become visible within a small part of the new middle classes, which already have the resources to arrange on individual footing more time sovereignty, self-expression and active participation.

• As 'a mere self-exploitation' wherever such unconventional forms of working and living arise at the margins of society through projects and associations, where the work is interesting but badly paid and secured, open for changes but combined with high risks.

Why should not there be a possibility to transform into integrative representations of well-being and welfare, what today takes the form of a privilege or a mere survival kit?

Notes

1) A first version of this paper has been discussed in the last plenary meeting of the research group (summer 1986). This version integrates further points raised in that discussion and a discussion of those national reports not available at that time. S. M. Miller shared our work as a senior advisor. We include references concerning his special contribution to this reader – a look at the European debate from the perspective of a researcher in the United States.

2) See: Social Policies beyond the 1980 in the European Region. Discussion paper prepared by the European Centre for Social Welfare, Training and Research, Vienna 1987 and Evers, A., 1987, Social Policy in Transition. An analysis of the country reports for the Conference of European Ministers responsible for social affairs in Warsaw 1987; both available from the European Centre.

3) Nine research teams from the following countries participated in the project: Austria: R. Pohoryles, D. M. Hoffmann, B. Rauscher, H. Wintersberger; France: G. Martin, G. Roustang, F. Sellier; Germany (Federal Republic of): A. Evers, I. Ostner, H. Wiesenthal; Hungary: E. Sik; Italy (B): P. Donati, I. Colozzi (University of Bologna); Italy (T): M. Bianchi, Ch. Saraceno (University of Trento); Poland: M. Ksiezopolski, I. Sienko; Sweden: I. Nilsson, A. Wadeskog; United Kingdom: St. Humble, A. Walker; Yugoslavia: I. Svetlik. S. M. Miller (USA) participated in the function of a senior adviser to the research group (see list of contributors).

List of Contributors

Bianchi Marina, Dipartimento di Politica Sociale, Università di Trento, Italy

Colozzi Ivo, Researcher of Sociology, Department of Sociology, University of Bologna, Italy

Donati Pierpaolo, Professor of Sociology, Director of the Study Centre on Social Policy (Ceposs), Department of Sociology, University of Bologna, Italy

Evers Adalbert, Research Fellow, European Centre for Social Welfare Training and Research, Vienna, Austria

Hoffmann D. Martin, Research Fellow, European Centre for Social Welfare Training and Research, Vienna, Austria

Humble Stephen, Director, Age Endeavours, United Kingdom

Ksiezopolski Miroslaw, Research Fellow, Department of Journalism and Political Science, Institute of Social Policy, University of Warsaw, Poland

Martin Gérard, Maître de Conférences, Institut d'Etudes Politiques de Grenoble; Directeur, Centre d'Etude et de Formation sur la Planification et l'Economie Sociales, Université de Grenoble, France

Miller S. M., Professor of Sociology and Economics, Boston University; Senior Fellow, Commonwealth Institute, Cambridge, USA

Nilsson Ingvar, Institute for SocioEcological Economics, Karlshäll, Järna, Sweden

Ostner Ilona, Professor of Women's Studies/Sociology, Fachhochschule Fulda, FRG

Pohoryles Ronald, Head of Research of the Interdisciplinary Centre for Comparative Research in Technology and Social Policy, Vienna; Visiting Faculty Member, Department for Political Science, University of Innsbruck, Austria

Rauscher Brigitte, formerly Secretary of the Austrian Committee on Social Welfare (ÖKSA), Vienna, Austria

Roustang Guy, Laboratoire d'Economie et de Sociologie du Travail, Centre National de la Recherche Scientifique, Aix-en-Provence, France

Saraceno Chiara, Professor of Sociology, Dipartimento di Politica Sociale, Università di Trento, Italy

Sellier François, Professeur émérite, Université de Paris X-Nanterre; Laboratoire d'Economie et de Sociologie du Travail, Centre National de la Recherche Scientifique, Aix-en-Provence, France

Sienko Irena, Research Fellow, Department of Journalism and Political Science, Institute of Social Policy, University of Warsaw, Poland

Sik Endre, Senior Research Fellow, Institute for Social Sciences, Budapest, Hungary

Svetlik Ivan, Professor, Faculty of Sociology, Political Science and Journalism, University E. Kardelj, Ljubljana, Yugoslavia

Wadeskog Anders, Institute for SocioEcological Economics, Karlshäll, Järna, Sweden

Walker Alan, Professor of Social Policy, University of Sheffield, United Kingdom

Wiesenthal Helmut, Wissenschaftlicher Angestellter, Fakultät für Soziologie, Universität Bielefeld, FRG

Wintersberger Helmut, Deputy Director, European Centre for Social Welfare Training and Research, Vienna, Austria